AUD

Auditing and Attestation

Written By:

Roger Philipp, CPA, CGMA

UWorld

9111 Cypress Waters Blvd

Suite 300

Dallas, TX 75019

accounting.uworld.com/cpa-review

MW01504804

Permissions

The following items are utilized in this program, and are copyright property of the American Institute of Certified Public Accountants, Inc. (AICPA), all rights reserved:

- Uniform CPA Examination and Questions and Unofficial Answers, Copyright © 1991 – 2021
- Audit and Accounting Guides, Auditing Procedure Studies, Risk Alerts, Statements of Position, and Code of Professional Conduct
- Statements on Auditing Standards
- Statements on Standards for Accounting and Review Services
- Statements on Quality Control Standards
- Statements on Standards for Attestation Engagements
- Accounting Research Bulletins, APB Opinions
- Uniform CPA Examination Blueprints
- Independence Standards Board (ISB) Standards

Portions of various FASB and GASB documents, copyright property of the Financial Accounting Foundation, 401 Merritt 7, PO Box 5116, Norwalk, CT 06856-5116, are utilized with permission. Complete copies of these documents are available from the Financial Accounting Foundation. These selections include the following:

Financial Accounting Standards Board (FASB)

- The FASB Accounting Standards Codification™
- Statements of Financial Accounting Concepts
- FASB Statements, Interpretations, and Technical Bulletins

Governmental Accounting Standards Board (GASB)

- GASB Codification of Governmental Accounting and Financial Reporting Standards and GASB Statements
- GASB Concepts Statements
- GASB Interpretations and Technical Bulletins

© 2023 UWorld, LLC. All rights reserved.

Reproduction or translation of any part of this work beyond that permitted by sections 107 and 108 of the United States Copyright Act without the permission of the copyright owner is unlawful.

Printed in English, in the United States of America.

About the Author

Roger S. Philipp, CPA, CGMA

Founder and Instructor, UWorld Roger CPA Review

Roger Philipp, CPA, CGMA, is one of the most celebrated motivators and instructors in the accounting profession. Roger believes you should enjoy what you do—in life, business, and learning. Guided by this philosophy, he strives to create dynamic and engaging instruction that makes learning concepts enjoyable. This focus has helped aspiring accountants across the globe reach career success for almost 30 years.

Roger launched Roger CPA Review in 2001 with the goal to create a CPA review course that would alter the landscape of accounting education. With the program now part of UWorld, Roger continues to act as a key inspiration and spark for company innovation. The success of the program is fueled by his unique approach to teaching, in which he breaks down and simplifies complex topics, with support from memory aids and mnemonic devices, to help students understand and retain information.

Roger's early career began in public accounting at Deloitte & Touche, where he earned his CPA designation, before transitioning to educational instruction. He was a lead instructor at Mark Dauberman CPA Review, before starting Roger CPA Review. Roger attributes his entrepreneurial success to the many doors his CPA license opened, as well as his passion for making professional education engaging and relevant for optimum effectiveness. In recent years, Roger was featured as one of Accounting Today's Top 100 Most Influential People in Public Accounting.

Today, Roger is a member of the AICPA, CalCPA, and has served on the Board of Directors for the American Professional Accounting Certification Providers Association (APACPA). He resides in San Francisco with his wife and co-founder of the company, Louisa, and their three children. He enjoys traveling with his family, enjoying the arts, and volunteering at his local food bank.

Acknowledgements

Keeping the course materials updated and accurate would not be possible without the contribution of our team of content experts. The team continues to be the driving force behind the updates and improvements for this year's textbooks.

Auditing & Attestation

Table of Contents

Introduction

Introduction

0.01 Course Introduction

How to Best Use Your Course

Welcome to the UWorld Roger CPA Review course! Our expert team is passionate about helping you succeed and have developed an award-winning program that is proven to yield results. Before you get started, please read through this helpful guide on how to best use your course so that you can master all of the topics laid out for you in the AICPA Blueprints and ultimately pass the CPA Exam.

Plan your Studies

> **Tip!**
> Download the app! This gives you access to everything your course offers while on-the-go.

When preparing for the CPA Exam, half the battle is setting yourself up for success with a solid plan from the get-go. This includes establishing short and long-term goals to ensure you're staying on track to pass within the 18-month window.

To get started, use the provided Study Planners in your course (located under "Study Resources"). Select either the 3-, 6-, 9- or 12-month planner and customize to meet your unique needs and schedule. It is important to follow your planner steadily so that you can ensure you hit your goals. If you miss a day, make it up!

Master the Concepts Through Active Learning

With this program, you will build your foundational knowledge and mastery of core exam topics through **active learning**. This evidence-based learning methodology centers around the principle that students *learn by doing* to maximize retention and improve learning outcomes. When preparing for the CPA Exam, the "doing" is working through exam-like questions.

- **Start with the QBank** – The QBank is where you work through multiple choice questions and simulations that align with the **AICPA Blueprints**. Start by creating a quiz, which can be customized down to the topic level. Begin with the first topic and work your way down the list. This granular level of filtering allows you to focus your energy around each concept, providing clarity as you run through groups of questions in the same area.

> **Tip!**
> Keep the quizzes to under 30 questions. This will help keep you focused and avoid burnout.

- **It's Okay to be Wrong** – You will be surprised at how much of the material you remember from school or in the field. However, if you answer questions incorrectly, don't worry! That's why you're here—to learn! And it's here in the questions that you are participating in active learning.

- **Learn Through the Answers** – Whether you've answered a question correctly or not, it's important that you know *why*. For this reason, questions are paired with clear and concise, expert-written answer explanations. Pay close attention to these because **this is where much of the learning happens!** Answer explanations include vivid imagery to summarize the concepts, plus a full breakdown of why each answer option is correct or incorrect.

Ultimately, explanations are designed to build your body of knowledge while teaching you the *what*, *why*, and *how* behind each concept.

Track Your Progress and Performance

As you complete each chapter, track your progress and performance using our signature **SmartPath Predictive Technology™**. SmartPath is a data-driven platform that provides recommended targets based on previous students who have passed the CPA Exam. This is an important tool to help you study efficiently and gauge whether you are *exam-ready*. Your goal is to hit both your progress target (Questions Attempted) and performance target (Score) for each chapter.

> **Tip!**
> Don't over-study. SmartPath™ helps determine when you can move on to the next topic.

As you work through the material, don't worry about hitting your "Score" target right away and focus your efforts on hitting the "Questions Attempted" target first. This approach may feel uncomfortable, but trust that you are building your knowledge as you absorb the answer explanations.

Once you've completed all the topics in a chapter, you can go back and focus your efforts on hitting the "Score" target. If you are falling short, drill down in the Performance tab to see which topics need extra attention.

Solidify the Concepts

Need extra help mastering the concept? Take advantage of the additional learning tools that are integrated into your course. For example, you could be working through a difficult question and find you need further explanation. No problem! There's a link to the supporting lecture right there in the question. Want to remember something for later review? Easily transfer content directly from the question to a digital flashcard. These are just a few ways we make it easy to navigate to and access the right tools you need at the right time.

These additional tools are designed to enhance your studies—**you do not necessarily need to read or watch all of this material!** Rather, use these tools as a means to improve on weak areas:

- **Video Lectures** – From the Lectures tab or directly integrated in the link at the bottom of each practice question, you have access to the profession's most motivating and effective lecturers, including lead instructor Roger Philipp, CPA, CGMA. Lectures break down difficult topics into simplified concepts and provide helpful memory aids. These are especially recommended for visual and auditory learners.

- **Textbooks** – Digital eTextbooks are accessible side-by-side with the video lectures or in a printed format with some of our course packages. These can be used as a reference if you need further explanation of a concept. Many students also find it beneficial to follow along in the textbook while watching the lectures and either take notes directly in the physical books or by using the Notes feature and highlighting tool in the platform.

- **Digital Flashcards –** Create custom flashcards directly from your practice questions by clicking on the lightning bolt symbol. Depending on your program package, your course may also be pre-loaded with an "Expert Deck" of flashcards covering the most heavily tested topics. You can review all your cards in Study Mode or using our **Spaced Repetition**

Technology. This is an evidence-based learning method that presents cards you've marked as *difficult* more frequently, and cards you've marked as *easy* less frequently. The spacing of how and when the flashcards are introduced has been proven to increase retention and strengthen memory recall.

Get Exam-Ready

The final days leading up to the exam are a critical time in which you're going to want to review your SmartPath data and ask, "Am I *exam-ready*?" If you have hit all the targets, you are in a really good spot. However, if any areas are still marked "Needs Improvement," now is the time to focus your efforts on meeting those targets.

Finally, we recommend you **take at least one full practice exam before exam day** (click on the "Exam Sim" tab in the QBank). This allows you to hone your test-taking skills in an exam-like environment that follows the same 5-testlet, 4-hour structure as the exam.

We hope you found some helpful information in this guide and that you can start the study process with confidence! As Roger always says, "You do not have to be a genius to pass the CPA Exam. If you study, you will pass!" You've got this. Happy Studying!

CPA Exam Blueprints

This course is based on the CPA Exam Blueprints, which are created by the American Institute of Certified Public Accountants (AICPA) to help candidates know what skills and content topics will be tested on the CPA Exam.

Not only are the CPA Exam Blueprints intended to assist candidates in preparing for the exam, but they also take into account the minimum level of knowledge and skills necessary for initial licensure once candidates become CPAs.

We have already used the blueprints to guide our course materials, so you are already on the right path. However, if you'd like to reference the blueprints to better understand what's required on the exam, we've provided a helpful guide below.

Overview of the CPA Exam

The blueprints provide an overview of how much time candidates have for each section and how many

Section	Time	MCQs	TBSs	WC
AUD	4 hrs	72	8	-
BEC	4 hrs	62	4	3
FAR	4 hrs	66	8	-
REG	4 hrs	76	8	-

questions by question type each section contains. Question types include Multiple Choice Questions (MCQ), Task-based Simulations (TBS), and Written Communication (WC).

Scoring Weight for All Question Types

Here candidates can see how the question types for each section are weighted and account for their overall score.

Section	MCQs	TBSs	WC
AUD	50%	50%	-
BEC	50%	35%	15%
FAR	50%	50%	-
REG	50%	50%	-

Skill Levels to be Assessed

Each exam section has a Skill Allocation framework based on the revised Bloom's Taxonomy of Educational Objectives. These are the skills that CPA candidates need to learn and successfully demonstrate on the CPA Exam.

Evaluation	The examination or assessment of problems and use of judgment to draw conclusions.
Analysis	The examination and study of the interrelationships of separate areas in order to identify causes and find evidence to support inferences.
Application	The use or demonstration of knowledge, concepts, or techniques.
Remembering & Understanding	The perception and comprehension of the significance of an area utilizing knowledge gained.

Skill Allocations

To break it down even further, here's how each of the skills above will be assessed on each section of the exam.

Section	Remembering & Understanding	Application	Analysis	Evaluation
AUD	25-35%	30-40%	20-30%	5-15%
BEC	15-25%	50-60%	20-30%	-
FAR	10-20%	50-60%	25-35%	-
REG	25-35%	35-45%	25-35%	-

Content Allocations

Below is an overview of the content allocation for each section of the exam.

AUD Content Area Allocation	Weight
I. Ethics, Professional Responsibilities & General Principles	15-25%
II. Assessing Risk and Developing a Planned Response	25-35%
III. Performing Further Procedures & Obtaining Evidence	30-40%
IV. Forming Conclusions and Reporting	10-20%

BEC Content Area Allocation	Weight
I. Enterprise Risk Management, Internal Controls & Business Processes	20-30%
II. Economics	15-25%
III. Financial Management	10-20%
IV. Information Technology	15-25%
V. Operations Management	15-25%

FAR Content Area Allocation	Weight
I. Conceptual Framework, Standard-Setting, & Financial Reporting	25-35%
II. Select Financial Statement Accounts	30-40%
III. Select Transactions	20-30%
IV. State and Local Governments	5-15%

REG Content Area Allocation	Weight
I. Ethics, Professional Responsibilities & Federal Tax Procedures	10-20%
II. Business Law	10-20%
III. Federal Taxation of Property Transactions	12-22%
IV. Federal Taxation of Individuals	15-25%
V. Federal Taxation of Entities	28-38%

How Skills are Applied to Exam Tasks (A Sample)

Each blueprint area is broken down further by content topic, skill, and representative task. This helps candidates identify the topics and subtopics they will be tested on in each section and which skill they will be required to demonstrate as they answer questions regarding those topics. Lastly, the representative task gives detailed, specific information on what they will be expected to perform on the exam related to those topics. As the AICPA points out though, the representative tasks are *not* an all-inclusive list of items that will appear on the exam.

To see how the content topic, skill, and representative tasks are presented in the blueprints, here is an excerpt from the AUD section:

Content group/topic	Remembering and Understanding	Skill			Representative task
		Application	Analysis	Evaluation	
A. Nature and scope					
1. Nature and scope: audit engagements	✓				Identify the nature, scope and objectives of the different types of audit engagements, including issuer and nonissuer audits.
2. Nature and scope: engagements conducted under Government Accountability Office Government Auditing Standards	✓				Identify the nature, scope and objectives of engagements performed in accordance with Government Accountability Office Government Auditing Standards.
3. Nature and scope: other engagements	✓				Identify the nature, scope and objectives of attestation engagements and accounting and review service engagements.
B. Ethics, Independence and professional conduct					
1. AICPA Code of Professional Conduct	✓				Understand the principles, rules and interpretations included in the AICPA Code of Professional Conduct.
	✓				Recognize situations that present threats to compliance with the AICPA Code of Professional Conduct, including threats to independence.
		✓			Apply the principles, rules and interpretations included in the AICPA Code of Professional Conduct to given situations.
		✓			Apply the Conceptual Framework for Members in Public Practice included in the AICPA Code of Professional Conduct to situations that could present threats to compliance with the rules included in the Code.
		✓			Apply the Conceptual Framework for Members in Business included in the AICPA Code of Professional Conduct to situations that could present threats to compliance with the rules included in the Code.
		✓			Apply the Conceptual Framework for Independence included in the AICPA Code of Professional Conduct to situations that could present threats to compliance with the rules included in the Code.

Conclusion

We hope you found this guide on how to read and understand the blueprints helpful. As we mentioned before, the UWorld Roger CPA Review course curriculum is directly mapped to and guided by these blueprints, so there is no need for you to spend considerable time studying the blueprints, as your course will guide you through the material. Rest assured that the practice questions in this course are designed to challenge critical thinking skills, ensuring you are thoroughly prepared to pass the CPA Exam.

To see the full AICPA Blueprints, visit
https://www.aicpa.org/becomeacpa/cpaexam/examinationcontent.

0.02 AUD Introduction

Plan Your Time!

Ensure success on the exam by following our recommendations for time allocation:

AUD Exam	
Testlet 1 *36 MCQ*	45 min
Testlet 2 *36 MCQ*	45 min
Testlet 3 *2 TBS*	30 min

Testlet 4 *3 TBS*	60 min
Testlet 5 *3 TBS*	60 min

Total Time: 4 hours

Things to consider:

- Use 75 seconds per multiple choice question as a benchmark.
- Allocate 15-20 minutes per task-based simulation, depending on complexity.
- Plan to use no more than 10 minutes per research question.
- Take the standard 15-minute break after the 3rd testlet; it doesn't count against your time.

AUD 1
Audit Basics &
Engagement
Planning

AUD 1: Audit Basics & Engagement Planning

1.01 Types of Audits

Overview

There are several types of audits that may be performed in relation to an entity. We introduce them all here, but we'll be focusing on the financial statement audit first. We'll come back to the details on these other types of audits in later chapters.

Type of audit	Focus	Performed by	Example
Compliance	Laws and regulations	Generally, a regulatory body	IRS audit, OSHA audt
Operational	Management policies and operations	Generally, internal auditors	Processes audits, internal control audits
Financial	Fairness of financial statements	Exclusively performed by CPAs	Financial statement audits, interim reviews
Performance	Efficiency and effectiveness	Generally, the government accountability office	Governmental project audits, nonprofit process audit

Compliance Audits

Compliance audits are often performed by or for governmental or regulatory organizations to determine if an entity is complying with applicable laws and regulations. Entities may be chosen for audit on a random basis or may be selected due to some indication that there may be one or more incidents of noncompliance (eg, tax returns with unusual deductions). Examples include:

- IRS audits
- Audits in accordance with *Generally Accepted Government Auditing Standards (GAGAS)**
- Agreed-upon procedures engagement* to determine compliance with provisions of a bond or note agreement

GAGAS and other attestation engagements are discussed in detail in a later chapter.

Operational (Performance) Audits

Operational (ie, performance) audits are generally performed to determine if management's policies are being followed appropriately and to evaluate the entity's compliance with internal controls and performance (ie, effectiveness, efficiency, and economy). Internal auditors and governmental auditors typically perform these audits, but external CPAs may also perform an operational audit as a consultant. Examples include:

- An internal auditor auditing a department or division of a corporation to see if it is meeting organizational goals

- A governmental auditor audtiting an organization to determine the effectiveness and benefit of specific government-funded programs

Financial Statement Audits

Financial statement audits are performed exclusively by CPA firms. A financial statement audit is an *examination* for the purpose of giving an *objective* (ie, unbiased) *opinion* as to the *fairness of financial statement presentations* in conformity with an **Applicable Financial Reporting Framework (AFRF)**.

Standards for the performance of financial statement audits in the United States are established by the:

- Auditing Standards Board (**ASB**) of the AICPA for audits of **nonpublic** entities

- Public Company Accounting Oversight Board (**PCAOB**) for audits of **public** entities

Financial Reporting Frameworks

A financial reporting framework (FRF) is a set of criteria used to determine measurement, recognition, presentation, and disclosure of all material items appearing in the F/S. It determines the form and content of the F/S. There are two types of FRFs.

- A **general purpose framework** is designed to meet the common financial information objectives of a wide range of users. General purpose frameworks include:

  - U.S. Generally Accepted Accounting Principles (**GAAP**), issued by the Financial Accounting Standards Board (**FASB**)

Generally Accepted Accounting Principles
• General-purpose accounting framework
• Encompasses rules, conventions, and procedures
• Defines accounting practices at a specific time
• Maintained and updated by FASB

  - International Financial Reporting Standards (**IFRS**), issued by the International Accounting Standards Board (**IASB**)

- A **special purpose framework** (ie, an other comprehensive basis of accounting—OCBOA) is a framework other than GAAP that could include the cash basis (modified cash), tax basis, regulatory agency basis, contractual basis, or an "other basis of accounting."

Applicable Auditing Standards

Standards for the performance of financial statement audits in the United States are established by the:

- Auditing Standards Board (**ASB**) of the AICPA for audits of **nonpublic** entities (ie, **nonissuers**)

  - These standards are individually referred to as Statements on Auditing Standards (SAS) and collectively referred to as Generally Accepted Auditing Standards (**GAAS**). They are codified as AU-C sections.

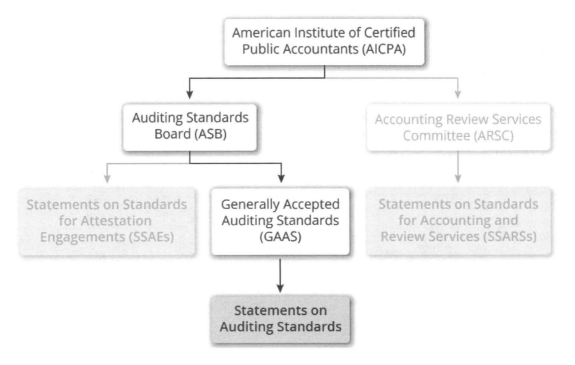

- Public Company Accounting Oversight Board (**PCAOB**) for audits of **public** entities (ie, **issuers**)

  - The PCAOB audit standards are referenced as PCAOB AS sections.

- Governmental Accountability Office (**GAO**) for audits of **governmental entities**

  - These standards are referred to as Generally Accepted Government Auditing Standards (**GAGAS** or **GAS**).

Auditor Requirements

The auditor should:

- Possess the appropriate qualifications to perform the audit.

- Apply **professional skepticism,** an attitude that includes a questioning mind and a critical assessment of audit evidence.

- Comply with relevant ethical requirements.

- Exercise professional judgment throughout the engagement.

- Comply with GAAS

  o **Interpretive publications** also shoud be considered in planning and performing the audit. Interpretive publications include auditing interpretations of GAAS, AICPA Audit and Accounting Guides, and AICPA Auditing Statements of Position (SOP).

  o **Other auditing publications** can be applied, but the auditor should exercise professional judgment in assessing the relevance and appropriateness of such guidance. These publications have no authoritative status.

Overall Objectives of a GAAS Audit

The overall objectives of the auditor in a GAAS engagement (AU-C 200) are to:

- *Obtain reasonable assurance* about whether the financial statements (F/S) as a whole are free from material misstatement, whether due to fraud or error, thereby enabling the auditor to *express an opinion* on whether the *F/S are presented fairly in accordance with an AFRF*, in all material respects.

- *Report* on the F/S and communicate the auditor's findings as required by GAAS.

Note: PCAOB audits require an integrated audit of F/S and internal control over financial reporting (ICFR). Additional objectives for integrated audits are discussed in a later section.

Assurance hierarchy

Cost and time to achieve →

Absolute assurance
- Ensures 100% accuracy
- Every financial item is looked at

Reasonable assurance
- Ensures a comfortable level of accuracy
- Financial items above a threshold are tested

No assurance
- Ensures no level of accuracy
- No items are tested

Inherent Limitations of an Audit

Due to inherent limitations in the audit, the auditor cannot obtain *absolute assurance* that the F/S are free from material misstatement. These limitations result in most audit evidence being persuasive rather than conclusive. Inherent limitations include the following items.

Nature of Financial Reporting. The preparation and fair presentation of F/S involves management's judgment and subjective decisions (eg, accounting estimates). Therefore, some items are subject to an inherent level of variability that cannot be eliminated with the application of audit procedures.

Nature of Audit Procedures. There are practical and legal limitations on the auditor's ability to obtain audit evidence. For example:

- Even though audit procedures are performed to obtain assurance that all relevant information has been obtained, the auditor still cannot be certain that management or others have provided complete information.

- Audit procedures may be ineffective at detecting intentional misstatements that may be concealed (ie, fraud).

- The auditor is not given specific legal powers (eg, the power of search) that would be required in an official investigation into wrongdoing.

Timeliness of Financial Reporting and the Balance Between Benefit and Cost. The relevance and value of information tends to diminish over time. It is also impracticable to address all information. Therefore, it is expected that the auditor will form an opinion on the F/S within a reasonable period of time to balance the benefits of the audit with its cost. This makes it necessary for the auditor to:

- Plan the audit so that it will be performed in an effective manner;

- Direct a larger proportion of audit effort to areas expected to contain risks of material misstatement; and

- Use testing and other means of examining populations for misstatements.

Reasonable Assurance

To express an opinion on the F/S, the auditor obtains reasonable assurance as to whether the F/S are free from material misstatement. Reasonable assurance is a high level of assurance, although it is not equivalent to absolute assurance.

- The scope of the audit is limited to items that are considered material.

- The auditor cannot look at evidence supporting all information in the F/S.

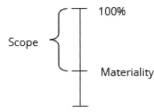

To obtain reasonable assurance, the auditor:

- Plans the work

- Properly supervises assistants

- Determines and applies appropriate materiality levels

- Identifies and assesses risks of material misstatement (RMM)
  - May be due to error or fraud
  - Based on auditor's understanding of entity and environment

- Obtains sufficient appropriate audit evidence

Steps in an Audit

Prepare for the Audit	Obtain understanding of client, its environment & I/C	Assess RMM & design further procedures	Perform tests of controls	Perform substantive procedures	Form opinion	Issue report

1.02 Auditor's Objectives & Reponsibilities

Overview

Financial statements (F/S) are **prepared by management** of an entity and belong to the entity.

The external auditor provides management and users with an objective and independent view of those F/S and provides credibility to those statements.

Responsibilities of management and auditor	
Management	• Prepare financial statements • Comply with laws and regulations • Establish and monitor internal controls • Provide auditor with relevant information
Auditor	• Provide reasonable assurance • Adhere to auditing standards • Understand regulatory environment • Assess internal controls

Objectives and Responsibilities

We will use the mnemonic **TIPICANOE** to provide a big-picture summary of the auditor's objectives and responsibilities.

These objectives and responsibilities can be broken up into three categories:

- **Responsibilities** that are applicable throughout the audit.
- **Performance** objectives that are applicable in the gathering of audit evidence.
- **Reporting** objectives that are applicable to the audit report.

Overall Objectives & Responsibilities of the Auditor (TIPICANOE)	
Responsibilities	**T**raining & professional judgment
	Independence & due care (ethics)
	Professional skepticism
Performance	**I**nternal controls
	Corroborative, sufficient appropriate audit evidence
Reporting	**A**ccounting principles in accordance with AFRF
	No new principles – consistency/comparability
	Omitted disclosures – none
	Express an opinion

Training & Professional Judgment

- AU-C 200 requires the auditor to exercise professional judgment in planning and performing the audit. **Professional judgment** is generally defined as the application of relevant **training**, **knowledge**, and **experience** to make appropriate decisions during the audit.

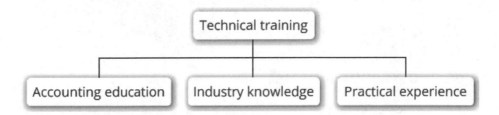

- Professional judgment is particularly necessary in making decisions related to:
  - Materiality
  - Audit risk
  - The nature, timing, and extent of audit procedures to be applied
  - Evaluations as to whether audit evidence is appropriate and sufficient
  - The evaluation of management's judgments
  - Drawing conclusions from the evidence obtained

Professional judgment applied throughout the audit should be adequately documented so that an experienced auditor will understand any significant judgments made in reaching conclusions.

Independence & Other Ethical Requirements, including Due Care

The auditor should be **independent in fact and appearance** of the entity and comply with all other relevant requirements of the AICPA Code of Professional Conduct. (AU-C 200)

- Independence enhances the auditor's ability to act with integrity and objectivity and maintain an attitude of professional skepticism.

- Independence includes the auditor, their spouse, dependent kids, or dependent relatives.

- There are circumstances under which an auditor will perform an audit *despite a lack of independence*:

  o GAAS provides for circumstances that allow the auditor to accept the engagement.

  o The auditor is required by law or regulation to accept the engagement.

Other ethical requirements include the AICPA Code of Professional Conduct, rules of state boards of accountancy, and other relevant regulatory agencies, as well as other requirements related to F/S audits.

Due care requires:

- **Planning** and adequately **supervising** the audit

- Acting with competence and diligence

- Having the **capabilities** to perform the audit

Professional Skepticism

The auditor should plan and perform the audit with **professional skepticism**, which recognizes that the F/S could be materially misstated. Professional skepticism includes:

- Having a questioning mind

- Being **alert** to the possibilities of misstatement due to **fraud** or **error**

- Critically assessing audit evidence

Applying professional skepticism reduces the risks associated with:

- Overlooking unusual circumstances

- Drawing conclusions from audit procedures that are over-generalized

- Making decisions regarding the nature, timing, and extent of audit procedures and evaluating the results of procedures, using inappropriate assumptions

Auditors may find it difficult to continually apply professional skepticism due to their biases, whether conscious or unconscious, and other cognitive tendencies.

- **Availability bias** – Auditors may place an undue amount of emphasis on events or experiences that come to mind easily (eg, management's explanation for a fluctuation), and ignore other possibilities that are more difficult to imagine.

- **Confirmation bias** – Auditors may place an undue amount of emphasis on information that confirms their existing beliefs or expectations. For example, the auditor may expect that internal controls are operating effectively so they tend to dismiss evidence to the contrary.

- **Overconfidence bias** – Auditors may overestimate their ability to make accurate risk assessments and quick judgments or decisions.

- **Anchoring bias** – Auditors may place and undue amount of emphasis on an early piece of information (eg, provided by management), which causes the auditor to use that information as an anchor against which all other information is improperly evaluated.

- **Automation bias** – Auditors may rely too heavily on the output from automated systems, even when conflicting information exists about whether it is reliable or suitable for the auditor's purpose.

- **Human bias** – If the auditor has a friendly relationship with client employees, the auditor may inadvertently favor the client when evaluating audit evidence. This is particularly true when there are incentives or pressure by the CPA firm to build and expand client relationships.

- **Misplaced trust in management** – Auditors who have worked with the client in previous years may build up a trust in management that is misplaced and unwarranted.

- **Time demands** – Unrealistic time budgets can result in auditors taking shortcuts in audit procedures, such as testing easily obtained evidence rather than evidence that is more difficult and time consuming to obtain and test.

Performance

Internal Controls – Rely ↑

- AU-C 315 requires the auditor to obtain an **understanding** of the entity and its **environment**, including its **internal control (I/C)**, to assess the risks of material misstatement (**RMM**) of the F/S whether due to **error or fraud**.

> Inverse relationship

Corroborative Audit Evidence – Substantive Testing ↓

- The objective of an audit is for the auditor to obtain **reasonable assurance** that the entity's F/S are free from material misstatement. In order to obtain reasonable assurance, the auditor needs to obtain **sufficient appropriate (Corroborative)** audit **evidence** to reduce audit risk to an acceptably low level. This allows the auditor to draw reasonable conclusions on which to base their opinion. (AU-C 200)
  - *Sufficiency* refers to the *quantity* of evidence needed.
  - *Appropriateness* refers to the *quality* of evidence needed.

Reporting

Accounting Principles in Conformity with AFRF (Explicitly stated)

AU-C 700 requires the auditor to evaluate whether the F/S are presented fairly, in all material respects, in accordance with the applicable financial reporting framework (eg, GAAP).

No new Accounting Principles applied – Comparability/Consistency (Implied)

AU-C 708 requires the auditor to evaluate whether the comparability (consistency) of the F/S between periods has been materially affected by a change in accounting principle or by adjustments to correct material misstatements.

The report should indentify circumstances in which *principles have not been consistently observed* in the current period in relation to the preceding period.

Omitted Informative Disclosures – None (Implied)

It is implied in an unmodified report that informative **disclosures** in the F/S are reasonably **adequate.** If they are inadequate, the report must be modified to say so. (AU-C 705)

Expression of an Opinion (Explicitly Stated)

AU-C 700 requires the auditor to express an **unmodified opinion** when the auditor concludes that the F/S *are presented fairly*, in all material respects, in accordance with the AFRF.

The auditor's opinion should be **modified** if:

- The F/S are materially misstated, or

- The auditor is unable to obtain sufficient appropriate audit evidence to conclude that the F/S are free from material misstatement.

1.03 Engagement Acceptance

Auditor Appointment

For entities with formal structures, the outside auditor meets with the **audit committee** of the BOD. The audit committee is a sub-committee made up of board members who are not officers or employees of the company (ie, they must be **independent**).

Entities that are not subject to the provisions of Sarbanes-Oxley (ie, **nonissuers**) may not have an audit committee. When that is the case, the individuals who oversee the accounting and financial reporting processes for the entity as well as the audit are considered to be the audit committee. In some cases, this may be only one person.

The prospective auditor negotiates with the audit committee to enter the audit engagement and establish an understanding. This understanding is required to be documented in the form of a written **engagement letter** or a comparable document and may be sent to the audit committee for the client's signature.

The auditor will also perform other preliminary engagement activities (AU-C 300), including:

Quality control for client acceptance

• Ensure association with clients whose management acts with integrity
• Provide reasonable assurance that the CPA firm
  ○ Is competent to perform engagement
  ○ Has needed capabilities
  ○ Can comply with legal and ethical requirements

- Evaluating compliance with relevant **ethical requirements** (eg, independence rules).
- Establishing an understanding with the client, documented in the form of an **engagement letter.**
  - The auditor is required to obtain management's agreement that it understands and acknowledges its responsibilities, regardless of whether the auditor contracts with management, exclusively with those charged with governance, or exclusively with a third party.

In the following sections we will focus primarily on the preconditions for an audit and other engagement requirements that are under the control of management rather than the auditor. Quality control, ethical requirements, and the engagement letter will all be discussed in more detail in later sections. In the meantime, the following is a quick checklist (**CLIP**) of how these items all work together to keep the auditor from accepting an engagement when they should not.

Prospective Client Acceptance Checklist (Don't CLIP the client)	
Capabilities of the firm	• Adequate training, skills, and experience • Firm's staffing resources • Reasonable deadline
Legal and ethical standards	• Auditor independence • Engagement does not violate laws or code
Integrity of the client	• Communicate with previous auditors • Assess the client's reputation • No scope limitations • Management tone at the top
Preconditions for an audit	• AFRF* is acceptable • Management accepts its responsibilities

*Applicable financial reporting framework

Preconditions & Other Requirements

Preconditions for an Audit

The first step in preparing for an audit is to decide whether to accept the engagement, which will depend on whether the preconditions for an audit have been met.

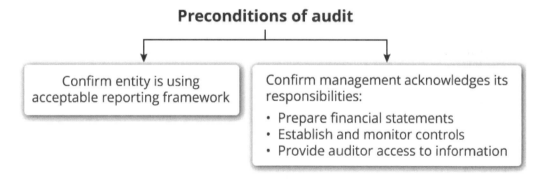

Preconditions of audit

Confirm entity is using acceptable reporting framework

Confirm management acknowledges its responsibilities:
• Prepare financial statements
• Establish and monitor controls
• Provide auditor access to information

Scope Limitations

A **scope limitation** imposed by the client that would require the auditor to issue a disclaimer of opinion would generally *preclude* the auditor from accepting the engagement. The auditor may, but is not required to, accept the engagement in such circumstances if the entity is required to have an audit by law or regulation (eg, employee benefit plans). The auditor can accept an engagement when a scope limitation is imposed by:

- Management, but it will likely result in a qualified opinion

- Circumstances beyond management's control

Considering a scope limitation

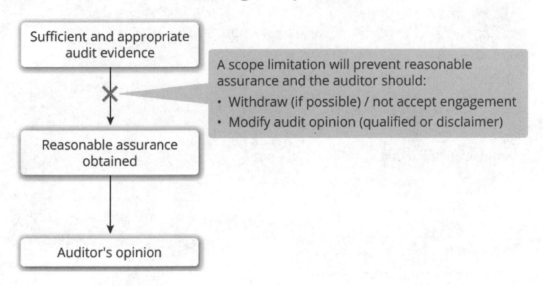

Timing of Engagement.

Accepting an audit engagement **after the fiscal year end** may create a **scope limitation** as the auditor may not be able to perform certain audit procedures (eg, observing year end inventory count). If such limitations can be remedied with alternative procedures (eg, reconciling the count to the reported inventory amount using perpetual inventory records), the auditor can accept the engagement.

Management's Integrity

An auditor will not wish to associate with an entity that has management who **lacks integrity**. Management has influence over every part of the day-to-day operations of the business and the financial records, and the F/S are, ultimately, the representation of management. If the auditor cannot trust the key officers of the business, all evidence related to the F/S will be subject to serious doubt.

Engagement Letter

Once the auditor has accepted the engagement, a **written** engagement letter is sent to the client. In it, the auditor will confirm the responsibilities of the various parties (ie, establish an understanding with the client). The engagement letter is signed by both the client and the auditor. It should include the following:

- Scope and objectives of the audit

- Auditor responsibilities – These include:

- o Conducting an audit in accordance with GAAS
- o Assessing and responding to the risks of material misstatement of the F/S, whether due to fraud or error
- o Obtaining an understanding of I/C relevant to the audit in order to design audit procedures
- o Communicating any significant deficiencies or material weaknesses in I/C
- o Evaluating the appropriateness of accounting policies used, the reasonableness of significant accounting estimates, and the overall presentation of the F/S
- o Concluding whether there are conditions or events that raise substantial doubt about the entity's ability to continue as a going concern for a reasonable period of time

- A statement that, due to the **inherent limitations of an audit and I/C**, material misstatements may not be detected (even though the audit is properly planned and performed in accordance with GAAS)

- Management (client) responsibilities – These include:
  - o Making all records available
  - o Not limiting the scope of the auditor's work
  - o Paying the fee based on the agreed-upon method
  - o Preparation and fair presentation of F/S
  - o Design, implementation, and maintenance (DIM) of I/C
  - o Management representation letter

- **Identification** of the applicable financial reporting framework (**AFRF**)

- Reference to the **expected form and content of the report** with an indication that the actual report may differ

- A request for management's acknowledgment, evidenced by their signature on the engagement letter, of receipt of the engagement letter and agreement to its terms (ie, **confirmation of engagement**)

- **Other relevant information** – Other matters may be referred to in the engagement letter, such as:
  - o Elaboration on the scope of the audit
  - o Matters related to the planning and performance of the audit
    - For example, the engagement team's composition, and the involvement of other auditors, specialists, internal auditors, and other entity staff
  - o Communication of key audit matters and other ways the auditor will communicate the results of the engagement
  - o The anticipation that management will provide written representations
  - o The expectation that management will provide access to all information that is relevant to the preparation and fair presentation of the F/S and disclosures
  - o Management's agreement to inform the auditor of subsequent events and subsequently discovered facts relevant to the F/S
  - o **Fees** and billing arrangements
  - o In an initial audit, arrangements to be made with the predecessor

- Restrictions, if any, on the auditor's liability
- The auditor's obligations, if any, to provide audit documentation to other parties
- Additional services to be provided by the auditor
- Any further agreements between the auditor and the entity

Elements of engagement letter

(FACSIMILE)

- **F**ees
- **A**uditor's responsibilities
- **C**onfirmation of engagement
- **S**cope and objective
- **I**nternal controls
- **M**anagement's responsibilities
- **I**rregularities (fraud)
- **Il**legal acts
- **E**rrors

 Engagement Letter Example

Mr. John Apple, Chairman of the Audit Committee
Budget Co.
555 State Street
San Francisco, California 94133

Dear Mr. Apple,

(Scope and Objectives of the Audit)

You have requested that we audit the financial statements of Budget Co., which comprise the balance sheet as of December 31, 20XX, and the related statements of income, changes in stockholders' equity, and cash flows for the year then ended, and the related notes to the financial statements. We are pleased to confirm our acceptance and our understanding of this audit engagement by means of this letter.

The **objectives** of our audit are to obtain **reasonable assurance** about whether the financial statements as a whole are free from material misstatement, whether due to fraud or error, and to **issue an auditor's report that includes our opinion**. Reasonable assurance is a high level of assurance but is not absolute assurance and therefore is not a guarantee that an audit conducted in accordance with auditing standards generally accepted in the United States of America (GAAS) will always detect a material misstatement when it exists. Misstatements can arise from fraud or error and are considered material if there is a substantial likelihood that, individually or in the aggregate, they would influence the judgment made by a reasonable user based on the financial statements.

(Responsibilities of the Auditor)

We will conduct our audit in accordance with GAAS. As part of an audit in accordance with GAAS, we exercise professional judgment and maintain professional skepticism throughout the audit. We also:

- Identify and assess the risks of material misstatement of the financial statements, whether **due to fraud or error**, design and perform audit procedures responsive to those risks, and obtain audit evidence that is sufficient and appropriate to provide a basis for our opinion. The risk of not detecting a material misstatement resulting from fraud is higher than for one resulting from error, as fraud may involve collusion, forgery, intentional omissions, misrepresentations, or the override of internal control.

- Obtain an understanding of **internal control** relevant to the audit in order to design audit procedures that are appropriate in the circumstances, but not for the purpose of expressing an opinion on the effectiveness of the entity's internal control. However, **we will communicate** to you in writing concerning any **significant deficiencies or material weaknesses** in internal control relevant to the audit of the financial statements that we have identified during the audit.

- Evaluate the **appropriateness of accounting policies** used and the reasonableness of significant accounting estimates made by management, as well as evaluate the overall presentation of the financial statements, including the disclosures, and whether the financial statements represent the underlying transactions and events in a manner that achieves fair presentation.

- Conclude, based on the audit evidence obtained, whether there are conditions or events, considered in the aggregate, that raise substantial doubt about Budget Co.'s ability to continue as a **going concern** for a reasonable period of time.

Because of the **inherent limitations** of an audit, together with the inherent limitations of internal control, an unavoidable risk that some material misstatements may not be detected exists, even though the audit is properly planned and performed in accordance with GAAS.

(Responsibilities of Management and Identification of the AFRF)

Our audit will be conducted on the basis that management acknowledges and understands that they have **responsibility for the preparation and fair presentation of the financial statements** in accordance with accounting principles generally accepted in the United States of America; for the **design, implementation, and maintenance (DIM) of internal control** relevant to the preparation and fair presentation of financial statements that are free from material misstatement, whether due to fraud or error; and to provide us with **access to all information of which management is aware** that is relevant to the preparation and fair presentation of the financial statements such as records, documentation, and other matters; additional information that we may request from management for the purpose of the audit; and **unrestricted access to persons** within the entity from whom we determine it necessary to obtain audit evidence.

As part of our audit process, we will request from management, **written confirmation concerning representations** made to us in connection with the audit.

(Other Relevant Information)

We will provide you with a **list of schedules** and information needed by our staff during the audit. It is our mutual understanding that in order to meet the audit deadlines, which we have established, your staff will provide that necessary information on a timely basis.

The **fees** for our services will be at our regular per diem rates plus out-of-pocket expenses. Invoices are payable upon presentation.

(Reporting)

We will issue a written report upon completion of our audit of Budget Co.'s financial statements. Our report will be addressed to the board of directors of Budget Co. Circumstances may arise in which our **report may differ from its expected form and content** based on the results of our audit. Depending on the nature of these circumstances, it may be necessary for us to modify our opinion, add an emphasis-of-matter paragraph or other-matter paragraph to our auditor's report, or if necessary, withdraw from the engagement.

Please sign and return the attached copy of this letter to indicate your acknowledgment of, and agreement with, the arrangements for our audit of the financial statements including our respective responsibilities.

Sincerely,
Roger Philip, Partner
Acknowledged and agreed on behalf of Budget Co. by

_____
(Signed) (Name and Title) (Date)

Recurring Audits

When the auditor is engaged for recurring audits, the auditor may determine that the terms of the preceding engagement may or may not need revision. If the terms do not need revision, the auditor should remind the client of the terms of the engagement, which may be done in writing or orally, but should be documented. Indications that the terms of the preceding engagement may need to be revised include:

- Indications that management does not understand the objective and scope of the engagement

- Revised or special terms

- A significant change in the entity's size or the nature of its business

- Changes to senior management or a significant change in ownership

- Changes to legal or regulatory requirements

- A change in the AFRF or other reporting requirements

First Year Audits – Communication with Predecessor Auditor

If the prior statements were audited, the auditor should request that management authorize the predecessor to:

- **Allow the successor to review the predecessor's documentation** – The auditor should read the most recent F/S and the predecessor's report. If the opinion is modified, the auditor should evaluate the effect on the current period F/S.

- **Respond fully to inquiries by the successor** – Once the client has authorized communication, the successor will generally make inquiries of the predecessor auditor about several key issues **(RID-C-U)**.

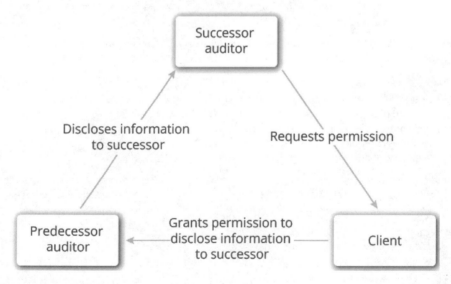

Client authorization required

- o **Reasons for change** – The successor needs to know why the predecessor understands that they are no longer the continuing auditor of the client.

- o **Integrity of management** – The predecessor should inform the successor whether they believe management can be trusted.

- o **Disagreements during audit** – If any conflicts arose regarding the application of accounting principles or the performance of auditing procedures during the time the predecessor was the auditor of the client, the predecessor should provide necessary details for the successor to understand the nature of the disagreements and how they were resolved.

- o **Communication with management or those charged with governance** – The predecessor should inform the successor of such communications regarding fraud and noncompliance with applicable laws and regulations, including illegal acts, as well as significant deficiencies and material weaknesses in I/C.

- o *Understanding of related party relationships/transactions and significant unusual transactions* – The predecessor should inform the successor of their understanding of the entity's related party relationships/transactions as well as any significant unusual transactions—ie, significant transactions outside the normal course of business or those that seem unusual due to timing, size, or nature.

Communication with predecessor auditor
(RID-CU)
Reasons for change
Integrity of management
Disagreements during audit
Communication with management or those charged with governance
Understand related party transactions and significant unusual transactions

If F/S audited by a predecessor auditor require *substantial revision*, it is the responsibility of the *successor auditor* to request that the client arrange a meeting among the three parties to attempt to resolve the matter.

The predecessor should cooperate as much as possible with the successor. If there is a legitimate reason (eg, attorney advice) that causes the predecessor to limit their response to the successor, the successor should inform the client of the limited response. This may affect the decision as to whether to accept the engagement.

Change in Engagement

Occasionally the client will request that the ongoing engagement be downgraded to a review or compilation. Similarly, an accountant performing a review may be asked to downgrade to a compilation, or vice versa. In such circumstances, the accountant should carefully consider:

- The reasons offered by the client for the changed engagement (eg, change in circumstances or a misunderstanding of the nature of an audit, review, or compilation).

- The additional effort and additional cost needed to complete the original engagement (if little time or effort is involved to complete the initial engagement, the auditor should look carefully at why the client wants the change – are they trying to hide something?)

If the request of the client is reasonable, the accountant will switch to the requested engagement. The report resulting from the new engagement makes no reference to the original engagement or the reasons for the change, as it would only serve to confuse the reader as to the nature of the work performed by the accountant.

If the reasons are not justifiable, the accountant should consider *withdrawing* from the engagement. If, while auditing an entity's F/S, management refuses to allow the accountant to correspond with the entity's legal counsel (ie, a scope limitation), the accountant is generally precluded from changing to a review engagement.

1.04 Communication with Management & Those Charged with Governance

Overview

During the conduct of an audit, there are several items that the auditor is required to communicate regarding the entity. In such cases, the auditor will communicate with those charged with governance, which may include management. (AU-C 260)

- Members of management may serve as executive members of the board of directors.
- In owner-managed entities, management and governance are the same.

Those charged with governance may also include:

- Members of the entity's legal structure, such as company directors
- Parties external to the entity, such as certain government agencies
- A collective group of people, such as a Board of Directors (BOD)

Those charged with governance are responsible for **overseeing the strategic direction** of the entity and the obligations related to accountability.

Management

Management includes those with executive responsibility for the **conduct of the entity's organization**. In some cases, all of those charged with governance are also involved in managing the entity. When that is not the case, there are additional items that are communicated to those charged with governance.

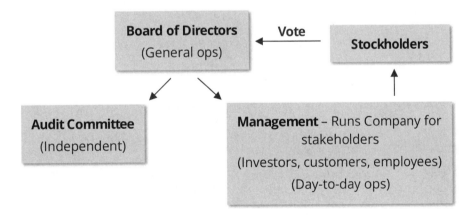

Objectives of Communication

Communication with those charged with governance is intended to promote a mutual sharing of relevant information. The objectives of establishing such communication are to:

- Provide those charged with governance with information about the auditor's responsibilities regarding the audit, including an overview of the **planned scope and timing**

- **Obtain information** (eg, regarding specific transactions or events) relevant to the audit from those charged with governance

- **Provide** those charged with governance with the **auditor's observations** arising from the audit that may be relevant to their role in the oversight of the financial reporting process

Matters to Be Communicated

Certain matters should be communicated to those charged with governance. While there are many matters that the auditor should communicate, the items that will be tested have been narrowed down to matters related to the following two subjects.

The planned scope and timing of the engagement – This includes communications regarding **significant risks** identified by the auditor that may require special consideration. However, the auditor should not discuss the detailed audit plan or specific audit procedures with the audit committee or management since it might reduce the effectiveness of the audit. Such communications might involve:

- **Issues of risk and materiality**

  o How will the auditor address *significant risks* of material misstatement (RMM) and areas of higher assessed RMM?

  o What factors will the auditor consider when determining *materiality*?

  o What are the entity's views of their objectives/strategies and the related *business risks* that may result in material misstatements?

- **Consequences of the auditor's work**

  o Will the auditor need to use any *specialists* to perform audit procedures or to evaluate results of procedures? If so, what is the nature and extent of the special skills or knowledge required?

  o Will the auditor need any assistance from the entity's *internal auditors*? If so, what is the nature and extent of the assistance required?

  o Is the entity aware of any matters that call for additional procedures to be performed by the auditor?

- **The entity and its environment**

  o What approach will the auditor take with respect to internal control over financial reporting (ICFR)?

  o Will the auditor be expressing an opinion on ICFR?

  o How will the auditor approach the implications for individual F/S and disclosures of significant changes in the applicable financial reporting framework (AFRF), the entity's environment, financial condition, or operations?

  o What are the attitudes, awareness, and actions of those charged with governance regarding ICFR, its effectiveness, and the detection or possibility of fraud?

  o What actions have been taken with respect to changes in law, accounting standards, corporate governance practices, etc.?

  o What actions have been taken with respect to previous communications with the auditor?

Additionally, certain disagreements with management should be reported to governance, including:

Disagreements with management to be reported to governance
Matters significant to the financial statements or the audit report • Scope of the audit • Wording of the auditor's report • Application of accounting principles • Basis for management's judgments about estimates • Disclosures to be included in the financial statements

The auditor *should not discuss* the detailed audit plan or specific audit procedures with the audit committee or management since it might reduce the effectiveness of the audit .**Deficiencies and material weaknesses in internal control (I/C)** is discussed in a later chapter.

Form, Timing & Adequacy of Communications

Those charged with governance should be informed by the auditor as to the form, timing, and expected general content of communications.

Form & Timing

Communications may be **oral** (eg, formal presentations or informal discussions) or in **writing**, and should be communicated on a timely basis. This may be during the audit or after the audit report is issued[1].

- Matters communicated orally should be **documented** by the auditor.

- Any written report should clearly indicate that it is intended solely for the information and use of the parties specified. That is, the report is **restricted** to those charged with governance, and management, if applicable.

- Written communications include the **engagement letter**.

- Whether communications are oral or written may depend on various circumstances, such as:
  - Whether the matter has been resolved, was previously communicated, or is discussed in the auditor's report
  - The size, operational structure, control environment, and legal structure of the entity
  - Legal or regulatory requirements
  - The expectations of those charged with governance

---

[1] *Under PCAOB AS 1301, the auditor is required to submit the communication to those charged with governance prior to issuance of the auditor's report.*

Adequacy

The auditor should evaluate the adequacy of the two-way communication with those charged with governance. If communication was inadequate, the auditor should evaluate the effect on auditor's RMM assessment and the ability to obtain sufficient appropriate evidence. Adequacy may be determined based on the auditor's observations, such as:

- Were actions taken in response to the auditor's communications appropriate and timely?

- Did those charged with governance appear to be open in their communications with the auditor?

- Were they willing and capable of meeting with the auditor without management being present?

- Did those charged with governance appear to fully comprehend the matters communicated?

1.05 Planning Procedures

Overview

Audit planning involves developing an **overall audit strategy** for the expected conduct, timing, and scope of the audit. The overall strategy is then used to develop an **audit plan** that details the specific audit procedures that should be performed. (AU-C 300)

Adequate planning helps the auditor:

- Dedicate adequate attention to critical audit items
- Solve potential problems in a timely manner
- Coordinate an efficient and effective engagement
- Select capable and competent engagement team members to address anticipated risks and allocate responsibilities to those team members
- Direct, supervise, and review team members' work
- Organize the work of other auditors and specialists, if applicable

Nature, Timing & Extent of Planning

The nature, extent and timing of planning will vary with:

- The size and complexity of the entity
- The auditor's experience with the entity
- Knowledge of the entity's business and industry
- Knowledge of the entity and its environment, including I/C

Overall Audit Strategy

The auditor's planning activities, applied in developing the overall strategy, include:

- Identifying characteristics of the engagement that affect the scope of the audit
- Determining the reporting objectives to plan the nature and timing of communications
- Considering other factors that the auditor deems significant to the direction of the audit
- Considering the preliminary activities and relevant knowledge gained from other engagements
- Ascertaining the nature, timing, and extent of resources needed to perform the engagement

Business & Industry Considerations

Different businesses have different types of transactions, regulatory environments, accounting policies, and systems of accounting and record keeping, each of which will affect the audit program.

Business Considerations

To gain an understanding of the client's business, the auditor should:

- Tour the client facilities, particularly any area related to production

- Review client's operating history (eg, read previous audit reports, minutes of BOD meetings, SEC filings, and tax returns)

- Obtain an understanding of the client's accounting practices

- Talk with client personnel and management about identified problems, concerns, and business risks

Industry Considerations

Specialized audit manuals developed by the AICPA can provide guidance in developing audit programs meeting the unique requirements of certain industries. In addition, *AICPA Accounting Trends and Techniques*, an annual publication summarizing disclosures of 600 industrial and merchandising corporations, is a useful source of information when evaluating disclosures.

Other Planning Considerations

- The entity's accounting policies and procedures

- The methods used to process accounting information, which influences the design of I/C

- F/S items likely to require adjustment

- Conditions that may require extension or modification of audit tests

- The nature of reports expected to be issued

Supervision & Review

The auditor with final responsibility for the audit is responsible for planning the nature, extent, and timing of direction and the supervision of engagement team members. The supervision and review of team members' work may depend on factors, such as:

- The size and complexity of the entity

- The area of the audit

- The assessed RMM

- The capabilities and competence of individual team members

Supervision includes:

- Tracking audit progress

- Considering the competence and capabilities of individual team members
- Addressing significant findings/issues arising during the audit and modifying the planned approach if necessary
- Identifying matters for consultation or consideration by qualified team members

Review responsibilities may be delegated to experienced team members. Such responsibilities may include considering whether:

- Work has been performed in accordance with professional standards and legal and regulatory requirements
- The nature, timing and extent of work performed is appropriate, documented, and supports the conclusions reached
- The objectives of the procedures have been achieved and evidence obtained is sufficient and appropriate to support the auditor's report

Steps in Planning the Audit

The steps in planning an audit include (**BRAINSTOPS**):

1. **Basic discussions with the client** about the nature of the engagement and the client's business and industry are performed first. In addition, the auditor meets the key employees, or new employees of a continuing client. The overall audit strategy or the timing of the audit may be discussed, but the specific audit procedures should not be.

2. **Review of audit documentation** from previous audits performed by the accounting firm (or a predecessor auditor, if available) will assist in developing an outline of the audit program.

3. **Ask about recent developments** in the company, such as mergers and new product lines, which will cause the audit to differ from earlier years.

4. **Interim F/S** are analyzed to identify accounts and transactions that differ from expectations (based on factors such as budgets or prior periods). The performance of **analytical procedures** (discussed later) is **mandatory** in the planning of an audit to identify accounts that may be misstated and that deserve special emphasis in the audit program.

5. **Non**audit personnel of the accounting firm who have provided services (such as tax preparation) to the client should be identified and consulted to learn more about the client.

6. **Staffing** for the audit should be determined and a meeting held to discuss the engagement.

7. **Timing** of the various audit procedures should be determined. For example, I/C testing needs to be performed early in the engagement, inventory counts need to be performed at or near the balance sheet date, and the client representation letter cannot be obtained until the end of the audit fieldwork.

Procedures performed before/after balance sheet date

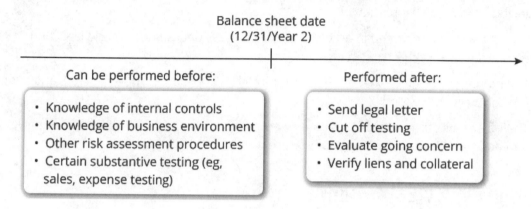

8. **Outside assistance** needs should be determined, including the use of a **specialist** (eg, a tax practitioner, an appraiser for special valuation issues, or an IT professional) and the internal auditors of the client. We'll discuss the use of specialists and others in more detail in a later section.

9. **Pronouncements** reflecting changes in accounting principles and audit standards should be read or reviewed to assist in the development of complete audit programs fitting the unique needs of the client's business and industry.

10. **Scheduling with the client** is needed to coordinate activities. For example, client-prepared schedules need to be ready when the auditor expects to examine them, and the client needs to be informed of dates when they will be prohibited from accessing bank safe deposit boxes to ensure the integrity of counts of securities held at banks.

Planning Documentation

The auditor should document the planning of the engagement, including:

- The overall audit strategy

- The audit plan

- Any significant changes made to either the overall strategy or the audit plan during the audit engagement, along with the reasons for the changes

Audit Plan/Program

An audit program (ie, a detailed audit plan) is a step-by-step **list of audit procedures**, which is **required** for every GAAS audit. It is written after sufficient planning procedures have been conducted and is designed so that:

- The planned procedures will achieve specific audit objectives, which relate to management's assertions.

- It supports the auditor's conclusion.

- It describes the **nature, timing, and extent** of audit procedures:

  o **Risk assessment procedures** are designed to provide an understanding of the entity and its environment, including I/C, in order to assess risk of material misstatement (RMM). However, on their own, they are not sufficient to support an audit opinion.

  o **Further audit procedures** at the relevant assertion level for each material class of transactions, account balance, and disclosure include tests of controls and substantive procedures.

    - **Tests of Controls (TOC)** – evaluate the operating effectiveness of I/C in preventing or detecting material misstatements. They are often used when the use of substantive procedures is not sufficient.

    - **Substantive Procedures** – detect material misstatements and include tests of details and substantive analytical procedures. Substantive procedures are required for all relevant assertions related to any material transaction class, account balance, and/or disclosure item.

Key factors to prepare an audit program

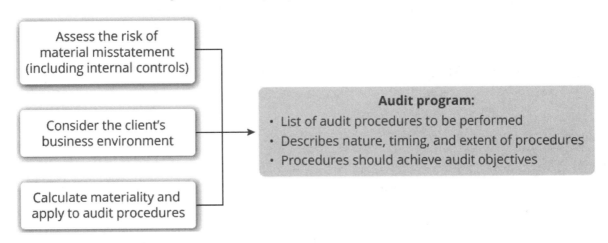

Audit procedure timing

For most clients, some testing can be conducted at an interim date (ie, prior to year end). There is some risk involved in testing earlier than year end, and the auditor must be satisfied that there are also procedures planned to extrapolate any results from the interim work. For example, the physical inventory count is typically performed before year end (assuming internal controls are strong), and the information is then rolled forward to year end balances.

Materiality

Misstatements and omissions are considered **material** if there is a *substantial likelihood* that, individually or in the aggregate, they would **influence the judgment** of a *reasonable user* based on the F/S.

- Professional Judgments about materiality consider:

  o Both *quantitative and qualitative information*

o *Surrounding circumstances*, including the size and nature of misstatements

o *The needs of F/S users as a group, rather than the effects of misstatements on individual users*

The auditor will apply the concept of materiality when:

- Deciding upon the risk assessment procedures to be performed in **obtaining an understanding** of the entity, its environment, and its I/C

- Assessing the risks of material misstatement

- Determining the **nature, timing, and extent** of further audit procedures

- Evaluating identified misstatements in the performance of the engagement and the effects of uncorrected misstatements on the F/S

- Forming an opinion on the F/S

Materiality in preliminary audit planning

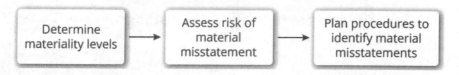

Misstatements will not always be considered immaterial when they are below the materiality threshold. Some misstatements may be *qualitatively* material due to the circumstances. For example, this might include misstatements:

- That affect trends of profitability

- That change losses into income

- That affect segment information

- That affect compliance with legal and contractual requirements

- With respect to related party transactions

Determining Materiality

In planning the engagement, the auditor determines materiality in relation to the F/S, which will be used to determine if the F/S, taken as a whole, are materially misstated.

Evaluating materiality of a misstatement

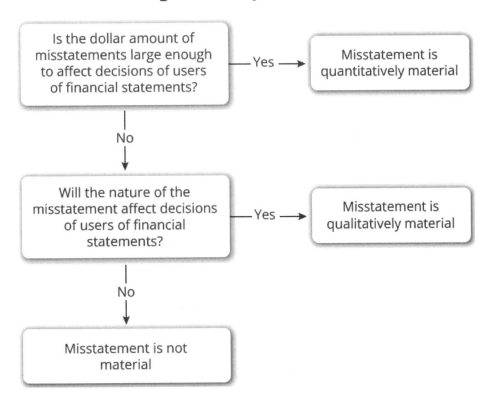

In addition, separate lower materiality levels may be established for specific classes of transactions, account balances, or disclosures. This would be the case when a misstatement to one of those items that is lower than the materiality level designated for the F/S, taken as a whole, would influence users of the F/S.

Materiality for individual or collective misstatements

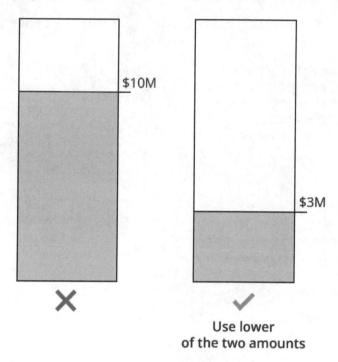

Materiality is often measured by applying a percentage to some **benchmark**. Common benchmarks include categories of income, including profit before tax, total revenue, gross profit, or total expenses; total equity; or assets. The selection of an appropriate benchmark will be influenced by a variety of factors, such as:

- The elements of the F/S (eg, assets, liabilities)
- Items on the F/S that are expected to be of particular interest to the users
- The nature of the entity, including its level of maturity, its industry, and the economic environment in which it operates
- The entity's ownership structure and how it is financed (eg, solely by debt or equity)
- The volatility of the benchmark

The percentage to be applied to the benchmark is a matter of professional judgment and will consider the nature of the benchmark. A higher percentage, for example, would be applied to a benchmark based on earnings, such as profit before taxes or gross profit, than would be applied to an item like total revenues.

Performance Materiality

The auditor also determines performance materiality. This considers that a misstatement that is *immaterial* in relation to the F/S as a whole may be material when combined with other identified misstatements. Thus, **performance materiality is lower** than materiality at the F/S level. It is estimated at an amount such that it is probable that the aggregate of uncorrected and undetected misstatements will not reach the level of F/S materiality.

Performance materiality can also refer to the amount(s) set by the auditor at less than the materiality level for particular classes of transactions, account balances, or disclosures.

Applying the concept of performance materiality to a particular sample is called **tolerable misstatement**. It is the *maximum* error in the population that the auditor is willing to accept.

Changing the Measurement of Materiality

During the engagement, the auditor may become aware of issues that will change the measurement of materiality.

Changing materiality levels

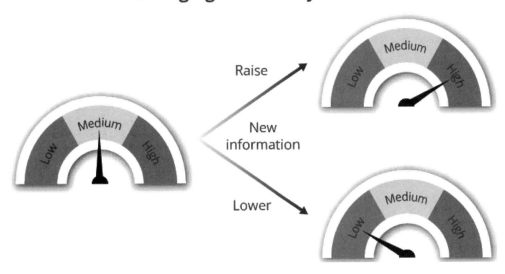

If, for example, materiality was measured as a percentage of sales and, as a result of audit procedures applied, the auditor determines that sales were overstated, the auditor will revise materiality accordingly.

- A decrease in the benchmark will result in a decrease in the measurement of what is material.

- This may also result in a decrease to the materiality level assigned to one or more specific classes of transactions, account balances, or disclosures.

- Previously identified misstatements that were considered immaterial may have to be reevaluated in relation to the reduced measurement.

 If materiality was to be measured at 5% of sales and the client's trial balance indicated sales of $5,000,000, a misstatement under $250,000 would not be considered material. A proposed adjustment reducing sales to $4,500,000 due to an overstatement found would reduce the measurement of materiality to $225,000. Thus, a misstatement between $225,000 and $250,000 would now be considered material.

Materiality Documentation

The auditor is required to document:

- Materiality for the F/S taken as a whole

- Materiality for specific classes of transactions, account balances, or disclosures, if appropriate

- Performance materiality

- Revisions to any of the materiality measurements occurring during the engagement

1.06 Audit Risk

Overview

Audit risk is the risk that the auditor may unknowingly **fail to** appropriately **modify the opinion** on F/S that are **materially misstated**. The risk exists because auditors are only required to obtain *reasonable* (not absolute) assurance that the F/S are free of material misstatement.

A **misstatement** is a difference between the reported amount and that which is required for the item to be presented fairly in accordance with the applicable financial reporting framework (AFRF). Misstatements can occur due to fraud or error. Misstatements are classified into three categories:

- **Factual** – there is no doubt about the misstatement

- **Judgmental** – differences between management and the auditor on how an item should be recognized, measured, presented, or disclosed

- **Projected** – auditor's best estimate of the misstatement(s) for the population

- A material misstatement would typically cause a reasonable person to change their judgment about an item(s). Auditors consider the level of misstatement at both the individual and aggregate levels.

Audit Risk

Audit risk (AR) is the product of two component risks:

- **Risk of Material Misstatements (RMM)** is the risk that the relevant assertions related to account balances, classes of transactions, or disclosures contain misstatements that could be material to the F/S when aggregated with other misstatements. RMM consists of:

  - **Inherent risk (IR)** – The risk that a material misstatement of an assertion will occur in the absence of any internal controls. This risk is a function of the susceptibility of the various items to being misstated and cannot be affected by the actions of either the client or auditor.

Examples of inherent audit risk
• Complex transactions
• Estimated account values
• Accounts susceptible to theft
• Unexpected asset obsolescence
• Decline in industry or product demand

  - **Control risk (CR)** – The risk that the client's I/C structure will fail to prevent or detect and correct a material misstatement on a timely basis. This is a function of the effort put forth by the client's management to safeguard assets and ensure reliable financial records. As a result, it is affected by the actions of the client but not the auditor.

Effect of control risk on substantive testing sample size		
Tests of controls findings	Control risk	Substantive testing sample size
Internal controls are not effective	Increased	Higher
Internal controls are effective	Reduced	Lower

- **Detection risk (DR)** – The risk that audit procedures will lead to an incorrect conclusion that a material misstatement does not exist in an account balance when, in fact, such a misstatement does exist. This is a function of the effort put forth by the auditor in performing tests of details of transactions and accounts, and analytical procedures. It is the only risk component that the auditor can affect. DR can be broken down into two components:

  - Test of details risk **(TD)**

  - Substantive analytical procedures risk **(AP)**

Failure of the audit can occur only when the **two component** risk events occur together.

Audit Risk Model

Although the assessment of RMM is a matter of *professional judgment*, the auditor should have an appropriate basis for that assessment. This basis may be obtained through risk assessment procedures performed to obtain an understanding of the entity and its environment, including its I/C, and through the performance of test of controls.

Audit risk model

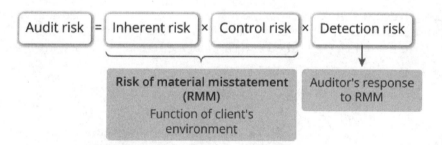

Detection risk bears an **inverse relationship to RMM** (IR × CR). The greater the RMM the auditor believes exists, the less the detection risk that can be accepted and vice versa. Regardless of the RMM, however, the auditor should perform substantive procedures for all relevant assertions related to all material classes of transactions, account balances, and disclosures.

Inverse relationship between RMM* and detection risk

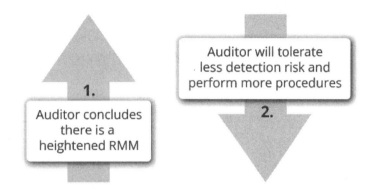

1.
Auditor concludes there is a heightened RMM

Auditor will tolerate less detection risk and perform more procedures
2.

Risk of material misstatement

Detection risk relates to the auditor's procedures and **can be altered** by adjusting the nature, timing, and extent of substantive procedures. Thus, the auditor performs the following procedures:

- **Determine** the acceptable level of **audit risk**, the risk that the auditor is willing to take, incorporating cost and benefit considerations, that a material misstatement may not be detected by the audit

- **Assess** the **RMM** by evaluating the inherent risk associated with financial statement elements and assessing control risk based on the auditor's understanding of I/C

- **Determine** the level of **detection risk** that is necessary to achieve the desired audit risk

The auditor may make a combined assessment of inherent risk and control risk or separate assessments of inherent risk and control risk. Audit risk and its two component risks can be expressed nonquantitatively (*high, medium,* or *low* risk), but the relationship between them is easier to understand when expressed mathematically:

- AR = IR × CR × DR, or AR = RMM × DR, thus acceptable **DR = AR / RMM**

- Also, AR = (IR × CR) × (TD × AP)

Impact of risk on audit testing

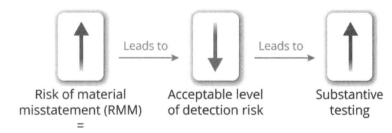

Leads to   Leads to

Risk of material
misstatement (RMM)
=
Inherent risk × Control risk

Acceptable level
of detection risk

Substantive
testing

Note: If the RMM decreases, the acceptable level of detection risk increases and substantive testing decreases.

Example

Audit Risk: Assume the auditor decides an audit risk of 6% is acceptable, indicating that the auditor is willing to accept that there will be a 6% probability that a material misstatement that would cause the auditor to modify the report will not be detected in the audit.

- **Inherent Risk:** The F/S include assets that are highly susceptible to theft, others that require significant estimates requiring high levels of judgment to determine their carrying values, and other items that are complex or involve very high volumes of transactions.

- As a result, the auditor would assess inherent risk as relatively high. Assume a value of 75%, indicating that there is a 75% probability that the F/S will be materially misstated if internal controls do not prevent or detect the misstatement and if the auditor does not detect it.

Control Risk: The client has established potentially effective internal controls in some key areas, but they are not universal throughout the organization or the processes relevant to financial reporting.

As a result, the auditor may assess control risk below maximum. Assume a value of 80%, indicating that, if a material misstatement does occur, there is an 80% probability that it will neither be prevented nor detected and corrected on a timely basis. To assess control risk below maximum (100%), the auditor is required to perform tests of controls to obtain evidence that the controls that are being relied upon are in place and being executed as designed.[2]

Based on an inherent risk of 75% and a control risk of 80%, RMM is 60% (75% × 80%). To achieve an audit risk of 6%, detection risk must be reduced to 10%.

RMM = IR × CR, so 75% × 80% = 60% RMM
AR = RMM × DR and AR / RMM = DR, so 6% / 60% = 10%

---

[2] *In many cases, the auditor will set control risk at maximum, despite the potential for some effective controls, if the auditor determines it is likely to be more efficient to ignore controls and perform substantive tests that will support a lower detection risk.*

1.07 Fraud vs. Errors

Misstatements

The **auditor's responsibility** is to plan and perform the audit to obtain **reasonable assurance** that **no errors or acts of fraud** have caused the financial statements (F/S) to be materially misstated.

The difference between an error and fraud is intent.

Fraud vs. error	
Fraud	**Error**
• Intentional • Always material • Always communicated	• Not intentional • May not be material • Generally communicated if material

Types of Fraud

There are two types of fraud that the auditor is concerned with: fraudulent financial reporting and misappropriation of assets.

Fraudulent financial reporting. This is a *misrepresentation of facts* (ie, lying) in the F/S (ie, "cooking the books"). It is generally committed by management to deceive users and may involve:

- Manipulation, falsification, or alteration of accounting records or supporting documents.
  - The inability to produce or locate relevant documents may be indicative of fraud.
- Misrepresentation or omission of events, transactions, or information.
- Intentional misapplication of accounting principles.

Misappropriation of assets. This involves the *theft or misuse of assets* and can be committed by management, employees, and/or third parties (collusion). Examples include:

- Stealing funds, physical assets (eg, inventory), or intellectual property
- Payments to fictitious vendors or employees
- Kickbacks to purchasing from vendors for approving inflated prices
- Using company assets as collateral for a personal loan

Fraud Risk Factors (Fraud Triangle)

There are three conditions (ie, the *fraud triangle*) that are generally assumed to be present whenever fraud occurs. These risk factors should be considered by the auditor when assessing fraud risk.

Incentive/pressure. Individuals generally have a **reason** or **motivation** to commit fraud, such as personal gain or pressure to meet certain objectives

Opportunity. A **lack of effective internal controls** allows for the opportunity to commit fraud. Individuals (particularly management) may have the authority to override controls or the ability to circumvent controls (eg, through collusion).

Rationalization. Individuals who commit fraud usually rationalize their behavior as justified. Some **rationalizations** (attitudes) include:

- Fraud isn't really wrong – after all, "everyone" does it.
- Revenge – they are justified in "getting even" with the company.
  - They have no choice since the repercussions of not perpetrating the fraud would be too severe (eg, the stock price will not meet an earnings expectation) and they will lose their job.

Consideration of Fraud in Planning the Audit

Due to the nature of fraud, the risk of not detecting it is higher than the risk of not detecting errors. Furthermore, the risk of not detecting *management fraud* is higher than the risk of not detecting employee fraud since management is generally in a better position to override controls and conceal it. Therefore, the auditor designs audit procedures to **obtain reasonable (not absolute) assurance** that the financial statements are free from material misstatement due to fraud or error.

Step 1. The auditor should gain an **understanding** of the nature and characteristics of fraud . Remember it is **management** that is responsible for designing and maintaining internal controls to prevent and detect fraud.

Step 2. A **brainstorming session** should be held with engagement team to discuss the risks of material misstatements due to fraud. This should include a discussion about the importance of maintaining **professional skepticism** regarding the potential for fraud. Other discussion items might include:

- How and where the F/S might be susceptible to fraud, how management could perpetrate fraud and conceal it, and how assets could be misappropriated (particularly revenue transactions)

- Known internal and external risk factors that may be creating motivation (incentives /pressures) for fraud, providing opportunities for fraud to occur, and indicating a culture or environment that enables management or others to rationalize committing fraud

- The risk of management **override of controls**

- Circumstances that might be indicative of earnings management or manipulation of other financial measures

- How the audit might respond to the susceptibility of F/S to material misstatement due to fraud

Step 3. The auditor should obtain the information needed to **identify risks of material misstatement due to fraud**. This might include:

- Inquiring of management and others (eg, internal auditors, audit committee) about:
  - Knowledge or suspicion of fraud
  - Management's assessment of the *overall risk* of fraud
  - Management's process for identifying and responding to fraud risk communications with those charged with governance
  - Whether the entity has entered any significant unusual transactions, and if so, the nature, terms, business purpose, and parties to such transactions

- Evaluating the results of analytical procedures performed in the planning of the audit. One of the most common ways in which F/S are fraudulently misstated is through the overstatement of revenue. As a result, the auditor is required to presume that revenue recognition represents a fraud risk.

- Considering *fraud risk factors*, which are events or conditions that create reasons or motivation to commit fraud, the opportunity to commit fraud, or the attitudes that allow the rationalization of committing fraud

The auditor will then **identify risks** that may result in a material misstatement to the F/S. Four questions should be used to assess identified risk:

- Which of the two types of risk is it?

- How significant is the risk?

- What is the likelihood of the risk occurring?

- How extensive (ie, pervasive) is the risk (eg, affects all of the F/S or just disclosures?)

Any fraud risks identified should be treated as **significant risks**, and the entity's internal controls should be evaluated to determine if such fraud risks are sufficiently mitigated.

Step 4. The auditor must **respond** to the fraud risk assessment in three areas:

- Overall, general response. Response examples include:

  o Assign and supervise personnel, considering their knowledge, skill, and abilities

  o Evaluate whether the entity's selection and application of accounting policies may be indicative of fraudulent financial reporting

  o Incorporate an element of unpredictability in the selection of the nature, timing, and extent of audit procedures

- Response for specific audit procedures. Typically, the auditor will revise the **nature, timing, and extent** of substantive procedures to respond to the fraud assessment results.

- Response for management override risks. Response examples include:

  o Test the appropriateness of journal entries and other adjustments

  o Review accounting estimates for bias

  o Evaluate the business purpose(s) for any significant unusual transactions

Step 5. The auditor **revises** the original fraud risk assessment throughout the audit, and will then **evaluate the accumulated audit evidence** at or near the end of the audit. The auditor will:

Evaluate results of audit procedures, including analytical procedures performed as substantive tests or as part of the overall review. Conditions which should cause concern include:

- Weak code of conduct

- Unexplained, frequent changes in accounting estimates

- Accounting policies and procedures not consistent with industry practice

- Missing evidence or unexplained discrepancies in evidence

If fraud is indicated, the auditor should:

- Consider the implications for the audit (eg, on materiality, management integrity, the reliability of evidence obtained, and possible need for additional evidence).

- Question their ability to continue the audit, consider withdrawing, if appropriate and possible.

Step 6. The auditor is required to **communicate** knowledge or suspicion of fraud to management and governance (as appropriate) on a timely basis. Risks that have I/C implications should be communicated if they represent significant deficiencies or material weaknesses in I/C.

Fraud detection audit steps

Gain an understanding of fraud

↓

Hold engagement team brainstorming session

↓

Identify risks of material misstatement (RMM) due to fraud

↓

Determine nature and timing of tests to detect fraud

↓

Evaluate results of tests

↓

Document

↓

Report

Disclosure to regulatory and legal authorities may also be appropriate when the auditor's legal responsibilities outweigh their duty to maintain confidentiality. For example, an audit of an entity receiving government financial assistance. Additional situations which might require disclosure include:

- To a successor auditor, with client permission

- In response to a subpoena

Step 7. The auditor is required to **document**:

- The brainstorming session during planning

- Identified risks of material misstatement due to fraud

- Procedures performed in response to the risks (including management override) identified and the results of such procedures

- Communications regarding fraud

- Reasons revenue recognition was not considered a fraud risk factor, if appropriate

Noncompliance with Applicable Laws and Regulations

Noncompliance with applicable laws and regulations (ie, **illegal acts**) is defined as acts of omission or commission by the entity, either intentional or unintentional, which are contrary to the prevailing laws or regulations. Such noncompliance may result in fines, litigation, or other consequences that may have a material effect on the F/S. (AU-C 250)

Audit procedures to identify illegal acts
• Read the minutes
• Inquire of management, in-house counsel, and external legal counsel concerning litigations, claims, and assessments
• Perform substantive tests of details of classes of transactions, account balances, or disclosures
• Examine large or unusual transactions

In obtaining an understanding of an entity and its environment, including its I/C, the auditor will obtain a general understanding of the legal and regulatory framework under which the entity operates and how it complies with that framework. The entity should have a system under which all laws and regulations to which the entity is subject are identified, interpreted, and complied with.

The auditor has **different responsibilities** for laws and regulations that have a **direct effect** (eg, tax law) on the amounts and disclosures in the F/S and for those that have only an **indirect effect**. Compliance with laws with an indirect effect (eg, environmental regulations) may be (1) fundamental to the operating aspects of the business and its ability to continue, or (2) necessary to avoid material penalties.

- For laws with a **direct effect,** the auditor should obtain *sufficient appropriate audit evidence* regarding material amounts and disclosures in the F/S that are determined by those laws and regulations.

- For laws/regulations with an **indirect effect**, the auditor need only identify noncompliance with those laws/regulations that may have a material effect on the F/S.

If the auditor becomes aware of noncompliance or suspected noncompliance with laws/regulations, the auditor should obtain:

- An understanding of the nature of the act and the circumstances in which it occurred

- More information to evaluate the effect on the F/S

If, after communicating suspected material noncompliance to management and those charged with governance, information is not provided to support that the entity is in compliance, the auditor should:

- Consider consulting with legal counsel

- Evaluate the effect of the lack of evidence on the auditor's opinion

    o The auditor may need to express a qualified opinion or disclaim an opinion on the F/S due to a scope limitation.

- Evaluate the implications of noncompliance on other aspects of the audit

If noncompliance has a material effect on the F/S, and it has not been adequately reflected in the F/S, the auditor should express a qualified or adverse opinion on the F/S.

Reporting illegal acts
(nonissuer)

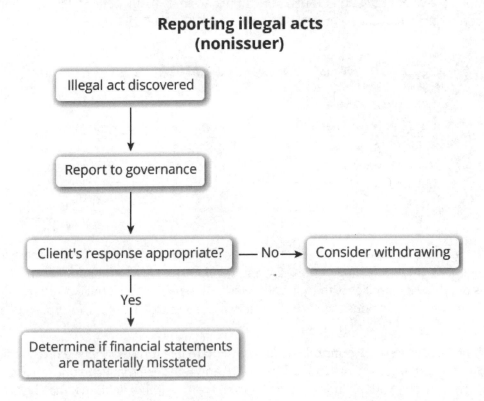

Documentation should include a description of the identified or suspected noncompliance and the results of the discussion with management and those charged with governance and other parties inside or outside the entity.

1.08 Quality Control

Overview

There are two main quality control standards a CPA exam candidate needs to be familiar with:

- QC 10, *A Firm's System of Quality Control* – **CPA firm quality control**
- AU-C 220, Quality Control for an Engagement Conducted in Accordance With Generally Accepted Auditing Standards – **Engagement-level quality control**

These quality control standards complement those that are applied primarily at the **individual level** (eg, the AICPA Code of Professional Conduct).

Statements on Quality Control Standards (SQCS), issued by the ASB, are explicitly limited in their application to a firm's **accounting and auditing practice**. That is, SQCS only apply to engagements governed by standards set by the Auditing Standards Board (ASB) or the Accounting and Review Services Committee (ARSC) of the AICPA. AU-C 220, also issued by the ASB, adds yet another layer of quality control that is specific to **GAAS audits**.

Fortunately, the objectives of these standards are essentially the same, so the elements of the standards are related and can be recalled with the same mnemonic. One need only think about the level at which the quality control is being applied.

Quality Control for CPA Firms

Objectives

QC 10 requires a CPA firm to establish a system of quality control designed to provide it with **reasonable assurance** of:

- Compliance with professional standards and applicable regulatory and legal requirements
- Issuance of reports that are appropriate in the circumstances

A system of quality control consists of policies designed to achieve these objectives and the procedures necessary to implement and monitor compliance with those policies, including communication of such policies and procedures to all firm personnel.

Considerations for CPA firm quality control policies and procedures
- Firm size
- Nature of firm's practice
- Organization structure
- Costs/benefits

Elements of CPA firm Quality Control

The 6 elements of CPA firm quality control include (**HEAL-ME**):

- ***H*uman Resources (ie, Personnel management)** – The firm should establish policies and procedures for effective hiring, development, assignment, compensation, and advancement of staff. Personnel management procedures are designed to ensure reasonable assurance that personnel:

  - Hired (eg, staff, partners) are sufficiently competent and technically trained to complete engagement responsibilities

  - Complete continuing professional education, as required

  - Promoted are properly qualified and compensated/rewarded

- ***E*thical Requirements (eg, Independence)** – The firm should establish procedures to ensure that independence is maintained (both in fact and appearance) in attest engagements, and that there is an appropriate means for identifying potential independence difficulties involving staff members. The purpose is to ensure that the firm will always be able to act with integrity and objectivity in the performance of work. Procedures include:

  - Annual, written confirmation by appropriate personnel of their independence

  - Appropriate rotation of firm personnel on engagements.

- ***A*cceptance and continuance of client relationships** Firms should establish policies and procedures before the acceptance of new clients and engagements and to determine if continued association with existing clients is warranted.

Quality control for client acceptance

• Ensure association with clients whose management acts with integrity
• Provide reasonable assurance that the CPA firm
   ○ Is competent to perform engagement
   ○ Has needed capabilities
   ○ Can comply with legal and ethical requirements

  - Firms should document their understanding with the client regarding the nature, scope, and limitations of the services to be provided, along with any issues related to acceptance and continuance decisions.

  - Firms should have established procedures for withdrawal, if necessary, which address:

  - Documentation of significant issues and conclusions

  - Discussions held with the client on any action taken related to issues, including names of all who participated in the discussion.

  - Consideration of legal, regulatory, or professional requirements for the firm to remain on the engagement, or if the firm is required to report the withdrawal.

- ***L*eadership responsibilities for quality ("tone at the top")** – The firm's leadership must assume ultimate responsibility for the firm's quality control. In particular:

- o Adequate, sufficient resources should be dedicated to developing, communicating, and supporting a quality control system.

- Quality is emphasized over profitability. This should be evident in performance evaluation, compensation, and advancement decisions.

- *Monitoring* – Should be performed by a partner, and includes the performance of conducting quality control reviews, post-issuance reports, and inspections of random engagements. Policies and procedures should be established for:

  - o Determining whether the system of quality control is relevant, adequate, and operating effectively

  - o Evaluating, communicating, remedying deficiencies, with appropriate documentation. Dealing with complaints and allegations of noncompliance

  - o Reviews of administrative records, working papers, reports, and financial statements

  - o Peer reviews (see below), which can replace some of the firm's inspection procedures

  - o Second partner reviews prior to issuance of client reports

- *Engagement performance* – The firm should establish policies and procedures for ensuring:

  - o The firm meets applicable professional standards in the performance of its engagements

  - o Consultations are undertaken for difficult issues

  - o Differences of opinions within the engagement team are resolved

  - o All engagements are evaluated to determine whether an engagement quality control review should be performed

Engagement quality reviewer responsibilities
• Perform an objective review
• Review documentation relative to significant judgments and conclusions
• Read financial statements and audit report
• Determine if nature, timing, and extent of work is appropriate
• Determine if sufficient appropriate audit evidence supports the report

Peer Review

One CPA firm reviews another CPA firm's compliance with its quality control system. Firm members of the AICPA must have a peer review once every 3 years. The reviewing firm issues a report of conclusions and findings. If the reviewed firm does not take corrective action where required, sanctions may be issued.

Deficiencies

Although an effective quality control system is conducive to compliance with GAAS, deficiencies in or instances of noncompliance with a firm's quality control system do not, in and of themselves, indicate that an engagement was not performed in accordance with the applicable professional standards.

Documentation

- Proper documentation of quality control procedures includes evidence of: issues identified and resolutions related to compliance with ethical requirements

- Nature, scope, and conclusions of consultations during the engagement

  o Completing final engagement files on a timely basis

  o Maintaining the confidentiality, safe custody, integrity, accessibility, and retrievability of engagement documentation

  o Retaining engagement documentation long enough to satisfy the needs of the firm, professional standards, laws, and regulations

- For an **engagement quality control review**:

  o The required procedures have been performed

  o The date the review was completed

- The reviewer is not aware of any unresolved matters that would give reason to believe that significant judgments made and the conclusions reached were inappropriate.

Quality control elements for a CPA firm (HEAL-ME)	
Element	**Policies provide reasonable assurance that:**
Human resources	• Employees are competent (ie, adequately trained) • Employees selected for advancement are qualified
Ethical requirements	• Firm complies with ethical requirements (eg, independence, integrity, and objectivity)
Acceptance and continuance	• Firm has resources to perform engagement • Firm does not associate with clients that lack integrity
Leadership responsibilities for quality	• Person(s) with responsibility for quality control has sufficient and appropriate experience and authority
Monitoring	• Firm policies are relevant, adequate, and operating effectively
Engagement performance	• Engagements meet professional/quality standards and legal and regulatory requirements

AUD 2
Professional
Responsibilities
& Ethics

AUD 2: Professional Responsibilities & Ethics

2.01 AICPA Code of Professional Conduct

There are a number of ways in which CPAs may distinguish themselves. Every CPA is required to obtain a CPA certificate, which is issued by the state to which the CPA applies and is administered by that state's board of accountancy. In addition, a CPA may be a member of the AICPA; a member of a state society of CPAs; and a member of various professional organizations, some of which are based on ethnicity, such as the Philippine Institute of CPAs (PICPA) and the National Association of Black Accountants (NABA), while others are based on some other factor, such as the segment of the profession in which its members operate like the Association of Governmental Accountants (AGA) or the Institute of Management Accountants (IMA).

A CPA may also be subject to various regulators such as the SEC or the PCAOB. Each of these agencies, organizations, regulators, and societies have rules and guidelines that affect the behavior of CPAs. One of the most comprehensive is the **AICPA Code of Professional Conduct (Code) (ET – for research)**. Many sets of rules and codes of ethics related to accountants are largely based on the Code, which is regularly tested on the CPA exam.

While the consequences of violating the Code will not be more severe than the loss of the CPA's membership in the AICPA, which is why the rules and guidelines are expressed as obligations of "members," violations of other codes of conduct (state board of accountancy) may result in a prohibition against performing certain types of services, the inability to serve certain regulated clients, or, in some cases, the suspension or loss (revocation) of the CPA certificate. This could result from the commission of a felony or the filing of a fraudulent tax return, whether for the CPA or for a client.

In addition to the Code, a CPA will consider the ethical requirements of all applicable bodies and agencies, which may include:

- State societies
- State boards of accountants and related regulatory agencies
- The SEC, PCAOB, GAO, and DOL
- Taxing authorities

The Code is organized in **four parts**: the Preface, which is applicable to all members; Part 1, which is applicable to members in public practice; Part 2, which applies to members in industry; and Part 3, which applies to all other members, including those retired or unemployed.

Each part is divided into topics. The **Preface** (applicable to all members) is divided into **six** topics consisting of:

- 0.100 – Overview of the code of Professional Conduct
- 0.200 – Structure and Application of the AICPA code
- 0.300 – Principles of Professional Conduct
- 0.400 – Definitions
- 0.500 – Nonauthoritative Guidance

- 0.600 – New, Revised, and Pending Interpretations and Other Guidance

The topics and subtopics or sections are similarly numbered and named in each of the remaining three parts. All of the enumerated topics and subtopics apply to Part 1, Members in Public Practice. Fewer apply to Part 2, Members in Industry, and only two apply to Part 3, Other Members. The subtopics are as follows:

- Part 1 – Members in Public Practice
  - 1.000 – Introduction
  - 1.100 – Integrity and Objectivity
  - 1.200 – Independence
  - 1.300 – General Standards
  - 1.310 – Compliance With Standards
  - 1.320 – Accounting Principles
  - 1.400 – Acts Discreditable
  - 1.500 – Fees and Other Types of Remuneration
  - 1.600 – Advertising and Other Forms of Solicitation
  - 1.700 – Confidential Information
  - 1.800 – Form of Organization and Name
- **Part 2** – Members in **Industry**
  - 2.000 – Introduction
  - 2.100 – Integrity and Objectivity
  - 2.300 – General Standards
  - 2.310 – Compliance With Standards
  - 2.320 – Accounting Principles
  - 2.400 – Acts Discreditable
- Part 3 – Other Members
  - 3.100 – Introduction
  - 3.400 – Acts Discreditable

Preface

The preface, applicable to *all members*, consists of **six topics:**

Topic 100 – Provides an **overview**, including an explanation of the structure of the Code; a requirement that members adhere to the Code's **rules** based on an understanding of the rules and the voluntary actions of the CPA; an indication that CPAs are expected to follow **interpretations**, and may be required to justify departures from them; and an indication that, when a CPA has multiple professional roles, the highest and most restrictive level of standards should be applied.

Topic 200 – Describes the **structure** of the Code and indicates its **applicability** to the services performed by a CPA. It indicates that, with few exceptions, the Code applies to all professional services performed by a CPA, except when rules identify services to which they do not apply. This topic also describes how certain terms are interpreted in a section related to drafting conventions.

- Rules requiring a member to **consider** something are requiring the CPA to *think about* the matters being addressed.

- Rules requiring a member to **evaluate** something are requiring the CPA to *measure a matter's significance.*

- Rules requiring a member to **determine** something are requiring the CPA to establish a *conclusion* related to a matter or make a decision in relation to it.

In addition, a CPA will apply professional judgment in determining whether or not to perform a procedure or take an action that the Code indicates that the CPA should consider.

Topic 300 – Describes the **principles** embedded in the Code. In the preamble, it reminds CPAs of their responsibility of **self-discipline** exceeding the simple compliance with applicable laws and regulations; **responsibilities to the public, to clients, and to colleagues**; and a commitment to **act with honor** despite the possibility of personal sacrifice that may result. Various principles support these premises:

- *Responsibilities* – Requires the application of sensitive professional and moral judgment at all times and cooperation with other members of the profession to improve the art of accounting, to maintain the public's confidence in the profession, and to carry out the profession's responsibility for self-governance.

- *Public Interest* – Requires a commitment to professionalism and acting in a manner that serves the public interest and honors the trust that the public has in the accounting profession. The public interest is the collective well-being of the community of people and institutions that are served by the accounting profession, which requires the accountant to act with integrity when confronted by conflicts among various stakeholders and perform services applying integrity, objectivity, and due professional care.

- *Integrity* – Requires that the highest level of integrity be applied through the CPA's honesty and candor, within the constraints of client confidentiality, and an unwillingness to subordinate service or the public trust to personal gain or advantage.

- *Objectivity and Independence* – Requires independence, both in *fact* and in *appearance*, when performing auditing and other attestation services, for which standards require independence, and that the CPA remain free of conflicts of interest and exercise impartiality and intellectual honesty in the performance of all professional services.

- *Due Care* – Requires compliance with technical and ethical standards while continuing to endeavor to improve the CPA's competence and quality of services, which is accomplished through a commitment to learning throughout the CPA's professional life, and diligence in the provision of professional services enabling performance to the best of the CPA's ability. Due care also requires a CPA to remain competent and to understand the limitations to that competence, which may result in consultation or the referral of services, and to adequately plan and supervise all professional activities for which the CPA is responsible.

- *Scope and Nature of Services* – Requires the CPA to evaluate whether or not services can be performed in a manner consistent with the principles of the Code by practicing in a firm with appropriate quality control policies and procedures commensurate with the services being performed; making certain that services performed for an audit client do not create a conflict of interest; and that activities in which the CPA participates are appropriate for members of the CPA profession.

Topic 400 – Provides **definitions** of terms that are used throughout the Code.

Topic 500 – Specifies that only the Code is authoritative and that guidance provided by the staff of the Professional Ethics Division of the AICPA is **nonauthoritative guidance**.

Topic 600 – Indicates the status of **new, revised, or pending interpretations and other guidance**. It specifies that new or revised authoritative interpretations and other guidance are effective as of the last day of the month in which the pronouncement or notice is published in the Journal of Accountancy.

Part 1 – Members in Public Practice

Part 1 is applicable to members in public practice, including government auditors who are part of a governmental audit agency responsible for auditing governments or component units of them, provided the auditor is either elected directly by the voters or appointed with removal subject to oversight or approval by a legislative body. When a CPA is serving both as a member in public practice and as a member in industry, both Parts 1 and 2 will apply.

Topic 1.000 – Introduction

This topic introduces a conceptual framework approach to applying the Code. It provides a member with a means of evaluating compliance with the code when confronted with a decision or other circumstance that is not directly addressed. Applying the conceptual framework approach cannot overcome a clear violation of the rules or interpretations of the Code. It can, however, assist the CPA in determining if the Code has been violated when it is not necessarily clear.

The *conceptual framework approach* involves a 3-step process:

- **Identify threats** that may interfere with the CPA's ability to remain in compliance with the Code. The CPA may, for example, be considering entering into a relationship that is not prohibited but that raises the possibility of a conflict of interest. The existence of one or more threats does not necessarily indicate that the CPA is in violation of the Code, but requires that the threat or threats be evaluated.

- **Evaluate the significance of identified threats**, both individually and in the aggregate, to determine if they are at an acceptable level. A threat is considered to be at an acceptable level when a reasonable and informed third party would conclude that the Code was not violated. The evaluation will consider qualitative and quantitative factors and should take into account existing safeguards that are in place and may reduce the threat to an acceptable level.

- **Identify and apply safeguards** to those threats that are not at an acceptable level. In some cases, a single safeguard may eliminate more than one threat while, in others, it may require several safeguards to reduce a single threat to an acceptable level. In cases where safeguards cannot be implemented to reduce the threat or threats to an acceptable level, providing those specific professional services would result in the member's compliance with the Code being compromised, the member should determine if declining or discontinuing the service or resigning from the engagement would be appropriate.

Threats

There are **seven categories of threats** identified in Topic 1.210 of the Code. They are not mutually exclusive in that a single threat may fall under more than one category. Threats are evaluated both individually and in the aggregate. The categories are:

- The threat of self-review exists when the accountant performs some form of evaluation of matters that were previously influenced by the accountant's judgment, such as when an accountant is performing an attest service in relation to a client's financial statements when the accountant's firm performed bookkeeping services for that client. The self-review threat is the threat that the accountant will assume a level of reliability without performing an appropriate level of testing or other due diligence.

- An **advocacy** threat exists when the accountant's actions effectively promote a client's interests or position. This would be the case if the accountant is:

  - Providing forensic accounting services to the client in a conflict with third parties.

  - Providing investment advice for an officer, director, or shareholder holding 10% or more of the client's shares.

  - Promoting or underwriting the client's securities, or acting as a registered agent for the client.

  - Endorsing the products or services of a client.

  - It does not result from testifying as a fact witness or defending the results of a professional service performed for the client. Advocacy is covered in detail in Topic 1.140.

- The threat of an **adverse interest** exists when the interests of the client are in conflict with the interests of the accountant, which may inhibit the accountant from applying objectivity. This would be the case, for example, if the client and the accountant were involved in, or anticipating, litigation against each other.

- The threat of **familiarity** results from a close and longstanding relationship with a client, potentially causing the accountant to become too sympathetic to the client's interests or too trusting of the client's work or products. Examples of the types of relationships that create a familiarity threat include:

  - The spouse, a family member, or a close friend of an engagement team member is employed by the client.

  - The member has a close and significant business relationship with an officer, director, or significant shareholder of the client.

  - Senior firm personnel have a long-standing relationship with the client.

- The threat of **undue influence** results from attempts by management or others to exercise an excessive amount of influence over the accountant. This may involve:

  - A client's threat to replace the accountant as a result of a disagreement.

  - A client exerting pressure to limit an engagement to reduce fees.

- The threat of **self-interest** occurs when the accountant has the opportunity to obtain a potential benefit from an interest in, or another relationship with, a client. This would be the case if:

  - The accountant has a financial interest in the client, the value of which may be affected by the results of the service being performed.

- o The accountant enters into an arrangement that involves a contingent fee rather than one that is predetermined.
  - o The accountant relies excessively on the fees earned from the client.
- The threat of **management participation** occurs when the accountant takes on the role of management for the client or performs management functions on behalf of the client. Assuming management responsibilities will generally impair a member's independence in relation to a client but will not necessarily, otherwise, indicate a violation of the Code. A member may still perform professional services for such a client provided the services do not require the accountant to be independent.

The performance of management functions does not impair independence as long as the member is not assuming management responsibility. The accountant may, for example, design a client's system of internal control provided the client takes responsibility for all decisions involving the allocation or use of resources, and the general requirements for the performance of nonattest services in section 1.295 of the Code, discussed later in this chapter, have been met. This includes designating someone from the client's organization, preferably a member of senior management, who will take responsibility for the services performed by the CPA.

Safeguards

Safeguards are controls that eliminate or reduce threats, ranging from prohibitions against circumstances that create threats to procedures that counteract the potential risk associated with a threat. Safeguards are considered effective if they eliminate a threat or reduce it to an acceptable level.

There are a number of factors that determine if safeguards are likely to be effective. The factors include the circumstances surrounding the situation, whether threats are identified properly, whether safeguards are designed appropriately, who applies the safeguards and who are subject to them, and how they are applied and the consistency with which they are applied.

Certain safeguards are imposed on the accountant by **requirements of the profession, or by legislation or regulation**. Examples include:

- Education, training, and continuing professional education (CPE) requirements
- Professional standards, combined with monitoring and disciplinary processes and external reviews of the firm's quality control
- Legislation
- Requirements related to competency and experience

Other safeguards result from **client characteristics or policies**. These, which act in combination with other safeguards, might include:

- Client personnel with an appropriate combination of skill, knowledge, and experience to oversee professional services provided by the accountant
- A tone at the top that emphasizes a commitment to fair reporting, compliance with laws and regulations, and ethical conduct
- Client governance related to the accountant's services that is structured and designed for appropriate decision making, oversight, and communication

- Policies limiting the client's use of the accountant for services that impair independence, encourage noncompliance with ethical requirements, or would not serve the public interest

Safeguards may be **implemented by the firm**. These may be many and varied, including:

- Leadership that stresses the importance of ethical behavior and acting in the interest of the public
- Policies and procedures designed to:
  - Implement and monitor quality control
  - Monitor compliance with firm policies
  - Monitor the firm's reliance on revenues from a single client
- Training and timely communication of firm policies and procedures
- Designating an appropriate individual from senior management to oversee the firm's quality control
- Disciplinary policies designed to encourage compliance with policies and procedures, and to empower staff to communicate noncompliance
- Discussing independence and ethics with the client's audit committee or the client's governance, and establishing policies and procedures for independence-related communication
- Disclosing to the audit committee the nature of services being provided and their related fees
- Consulting with interested third parties
- Rotation of senior attest engagement personnel
- Use of another firm to re-perform and take responsibility for portions of engagements

Another safeguard that can be initiated by the firm would be to establish a **consultation function**. It would be staffed with experts in accounting, auditing, independence, or other relevant issues. They would assist the attest engagement team in assessing issues that are highly technical, require a great deal of judgment, or for which there is no guidance. They would also assist the engagement team in resisting undue pressure from the client when there are disagreements regarding those matters.

Ethical Conflicts

Ethical conflicts may arise as a result of various circumstances, but most relate to a circumstance where internal or external pressures create obstacles that interfere with following an appropriate course of action; where conflicts arise in applying relevant professional and legal standards, such as when reporting suspected fraud may be a violation of client confidentiality rules; or some combination of these.

Departures from rules or laws may require justification when the member believes them to be appropriate in the circumstances. Members may suffer consequences, however, when resolution is not achieved in a manner that permits compliance with all applicable rules and laws.

A CPA should consider consulting with others within their employing firm or organization before taking a course of action. If a course of action is not effective and an ethical conflict is not resolved, regardless of whether consultation occurred or not, the accountant should consider consulting with others or obtaining advice from a professional body or from legal counsel. When conflicts remain unresolved, it is likely that the CPA will be in violation of one or more rules and the CPA should consider whether it is appropriate to continue a relationship with the engagement team, assignment, client, firm, or employer.

Topic 1.100 – Integrity and Objectivity

In performance of **any** professional service, a member shall maintain objectivity and integrity, avoid conflicts of interest, and not knowingly misrepresent facts or subordinate their judgment to others.

Topic 1.110 – Conflicts of Interest

Conflicts of interest arise when a CPA is performing professional services related to a matter for two or more clients with conflicting interests or when the interests of the CPA or the CPA's firm conflict with those of the client. Before accepting an engagement or a relationship, the CPA should evaluate a potential conflict of interest by identifying:

- The relationships among parties involved and the natures of their relevant interests, which may change during the course of the engagement; and

- The nature and implications of the service being provided.

Safeguards may reduce the threat of a conflict of interest to an acceptable level. Maintaining separate engagement teams, for example, with clear policies and procedures for maintaining confidentiality may be an adequate safeguard to reduce the threat of a conflict of interest to a reasonable level when the conflict arises from performing services for two or more clients with conflicting interests related to the subject matter of the engagements.

Serving as a director on the board of an entity may create a conflict of interest if the entity, such as a bank, enters into or considers transactions with the CPA's clients. The member may consider limiting the relationship to a consulting arrangement, excluding transactions that may involve the CPA's clients. If, however, the CPA does serve as a director, threats and safeguards should be evaluated to make certain that threats are at an acceptable level.

When a conflict of interest does exist, even when threats are reduced to an acceptable level, the accountant is *required to disclose* the nature of the conflict to clients and others affected by it and to obtain their consent for the performance of the professional services.

Topic 1.120 – Gifts and Entertainment

Offering gifts or entertainment to a client or accepting gifts or entertainment from a client may create various threats to the CPA's compliance with the Code, including threats associated with self-interest, familiarity, and undue influence. Threats cannot be reduced to an acceptable level when the offer or acceptance of gifts is in violation of member or client policies or applicable laws, rules, or regulations if the member is aware of the violation or is unaware due to recklessness.

Threats may be reduced to an acceptable level when gifts or entertainment are *reasonable* in the circumstances when considering such factors as the nature of the item, the occasion giving rise to it, the cost, and other facts and circumstances surrounding it.

Topic 1.130 – Preparing and Reporting Information

In order to comply with the rule regarding integrity and objectivity, a member who is responsible for recording, maintaining, preparing, approving, or presenting information has an obligation to adhere to the relevant reporting framework when there is one. When there is not, the accountant should apply professional judgment, taking into consideration the purpose for which the information is being presented and the audience it is intended for. The information should not be presented in a manner intended to mislead, nor should there be omissions that cause the information to be misleading.

Making materially false and misleading entries in an entity's financial statements or records, or permitting or directing another to do so; failing to correct materially false and misleading financial statements or records of an entity with the authority to do so; and signing a document containing false and misleading information, or permitting or directing another to do so, create threats to compliance with the rule regarding integrity and objectivity that could not be reduced to an acceptable level.

Differences of opinion between a member and supervisors or other individuals within the member's organization may create self-interest, familiarity, or undue influence threats to the members' ability to comply with the integrity and objectivity rules as a result of the potential of subordinating the member's judgment. A supervisor, for example, may take a position that the member believes is not in compliance with standards, represents a material misstatement of facts, or violates applicable laws or regulations. In such cases, threats cannot be reduced to an acceptable level and the member should:

- Discuss concerns with the supervisor.

- Discuss concerns with an appropriate higher level of management within the member's organization when the difference of opinion cannot be resolved through discussion with the supervisor. Appropriate actions in response might involve:

  o Correcting the information.

  o Informing those to whom the information has already been given of the correct information.

- If the member concludes that appropriate actions are not taken, the member should follow certain safeguards to *reduce or eliminate the threats* to an acceptable level:

  o Consult with an appropriate professional organization or body.

  o Determine if the member's organization has internal policies and procedures for reporting differences of opinion.

  o Determine whether the member is responsible for communicating with third parties, such as regulatory agencies, keeping confidentiality requirements in mind.

  o Consult with legal counsel.

  o Document an understanding of the facts, the matters involved, and the conversations held, identifying the parties with which they were held.

If threats can be reduced to an acceptable level, the member will discuss conclusions with the other party and take no further action.

Upon a conclusion that no safeguards can eliminate the threats or reduce them to an acceptable level, the member should not be willing to continue to be associated with the information, consider whether it is appropriate to continue in a relationship with the organization and should take steps to eliminate exposure to having subordinated judgment.

Pressure may be explicitly or implicitly placed upon a member to breach the rules of conduct, the rules related to integrity and objectivity most commonly. Pressure may be imposed by colleagues or supervisors within the member's organization or from external sources, such as customers or vendors, lenders, or others. A member should neither yield to such pressure resulting in a breach to the Code nor exert pressure on others such that a breach may result.

Pressure may relate to any combination of:

- Conflicts of interest;

- Presentation or suppression of information;

- Performing tasks without an appropriate level of competence or due care;

- Advancing the interests of those with financial interests; and

- Gifts and entertainment.

The member should make a determination whether the pressure could result in a breach, consulting with others, as appropriate, taking into consideration the implications of the interpretation "Confidential Information Obtained from Employment or Volunteer Activities." If the member concludes that the pressure would result in a breach, there are a number of safeguards that may be considered. The member might:

- Try to resolve the matter by discussing it with the individual exerting the pressure.

- Discuss the matter with a supervisor or parties at a higher level, such as management, internal and independent auditors, or members of those charged with governance.

- Request a change in responsibilities, removing the member from the influence of the party exerting the pressure.

- Expose the matter using the mechanisms within the organization, such as whistleblower policies.

- Consult with legal counsel.

If the member determines that the pressure to breach cannot be eliminated, the member should not undertake, or should cease undertaking, the activity that would result in the breach and consider whether to remain involved in a relationship with the organization. The member should also document an understanding of the facts, the matters involved, the conversations held, identifying the parties with which they were held, and how the matters were addressed.

Topic 1.140 – Client Advocacy

When performing certain nonattest services for a client, such as tax or consulting services, the member may be in position to act as an advocate for the client in supporting the client's position on accounting or financial reporting issues to other engagement team members or to standard setters or regulators. These services may pose threats to the member's ability to comply with the integrity and objectivity rules that should be evaluated.

Topic 1.150 – Use of a Third-Party Service Provider

Use of a third-party service provider in a professional engagement may expose the third party to confidential information posing a threat to the member's ability to comply with the integrity and objectivity rules. Before disclosing confidential client information to a third-party service provider, the member should inform the client, preferably in writing.

Topic 1.200 – Independence

A member in public practice shall be independent in the performance of professional services when independence is required by applicable professional standards.

Independence is the ability to act with **integrity and objectivity** and applies to a *covered member and to the member's immediate family,* including the member's spouse or spousal equivalent, and all dependents, whether related or not. A **covered member** would be any of the following:

- A member of an attest engagement team or an individual in a position to influence the attest engagement

- A partner, partner equivalent, or manager providing more than 10 hours of nonattest services to the attest client within a fiscal year

- A partner or partner equivalent in the same office in which the lead engagement partner for the attest engagement practices

- The firm and its employee benefit plan

- An entity under the control of any one of the other covered members described and two or more of those individuals or entities acting together

- With agreed-upon procedure engagements only, covered members may be limited to those participating in or directly supervising the engagement, and individuals consulting with the engagement team on technical or industry-related issues.

A covered member—

- Must maintain independence for **attest services (ERAS):**
  - Examinations / Audits
  - Reviews
  - Agreed-upon procedure engagements leading to findings
  - Special reports

- Need not be independent for:
  - Compilations – Independence is expected, but not required; lack of independence must be disclosed.
  - Taxes
  - Consultations
  - F/S Preparation Engagement
  - Other nonattest services, such as bookkeeping or payroll

Independence should be maintained in both:

- **Fact** – State *"of mind"*
- **Appearance** – How it appears to the public

The Code provides some specific guidance as to certain events, circumstances, or conditions that will create threats to independence that cannot be reduced to an acceptable level. If, for example, a member has any direct financial interest in a client, independence is impaired and no safeguards could reduce the threat to independence to an acceptable level.

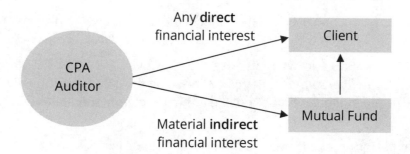

When events, circumstances, or conditions that might impair independence *are not addressed* directly in the Code, *the member is required to apply the conceptual framework approach*, applied in the same manner as the conceptual framework approach related to the Code itself.

Topic 1.210 – Conceptual Framework Approach

Rules of conduct incorporated in the Code provide indications as to when independence is in fact impaired, such as a *direct financial interest* in a client or having the authority to sign checks on a client's bank account. Even when a CPA has not engaged in any activity or relationship that would specifically impair independence, however, threats to independence may be at an unacceptable level.

Threats to independence are considered to be at an acceptable level when a reasonable and informed third party, aware of the relevant information, would conclude that the member's independence is not impaired. As a result, the member will focus on the *appearance* of independence when applying the conceptual framework.

Threats to independence include:

- **Adverse interest threat** – When a member's interests are in opposition to the clients, such as when they are involved in, or anticipating, litigation, the member may not act objectively.

- **Advocacy threat** – A member may compromise independence when promoting a client's position, depending on the degree to which the member promotes it. This may be the case when the member is promoting the client's securities in an initial public offering, serving as an expert witness on behalf of the client, or representing the client in tax court or elsewhere.

- **Familiarity threat** – A long relationship with a client may make a member sympathetic to a client's interests or accepting of the client's work or product, such as when there has been a history of work that has been essentially error-free in the past. The degree to which this occurs may cause a threat to the member's independence, particularly when an immediate family member or close relative holds a key position with the attest client; a partner of the firm, or the equivalent, has been on the engagement team for the attest engagement for an extended period of time; or a member of the engagement team's firm has recently been a director or officer of the attest client or has a close friend in a key position.

- **Management participation threat** – A member who serves as an officer or director of an attest client; accepts responsibility for the design, implementation, or maintenance of internal control for an attest client; or hires, supervises, or terminates employees of the attest client, creates a management participation threat to independence. An auditor, for example, may decide to ignore a significant deficiency in internal control when the auditor's firm has accepted responsibility for their design and implementation of internal control. When this is the case, of course, the accountant would not be independent since accepting responsibility for the design and implementation of internal control involves assuming a management responsibility. Doing so raises the management participation threat to an unacceptable level in relation to independence. In such a case, no safeguards would be able to reduce the threat to an acceptable level.

- **Self-interest threat** – When a member may benefit from an interest in, or relationship with, an attest client, a self-interest threat to independence is created. The benefit may be financial or nonfinancial, including a direct financial interest or material indirect financial interest in an attest client; a loan from the client, an officer or director, or a significant shareholder of the attest client; an excessive reliance on fees from a single attest client; or a material joint venture or business arrangement with an attest client.

- **Self-review threat** – When a member or the member's firm performs nonattest services for an attest client, there is the possibility that either the member will not test the information with an appropriate level of due diligence, or may overlook an error or other discrepancy to preserve the reputation of the firm and the relationship with the client, creating a self-review threat to the member's independence.

- **Undue influence threat** – An undue influence threat is the threat that the member will subordinate judgment to a third party as a result of a third party's reputation or expertise, aggressive or dominant personality, or attempts to coerce or exercise excessive influence; or to someone associated with the attest client due, perhaps, to a threat to replace the member or the member's firm over a disagreement, pressure to reduce procedures as a means of reducing fees, or receiving gifts from the attest client or related parties.

Similar to the approach used in evaluating threats to compliance with the Code, the member will evaluate safeguards to determine if there are those that are already in place that reduce threats to independence to an acceptable level. If threats are not already reduced to an acceptable level, the member will evaluate other safeguards that may be implemented that may so reduce it.

The member will consider safeguards imposed by the requirements of the profession or by laws or regulations; those resulting from client characteristics or policies; and those implemented by the firm.

Topic 1.220 – Accounting Firms

When a firm is part of a **network** of firms, all firms within that network are required to comply with the independence rules in relation to an attest client of any of the firms within that network if the use of the audit or review report for the client is not restricted. In other cases, the covered member should consider any threats to independence that the covered member knows of or has reason to believe may be created by the interests or relationships of other firms within the network.

A firm is considered to be part of a network of firms if the firms cooperate to enhance their ability to provide professional services through cross referrals and other means and has one or more of the following additional characteristics:

- A common brand name or initials that are part of the firm name
- Common control through ownership or management
- Sharing of profit and costs with the exception of certain costs such as those of operating the association and other costs that are not material to the firm
- Collaboration to create a common business strategy that member firms are held accountable for implementing
- Sharing of significant professional resources, such as systems and staff
- Uniform quality control policies monitored and enforced by the association

A covered member may also be part of an **alternative practice structure (APS)**, which is required to comply with independence rules; is required to be organized in a form allowed by applicable laws, rules, and regulations; and is required to comply with the rules in the Code related to the form of an organization and its name (1.800).

An APS is an organization in which a firm provides attest services while other professional services are performed by another public or private organization that is closely aligned, such as a CPA firm with a closely aligned consulting entity. Independence rules apply to both covered members and direct superiors in an APS.

- Covered members include employed and leased individuals otherwise having the characteristics of a covered member.
- Direct superiors are covered members who can directly control the activities of an engagement partner or manager.

Indirect superiors, those one or more levels above direct superiors, can impair independence by having a material relationship with an attest client that is prohibited as a financial interest (1.240); acts as a trustee or executor (1.245); has a prohibited loan (1.260); maintains joint closely held investments with the attest client (1.265); or is involved in any of a variety of specific relationships. An indirect superior may, however, perform nonattest services that would be prohibited to the firm performing attest services without impairing independence.

When an attest firm allows members of another firm which is not independent of an attest client to participate in an attest engagement, threats to independence cannot be reduced to an acceptable level and the attest firm's independence will be impaired. Members of the firm that is not independent, however, may serve in a capacity similar to that of an internal auditor as long as the firm complies with auditing standards.

A member whose independence becomes impaired after the issuance of a report may reissue the report provided the member or the member's firm does not perform procedures associated with updating or dual dating the report.

An indemnification clause in an engagement letter, in which an attest client holds the member harmless from liability resulting from knowing misrepresentations by management does not impair independence. Independence would be impaired, however, if an attest firm indemnifies an attest client from liability arising directly or indirectly from the acts of the attest client. An alternative dispute resolution clause in an engagement letter would not impair independence.

Topic 1.230 – Unpaid Fees

When fees for services that were performed *more than one year* before the date of the current-year report remain unpaid, this creates a threat to independence that cannot be reduced to an acceptable level. This is true even if the fees have not been billed to the client and if the client has signed a note for the amount owed. This does not apply, however, to unpaid fees due from a client in bankruptcy.

Topic 1.240 – Financial Interests

In general, a member who possesses or has a commitment to acquire a **direct or material indirect** *financial interest* in an attest client creates a self-interest threat that cannot be reduced to an acceptable level and the member's independence would be impaired. The same would be true if a partner or professional employee of the firm, including the partner's immediate family or any group of those individuals acting together, owned more than *5 percent* of an attest client during the period of the attest engagement.

Certain other financial interests may or may not create threats to independence that cannot be reduced to acceptable level, impairing independence.

- Threats to independence may be reduced to an acceptable level when a member *receives an unsolicited direct or indirect financial interest in an attest client*, such as through a gift that is not material to the member, if the member applies two safeguards:

  o The financial interest is disposed of within 30 days of learning of the interest, or sooner if practicable; and

  o The member does not participate on the attest engagement team during the period in which the covered member does not have the right to dispose of the financial interest.

- Ownership of shares of a *mutual fund* constitutes a direct financial interest in the mutual fund. Ownership of the underlying investments of the mutual fund may be direct or indirect, depending on the proportion of the mutual fund owned by the member and the diversity of the mutual fund's holdings.

  o Ownership of 5% or less of a diversified mutual fund results in an immaterial indirect financial interest in its investments.

- Ownership of more than 5% of a diversified fund, or an ownership interest in an undiversified fund, should be evaluated to determine if the member holds a material indirect interest.

- Financial interests in *retirement, savings, compensation, or similar firm-sponsored plans* may be direct or indirect financial interests, based on circumstances.

  - Investments in a firm-sponsored plan are direct financial interests of the firm.

  - The ability to supervise or participate in a plan's investment decisions creates a direct financial interest while the inability to do so results in an indirect financial interest.

  - Financial interests held by a defined benefit plan are only considered the financial interest of a member who is a trustee or otherwise supervises or participates in the plan's investment decisions.

  - Allocated shares held in an employee stock ownership plan (ESOP) are indirect financial interests until the member has the right to dispose of the allocated shares of the ESOP.

  - Interests resulting from share-based compensation arrangements, including rights to acquire equity interests and restricted stock awards are direct financial interests even if they are not vested or exercisable.

- A *partnership interest* is a direct financial interest in a general or a limited partnership.

  - A general partner has a direct financial interest in the partnership's financial interests.

  - A limited partner has an indirect financial interest in the partnership's financial interests unless the limited partner controls the partnership, supervises or participates in the partnership's investment decisions, or has the ability to replace the general partner or participate in investment decisions, in which case the interest is direct.

- An ownership interest in a *limited liability company* (LLC) is a direct financial interest in the LLC.

  - The managing member and those with the ability to control, supervise, or participate in the LLC's investment decisions have direct financial interests in the LLC's financial interests.

  - Others without the ability to control, supervise, or participate in the LLC's investment decisions have indirect financial interests.

- The account owner of a *Section 529 plan* (Education savings plan) has a direct financial interest in the plan, but beneficiaries do not have a direct or indirect financial interest in the plan.

Topic 1.245 – Trusts and Estates

If an estate or trust has any direct or any material indirect financial interest in an attest client, a threat to the member's independence would not be at an acceptable level if the member served as trustee of the trust, or executor or administrator of the estate, during the period of the professional engagement if any of the following also applied:

- The member had the authority to make investment decisions for the trust or estate;

- The trust or estate either owned, or was committed to acquire, an equity interest in excess of 10% of the attest client's outstanding equity securities; or

- The value of the equity interest in the attest client exceeded 10% of the total assets of the trust or estate.

When the CPA is the grantor of a trust, the trust and its investments are considered direct financial interests of the CPA, even if the trust is a blind trust, if the trust's investments ultimately revert to the CPA, or if the CPA:

- Can amend or revoke the trust;

- Has the authority to control the trust; or

- Has the ability to participate in, or supervise, the trust's investment decisions.

If none of those circumstances apply, the CPA has a direct financial interest in the trust and an indirect financial interest in the trust's underlying investments.

Topic 1.250 – Participation in Employee Benefit Plans

When a CPA is a participant in an employee benefit plan that is either sponsored by an attest client or is, itself, an attest client, independence is generally impaired due to the self-interest threat. The threat would be reduced to an acceptable level, however, in certain circumstances the CPA is a participant in a public employee retirement plan that is sponsored by more than one governmental organization, one of which is the employer of the CPA. In addition:

- The CPA is required as an employee to participate in the plan, which is offered to all employees in comparable positions;

- The CPA does not influence or control key aspects of the plan such as investment strategy, benefits, or other management activities; and

- The CPA may not serve in a role prohibited by ET 1.275, *Current Employment or Association with an Attest Client*.

When, as a result of an immediate family member's employment, that family member is a participant in a plan that is an attest client or is sponsored by an attest client, the requirements of ET 1.270, *Family Relationships with Attest Clients*, are to be complied with.

Topic 1.255 – Depository, Brokerage, and Other Accounts

A firm may have funds on deposit at an attest client that is a bank or similar depository institution without impairing its independence as long as the firm concludes that the likelihood that the institution will experience financial difficulties is remote. An individual's independence would not be impaired as long as:

- The balance on deposit is fully insured; or

- The aggregate of uninsured amounts is not material to the individual; or

- Uninsured amounts that are considered material are reduced to an amount that is not material within 30 days of when it became, or becomes, material to the individual.

When a CPA maintains brokerage or other accounts with an attest client that is an insurance company, investment advisor, broker-dealer, bank, or other member of the financial services industry, impairment of independence may be avoided if certain safeguards are in place:

- The attest client is providing services applying its normal terms, procedures, and requirements; and

- Any risk of loss, such as from the client's bankruptcy, insolvency, fraud or illegal acts, or other circumstances, is not material to the individual after considering protections from federal, state, or other insurers or from other sources.

An insurance policy from a stock or mutual life insurance company is not considered a financial interest unless the policy offers the policy holder an investment option. Holding such a policy would create a self-interest threat to independence only if the policy was not obtained under the issuing entity's normal terms, procedures, and requirements.

When a CPA holds an insurance policy with an investment option, independence may be impaired.

- If not obtained under the insurer's normal terms, procedures, and requirements, threats to independence would not be at an acceptable level.

- When obtained under the insurer's normal terms, procedures, and requirements, a direct financial interest would be created if the CPA participates in or oversees investment decisions and the self-interest threat would be at an unacceptable level

Topic 1.260 – Loans, Leases, and Guarantees

Loans to or from an attest client, an officer or director of an attest client, or an individual owning 10% or more of an attest client's outstanding ownership interests create a *self-interest threat* that may not be at an acceptable level. Unsecured loans that are not material to the CPA's net worth, home mortgage loans, and secured loans will not raise the threat to an unacceptable level if certain safeguards are all in place:

- The loan was obtained under the institution's normal terms, procedures, and requirements.

- The loan was obtained prior to the institution becoming an attest client; from a lender that was not an attest client but was subsequently sold to an attest client; or prior to the CPA becoming a covered member.

- The loan has been maintained as current at all times as long as the borrower has been a covered member and there have been no changes to the terms of the loan not provided for in the original agreement.

- The estimated value of collateral at least equals the outstanding balance of the home mortgage or secured loan.

Obtaining one of the following from a lending institution under its normal lending procedures, terms, and requirements would *not impair* a CPA's independence as long as the CPA is in compliance with the terms of the agreement at all times:

- Automobile loans or leases collateralized by the automobile;

- Loans fully collateralized by the cash surrender value of an insurance policy or cash deposits at the same institution; or

- Credit cards and overdraft protection with an aggregate balance of no more than $10,000 after payment of the most recent monthly statement, made within the grace period.

A *lease arrangement* with an attest client would not raise threats to an unacceptable level if all the following safeguards are in place:

- The lease meets the criteria to be accounted for as an operating lease under GAAP.

- The terms and conditions are comparable to other similar leases.
- All payments are made in accordance with the lease terms.

Topic 1.270 – Family Relationships with Attest Clients

In general, members of a CPA's **immediate family,** which include the CPA's spouse or spousal equivalent, and all dependents, whether related or not, are required to comply with the independence rules to avoid impairing the independence of the CPA. Any financial interests of immediate family members are attributed to the CPA, including when determining the materiality of an indirect financial interest. Without impairing a CPA's independence, an immediate family member may:

- Be employed by an attest client provided it is not in a key position, which would create the threats of management participation, familiarity, and self-interest.

- Participate in an employee benefit plan that is an attest client or is sponsored by an attest client as long as the family member is not in a key position with the client, the plan is offered to all employees in comparable positions, the family member is not part of the plan's governance, and the family member does not participate in or oversee investment decisions.

- Participate in a retirement plan that is not an attest client or sponsored by an attest client but that holds an investment in an attest client provided:

  o The CPA does not participate in, and cannot influence, the attest engagement;

  o The family member has no other investment options available; and

  o If given the opportunity to invest in a nonattest client or a nonclient, the family member disposes of financial interests in the attest client as soon as is practicable, no later than 30 days after the option becomes available.

Actions and circumstances related to **close relatives**, which are parents, siblings, and nondependent children, may also result in an impairment of a member's independence. This would be the case if either a member of the engagement team, or an individual in a position to influence the engagement team or any partner or partner equivalent in the office of the engagement has a close relative:

- In a key position with the attest client during the period covered by the engagement or during the period of the engagement; or

- With a financial interest in the attest client that is known or believed to be material to the relative or enables the relative to exercise significant influence over the attest client.

Topic 1.275 – Current Employment or Association with an Attest Client

When a member is employed or associated with an attest client as a director, officer, employee, promoter, underwriter, voting trustee, or trustee of a pension or profit-sharing plan during the period covered by financial statements or during the period of the professional engagement, the familiarity, management participation, advocacy, or self-review threats will be raised to an unacceptable level and independence will be impaired. The member may serve as an adjunct faculty member for an attest client educational institution provided the member:

- Is not in a key position with the educational institution;

- Does not participate on, nor can influence, the engagement team;

- Is employed by the educational institution in a nontenured or part-time position;

- Is not a participant in an employee benefit plan to the extent that it is not required; and

- Does not assume management responsibilities or set policy for the institution.

Threats would be at an acceptable level if a member's association with an attest client consisted of:

- Serving as an honorary director or trustee for an attest client not-for-profit organization provided the position is clearly honorary and held in name only; the member does not vote or otherwise participate in board or management responsibilities; and, if named in letterheads or materials that are circulated externally, is identified as an honorary director or trustee.

- Serving on the advisory board of an attest client provided the responsibilities are truly advisory in nature; the advisory board is neither authorized to make nor does it appear to make management decisions; and the advisory board is distinct from the decision-making body with a minimum of common members.

- Serving on a committee established to study possible changes in the form of an attest client county government, or the government of the state in which the attest client county government resides, and advising the county government client.

- Serving as the treasurer for a mayoral campaign when the attest client is the candidate's political party or the municipality in which the candidate is running. Independence would be impaired, however, if the campaign organization itself was the attest client.

A CPA may not serve on the engagement team, or be in a position to influence the engagement team, of an attest client at which the CPA had been employed as an officer, director, promoter, underwriter, voting trustee, or trustee for the entity's pension or profit sharing trust during any portion of the period or periods to which the attest engagement applies.

Independence will not be impaired if a CPA fails to disassociate from an attest client before becoming a covered member if certain safeguards are all met:

- The member discontinues participation in the client's employee health and welfare plans unless the client is legally required to allow the member to participate and the member pays 100% of the cost of participation on a current basis;

- The member discontinues participation in all other employee benefit plans and disposes of all vested benefits from the plan at the earliest date permitted by the plan;

    o Disposal is not required if the member would be subject to a significant penalty

    o The covered member must not participate on the attest engagement team or be in a position to influence the engagement.

- The member disposes of any direct and any material indirect financial interest in the client;

- The member collects or repays any loans to or from the client' and

- The covered member evaluates whether other relationships with the attest client create additional threats that must be addressed.

Seeking or discussing *potential employment* or other association with an attest client, including receiving a specific offer of employment, would impair independence unless:

- The circumstances are promptly reported to an appropriate party at the firm; or
- The individual discontinues participation in the engagement or providing services to the attest client until either the offer is rejected or employment with the client is no longer being sought.

A member who leaves from a CPA firm to take a key position with an attest client would potentially have created the threat of familiarity, self-interest, undue influence, or management participation. Independence will be impaired unless:

- Amounts due to the member from the firm are not material to the firm;
- The member cannot influence the firm's operations or financial position; and
- The member is not associated with the firm and does not participate, or appear to participate, in the firm's business once employed or associated with the attest client, even if compensated for doing so.

In addition, the ongoing engagement team should consider whether to modify engagement procedures. If the member left the firm within one year of an engagement, an appropriate firm member should review the subsequent attest engagement and ascertain that an appropriate level of professional skepticism was applied, considering:

- The position the member holds with the attest client'
- The position the member held with the firm; and
- The nature of services performed by the member for the attest client while associated with the firm.

Employment with Audit Client
<ul><li>**Prior to leaving:**<ul><li>Must inform audit firm of conversations with client about possible employment.</li><li>Immediately be removed from the audit.</li><li>Once removed, the audit firm must review the work performed by the departed auditor.</li></ul></li><li>**After employed by the audit client:**<ul><li>Audit firm must consider modifying the audit plan.</li><li>Assure remaining audit team is objective.</li></ul></li><li>The next annual audit must be separately reviewed by an audit firm professional uninvolved in the audit.</li></ul>

Topic 1.280 – Memberships

Although memberships do create or enhance threats associated with management participation, self-review, and self-interest, they do not necessarily impair independence.

- A pro rata share of a club's equity or debt securities held by a CPA belonging to an attest client social club would not be considered a direct financial interest if the club membership is essentially a social matter.

- Membership in an attest client trade association would not impair independence unless the CPA serves in an inappropriate position, as indicated in ET section 1.275, such as a director, officer, or employee during the period covered by the financial statements subject to the attest engagement or during the period of the engagement.

Subject to those restrictions related to depository accounts and loans, membership in an attest client credit union would not impair the CPA's independence if membership was based on the CPA's qualifications or characteristics other than the fact that the CPA provides professional services to the credit union. If membership is due to providing professional services to the credit union, independence would be impaired.

Topic 1.285 – Gifts and Entertainment

Offering a gift to, or accepting a gift from, an attest client, an individual in a key position with an attest client, or an individual owning 10% or more of an attest client's outstanding equity may impair independence if the threats of undue influence or self-interest are increased to an unacceptable level. To avoid impairing independence:

- A gift may only be accepted from an attest client if it is clearly insignificant to the recipient.

- Being entertained by an attest client is acceptable if it is reasonable under the circumstances.

- A CPA may only offer gifts or entertainment to a client that is reasonable under the circumstances.

In determining if a gift or entertainment is reasonable under the circumstances, the CPA will consider:

- The nature of the item and the occasion giving rise to it

- The cost or value

- The nature, value, and frequency of other gifts or entertainment offered or accepted

- Whether business was actively conducted before, during, or after entertainment

- Whether or not other attest clients participated

- The individuals from the attest client involved

Topic 1.290 – Actual or Threatened Litigation

Litigation, whether actual or the expressed intention to begin litigation may create an adverse interest or a self-interest threat that could be at an unacceptable level. The materiality of such actual or threatened litigation to the CPA, the CPA's firm, and to the client should be evaluated by the CPA in making a determination. Whether or not independence is impaired will depend on the facts and circumstances surrounding each situation and will require the CPA to apply professional judgment.

Some, but not all, actual or threatened **litigation between a CPA and an attest client** will impair independence. Independence will not be impaired by litigation that is not related to the client's attestation engagement and is not material to either the CPA or the attest client. Examples of litigation that will *impair independence* include:

- Deficiencies in audit work performed for the attest client alleged by its present management

- Allegations by the CPA of fraud or deceit by management

Any threats to a CPA's independence due to actual or threatened litigation is eliminated when the parties reach final resolution and the matter no longer affects the relationship with the attest client. This is a matter of the CPA's professional judgment.

Topic 1.295 – Performance of *Nonattest* Services and Independence

Many CPA firms provide a variety of nonattest services for their attest clients, the most common of which include bookkeeping; tax compliance; and nontax disbursement services; such as payroll services. The performance of nonattest services may create *self-review, management participation, or advocacy threats to independence.* When significant threats to independence exist during either the period during which the professional engagement is being performed, or the period covered by the financial statements that are the subject of the attest service, they must be reduced to an acceptable level or independence will be impaired.

Certain nonattest services, and certain conditions under which nonattest services are performed create threats to independence that cannot be reduced to an acceptable level. These will not prevent the CPA from performing an attest service for such a client if:

- The nonattest services were performed prior to the period in which the attest services were performed;

- The nonattest services relate to periods prior to the periods covered by the financial statements that are the subject of the attest services; and

- The financial statements for the period during which the nonattest services were performed were attested to by another CPA.

  - If the attest engagement is an audit, the prior financial statements were audited by another CPA.

  - If the attest engagement is a review, the prior financial statements were audited or reviewed by another CPA.

In addition to bookkeeping, tax compliance, and payroll, other nonattest services include advisory services; appraisal, valuation, and actuarial services; benefit plan administration; business risk and corporate finance consulting; executive or employee recruiting; forensic accounting; information systems design, implementation, or integration; Internal audit; and investment advisory or management services. Preparing the financial statements for an attest client and performing a cash-to-accrual conversion or reconciliations as part of the financial statement closing process are also nonattest services.

Although a CPA may not perform certain nonattest services for an attest client because they create threats to independence that cannot be reduced to an acceptable level, many nonattest services may be performed for an attest client **without impairing independence**. To make certain that independence is not impaired when performing nonattest services for an attest client, the CPA will address **three distinct components** of the Code.

1. The CPA will evaluate the *cumulative effect* of all nonattest services being performed for the client, using a conceptual framework approach, to determine if threats to independence are at an acceptable level.

2. The CPA will apply the *three general requirements* for performing nonattest services enumerated in the Code.

3. The CPA will evaluate the *specific services* being performed to make certain that none of them individually raise threats to independence to an unacceptable level.

1. Cumulative Effect of Multiple Nonattest Services

When a CPA performs multiple nonattest services for an attest client, the self-review and management participation threats may be elevated and the accountant should evaluate whether or not they are at an acceptable level and, if they are not at an acceptable level, whether safeguards that are in place, or that may be put into effect, will reduce them to an acceptable level.

- The **self-review threat** is the threat that occurs when a CPA uses the results of performing a service for a client, such as bookkeeping services, as a component of another service, such as a review or an audit of the client's financial statements, without appropriately evaluating the service previously performed, including the judgments made while performing that service.

- The **management participation threat** is the threat that the CPA will assume management responsibilities.

The three general requirements for performing nonattest services for an attest client are designed to reduce the self-review and management participation threats to an acceptable level. The fact that the three general requirements have been complied with does not, however, eliminate the need to evaluate the services performed in relation to all potential threats to independence as well as the cumulative effect of multiple nonattest services being performed for the attest client.

2. Apply the 3 General Requirements for Performing Nonattest Services

The performance of nonattest services for an attest client increases threats to the CPA's independence and the CPA should apply safeguards to avoid impairment. Specific nonattest services that a CPA may perform for an attest client raise threats to independence to an unacceptable level, which cannot be reduced to an acceptable level through the implementation of safeguards. When that is not the case, however, complying with the general requirements will reduce threats to an acceptable level.

The general requirements fall into **three categories**:

A. The client must accept its responsibilities;

B. The accountant's responsibilities must be limited; and

C. A written understanding must be established with the client.

    A. Client Responsibilities – The first of the general requirements is that the client and its management must agree to assume all management responsibilities. **Management responsibilities** involve:

    o Leading and directing an entity; and

    o Making decisions regarding human, financial, and intangible resources, including their acquisition, use, control, and disposal.

Examples of management responsibilities that the auditor may **NOT assume** include:

- Setting policy or strategic direction for the client

- Directing, or taking responsibility for, the actions of client employees
- Authorizing, executing, or completing transactions, or having the authority to do so
- Preparing source documents
- Having custody of client assets
- Deciding upon which recommendations of the CPA or others should be implemented
- Reporting to those charged with governance on behalf of management
- Serving as a stock transfer or escrow agent, registrar, general counsel, or in a similar role for an attest client
- Accepting responsibility for a client project
- Accepting responsibility for the preparation and fair presentation of the entity's financial statements in accordance with an applicable financial reporting framework (AFRF)
- Accepting responsibility for designing, implementing, or maintaining (DIM) internal control
- Performing monitoring procedures by evaluating internal controls on an ongoing basis

In addition, management must *accept responsibility for oversight* of the nonattest service being performed by the accountant for the client. The client does this by designating an individual with appropriate skill, knowledge, and experience, preferably someone in senior management, to fulfill the role. The party is not required to be able to perform the service but should have an adequate understanding to oversee it.

The client must also agree to *evaluate the adequacy and results* of the service performed and *accept responsibility* for the results of the service.

B. **Limitation on Accountant's Responsibilities** – To maintain independence, the accountant **may not** assume any management responsibilities. In addition, the accountant must be satisfied that the client will be able to meet the criteria it agrees to in the form of accepting all management responsibilities and the oversight and responsibility for the nonattest services being performed by the accountant on its behalf.

The accountant should also be satisfied that **the client will**:

o Make an informed judgment in regard to the result of the service; and

o Accept responsibility for significant judgments and decisions for which it has responsibility.

C. **Written Understanding** – In order to preserve independence, the accountant must enter into an understanding with a client regarding the nonattest services to be performed. The understanding is *required to be in writing* and is generally in the form of an **engagement letter**. It is required to include:

o The objectives of the engagement;

o The services to be performed;

o An acknowledgement by the client that it is accepting its responsibilities;

o An indication of the CPA's responsibilities; and

o Limitations on the engagement, if any.

3. Nonattest Services that Do or Do Not Impair Independence

As indicated, certain nonattest services, and certain conditions under which nonattest services are performed create threats to independence that cannot be reduced to an acceptable level. The AICPA Code of Professional Conduct has **provided guidance** for when the accountant is performing certain **types of nonattest services**. These include:

- Advisory services

- Appraisal, valuation, and actuarial services

- Benefit plan administration

- Bookkeeping, payroll, and other disbursements

- Business risk consulting

- Corporate finance consulting

- Executive or employee recruiting

- Forensic accounting

- Information systems design, implementation, or integration

- Internal audit

- Investment advisory or management

- Tax services

- Attestation services

Advisory Services – When a CPA provides advisory services to a client, the management participation and self-review threats are affected. These threats will be at an acceptable level, however, if the services are exclusively advisory in nature and the accountant does not assume any management responsibilities. Without raising threats to an unacceptable level, **a CPA may**:

- Provide advice, resources for research, and make recommendations to management to assist it in performing its functions and making its decisions;

- Attend board meetings as an advisor with no voting rights;

- Provide interpretations of financial statements, forecasts, or other analyses; or

- Advise management regarding its anticipated plans, strategies, or relationships.

Appraisal, Valuation, and Actuarial Services – When a CPA provides appraisal, valuation, and actuarial services, the management participation and self-review threats are affected. When these services both involve a significant degree of subjectivity and are material to the client's financial statements, either individually or in combination with other valuation, appraisal, or actuarial services, threats would not be at an acceptable level and could not be reduced to an acceptable level by the application of safeguards.

Valuations of ESOPs or business combinations, and appraisals of assets or liabilities generally require a significant degree of subjectivity and impair independence if the results are material to the client's financial statements. An actuarial valuation of pension or postemployment benefit liabilities do not generally require a significant degree of subjectivity and would not raise threats to independence to an unacceptable level. In addition, appraisals, valuations, and actuarial services that are performed for nonfinancial statement purposes would not raise threats to an unacceptable level.

Benefit Plan Administration – When a CPA provides benefit plan administration services, the management participation and self-review threats are affected. Without raising threats to an unacceptable level, however, **a CPA may**:

- Communicate summary plan information to a trustee of the plan;

- Provide management advice regarding the application and impact of provisions in a plan document;

- Process transactions initiated by plan participants or approved by administrators such as processing investment or benefit elections, processing changes in contributions to the plan, performing data entry, preparing participant confirmations, and processing distributions and loans;

- Prepare account valuations for plan participants; and

- Prepare and transmit participant statements.

Threats, however, would be raised to an unacceptable level and the accountant would not be able to reduce them to an acceptable level through the application of safeguards if the accountant (**Cannot do**):

- Makes policy decisions for management;

- Interprets plan provisions for a participant without management concurrence;

- Disburses funds on behalf of the plan;

- Has custody of plan assets; or

- Serves in a fiduciary capacity, as defined in ERISA.

Bookkeeping, Payroll, and Other Disbursements – When a CPA provides bookkeeping, payroll and other disbursement services, the management participation and self-review threats are affected. Without raising threats to an unacceptable level, however, **a CPA may**:

- Record transactions, for which the client has approved or determined the account classification, in the client's general ledger;

- Post transactions, coded by the client, to the client's general ledger;

- Prepare financial statements based on the client's trial balance;

- Post entries that have been approved by the client to the client's trial balance;

- Propose entries or changes to the financial statements that are reviewed by the client, provided the accountant is satisfied that the nature and financial statement impact are understood by the client, before posting;

- Generate unsigned checks from information provided and approved by the client;

- Process payroll for a client based on payroll records that have been provided and approved by the client;

- After client review and authorization, transmit payroll or other disbursement information to a bank, provided:

- o Prior to transmission, the client has made arrangements to limit such payments as to amounts and payee; and

  - o Once transmitted, the client has authorized the bank to process the information; and

- Prepare a bank, accounts receivable, or other reconciliation.

Threats, however, would be raised to an unacceptable level and the accountant would not be able to reduce them to an acceptable level through the application of safeguards if the accountant (**Cannot do**):

- Determines or changes, without prior approval from the client, journal entries, coding, classifications, or accounting records;

- Authorizes or approves transactions;

- Prepares source documents, such as purchase orders or invoices, or makes changes to them without client approval;

- Accepts responsibility for authorizing client payments, other than certain electronic payroll tax payments provided certain requirements are complied with;

- Accepts responsibility as a check signer;

- Has custody of client funds; or makes credit or banking decisions for the client; or

- Approves invoices from vendors for payment.

Business Risk Consulting – When a CPA provides business risk consulting services, the management participation and self-review threats are affected. Without raising threats to an unacceptable level, however, **a CPA may**:

- Assist management in assessing its business risk control processes; or

- Recommend, and assist in the implementation of, improvements to the client's business risk control processes.

Threats, however, would be raised to an unacceptable level and the accountant would not be able to reduce them to an acceptable level through the application of safeguards if the accountant (**Cannot do**):

- Makes or approves business risk decisions; or

- Presents considerations of business risk to the board of directors on behalf of management.

Corporate Finance Consulting – When a CPA provides corporate finance consulting services, the advocacy, management participation, and self-review threats are affected. Without raising threats to an unacceptable level, however, **a CPA may**:

- Assist management in developing corporate strategies and identifying capital sources, based on client criteria;

- Introduce sources of capital to the client, based on client criteria;

- Assist management in determining effects of potential transactions with possible buyers, sellers, or providers of financing;

- Advise the client during negotiations and assist the client in drafting its offering documents;

- Participate, in an advisory capacity, in transaction negotiations; or

- Be named as the client's financial adviser in a private placement memorandum or an offering document.

Threats, however, would be raised to an unacceptable level and the accountant would not be able to reduce them to an acceptable level through the application of safeguards if the accountant (**Cannot do**):

- Commits the client to a transaction;

- Consummates a transaction on behalf of a client;

- Acts as promoter, underwriter, broker-dealer, or guarantor of client securities;

- Acts as distributor of a client's private placement memorandum or offering documents; or

- Maintains custody of the client's securities.

Executive or Employee Recruiting – When a CPA provides executive or employee recruiting services, the management participation and self-review threats are affected. Without raising threats to an unacceptable level, however, **a CPA may**:

- Recommend candidate specifications or a position description to the client;

- Solicit and screen candidates who conform to client criteria;

- Recommend candidates who appear qualified based on client criteria; and

- Participate, in an advisory capacity, in hiring or compensation discussions.

Threats, however, would be raised to an unacceptable level and the accountant would not be able to reduce them to an acceptable level through the application of safeguards if the accountant (**Cannot do**):

- Commits the client to employee compensation or benefit arrangements; or

- Hires or terminates client employees.

Forensic Accounting – A CPA may provide forensic accounting services, consisting of investigative services and litigation services. Investigative services include all forensic services that do not involve litigation and affect the management participation and self-review threats to independence. Litigation services pertain to actual or potential proceedings, legal or regulatory, before a trier of facts to resolve a dispute between parties. Litigation services include expert witness services, litigation consulting services, and other related services.

- In general, performing *expert witness* services increases the advocacy threat to an unacceptable level that could not be reduced to an acceptable level by safeguards.

- Threats would be at an acceptable level if the services were being performed for a large group of plaintiffs or defendants, including the client; and

- The clients make up less than 20% of the members of the group, no client is designated as lead plaintiff or defendant, and no client has sole decision-making authority to determine who will serve as expert witness.

- Acting as a *"fact witness"* is not considered a nonattest service and would not impair an accountant's independence if the accountant responds to requests for providing an opinion regarding matters within the accountant's expertise.

Litigation consulting services, in which the accountant provides advice about facts, issues, or strategy, elevate the advocacy and management participation threats to independence.

Provided that the general requirements for performing nonattest services have been met, threats would be at an acceptable level and independence would not be impaired. Subsequent agreement to serve as an expert witness, however, elevates threats to an unacceptable level, which could not be reduced to an acceptable level through the application of safeguards.

The advocacy threat would also be raised to an unacceptable level, which could not be reduced to an acceptable level through the application of safeguards, if the accountant is serving as a trier of fact, special master, court-appointed expert, or arbitrator in a matter involving a client. Threats, on the other hand, would be at an acceptable level if the accountant agrees to serve as a mediator in a circumstance where the accountant is facilitating negotiations in which the parties are reaching their own agreement.

Information Systems Design, Implementation, or Integration – Performing information systems design, implementation, or integration services affect the management participation and self-review threats to the accountant's independence. Threats would not be elevated to an unacceptable level if the accountant performs any of the following services (**A CPA may**):

- Installation or integration of a client's financial information system that was designed or developed by parties other than the accountant;

- Assisting the client in establishing a *chart of accounts* and formats for financial statements in the client's financial information system;

- Designing, developing, installing, or integrating an information system that is not related to the client's accounting records or financial statements;

- Training or instructing client employees in regard to the information and control systems; or

- Performing network maintenance, updating virus protection, applying routine updates and patches, or configuring user settings based on requests from management.

Threats to independence would be at an unacceptable level and would not be able to be reduced to an acceptable level by safeguards if the accountant (**Cannot do**):

- Designs or develops the client's financial information system;

- Makes modifications to source code related to the client's financial information system, unless inconsequential;

- Supervises client personnel in the operation of the client's financial information system; or

- Operates a client network.

Internal Audit – Internal audit services consist of assisting the client in its internal audit, or internal control activities. If a client outsources its internal control activities to the accountant, such that the accountant essentially manages the client's internal audit activities, including accepting responsibility for the Design, Implementation, and Maintenance (DIM) of internal control, threats to independence would not be at an acceptable level and applying safeguards could not reduce threats to an acceptable level.

Other than outsourcing services, the CPA may assist the client in performing financial and operational internal audit activities provided, to the accountant's satisfaction, management:

- Designates someone to be responsible for the internal audit function who possesses suitable skills, knowledge, and experience, preferably from within senior management;

- Makes all decisions regarding the scope, risk, and frequency of internal control activities, including those performed by the CPA or by others;

- Evaluates all findings and results that emanate from the internal audit activities, whether performed by the accountant or others; and

- Evaluate the adequacy of the procedures performed and the results of those procedures.

Activities that the **CPA may not perform** without raising threats to an unacceptable level, without the ability to reduce them to an acceptable level by applying safeguards, include:

- Performing ongoing evaluations or control activities that affect either the execution of transactions or ensuring that they are properly executed and accounted for;

- Performing routine activities related to an ongoing compliance or quality control function in connection with client operating or production processes;

- Performing routine operations built into the client's business process, such as separate evaluations on the effectiveness of specific significant controls;

- Providing the primary basis for management's assertions regarding the design or operating effectiveness of internal controls;

- Determining which recommendations for the improvement of the client's internal control system should be implemented, if any;

- Reporting to the board of directors on behalf of management in regard to the internal control function;

- Taking responsibility for, or approving, the internal audit work plan, including scope, priorities, and frequency of performance; or

- Taking a *management role* in relation to the client.

Evaluating whether components of a client's internal control system have been put in place and are operating properly is part of the monitoring process. Ongoing evaluations that are incorporated in the client's system are the responsibility of management and would raise the management participation threat to an unacceptable level that could not be adequately reduced by the application of safeguards. The performance of separate evaluations, applied periodically to determine if controls are present and functioning, do not create a significant management participation threat to independence.

Because of the nature of internal audit services, the accountant will be required to apply judgment in determining when threats have been raised to an unacceptable level and whether or not they can be reduced to an acceptable level through the application of safeguards.

Performing services that are normally associated with the attest function, such as confirming accounts receivable or analyzing fluctuations in account balances, are not internal audit services and do not impair the accountant's independence, even when they exceed the scope of the accountant's responsibilities for the nature of attest service being performed for the client.

Investment Advisory or Management – When a CPA provides investment advisory or management services, the management participation and self-review threats are affected. Without raising threats to an unacceptable level, however, **a CPA may:**

- Apply client criteria, such as rate of return, to recommend an allocation of funds among various investments or asset classes

- Maintain records of the client's portfolio, prepare reports, and provide analysis of investments in comparison with third party benchmarks

- Evaluate the management of the portfolio to assess if managers are following the client's investment policy guidelines, meeting the client's investment objectives, and conforming to the client's parameters, including its risk tolerance

- Submit to a broker-dealer the client's investment selection provided the client has consented to the submission and authorized the broker-dealer to execute the transaction

Threats, however, would be raised to an unacceptable level and the accountant would not be able to reduce them to an acceptable level through the application of safeguards if the accountant (**Cannot do**):

- Makes investment decisions on behalf of the client'

- Has discretionary authority over client investments;

- Executes a transaction to trade a client's investments; or

- Has custody of client assets, even temporarily.

Tax Services – Tax services include:

- Tax return preparation or transmittal;

- Transmittal of a tax payment to a taxing authority

- Signing and filing a tax return or having a power of attorney limited strictly to tax matters; and

- Representing a client before a taxing authority in an administrative proceeding.

Preparing a tax return and transmitting the return and related payment to a taxing authority may create or increase the management participation and self-review threats to independence. In such circumstances, the accountant's independence would not be impaired if the accountant does not have control or custody over client assets. In addition, the individual designated to oversee the tax services must review and approve the tax return and related payments; and if the return is required to be signed for filing, signs the tax return prior to it being transmitted by the accountant to the taxing authority.

In addition, provided certain conditions are met, signing and filing a tax return on behalf of a client, assuming the accountant has the legal authority to do so, **would not impair** the accountant's independence. Nor would:

- Serving as the client's authorized representative in an administrative proceeding; or

- Having a power of attorney that is limited strictly to tax matters.

Representing a client in court to resolve a tax dispute would raise threats to independence to an unacceptable level and applying safeguards would not be able to reduce threats to an acceptable level.

Attestation Services – Independence requirements apply to the performance of all attest services, including services performed in accordance with **attestation standards**. The CPA is not required to be independent of an individual or entity engaging the CPA to perform an attestation engagement if the individual or entity is not the responsible party, the party responsible for the assertion to which the accountant is attesting. Modifications to the independence requirements in relation to the attestation standards include:

- Restrictions on nonattest services only apply to those nonattest services performed in relation to the subject matter of the nonattest services.

- Covered members who must comply with the independence requirements in an agreed-upon procedures engagement may be limited to those participating on the engagement; those who directly supervise the engagement partner or partner equivalent; and individuals consulting with the engagement team regarding technical or industry-related issues relevant to the engagement.

Topic 1.300 – General Standards

A member must comply with the following standards for all professional engagements:

- Only accept engagements expected to be completed with **professional competency**.

- Exercise **due professional care**.

- Adequately **plan and supervise** engagements.

- Obtain **sufficient relevant data** to afford a reasonable basis for conclusions and recommendations.

A member who performs auditing, review, compilation, consulting services, tax or other services shall comply with standards promulgated by bodies designated by Council. The bodies include:

- FASB

- GASB

- PCAOB (SOX)

- IASB for IAS

- AICPA bodies

  - ARSC – Accounting and Review Services Committee

  - ASB – Auditing Standards Board

  - Management Consulting Standards Executive Committee

  - Attestation Standards

  - Tax Executive Committee

  - Forensic and Valuation Services Executive Committee

  - Personal Financial Planning Executive Committee

A member may not provide positive or negative assurance that financial statements are in conformity with a financial reporting framework (GAAP, IASB, PCAOB, GASB, and FASAB statements) if statements contain departures from that framework having a material effect on statements taken as a whole except when unusual circumstances would make financial statements *misleading* if the requirements of the framework had been followed. May depart from GAAP/GASB without modifying report if new legislation or a new form of business transaction exists.

Topic 1.400 – Acts Discreditable

A member should NOT commit certain acts that are discreditable to the profession. These might include:

- Discrimination and harassment in employment practices
- Failing to file a tax return or pay a tax liability
- Retaining client records to enforce payment of a bill.
- Providing a fee estimate to a client for services, when the accountant expects the actual fee to be substantially higher (Deliberate underbidding).
- Negligence in the preparation of Financial Statements.
- Filing a fraudulent tax return for self or client.
- Commission of a Felony.
- Noncompliance with applicable requirements of governmental bodies; commissions, or other regulatory agencies when operating within their jurisdiction, including the SEC, Federal Communications Commission, or the PCAOB;
- Solicitation or disclosure of CPA examination questions and answers.
- False, misleading, or deceptive acts in promoting or marketing professional services
- Inappropriate use of the CPA credential

Topic 1.500 – Fees and Other Types of Remuneration

A member may NOT prepare an original or amended tax return for a contingent fee or accept contingent fees for services involving, or from a client for whom the CPA performs such services:

- An audit or review
- A compilation of financial statements expected to be used by third parties without indicating the lack of independence
- An examination of prospective financial statements

Contingent fees are permitted when performing certain tax-related services, including:

- Representing a client in an examination of an income tax return
- Filing an amended income tax return claiming a refund:
  - Based on a tax issue subject to a test case or an evolving position
  - In an amount greater than the threshold for review by the Joint Committee on Internal Revenue Taxation or state taxing authority

A member may accept commissions and referral fees only if both:

- Nonattest engagement client.
- Payment fully disclosed to client.

No commission may be accepted if the accountant is required to be independent for the service provided.

Topic 1.600 – Advertising and Other Forms of solicitation

A member may NOT engage in false, misleading, or deceptive advertising.

Topic 1.700 – Confidential Information

Information is considered confidential, not privileged. Must not reveal information without client permission with certain **exceptions:**

- Valid subpoena or summons.

- Inquiry by AICPA trial board.

- A request made as part of a Quality control peer review program.

A CPA may not give information to another CPA as a professional courtesy and may not take copies of client files when leaving the firm.

Topic 1.800 – Form of Organization and Name

A member may practice public accounting in any form of organization that is permitted by law or regulation with characteristics consistent with those approved in resolutions of the AICPA Council.

- Form and name should not be misleading.

- A firm cannot designate itself as "members of the AICPA" unless all of its CPA OWNERS are members of the AICPA.

- An individual may practice in name of a former partnership for up to 2 years (applies when all other partners have died or withdrawn).

- A firm name may include names of past partners.

Part 2 – Members in Industry

Part 2 is applicable to members in private industry. A member who is both in private industry and public practice, the requirements applicable to a member in public practice will apply.

Topic 2.000 – Introduction

This topic indicates that this part applies to members in private industry. It also requires a conceptual framework approach to determining when threats to compliance with the Code are at an acceptable level and when they require the application of safeguards to eliminate the threat or reduce it to an acceptable level. The conceptual framework is comparable to that for members in public accounting.

Topic 2.100 – Integrity and Objectivity

As is true for members in public accounting, those in private industry shall maintain objectivity and integrity, avoid conflicts of interest, and not knowingly misrepresent facts or subordinate judgment in the performance of any professional service.

Topic 2.300 – General Standards

A member must comply with the following standards for all professional engagements:

- Only accept engagements expected to be completed with professional competency.

- Exercise due professional care.

- Adequately plan and supervise engagements.

- Obtain sufficient relevant data to afford a reasonable basis for conclusions and recommendations.

Topic 2.400 – Acts Discreditable

A member should NOT commit certain acts that are discreditable to the profession. These might include:

- Violations of laws related to discrimination or harassment in the workplace.

- Solicitation or disclosure of CPA examination questions and answers.

- Nonpayment of a tax liability or not filing a return

- Preparing financial statements in a negligent manner

Part 3 – Other Members

Part 3 is applicable to members who are **neither in public accounting or private industry**, such as a member who is *retired or unemployed*.

Topic 3.000 – Introduction

This topic indicates that this part applies to members who are neither in public accounting or private industry.

Topic 3.400 – Acts Discreditable

A member should NOT commit certain acts that are discreditable to the profession. These might include:

- Violations of laws related to discrimination or harassment in the workplace.

- Solicitation or disclosure of CPA examination questions and answers.

- Nonpayment of a tax liability or not filing a return

- Disclosing confidential information obtained as a result of previous relationships

2.04 Sarbanes-Oxley Act

As a result of numerous incidents involving fraudulent financial reporting involving such companies as Enron, WorldCom, Global Crossing, and others, Congress passed the Sarbanes-Oxley Act (SOX). SOX was created to restore investors' confidence. It established the **P**ublic **C**ompany **A**ccounting **O**versight **B**oard (**PCAOB**) to regulate auditors of public companies (**issuers**), subject to SEC oversight. This eliminated a significant portion of the accounting profession's system of self-regulation.

SOX also led to *"integrated audits"* in which auditors report on audits of both the financial statements and on internal control over financial reporting (ICFR) for public audit clients.

Title I – Public Accounting Oversight Board

- **101** – Establishes the Board (PCAOB), which consists of five (5) full-time members, two (2) of which are CPAs, all appointed by the SEC.

- **102** – Requires public accounting firms to register with the Board in order to issue or participate in the issuance of an audit report for an issuer.

- **103** – Authorizes the Board to establish audit standards*, quality control standards, and ethics standards to be used by registered public accounting firms in the preparation and issuance of audit reports. The board also inspects, investigates, and disciplines public accounting firms and enforces compliance with the act.

  - A second partner is required to review all audit reports.

A list of the PCAOB standards along with short descriptions can be found in the Research Appendix.

- **104** – Provides for Quality Control *Peer Review Inspections* to be conducted by the Board:

  - Must be performed every year for firms that provide more than 100 audit reports annually.

  - At least every three (3) years if 100 or less annually

    - A written report of findings, including deficiencies discovered, is provided to the SEC and made available to the public.

- **105** – Gives Board authority to conduct investigations and obtain all relevant info.

  - Power to suspend auditors, revoke the registration of the accounting firm, or impose penalties for violations or for unwillingness to cooperate with an investigation.

  - Provisions apply to both domestic and foreign auditors.

  - Monetary penalties for violation of board rules or securities law capped at $100K for an individual and $2M for an entity (if intentional breach $750K and $15M).

- **106** – Regulates foreign public accounting firms furnishing an audit report to an issuer and requires them to comply with board requests.

- **107** – Gives SEC oversight and enforcement authority over the Board and its decisions.

- **108** – Amends the Securities Act of 1933 to allow the SEC, which has the authority to establish accounting standards, to adopt the accounting standards established by a standard setting body that meets certain qualifications, such as the FASB.
  - Required study of accounting principles, including content, structure, and standard-setting process.
  - Made recommendations to FASB, resulting in development of the Codification, and adopted FASB standards as amended by SEC pronouncements.
- **109** – Calls for funding of the Board and the designated accounting standard-setting body (FASB) to be funded from fees imposed upon public companies.

Title II – Auditor Independence

- 201 – *Prohibits* any registered public accounting firm from providing the following nonaudit services to Audit clients:
  - Bookkeeping or other services related to the accounting records.
  - Financial info systems design or implementation.
  - Appraisal or valuation services, or providing fairness opinions or contribution-in-kind reports.
  - Actuarial services.
  - Internal audit outsourcing services.
  - Management functions or human resources.
  - Broker or dealer investment advisor or investment banking services.
  - Legal services and expert services that are unrelated to the audit.
  - Any other service the board determines impermissible.
    - Tax services are still permissible if preapproved by the audit committee and disclosed to the SEC.
    - May still perform these services to nonaudit clients or to private companies.
- 202 – Requires the issuer's audit committee to preapprove all auditing and nonauditing services to be provided to an issuer.

  All nonaudit services that are not prohibited are also required to be preapproved unless they are considered de minimis. De minimis nonaudit services entail fees that do not exceed 5% of the total fees paid to the auditor. In addition, the client must not have recognized the services as nonaudit services at the time of the engagement and the services were promptly brought to the attention of the audit committee and approval was obtained prior to the completion of the audit.
- 203 – Establishes mandatory and substantive rotation of audit partner and partner responsible for review every 5 years (not audit firm rotation).
- 204 – Requires audit firm to report to the audit committee:
  - Critical accounting policies and practices
  - Alternative accounting treatments within GAAP discussed with management
  - Material written communications between auditor's firm and management of the issuer

- **205** – Defines the term audit committee and indicates that the entire board of directors is considered the audit committee when one has not been designated.

- **206** – Prohibits the audit firm from providing audit services for issuer if the CEO, controller, CFO, CAO or any person serving in the equivalent capacity was employed in the audit practice of the accounting firm during the one-year period prior to the audit.

Title III – Corporate Responsibility

- **301** – Makes audit committee, which must be independent, responsible for appointment, compensation and oversight of any audit work performed by the audit firm. Allows the SEC to de-list any issuer not in compliance with title III.

- **302** – Requires principal executive and principal financial officers to certify, in each annual or quarterly report:

  o That they reviewed the report

  o The report does not contain any untrue statement of material fact or omission of a material fact

  o Financial position and results of operations are fairly presented

  Officers also certify that they:

  o Are responsible for establishing and maintaining effective internal control

  o Have evaluated the effectiveness of the controls within 90 days prior to the report

  o Have presented their conclusions as to the effectiveness of internal control

  o Signing officers required to disclose to auditors and audit committee:

  o Significant deficiencies in the design or operation of internal controls

  o Any fraud, regardless of whether or not material, that involves management or employees involved in internal controls

  Report of signing officers also indicates changes in internal controls over financial reporting.

- **303** – Prohibits an officer or director of an issuer to fraudulently influence, coerce, manipulate, or mislead the auditor.

- **304** – Requires executives of an issuer to forfeit any bonus or incentive based pay or profits from the sale of stock, received in the 12 months period after the date of issuance of financial statements subject to an earnings restatement (**Claw-back Policy**).

- **305** – The SEC may bar any person who has violated federal securities laws from serving as an officer or director of an issuer.

- **306** – Prohibits trading by officers and directors during blackout periods established between the end of a quarter and the earnings report date.

Title IV – Enhanced Financial Disclosures

- **401** – Requires all financial statements prepared in accordance with GAAP to reflect all material adjustments identified by the auditors.

  o Also required the SEC to establish standards to address off-balance sheet transactions.

  o Result was rules for consolidation of variable interest entities

- **402** – Prohibits personal loans to directors and executive officers.

- **403** – Requires directors, officers, and principal shareholders to disclose the amount of all equity securities in which they hold a beneficial interest and any changes in their interests since the previous filing.

- **404** – Requires that management acknowledge its responsibility for establishing and maintaining adequate internal control over financial reporting and that management assess the effectiveness of internal control as of the end of the period. Also *requires the auditor to examine the design and operating effectiveness of internal control over financial reporting to provide a sufficient basis to report on management's assessment.*

  o The auditor should conduct the attestation in a manner consistent with the Statements on Standards for Attestation Engagements and PCAOB Standards.

  o Note that the auditor is not attesting to the effectiveness or the efficiency of internal control but on management's assessment of internal control.

  o The Act does not specify a date by which the auditor's report is to be submitted.

- **405** – Exempts investment companies registered under the Investment Company Act of 1940 from sections 401, 402, and 404.

- **406** – Requires an issuer to disclose whether it has adopted a code of ethics for senior financial officers and, if not, the reasons for not having done so.

- **407** – Must disclose whether at least one member of its audit committee is a "**financial expert.**"
  The audit committee of an issuer is required to be made up of independent directors, and at least one member of the audit committee is required to be a *financial expert*. If there is not a financial expert on the audit committee, the *reasons* must be disclosed. A financial expert has:

  o An understanding of GAAP and F/S

  o Experience preparing or auditing comparable F/S and experience in applying financial statement or audit knowledge to the accounting for estimates, accruals, and reserves

  o Experience with internal accounting controls

  o An understanding of the functions of the audit committee

    ▪ Need not be a CPA

- **408** – Provides for enhanced review of periodic disclosures by Board.

- **409** – Requires issuers to disclose material changes in the financial condition or operations on a rapid and current basis.

Title V – Analyst Conflict of Interest
Title VI – Commission Resources and Authority
Title VII – Studies and Reports
Title VIII – Corporate and Criminal Fraud Accountability

- Auditors are required to maintain all audit working papers for seven (7) years.

- It is a felony to knowingly destroy or create documents (including audit working papers) to impede, obstruct or influence any existing or contemplated federal investigation.

- The statute of limitations on securities fraud claims is extended to five (5) years from the fraud, or two (2) years after the fraud was discovered.

- Employees of CPA firms (and audit clients) are extended whistleblower protection that would prohibit the employer from taking certain actions against employees. Whistleblower employees are also granted a remedy of special damages and attorney's fees.

- Securities fraud by CPA's (and audit clients) is punishable of up to 10 years in prison.

Title IX – White Collar Crime Penalty Enhancements

- **906 – Requires that management certify that the reports filed with the SEC (10Q, 10K)** comply with relevant securities laws and also fairly present, in all material respects, the financial condition and results of operations of the company.

Note: Violations of rules of the PCAOB are treated as violations of the Securities Exchange Act of 1934 with its penalties, and the Act contains provisions for future rulemaking.

2.05 Other Regulatory Bodies & Responsibilities

Private Securities Litigation Reform Act of 1995

Although the Private Securities Litigation Reform Act of 1995 was primarily designed to limit frivolous lawsuits related to the securities laws, it imposes requirements on an auditor to perform certain tests and to notify the SEC of noncompliance with applicable laws and regulations.

- Imposes requirements to include audit tests to detect (RIG):
  - **R**elated party transactions
  - **I**llegal acts (noncompliance with laws and regulations)
  - **G**oing concern doubts
- Requires quick notice of illegal acts (noncompliance with laws and regulations) unless clearly inconsequential.
  - Auditor must inform board of directors within one business day.
  - Board must notify SEC by next business day.
  - Auditor must resign or notify SEC within one business day after that, if board fails to notify SEC and provide auditor with proof of notice (auditor cannot be sued privately for negative effect of SEC notice on the company's securities).

Securities and Exchange Commission (SEC)

"The mission of the SEC is to protect investors, maintain fair, orderly, and efficient markets, and facilitate capital formation." As will be discussed in Regulation (REG), the Securities Act of 1933 and the Securities and Exchange Act of 1934 were designed to protect the public from potentially unscrupulous practices of publicly traded companies.

They established the SEC and gave it the authority to require publicly held companies to issue audited financial statements, designate the acceptable basis or bases of accounting for publicly held companies, and oversee auditors of publicly held companies. The SEC has designated the PCAOB to regulate auditors of publicly held entities and to develop and maintain auditing standards applicable to their audits.

In some cases, the requirements imposed are **more restrictive** than those imposed on auditors of nonpublic entities, such as the prohibition against performing almost any nonassurance services for an audit client and the requirement to disclose audit and nonaudit fees earned. In most cases, however, the Auditing Standards Board (ASB) of the AICPA has evaluated GAAS with the intention of eliminating as many differences between those requirements and those of the PCAOB as is reasonably possible.

Government Accountability Office (GAO) Government Auditing Standards

If performing an audit of a nonfederal governmental agency or an entity receiving governmental financial assistance, the engagement is performed in accordance with **Generally Accepted Government Auditing Standards (GAGAS)** (ie, the "**Yellow Book**") and the auditor must comply with the ethical requirements of the Government Accountability Office (GAO)—an agency of Congress responsible for investigating how the federal government spends taxpayer money.

Ethical Principles

There are five ethical principles to keep in mind when applying GAGAS:

- **The public interest** – Integrity, objectivity, and independence are critical in performing the auditor's professional responsibilities to honor the public trust (ie, the collective well-being of the community of people and entities served.)

- **Integrity** – This includes maintaining an attitude that is *objective, fact-based, nonpartisan,* and *nonideological* with regard to the audited entities and users of the audit reports.
  - Auditor integrity is important to maintaining public confidence in government.
  - Inappropriate, conflicting pressures (eg, from management or others) encountered should be resolved with decisions that are consistent with the public interest.

- **Objectivity** – This includes being independent, intellectually honest, and free of conflicts of interest as well as maintaining an attitude of impartiality.

- **Proper use of government information, resources, and positions** – Such information (which may be sensitive or classified), resources, and positions should not be used for personal gain or handled in a way that is illegal, improper, or detrimental to the interests of the audited entity or audit organization.

- **Professional behavior** – The auditor should comply with all laws, regulations, and professional obligations and avoid conduct that could bring discredit to their work.

Independence Requirements

The GAO's separate, and somewhat *more restrictive*, independence requirements apply when performing an engagement in accordance with GAGAS. It indicates that: *"In all matters relating to the GAGAS engagement, auditors and audit organizations must be independent from an audited entity."* This includes:

- **Independence of mind**, indicating that the auditor is free of influence that might compromise the auditor's judgment

- **Independence in appearance**, meaning no circumstances exist that would cause reasonable and informed third parties to conclude that the auditor's judgment was compromised

GAGAS incorporates an **independence conceptual framework** similar to the AICPA professional standards in which government auditors are expected to:

- **Identify threats** to independence

- **Evaluate the significance** of the threats, individually and collectively

- **Apply safeguards** to eliminate/mitigate the threats so that they are reduced to an acceptable level

The framework is applied by first identifying facts and circumstances that create **threats to independence**. There are 7 categories of threats to independence in the Yellow Book. The first two here are different and the rest are very similar to the AICPA code of conduct:

★ A **bias** threat occurs when the auditor is not objective with regard to the client due to political, ideological, social, or other beliefs.

★ A **structural** threat occurs when the audit entity's placement within the government entity it is auditing, along with the structure of the government entity, impairs the auditor's ability to remain objective in performing the audit work and reporting the results.

- A **self-interest** threat occurs when the auditor has a financial or other interest in the entity that might affect the auditor's judgment.

- A **self-review** threat occurs when the extent of nonattest services performed by the auditor for the client raise a question as to whether the auditor will be reviewing judgments and estimates that the auditor participated in the development of.

- A **familiarity** threat occurs as a result of the duration and closeness of the relationship between the auditor and the client.

- An **undue influence** threat occurs when external sources create influence or pressure that may affect the auditor's ability to make objective judgments.

- A **management participation** threat occurs when the auditor takes on the role of management or performs management functions for the client.

If the threat to independence results from the performance of nonaudit services, the auditor will first determine if the service was prohibited. If so, independence is impaired and the auditor will not be able to perform the engagement. **Prohibited nonaudit services** include:

- Performing *management responsibilities*, such as strategic planning for the entity, developing entity program policies, directing employees, making decisions regarding the acquisition, use or disposition of resources, custody of assets, reporting to governance, accepting responsibility for internal controls, and voting in the management committee or board of directors

- Performing certain *accounting functions without obtaining management approval,* such as determining or changing journal entries, authorizing or approving transactions, and preparing or altering source documents*

- Providing *internal audit assistance* in the form of setting policies, strategic direction, or scope for the internal audit function, or performing internal control procedures

- *Accepting responsibility* for the design, implementation, or maintenance (DIM) of internal control, or its monitoring

- Participation in *information technology services* including the design, development, or alteration of IT systems that manage aspects of the operations that will be audited, or operating or supervising the operation of such a system

- Providing *valuation services* that materially impact information included in the financial statements

- Performing specific *additional services* related to advisory services, benefit plan administration, business risk consulting, executive or employee recruiting, and investment advisory or management

Note that the preparation of the financial statements in their entirety from a client-provided trial balance or underlying accounting records is no longer a prohibited service, but it is considered to create significant threats to independence.

The auditor will evaluate the magnitude (significance) of any threats, individually and in the aggregate, to determine if they are at an acceptable level. If they are not at an acceptable level (ie, threats are significant), the auditor will consider **safeguards** to mitigate or eliminate those threats.

- If safeguards are **sufficient** to reduce threats to an acceptable level, the auditor will document the analysis and may perform the audit engagement.

- If safeguards are **not sufficient,** the auditor's independence is impaired and the auditor may not perform the engagement.

To support the auditor's consideration of independence, **documentation** should include:

- Threats to independence and the safeguards applied;

- The safeguards applied if the audit organization is structurally located within a government unit and is considered independent as a result of those safeguards;

- Consideration of management's ability to oversee nonaudit services provided; and

- The understanding with the audited entity regarding the performance of nonaudit services.

- The evaluation of the significance of certain nonaudit services, including

  - Recording transactions that management has approved.

  - Preparing certain line items or sections of the financial statements based on the trial balance.

  - Posting entries that management approved.

  - Preparing account reconciliations for management's evaluation.

Department of Labor & Employee Retirement Income Security Act of 1974 (ERISA)

An accountant performing audits of employee benefit plans is required to comply with the independence requirements of the Department of Labor (DOL). Employee benefit plans must be audited in accordance with the Employee Retirement Income Security Act of 1974 (ERISA), as enforced by the DOL. ERISA indicates that the audit is to be performed by an *independent* qualified public accountant (IQPA) and, in the DOL's view, "an accountant's independence is at least of equal importance to the professional competence he or she brings to an engagement to render an opinion and issuing a report on the financial statements of an employee benefit plan." The DOL independence requirements are a bit **more restrictive** than the AICPA requirements.

The rule specifies three types of relationships that will impair an accountant's independence. The requirements apply to the accountant and the accountant's firm and relate to the period of the engagement as well as the period covered by the engagement. **Independence is impaired by:**

- Having, or committing to acquiring, any direct financial interest or any material indirect financial interest in the plan

- Acting as the plan's, or plan sponsor's, promoter, underwriter, investment advisor, voting trustee, director, officer, or employee

- Maintaining financial records for the plan

Independence is not impaired if the accountant is engaged by the plan's sponsor for a professional engagement, provided it does not involve an activity that is prohibited. In addition, independence is not impaired if the plan uses the services of an actuary that is associated with the accountant.

AUD 3
Understanding
an Entity & its
Environment

3.01 The Entity & Its Environment

Overview

Steps in an Audit

Prepare for the audit	**Obtain understanding of client, its environment & I/C**	Assess RMM & design further procedures	Perform tests of controls	Perform substantive procedures	Form opinion	Issue report

The **objective** of AU-C 315[1] is for the auditor to identify and **assess** the risk of material misstatement (**RMM**), whether due to *fraud or error*, at the financial statement and relevant assertion levels. This is accomplished by **understanding** the **entity** and its **environment**, including internal control (**I/C**). This understanding will provide a basis for designing and implementing responses to the assessed RMM.

GAAS Versus PCAOB Audits

GAAS Audits

Auditors of entities that **do not report to the SEC** (aka, **nonissuers**) are required to follow GAAS. GAAS require the auditor to obtain and document an understanding of the client's I/C to assess the risk of material misstatement (RMM) of the financial statements (F/S). The RMM, which consists of inherent risk (IR) and control risk (CR), is then used to determine the extent to which detection risk (DR) must be reduced to keep audit risk (AR) at an acceptable level.

When an auditor believes that the nature, timing, or extent of substantive testing can be limited due to effective I/C, the auditor must perform **tests of controls** to verify that they are operating effectively as designed and intended. Based on those tests, the auditor draws a conclusion as to whether the controls can be relied upon for the entire period for which controls were tested.

PCAOB Audits

Auditors of entities that **do report to the SEC** (aka, **issuers**) are also required to obtain an understanding of I/C. Like auditors of nonissuers, they are required to obtain and document the understanding to assess RMM of the F/S and to plan and perform the audit.

Sarbanes-Oxley, however, requires auditors of issuers to perform an **integrated audit** of both internal control over financial reporting (ICFR) and of the F/S. As a result, in addition to obtaining sufficient evidence to support the auditor's CR assessment, the auditor is required to obtain sufficient evidence to support an **opinion on ICFR** as of a **specific point in time**, the date of the F/S.

---

[1] *Understanding the Entity and Its Environment and Assessing the Risks of Material Misstatements*

Control Risk is High

Auditors of both issuers and nonissuers may conclude either that internal controls are not sufficiently reliable to limit the nature, timing, or extent of substantive testing or that the cost of testing controls exceeds the potential benefit. In either case, the auditor will not perform tests of controls for the purpose of reducing RMM and will, instead, perform substantive tests based on CR set at maximum.

Setting CR at maximum means that if an error or fraud were to occur, the auditor believes there is a 100% probability that I/C will neither prevent nor detect it to allow correction on a timely basis. When the auditor is also performing an examination of I/C (always the case for issuers), the auditor is required to perform tests of the operating effectiveness of I/C. This is true even when controls are not expected to be effective or the cost of testing controls is expected to exceed the cost reductions in substantive testing.

- An entity's I/C cannot be considered effective if one or more material weaknesses exist.

- The auditor must plan and perform the examination to obtain reasonable assurance as to whether material weaknesses exist as of the specified date.

- Material weaknesses may exist when the F/S are not materially misstated.

Evaluating Controls

Entity Level

Controls are evaluated at the entity level, seeking assurance as to the general reliability of the financial reporting process and the desire and intention of the entity to operate in an ethical environment, free of fraud and significant errors, with systems and procedures to provide assurance as to the three **primary objectives** of a system of **I/C** (**ACE**):

- Accurate & reliable financial reporting

- Compliance with applicable laws and regulations

- Efficient and effective operations

Assertion Level

Controls are also evaluated at the assertion level. When management is presenting F/S, there are various assertions embedded in which management is indicating that the financial information contains certain characteristics. When a misrepresentation may result in a material misstatement to the F/S, the assertion affected is considered a relevant assertion.

When performing an audit, the auditor is required to obtain sufficient appropriate audit evidence to support every relevant assertion. This can be accomplished by:

- Demonstrating through the use of **tests of controls** that internal controls are sufficient to prevent a material misstatement in regard to that assertion or to detect and correct such a misstatement on a timely basis;

- Obtaining evidence through the performance of **substantive tests** to demonstrate that the information presented is free of material misstatement, regardless of the existence of internal controls; or

- Some **combination** of those approaches, which is most frequently the case.

F/S Assertions

There are several F/S assertions (**U-PERCV**). These assertions can be expanded out into three categories to correlate with how they apply to the F/S: events and transactions (income statement), account balances (balance sheet), and presentation and disclosure.

Management Assertions
Understandability & Classification
Presentation & Disclosure
Existence or Occurrence
Rights & Obligations
Completeness & Cutoff
Valuation, Allocation & Accuracy

Events & Transactions

The first five assertions relate to events and transactions that occurred during the period of audit, as generally presented on an entity's *income statement* (**CPA-CO**):

- **Completeness** – All events/transactions pertaining to the entity that occurred have been reported.

- **Period cutoff** – All events/transactions have been reported in the appropriate period.

- **Accuracy** – All events/transactions have been reported in the appropriate amounts.

> Just remember that if all revenue and expenses are properly reported, the **CPA-CO** will have no problem preparing your taxes.

- **Classification** – All events/transactions are included in appropriate accounts or categories.

- *O*ccurrence – All events/transactions did occur.

Account Balances

The next four assertions relate to **account balances**, amounts reported as of the date of the F/S, as generally presented on the *balance sheet* (**RACE**):

- **Rights & obligations** – The entity has rights to those items reported as assets, and liabilities are the obligations of the entity.

- **Allocation & valuation** – All assets, liabilities, and equity-related items are reported in amounts that are appropriate as of the date of the F/S.

- **Completeness** – All assets, liabilities, and equity that should have been reported are included on the F/S.

> Of course, if an entity has a healthy balance sheet, it is running at good **RACE**.

- **Existence** – Assets, liabilities, and equity reported on the F/S exist as of the F/S date.

Presentation of the F/S & Disclosures

The final five assertions relate to the presentation of the F/S and the F/S disclosures **(RACOUn)**:

- **Rights & obligations** – All information presented and disclosed is related to events, transactions, and other matters that pertain to the entity.

- **Accuracy & valuation** – Both financial and nonfinancial information is fairly presented, properly disclosed, and provides appropriate amounts.

- **Completeness** – All information that should be presented is disclosed.

- **Occurrence** – Disclosed events, transactions and other matters have occurred and pertain to the entity.

> **RACOUn's** are always presenting and disclosing my garbage at night!!

- **Understandability & classification** – Financial information is appropriately presented and described, and disclosures are expressed in a clear manner.

Operating Cycles & Business Processes

An auditor divides the audit into different **operating cycles** that make up the flow of transactions and business processes for the entire company. A **business process** is a combination of procedures performed in a particular sequence for a desired result. The most common operating cycles include the following:

Revenue cycle | Spending cycle | Production & conversion cycle | Investing & financing cycle | Fixed assets | Personnel & payroll cycle

All related accounts within each cycle are audited together. Within each cycle, the auditor is concerned with:

- What each specific employee does

- The documents and records they handle

- Whether there is appropriate segregation of duties and other necessary control activities

In obtaining an understanding of an entity's I/C, the auditor will identify the different **types of transactions/events** within business processes that occur on an ongoing basis that affect an entity's operations or financial position. The auditor will then obtain an understanding of the components:

- **Start** – The auditor should determine what event or circumstance **initiates** a transaction.

- **Authorization** – Before committing resources to a transaction or responding to an event or circumstance, an entity will determine that the counterparty to the transaction is a legitimate party with the intent and ability to perform or that the event is real.

- **Completion (execution)** – The entity should have policies and procedures to make certain that its obligations in transactions and its responses to recurring events/circumstances are being performed in accordance with management's directives. This will include the flow of documents, services, goods, and other resources throughout the system.

- **Recording** – The entity should have a system for making certain that all transactions, events, or circumstances that affect operations or financial position are properly captured and reflected in the entity's financial records.

- **E**valuate **d**efenses – Each system should have checks and balances (ie, **verifications**) to make certain that each function is performed properly and in the appropriate sequence.

  - This may involve policies requiring the **matching of documents** (manually or automated). For example, requiring the shipping department to compare a customer's purchase order with an internal sales order and to a list of goods transferred from stores before shipping the goods.

    > It should be easy to remember that a good system of I/C is **SACREd** to a business.

  - It may also involve accounting for the sequence of **prenumbered documents**, checking for **authoritative signatures**, or periodically **reconciling** recorded amounts to physical assets.

3.02 Five Components of Internal Control

COSO's Internal Control Framework

The most commonly used framework to benchmark internal controls in the U.S. is *Internal Control – Integrated Framework* developed by COSO. COSO describes internal control (I/C) as a process, effected by the entity's board of directors, management, and other personnel designed to provide reasonable assurance regarding the achievement of objectives in the categories of (**ACE**):

- **Accurate and reliable financial reporting** – This is the primary interest of the outside auditor since it relates to the fair presentation of the F/S being audited.

- **Compliance with laws and regulations** – This is primarily relevant to *compliance auditing*, which may occur in connection with audits under government auditing standards. The financial statement auditor would, however, be concerned about compliance with laws and regulations that could have a material direct or indirect effect on the F/S.

- ***Effectiveness and efficiency of operations*** – This is generally not addressed by the financial statement auditor, but is addressed in consulting engagements and *operational audits*.

> The mnemonic **ACE** will remind management that it should try to establish a strong I/C structure so as to have an ACE in the hole.

COSO defines five components of I/C:

- Control **E**nvironment
- **R**isk assessment
- **C**ontrol activities
- **I**nformation and communication
- **M**onitoring

> The mnemonic **CRIME** reminds management that it would be a crime not to consider all the I/C elements when designing the system.

AU-C 315 requires the auditor to obtain an understanding of all five components of I/C under COSO to:

- Evaluate the design of relevant controls and determine whether they have been implemented

- Assess the risk of material misstatement (RMM)

- Design the nature, timing, and extent of further audit procedures

Control *Environment*

Defined

The first component of the COSO framework is the control environment, also referred to as the tone at the top. The control environment sets the tone of an organization, influencing the control consciousness of its people. It is the foundation for all other components of I/C, providing discipline and structure. Control environment factors include the following (**CHOPPER**):

- **Commitment to competence** – Effective control requires a sincere interest on the part of the employees in performing good work.

- **Human resource policies & practices** – A company can minimize the control difficulties created by new employees with sound hiring practices and training policies.

- **Organizational structure** – A company that operates all over the world has different I/C problems than one operating entirely within a single building.

- **Participation of those charged with governance** – An audit committee of the board of directors that actively monitors the internal audit function produces more attentive management of control issues.

- **Philosophy of management & management operating style** – The belief (or lack of it) in the importance of I/C by management will affect the seriousness with which it is taken by the rest of the employees. This is especially the case when decision-making in the company is dominated by a single individual.

- **Ethical values & integrity** – Honest employees will be less likely to cause I/C difficulties related to fraud and improve the opportunity for errors to be effectively detected and corrected.

- **Responsibility assignment** – The way authority, responsibility, and accountability are assigned to different employees determines the controls that will be needed. Again, the domination of decision-making by a single individual holds significance since such power makes it extremely difficult for I/C to be trusted.

Principles

There are five principles related to the control environment. They indicate that management and those charge with governance:

1. Demonstrate a commitment to integrity and ethical values

2. Exercise their oversight responsibility

3. Establish structure, authority, and responsibility

4. Demonstrate a commitment to competence

5. Enforce accountability

Entity-Level Controls

The auditor is responsible for determining if the control environment, influenced by management with the oversight of those charged with governance, has established an honest culture, promoting ethical behavior. The control environment, consisting of entity-level controls, should provide a *foundation for the overall I/C structure* and for assuring that internal controls are not undermined by deficiencies in the control environment.

Entity-level controls deal with company-wide issues and set the tone of the organization, involve the assignment of authority and responsibility, and address conduct. Entity-level controls include:

- A **mission statement** that is part of the entity's culture

- A **code of conduct** that applies to all members of the organization, including management

- **Organization charts and job descriptions** that indicate the roles of individuals within the organization

- The **behavior of management and executives**, which is often considered one of the more significant components

The auditor obtains knowledge of entity-level controls through inquiries made of management and others and through observations. The auditor can often learn a great deal about the control environment by simply observing the relationship between employees and their supervisors and management and, particularly, whether employees at all levels are shown an appropriate level of respect.

*R*isk Assessment

Defined

An entity's risk assessment for financial reporting purposes is its identification, analysis, and management of risks relevant to the preparation of F/S that are fairly presented in conformity with the applicable financial reporting framework (AFRF). Risk assessment includes risks that may affect an entity's ability to properly record, process, summarize, and report financial data.

Risk assessment, for example, may address how the entity considers the possibility of unrecorded transactions or identifies and analyzes significant estimates recorded in the F/S.

Factors

Risks relevant to financial reporting include **external** and **internal factors.** Examples are provided in the table below.

External Factors	Internal Factors
• Economic environment o Interest rates o Exchange rates o Credit availability o Economic growth o Inflation • Industry • Accounting pronouncements • Technology o Rate of change o Disruption • Social climate • Political/legal environment o Political stability o Taxation o Labor & trade limitations o Laws & regulations	• Selection of accounting policies • Corporate restructuring o Ownership structure o Governance structure • New investments and financing plans • Operating environment o Personnel/management turnover o Changes in entity objectives/strategies o New lines of business/products o Business process reengineering o Information systems infrastructure ▪ Cloud computing or hosting arrangements ▪ Enterprise Resource Planning (ERP) Software ▪ Custom or packaged software applications • Rapid growth

Principles

There are four principles related to risk assessment. They indicate that management and those charged with governance:

1. Specify suitable objectives

2. Identify and analyze risk

3. Assess fraud risk

4. Identify and analyze significant change

Control Activities

Defined

Control activities are policies and procedures that help ensure that management directives are carried out. These include (**PIPS-ARCC**):

- **Performance reviews** – Controls involving the evaluation of performance against some criteria, such as:

  o Comparing actual amounts to budgeted amounts

  o Comparing current period results to those of prior years

   o Evaluating financial data in relation to nonfinancial data

- *Information processing* – Controls that prevent the processing of information unless certain criteria are met, such as the **matching** of certain documentation before recording a sale. In an information technology (IT) environment, there are **general controls** that relate to the overall operation of the system, including the structure of the organization and access to information; and **application controls** that relate to specific functions being performed.

- *Physical controls* – Controls that limit **access** to physical assets (eg, locks) as well as computer programs and data (ie, proper **authorization**). This may also include comparing **physical counts** to the accounting records (eg, inventory counts).

- *Segregation of duties* – Segregating certain duties reduces the opportunities for any person to be able to both *perpetrate and conceal errors or fraud*. This involves assigning different people to the following responsibilities (**ARCC**):

   o **Authorization** of transactions

   o **Recording** (posting) transactions

   o **Custody** of assets

   o **Comparisons** (ie, performing reconciliations or comparisons)

The auditor will have to identify control activities and determine if they are relevant to the audit. Some will be relevant in the professional judgment of the auditor. This will be the case, for example, when all of the following are true:

- The auditor determines that a control reduces the RMM in relation to a management assertion.

- The auditor has a basis for testing the control activity to determine if it was properly designed and being applied properly during the period under audit.

- The nature, timing, and extent of further audit testing can be reduced as a result of relying on the control activity if the tests of controls indicate that it is effective.

There may also be certain risks that could result in a material misstatement to the F/S that cannot be evaluated based on substantive evidence alone. This might be the case, for example, for transactions processed automatically with a minimum of manual intervention, where much of the information related to the initiation, authorization, recording, processing, and reporting is in electronic form. The reliability of data derived from such transactions would be dependent on the controls related to the processing of those transactions.

Principles

There are three principles related to control activities. They indicate that management and those charged with governance:

1. Select and develop control activities

2. Select and develop general controls over technology

3. Deploy controls through policies and procedures

Information & Communication

Defined

The information and communication component of I/C relates to the flow of information to and from the entity as well as within the entity.

Internal Communications

Information should flow in all directions so that management's directives can be properly communicated to those who are expected to work toward achieving them and so that management can obtain feedback to determine if objectives are being achieved.

External Communications

Communication with external parties facilitates the flow of goods and services and enhances the efficiency with which business can be conducted. It also enables parties and other entities with which an entity does business to assist in the enforcement of the entity's internal controls. For example, if customers are informed that all sales are to be reported on a prenumbered sales form, customers may prevent a salesperson from inappropriately taking an order without completing the required form.

Financial Reporting Systems

The auditor is particularly concerned with information systems relevant to financial reporting. Thus, the auditor should obtain an understanding of how:

- The *information systems* consist of methods and records used to *record, process, summarize and report* the company's transactions to maintain accountability for the related accounts.

- Individual duties and responsibilities related to I/C are established and *communicated* to involved personnel.

- Transactions are initiated, authorized, and processed, including which components are performed manually and which are performed electronically.

- Transactions, events, and conditions are reported.

- Accountability is maintained for assets, liability, and equity, including the maintenance of records supporting information or specific items in the F/S.

- The incorrect processing of transactions is identified and resolved.

- Recurring and nonrecurring journal entries, unusual transactions, and other adjustments are identified and prepared.

- System overrides or bypasses to controls are processed and accounted for.

- Information is transferred from the processing systems to the general ledger.

- Events and conditions, including depreciation and amortization of assets and collectability of receivables, are identified, and how information (ie, data) is captured.

- F/S are prepared, including the development of estimates.

- Information that is required to be disclosed is identified, accumulated, recorded, processed, summarized, and properly reported.

Principles

There are three principles related to information and communication. They indicate that management and those charge with governance:

1. Use relevant information
2. Communicate internally
3. Communicate externally

Monitoring

Defined

Monitoring activities are how management determines if internal controls are being followed and if they are effective. Controls are monitored through some combination of ongoing activities, which are generally part of recurring activities, such as the supervision of employees and separate evaluations.

Internal Audit

When the entity has an internal audit function, understanding the role it plays contributes to the auditor's understanding of the entity, its environment, and its I/C. In some circumstances, the auditor may use the work performed by the entity's internal auditor's either to modify the nature, timing, or extent of other audit procedures to be performed, or to assist in the performance of audit procedures under the oversight of the auditor. This is discussed in more detail in a later section.

Reliability of Data

In addition to obtaining an understanding of how the entity monitors its I/C, the auditor should also obtain an understanding of the data (information) that is used in the entity's monitoring activities, the sources of that data, and the basis upon which the reliability of the data is evaluated.

Principles

There are two principles related to monitoring. They indicate that management and those charge with governance:

1. Conduct ongoing and/or separate evaluations
2. Evaluate and communicate deficiencies

Inherent Limitations

A system of I/C can be designed to provide only *reasonable assurance* of achieving an entity's objectives. That is, even with an effective system of I/C, the following **inherent limitations (COP)** may result in failures (ie, fraud and error):

- **Collusion** – Control activities that depend on segregation of duties will not be effective if those engaged in the segregated functions conspire with one another.

- **Override by management** – Since management designs and implements the system of I/C, they are able to override it.

- **Poor human judgment and errors** – If control procedures are erroneously applied, they will not be effective. I/C cannot be expected to prevent mistakes in human judgment.

Fraud

Error

3.03 Understanding the I/C Structure

Overview

An auditor performs the following procedures to obtain and apply an understanding of internal control (I/C) to an audit (AU-C 315):

- **Step 1** – Obtain an understanding of the design of all five components of the entity's I/C (CRIME) through the performance of risk assessment procedures.

- **Step 2** – Document the understanding of I/C.

- **Step 3** – Assess Risk of Material Misstatement (RMM), which consists of inherent risk (IR) and control risk (CR). RMM = IR × CR.

- **Step 4** – Develop an audit strategy to either:

  - (**NOT Rely**) Decide **not** to perform tests of controls (TofC), assessing CR at the *maximum level* as if the controls did not exist; or

  - (**RELY**) **Perform TofC** to determine if CR is *below maximum*, allowing for the modification of further audit procedures (substantive tests).

- **Step 5** – Reassess RMM and evaluate results.

  - For controls for which TofC were performed, evaluate results to reassess RMM and determine if it is appropriate to modify further audit procedures.

- **Step 6** – Document conclusions and develop or revise audit program for further audit procedures.

Step 1: Understand the Design of CRIME

Have the controls been **implemented** (ie, put into use)? To evaluate the implementation of a control means to determine whether a control is actually being used by the entity. The auditor first considers the **design** of the control (ie, what is the form of I/C?). If the control is improperly designed, it may represent a material weakness in the entity's I/C.

Risk Assessment Procedures

An auditor obtains an **understanding of the entity and its environment**, including its I/C (CRIME) through the performance of risk assessment procedures. These procedures are designed to gather information to enable the auditor to effectively assess the RMM and the controls that should be in place to mitigate such risks. Required risk assessment procedures include (**AIIO**):

- **Analytical procedures** (study of data comparisons and relationships) using high-level data

- **Inquiries** of management and others within the entity, including internal auditors

- **Inspection** of documents and records (eg, examining documents that are used in I/C, such as authorization forms and procedures manuals)

- **O**bservation (eg, observing the application of manual controls)

The knowledge obtained through risk assessment procedures is used to:

- Identify the types of potential misstatements (ie, errors or fraud).
- Consider factors that affect the RMM.
- Design TofC and substantive procedures.

Other Procedures for Understanding I/C

In addition to the risk assessment procedures above, the auditor may need to perform other procedures to understand I/C. As part of obtaining an understanding of I/C sufficient to plan the audit, the auditor should evaluate whether the client's programs and controls that address the identified risks of material misstatement have been suitably **designed** and **implemented** (ie, placed into operation). Understanding **does not** require evaluating their **operating effectiveness**.

- The **goal** of this understanding is to identify those controls that might reduce the risk of misstatements. If the auditor believes that these controls can be relied upon, TofC will be performed to evaluate their operating effectiveness. Assuming they prove effective, the auditor will be able to reduce substantive testing.
- If the auditor decides to assess CR as high, the auditor will not rely on I/C so there is no point in determining whether the controls are effective.

Most of the initial information that an auditor obtains about an entity's I/C will be the result of **inquiries*** made of management and others. If the auditor is a continuing auditor, much information will be derived from reviewing **prior period engagement files**.

*Note that the auditor may not rely exclusively on inquiries to evaluate the design of controls or whether they have been implemented.

The auditor will initially evaluate the design of a control to determine whether it has the **potential of reducing RMM**.

- If the control has **no potential** of reducing RMM, the control is **not relevant** to the audit and no determination will be made as to whether it has been implemented.
- If it does have the potential to reduce RMM, however, the auditor can perform a walkthrough to determine whether the control has been implemented and is operating as it was designed.

A **walkthrough** involves tracing transactions through the system and may include (**RIIO**):

- **R**eperformance of activities to determine whether automated controls exist
- **I**nquiries of personnel who perform the process
- **I**nspection of documents or other items that will provide evidence that controls are in place
- **O**bservation of controls being applied

When an auditor needs to gain an understanding of the controls at a **service organization**, a **SOC 1 Report** will need to be obtained. There are two types of SOC 1 Reports (ie, a report on ICFR):

- **Type 1** – Report on the fairness of the presentation of management's description of the service organization's system and the suitability of the **design** of the controls to achieve the related control objectives included in the description as of a specified date.

- **Type 2** – Report on the fairness of the presentation of management's description of the service organization's system and the suitability of the **design and operating effectiveness** of the controls to achieve the related control objectives included in the description throughout a specified period.

SOC Reports are discussed in further detail in a later section.

Step 2: Document Understanding

The auditor is **required** to document the following:

- Key elements of the understanding of the entity and its environment, as well as each of the five components of I/C (**CRIME**)

- The sources of information from which the understanding was obtained

- The risk assessment procedures performed

There are several different techniques that are commonly used for documenting the auditor's understanding of the I/C structure (**FIND**); however, there are no specific requirements for their use. The **form and extent** of documentation needed are influenced by the **size and complexity** of the entity. That is, larger, more complex entities may need flowcharts, questionnaires, and/or decision trees, while a relatively small and simple entity may require only a narrative. If the client has good documentation of its system, the auditor can reference it and need not recreate it.

Flowcharts
System flowchart
Document flowchart
Internal control questionnaire
Narrative or memorandum
Diagrams
Process diagram
Data flow diagram (DFD)
Entity-relationship (ER) diagram
Decision table/tree

Internal Control Questionnaire

One common form of documentation is the internal control questionnaire (ICQ). A questionnaire always phrases questions in a form that requires a **yes or no** answer for each question. A yes answer indicates the presence of a potentially useful control, and a **no** response indicates a **weakness**.

A well-designed questionnaire will include questions related to each of the different types of **control activities** that may be utilized in an I/C structure. The following list of questions (**PIPS-ARCC**) can be adapted for TBS questions by referring to documents and personnel in the department being tested:

Control activities
• Performance reviews
• Information processing
• Physical security
• Segregation of duties (ARCC)
• Authorization
• Recording
• Custody
• Comparisons
Risk assessment
Information & communication
Monitoring
control Environment

- **Performance reviews** – Are there written department policies and procedures? Are unusual or uncompleted transactions periodically investigated?

- **Information processing** – Are there controls that prevent the processing of information unless certain criteria are met, such as the matching of certain documentation before recording a sale? Are there *IT general controls* that relate to the overall operation of the system, including the structure of the organization and access to information? Are there *application controls* that relate to specific functions being performed?

- **Physical controls** – Is proper *security* maintained over valuable department assets? Are there adequate safeguards over unused documents?

- **Segregation of duties** – Are the principal functions of each process—authorization, recording, custody, and comparison (ARCC)—independent of one another?

  - **Authorization** of transactions – Are transactions authorized by personnel at least one level above the request level? Are third parties involved in transactions approved in advance?

  - **Recording** (posting) transactions – Are transactions documented as to all relevant terms and descriptions? Are documents *prenumbered* and periodically accounted for?

  - **Custody** of assets – Is custody limited to those with a need to have access? Are those with access subjected to bonding or appropriate background checks?

  - **Comparisons** – Are physical assets periodically reconciled to recorded amounts? Are normal activities subject to comparisons of recorded amounts to support documents? For example, are daily deposits compared to remittance listings?

The preparation of an ICQ involves the application of a systematic process that consists of the following steps:

1. Identify the **cycle** (eg, revenue cycle) and the **business processes** that are being evaluated.

2. Determine what **account balances** or **classes of transactions** (eg, sales transactions) are affected.

3. Determine where in the process (**SACREd**) there should be control activities (**PIPS-ARCC**) for each of the relevant assertions (**RACE, CPA-CO**).

4. Anticipate the **forms** that the client should use to capture pertinent information, what that information should be, **how many copies** of each form will be needed, and **how** those copies should be **distributed**.

Start (initiation) of a transaction/event
Authorize transaction/event
Complete (execute) transaction/event in accordance with policies/procedures
Record transaction/event
Evaluate **d**efenses (verify)
Matching documents Authoritative signatures Prenumbered documents Periodic reconciliations

Flowcharts, Diagrams & Narratives

Flowcharts and diagrams are visual depictions of the I/C structure and the client's IT system. There are several different types of flowcharts and diagrams that are commonly used to show the different aspects and levels of detail in a system. You'll see some examples below.

- **System flowchart** – This is generally a high-level depiction of the client's entire system. It typically shows:
  - Inputs (eg, documents, data entry)
  - The overall flow of manual and automated processes
  - Outputs (eg, documents, reports)
  - Electronic data stores and any physical storage of documents

- Process diagram –This shows:
  - A business process from beginning to end
  - Which departments or groups of employees are responsible for each function
  - The interaction among departments or groups of employees

- **Document flowchart** – This shows only the documents that are used in a business process and how they are distributed and disposed of.

- **Data flow diagram (DFD)** – Depending on the level of detail, a DFD shows how data flows within a system or a specific business process.

- **Entity-relationship (ER) diagram** – ER diagrams are typically used to describe details related to data structures, such as tables in a relational database, and how those structures relate to each other. An ER model uses three basic components to diagram data structures:
  - **Entities** – Any object, event, or business process that requires data storage (ie, a table)
  - **Relationships** – How entities are related (ie, one-to-one, one-to-many, and many-to-many)
  - **Attributes** – The characteristics of the entities (ie, fields in a table)

- **Decision table/tree** – Parts of an I/C structure may require an employee to choose from several alternative actions, depending on the conditions faced, and document such activities. This may best be accomplished by preparing a decision table that lists each possible condition and the actions that will result from each (ie, it depicts the logic of an operation or process).

A **narrative or memorandum** is in the form of a detailed written description of the I/C structure. It generally describes the system in a manner similar to how it is depicted in a flowchart or diagram but with words rather than symbols.

Flowcharts, diagrams, and narratives perform essentially the same function in that they generally:

- Describe each step in a cycle in sequence

- Identify the party or department responsible for performing the procedure

- Indicate what forms enter the cycle (eg, a customer's purchase order) or are created in the cycle (eg, material requisition form), how many copies are created, and how those copies are distributed; and most other aspects of the cycle

An *advantage of the narrative* is that it is easy to understand and often provides users a clearer view of the interaction among the participants than other forms of documentation. *Disadvantages*, however, are that it is often difficult to identify whether responsibilities are properly segregated, and it may be difficult to trace the flow of documents.

Flowcharts & Business Process Diagrams			
Symbol	**Description**	**Symbol**	**Description**
	Manual operation (Prepare, compare, or match)		Manual input (keyboard)
	Computer operation or Process (Prepare, match, Print PO)		Input or output (general ledger)
	Document (Invoice, PO, error listing)		Magnetic tape (Sequential access storage)
	On page connector (to connect to another location without a connecting line)		Off page connector (eg, from customer)
	A decision (granting credit, If, then, else)		Off-line storage (file by name, date, order number)

Flowcharts & Business Process Diagrams

Symbol	Description	Symbol	Description
(cylinder)	Magnetic disc storage (Database)	(open-ended cylinder)	On-line storage (disc, drum)
(oval)	Start/finish	(horizontal cylinder)	Direct access storage

Data Flow Diagrams

Symbol	Description	Symbol	Description
(rectangle)	Origin/destination of data	(circle)	Process
(line)	Data storage	(arrow)	Data flow

Entity-Relationship Diagrams

Symbol	Description	Cardinality Notation	Relationship Description
(rectangle)	Entity	(line)	One to one
(diamond)	Relationship	(line with crow's foot)	One to many
(oval)	Attribute	(crow's foot both ends)	Many to many

Sales System Flowchart Example

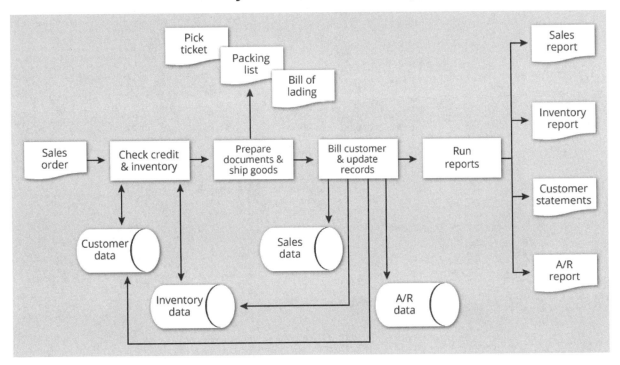

Collections Process Diagram Example

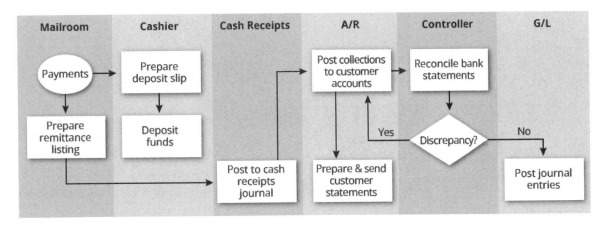

Document Flowchart for Sales Process Example

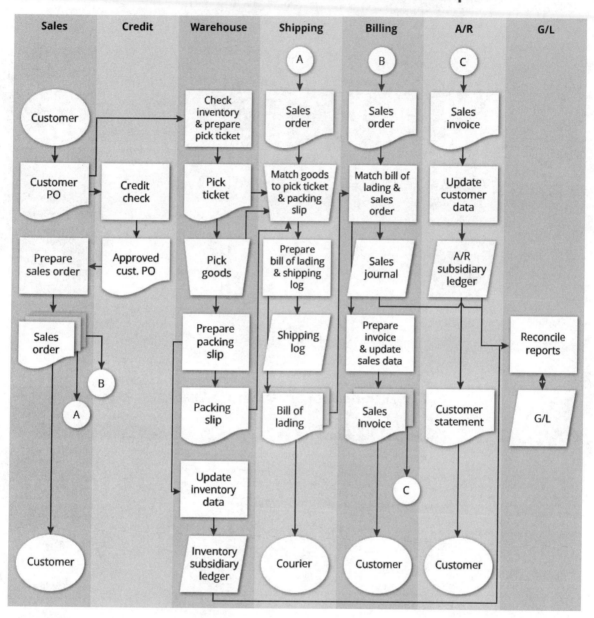

Data Flow Diagram Example

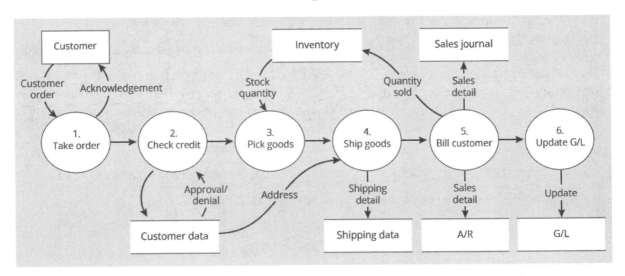

ER Diagram Example

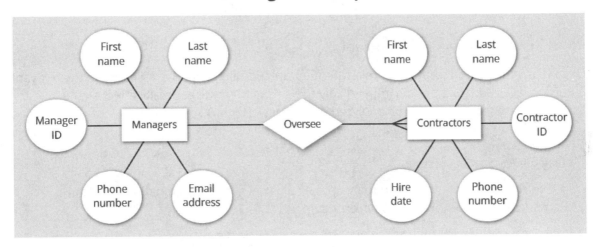

Step 3: Assess Risk of Material Misstatement

The auditor should perform the risk assessment to identify and assess the risks of material misstatement (RMM) at the F/S level and at the relevant assertion level for classes of transactions, account balances, and disclosures.

RMM at F/S Level

The auditor first assesses RMM at the F/S level by evaluating the entity's ability to prepare F/S that are fairly presented in accordance with the AFRF. The following are examples of factors that may increase the risk that the F/S, taken as a whole, will be materially misstated:

- The auditor's perception of the competency of the entity's accounting personnel

- An evaluation of the entity's ability to develop estimates and interpret accounting principles

- Whether the auditor considers management aggressive or believes management is under pressure to achieve difficult financial goals

- Whether the industry or the economy has created particular challenges

- Whether the entity is seeking financing or anticipating entering into a substantial transaction

The auditor also assesses risk at the F/S level by identifying those items that may have a propensity for misstatement. This may be individual accounts, such as items on the balance sheet; classes of transactions, such as items on the income statement; or disclosures, including footnotes as well as descriptions and notations on the F/S themselves. Items will represent a greater risk of misstatement for a variety of reasons. It may be *due to error* as a result of:

- The difficulty of obtaining information needed to accurately record the transaction; or

- The complexity of the requirements for accounting for an item.

An item may be more susceptible to *fraud* because:

- It is a valuable item that might be misappropriated by employees or others;

- It is an item for which it is easy to conceal a misstatement; or

- A misstatement to the item has the potential of influencing other actions, such as the payment of a commission or the earning of a bonus based on performance.

RMM at Relevant Assertion Level

Once items that are susceptible to misstatement are identified, RMM is assessed at the relevant assertion level. The fact that an item is likely to be misstated will generally affect all the assertions and the risk should be analyzed accordingly.

Risk of Overstating Results

- For an entity that might tend to overstate sales because it is competing in capital markets, the auditor will be concerned about:

  o Occurrence, since the entity may record sales that did not occur

  o Cutoff, since the entity may record sales from the next period in the current period

  o Accuracy, since the entity may record sales in amounts greater than the actual transactions

  o Classification, since the entity may wish to characterize the proceeds from the issuance of debt or from the sale of assets that do not generate revenues into sales

- The auditor would be less concerned with completeness, however, since an entity wishing to overstate sales would not omit sales.

Items susceptible to misstatement due to error or fraud are generally identified by applying a **"what could go wrong?"** (ie, risk) analysis at the assertion level.

Next, the auditor will **determine if there are controls** that would either prevent or detect and correct the issue on a timely basis.

- If there are **no controls** to deal with the issue, the auditor would likely conclude that a **control deficiency** has been identified. The auditor will determine if it is a significant deficiency or a material weakness, either of which **must be communicated** to those charged with governance.

    o The controls may be built into the system, which the auditor can determine by reviewing the documented understanding.

    o Otherwise, the auditor will inquire as to whether management has considered the possibility and developed a separate control, of which the auditor is not yet aware, to deal with the issue.

- If there are **controls** intended to deal with the issue, the auditor will evaluate the design of the controls and decide as to whether the design is suitable and if the controls are likely to be effective.

    o If the controls are expected to be effective, the auditor will perform a **walkthrough** involving **RIIO**.

    o If not, the auditor will not attempt to verify that the controls have been implemented as it is irrelevant.

Finally, the auditor will **develop an audit program** with procedures designed to verify that the information reported in the F/S is correct.

For example, an auditor is evaluating the occurrence assertion in relation to sales. The auditor determines that, since sales personnel are highly incentivized by a liberal commission system, they may be motivated to overstate sales. The following may result:

- What could go wrong? Sales personnel may submit paperwork for sales that did not actually occur.

- Next, the auditor will determine if there are controls that would either prevent the recording of sales that did not occur or would cause them to be detected and corrected on a timely basis.

- Finally, the auditor will determine further audit procedures to provide evidence that recorded sales did actually occur.

    o To test the assertion of occurrence, the auditor will likely select a sample from the population of recorded sales and trace them to supporting documentation to verify that they actually occurred.

Step 4: Develop an Audit Strategy

The auditor will then determine an audit strategy. The auditor may use either a **substantive approach**, in which substantive procedures are emphasized, or a **combined approach**, in which both tests of controls and substantive procedures are used.

Intend to Rely on Controls?

- **No, Substantive approach** – The risk assessment may **not** include an expectation that controls operate effectively when:

- o Controls appear inadequate, ineffective, or weak, or

- o Auditor believes that performing extensive substantive procedures is likely to be more *cost effective* than performing tests of controls.

- o In this case:

  - CR will be assessed at the *maximum level* as if the controls did not exist.

  - RMM will be equal to the assertion's inherent risk under the assumption that there are no relevant controls in place.

  - The auditor will *not* perform tests of controls.

  - The auditor will develop a program to test the assertion by applying *substantive audit procedures* that the auditor believes will provide sufficient appropriate audit evidence.

RELY?
NO – RMM ↑ Substantive Approach
YES – RMM ↓ Combined Approach

- **Yes, Combined approach** – If the controls **appear effective**, tests of controls will be performed when:

  - o The auditor's risk assessment includes an expectation of **operating effectiveness of controls** because the likelihood of material misstatement is lower if the control operates effectively (cost effective), or

  - o When **substantive procedures alone** do not provide sufficient audit evidence.

  - o In this case:

    - RMM will be reduced from IR, considering the effect of CR being below the maximum.

    - The auditor will *perform tests of the controls* selecting from a population that covers the entire period during which the auditor is anticipating that the controls were in place.

    - This generally allows the nature, timing, and extent of further audit procedures (ie, substantive tests) to be modified.

Tests of Controls (Combined Approach)

If the risk assessment is based on an expectation that controls are operating effectively, the auditor should test the operating effectiveness of controls (TofC) that have been determined to be suitably designed to prevent or detect material misstatements.

> What is the substance of I/C?

Since TofC alone are not normally sufficient upon which to base an audit opinion, further audit procedures will be composed of TofC *and* substantive tests. Thus, TofC will be performed when a combination of TofC and a decreased scope of substantive tests is more cost effective than performing more extensive substantive tests.

The overall approach here, as it relates to controls is to:

- Identify controls that are relevant to specific assertions that are likely to prevent or detect material misstatements, and

- Perform tests of controls to evaluate the effectiveness of those controls.

To test the effectiveness of the design and operation of a control, the auditor must consider:

- *How* the control was applied,

- The *consistency* with which it was applied, and

- *By whom* it was applied.

TofC generally consist of four types of procedures (**RIIO**):

- **Reperformance** – The auditor applies the control that the client personnel presumably performed to determine if the procedure was performed properly.

- **Inspection** – The auditor examines controls, documents, and reports that provide documentary evidence.

- **Inquiry** – The auditor asks client personnel involved in controls to state how effectively certain controls were enforced.

- **Observation** – The auditor watches client personnel performing their regular functions to see if they follow the controls that were designed and implemented.

> Test the cycles for **ARCC**'s by doing **RIIO**

These different types of TofC can be very effective in determining if a system features appropriate **segregation of duties**. In general, however, the **most effective** type of TofC is **observation**.

Prior Audits

An auditor may plan to use audit evidence about the operating effectiveness of controls obtained in prior audits when the controls have not changed since they were last tested. However, the auditor should test the operating effectiveness of such controls at least **once every three years**. The auditor will determine that controls have not changed since they were last tested through the performance of risk assessment procedures.

Step 5: Reassess RMM to Determine Detection Risk

When an auditor decides to rely on controls, TofC are performed to determine if the controls were working effectively as they were designed for the period under audit. Based on the results of the TofC, the auditor will determine whether it is necessary to modify the scope of substantive tests.

- If the I/C **operates effectively as expected**, there will generally be no need to change the scope of planned substantive tests.

- Conversely, if the system does **not** operate as effectively as expected:

  o **CR** will be **reset to maximum** as if there were no controls.

  o The scope of **substantive tests** for the relevant assertions will **increase** to keep detection risk at an acceptable level.

  o AR / (IR × CR) = DR, which tells you how much substantive testing to do.

Step 6: Document Conclusions & Develop Audit Programs

The auditor needs to document the following:

- The assessment of the risks of material misstatement at the F/S and relevant assertion levels and the basis for that assessment

- Significant risks identified and related controls evaluated

- Risks identified and related controls evaluated that require TofC to obtain sufficient audit evidence

- The procedures performed and the conclusions reached

In addition, audit programs need to be developed or revised to indicate the further audit procedures that are necessary to draw a conclusion related to a management assertion. Further audit procedures are discussed in more detail in a later section.

3.04 IT Environment & Infrastructure

Overview

The use of Information Technology (IT) affects the initiation, authorization, recording, processing, and reporting of transactions. It may affect any of the five components (CRIME) of internal control (I/C). Since virtually every client has incorporated sophisticated software of some description to manage its business and accounting processes, IT has become very important on the exam.

 While IT is also tested in the BEC exam, AUD exam questions will focus on the auditor's understanding of the client's IT environment to perform an effective and efficient audit.

Overall Impact of IT on the Audit Approach

Although the existence of an electronic system does not change the basic objectives of an audit engagement, it has a major impact on the approach used to achieve those objectives. The auditor cannot give an opinion on the effectiveness of internal control if the "auditing *around* the computer" approach is used. Thus, the auditor may use a combination of approaches that also involve "auditing *through* the computer" and "auditing *with* the computer."

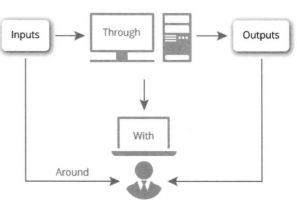

- **Auditing around the computer** – In some less complex IT environments, the same documents that would have been audited in a manual system can be printed out. This allows the auditor to perform the audit without obtaining extensive knowledge of the IT system. In this case, IT controls would not be tested and a *substantive approach* will be used.

- **Auditing through the computer** – In more complex IT environments, some processes may produce evidence that exists only in electronic form. In this case, the auditor has no choice but to test the controls to understand whether they operate effectively and produce reliable information. If the controls are operating effectively, the amount of substantive testing necessary can generally be reduced (ie, a *combined approach*).

- **Auditing with the computer** – *In either of the two scenarios above*, the auditor may choose to perform some auditing procedures using *computer-assisted auditing techniques (CAATs)*. CAATs, for example, might include the use of generalized audit software (GAS) to perform audit data analytics (ADAs) and other procedures. CAATs are discussed in greater detail in a later section.

Characteristics of an IT Environment

The IT environment is largely dependent on the size of the company and the number of employees and type of computers involved. Historically, a few large computers were operated exclusively by IT personnel. With servers, personal computers, tablets, and phones networked together, all employees use some type of electronic device daily. While the diversity of devices has proven to be extremely useful in the efficiency and effectiveness of business processes, the increase in access points creates more risk for an IT system.

Benefits of IT

The auditor should obtain audit evidence about the accuracy and completeness (ie, reliability) of data produced by the entity's IT system when that data is used in performing audit procedures. Thus, the primary **advantage** of IT as it relates to an audit is that a computer is not as subject to random errors as a human. That is, computers are **consistent**; they process data the same way every time.

As a result, an auditor who is able to **verify** that a computer **program** is working properly will **not** have to **test individual transactions** to be sure the outputs are reliable (ie, complete and accurate). An audit of a computerized system can, therefore, rely more heavily on the I/C structure and reduce the need for substantive testing, making the audit potentially more efficient. Other benefits of IT include:

- **Timeliness** – Electronic processing and updating is normally more efficient.
- **Analysis** – Data can be accessed for analytical procedures more conveniently (with proper software).
- **Monitoring** – Electronic controls can be monitored by the computer system itself.
- **Circumvention** – Controls are difficult to circumvent when programmed properly, and exceptions are unlikely to be permitted.
- **Segregation of duties** – Security controls can prevent the performance of incompatible functions by the same individual or group through security controls in applications, databases, and operating systems.

Risks of IT

There are two risks of major concern to the auditor:

- **Unauthorized access** – Disclosure, destruction, and alteration of large amounts of data are possible if unauthorized access occurs. This can cause more damage to the accounting system as a whole than in a manual system where it is difficult for one person to access, change, or destroy all the different records of the system.
- **Audit trail** – The audit trail is an electronically visible trail of evidence enabling one to trace information contained in statements or reports back to the original input source. An audit trail is also important to the client for the proper functioning of the system during the year; such a trail allows monitoring of activities, providing a deterrent to fraud and making it possible to answer queries by examining the source data. This would require the auditor to establish the reliability and extent of the audit trail.

Other IT risks include:

- **Overreliance** – Without clear output, IT systems are often assumed to be working when they are not.

- **Changes in programs** – Severe consequences without detection are possible if unauthorized program changes occur.

- **Failure to change** – Programs or systems are sometimes not updated for new laws, rules, or activities.

- **Manual intervention** – Knowledgeable individuals can sometimes alter files by bypassing the appropriate programs.

- **Loss of data** – Catastrophic data loss is possible if appropriate controls aren't in place.

IT Department

To control these risks, it is important that IT systems are operating as designed. This is generally the responsibility of the IT department.

- Large companies will have a separate IT department.

- Others will have some IT functions outsourced or partially outsourced and partially performed by end users.

- An IT department will normally include systems development and maintenance, operations, and other technical services.

  - Systems development and maintenance might include the following roles:

    - A **systems analyst** designs the information system using systems flowcharts and other tools and prepares specifications for applications programmers, as well as acting as an intermediary between the users and programmers.

    - An **application programmer** writes, tests, and debugs programs that will be used in the system. The programmer also develops instructions for operators to follow when running the programs.

    - A **database administrator** is an individual or department responsible for the security and information classification of the shared data stored on a database system. This responsibility includes the design, definition, and maintenance of the database.

  - **Operations** might include the following roles:

    - The **data control department** is responsible for collecting data for input into a computer's batch processing operations as well as the dissemination of the finished reports. A **data control clerk** schedules jobs for the computer and manages the distribution of reports and other output. Data control clerks may be involved in coding activities, calculating, and checking batch totals, and related clerical tasks.

    - **Data entry** includes keyboard entry, scanning, and voice recognition. When transactions are entered (batch data entry), they are just stacks of source documents to the keyboard operator. Deciphering poor handwriting from a source document is a judgment call that is often error prone. In online data operations, in which the operator takes information in person or by phone, there is interaction and involvement with the transaction and less chance for error.

- A **computer operator** operates a computer in a datacenter and performs such activities as commanding the operating system, mounting disks and tapes, and placing paper in the printer. Operators may also write the job control language (JCL), which schedules the daily work for the computer.

- **Librarians** are the individuals responsible for the safeguarding and maintenance of all program and data files.

o **Other technical services** might include the following roles:

- A **network administrator** is responsible for maintaining and enhancing computer networks and network connections.

- A **systems programmer** is responsible for updating and maintaining the operating systems (typically for mainframe computers).

- A **systems administrator** or **technical support** typically installs, upgrades, and monitors software and hardware.

- A **security administrator** is responsible for security of the system including control of access and maintenance of user passwords.

Centralized vs. Distributed Processing

Centralized Processing

In the early days of computers, each device was so expensive that a company rarely had more than one and all activity had to take place on that single computer. Although different people could connect to that single computer using **remote terminals**, these were simply input and output devices (essentially equivalent to just the keyboard and monitor on a current desktop). All activity had to take place on the one computer, known as **centralized processing**.

Distributed Processing

Today, computers are so reasonably priced that, in many businesses, employees each are assigned their own computers. This allows the allocation of a large volume of tasks to different employees and computers at different locations, known as **distributed processing**. Since the data utilized by the company is no longer on a single computer, it is necessary for them to be able to connect to each other in some way to form a **network**.

Networks

In a computer network, computers are connected to one another to enable sharing of peripheral devices, data, and programs stored on a **file server.** A file server is a high-capacity disk storage device or a computer that stores data centrally for network users and manages access to that data. File servers can be dedicated so that no process other than network management can be executed on that server while the network is available. Nondedicated file servers allow the standard user applications to run while the network is available.

The networking of different computers allows more than just the transfer of information from one to another. It also allows one computer to be used to operate the other.

Types of Networks

Networks may involve any size group from two (as in the case of many home networks) to the entire world.

- The **Internet** is a worldwide network that allows virtually any computer system to link to it by way of an electronic gateway. The Internet facilitates data communication services, such as remote login, file transfer, email, and newsgroups.

- An **Intranet** is a network that is limited to the computers of a single company.

- An **Extranet** is similar to an Intranet, since it is primarily for users within a single company, but select customers and vendors are able to participate as well.

Network Configurations

- **Local area networks (LANs)** – A LAN is a communications network that serves several users within a specified geographical area. A personal computer LAN functions as distributed processing in which each computer in the network does its own processing and manages some of its data. Shared data are stored in a file server that acts as a remote disk drive for all users in the network.

- **Wide area networks (WANs)** – A WAN is a computer network that connects different remote locations that may range from short distances (eg, a building) to extremely long transmissions that encompass a large region or several countries.

- **Value-added network (VAN)** – A VAN links computer files of different companies together.

- **Virtual Private Network (VPN)** – A VPN allows users to access network resources from remote locations. A VPN may or may not be incorporated as part of a larger cloud computing strategy (discussed later).

The need for solid physical transmission media in LANs has been overcome through the development of **wireless local area networks (WLANs).** Short-range radio transmission allows different computers to communicate with each other and share printers, Internet connections, and other devices. The two prominent standards for WLANs are **Wi-Fi** and **Bluetooth**. Any devices (eg, cell phones) that are in the vicinity of each other and which follow the same standard can communicate.

Enterprise Resource Planning (ERP) Systems

ERP systems can be broadly defined as information system packages that integrate information and information-based processes within and across functional areas of an organization. An ERP system is a packaged* business software system that enables a company to manage resources (eg, material, human, financial) more efficiently and effectively by providing an integrated solution for the organization's information processing needs.

Packaged applications broadly refer to any pre-packaged or "off-the-shelf" software application.

Advantages

ERP systems have many advantages, including but not limited to:

- **Timely information analysis** – ERP systems collect and distribute information in a timelier fashion; thus, they help managers improve their ability to process and analyze information.

- **Unified systems** – ERP systems usually replace multiple systems, each of which was designed and managed for support of a much more discrete grouping of business functions. The consolidation of these functions allows for the implementation of unified application controls within a single system with a single database.

- **Interactivity** – ERP systems can interact with IT systems of customers and vendors.

- **Continuous audit** – ERP systems enable the use of continuous auditing practices through embedded audit and monitoring modules.

- **Clear audit scope** – ERP systems can make the consideration of audit scope less complex, as the interfaces to business function modules are contained within one overarching system with a unified database.

Risks

- **Implementation & operation risks** – Due to the size and complexity of an ERP system, the implementation of a new system is likely to disrupt operations. Likewise, any failure in the system has the potential to halt operations throughout the organization.

- **Reduced segregation of duties** – A unified ERP system that consolidates business functions can lead to reduced segregation of duties and increased security risk without proper access controls.

- **Data access** – Complex data structures (eg, database tables, data flows) used within an ERP system can inhibit access to data. Data access is one of the main audit challenges to an engagement. Large, automated systems inhibit transparency by placing computer procedures and configurable controls between the auditor and data.

- **Business process risks** – An organization that utilizes packaged ERP software may need to change business processes to accommodate system data flows and functions. This can increase process interdependence risk, where one business process becomes a single point of failure for the whole system.

Custom vs. Packaged Software

The alternative to packaged software is the development of custom applications. Custom applications are developed by, or at the behest of, an enterprise to meet specific business needs.

These applications may serve similar business functions as those provided by packaged applications, or fulfill a business need where no suitable packaged application is available.

Custom applications tend to be more **expensive** overall than their packaged counterparts; however, they offer more **flexibility** along with the ability to better conform with established business processes and best practices.

Custom applications can present a challenge to an auditor since they usually require the development of custom audit packages. In addition, complexities in defining the audit scope can arise when considering the custom application system and its interfaces with other applications.

	Packaged Applications	Custom Applications
Purpose	Mass produced for general use	Custom produced for specific use
Upfront Costs	Lower	Higher
Ownership	Licensed	Wholly owned
Features	May not meet all business requirements	Should meet all business requirements
	Difficult to customize	Can alter as required
Business Processes	General business processes that conform to best practices	Customized business processes
Maturity Model	Mature	Varies
	Tested in a variety of settings	Tested in a development setting

Applications Maturity Model

A maturity model is useful for evaluating risk and creating a metric to be used in risk calculations. Both packaged and custom applications create risks associated with business interruption, system security, database security, and process interdependency. The degree to which those risks have been addressed generally correlate to where an application is on the maturity model. The maturity model has the five phases. See the table below.

Phase	People	Processes	Programs
Initial	Uncoordinated activities; no set staff	No formal security or access processes	No security or controls
Developing	Leadership established; informal communication	Basic governance & risk management processes	Basic controls with limited or no documentation
Defined	Roles & responsibilities established	Security & access processes in place; minimal verification	Controls implemented & documented; controls reliant on individual IT staff
Managed	Roles & responsibilities clearly defined; increased focus on resources	Formal security processes established; verification & measurement processes established	Controls monitored & measured; compliance levels established; some controls are automated
Optimized	Continuous improvement culture; established staff focus on security, processes, & technology	Comprehensive surety & risk management processes in place; risks are understood & quantitatively evaluated	Controls fully implemented, automated, & continuously monitored; controls subject to continuous improvement processes

(Risk — arrow indicating increasing direction)

Client-Server Computing vs. Cloud Computing

Client-Server Computing

In client-server computing, the users of **client** computers will be able to access a **server** computer. Users can be given access to add, edit, or delete data on the server; operate programs running on the server; and download and/or transfer files to the server. The physical device used to access the server is called a **workstation**. The server doesn't have a particular user and doesn't need a monitor or keyboard, except for initial set up.

Cloud Computing

Cloud computing is a model that allows organizations to use the Internet to access and use services and applications that run on remote third-party technology infrastructure.

- Cloud computing is the integration of virtual machines, remote services for hardware and software, and Web access.

- Working in the cloud can mean simply using a remote server for data storage or using a browser to access Web-based applications.

- Because cloud computing utilizes third-party hardware and software, it usually has lower upfront costs for equipment and maintenance.

- Cloud computing can introduce risks to secure sensitive corporate information, as there are security risks to transmitting information over the Internet.

- Common implementations of cloud computing involve off-the-shelf software that is not developed or modified in-house, with generally limited configuration and program modification options.

- Both packaged and custom applications require IT hardware infrastructure to host application code, house databases, and provide functionality to the enterprise. Cloud computing and application hosting arrangements (aka, cloud-based service arrangements) can offload some or all the back-end hardware requirements. This can reduce the need for on-site IT resources.

Common Cloud-Based Service Arrangements

- Software as a Service (SaaS)

  - SaaS is a method of **software** (application) **delivery** that allows a person to use the program over the internet without having the software on their device. In this web-based model, external service providers host and maintain the servers, databases, and code for an application or suite of applications.

  - SaaS is primarily concerned with third-party owned and maintained software that is delivered over a network. Users purchase licenses to use the vendor-hosted software on a subscription basis and access the software from remote devices using the Internet. This arrangement requires little to no technical staff on the part of the SaaS user.

  - Access controls are maintained by the SaaS user, while controls related to availability, data storage, and IT hardware are the responsibility of the SaaS provider.

- Platform as a Service (PaaS)

  - PaaS provides access to **hardware, storage, and operating systems** to a business **over a network**. PaaS facilitates deployment of applications by unifying and standardizing a system across an organization. This reduces complexity and costs associated with both software and hardware management.

  - In a PaaS arrangement, all software applications and controls are the responsibility of the PaaS user. Additionally, the development and deployment of applications is overseen by the PaaS user, requiring some IT staff.

  - PaaS providers are generally responsible for availability and all operational activities, maintenance, and management of the provided hardware, storage, and operating systems.

- Infrastructure as a Service (IaaS)

  - IaaS provides **physical resources and equipment**, such as network hardware, to a business. This helps reduce or eliminate direct upkeep and maintenance of IT equipment by the business.

  - Providers of IaaS generally undertake responsibilities related to physical security, environmental control, and monitoring services for the IT infrastructure.

o This model allows the IaaS user freedom to deploy their systems in a manner consistent with their needs, but also requires a larger technical staff to maintain all software and systems.

Cloud-based service arrangements can use two or more of the above models in conjunction with each other. For example, consider a company that offers a payroll system as a service (SaaS) who in turn relies on Amazon's Web Services (AWS) to provide their infrastructure (IaaS).

Auditors generally do not have direct access to the systems and subsystems used by the SaaS and IaaS providers; thus, auditors generally rely on **SOC 1** and **SOC 2 reports** to review the controls and the results of control testing for these **service organizations**. SOC reports and service organizations are discussed in further detail in a later section.

Cloud Deployment Models

Cloud computing technology is deployed in four general types, based on the level of internal or external ownership and technical architectures:

- **Public Cloud** – Cloud computing services from vendors can be accessed across the Internet or a private network. This uses systems in one or more data centers, shared among multiple customers, with varying degrees of data privacy control.

- **Private Cloud** – Computing architectures are modeled after Public Clouds, yet built, managed, and used internally by an enterprise. This uses a shared services model with variable usage of a common pool of virtualized computing resources. Data is controlled within the enterprise.

- **Hybrid Cloud** – A mix of vendor Cloud services, internal cloud computing architectures, and classic IT infrastructure form a hybrid model that uses the best-of-breed technologies to meet specific needs.

- **Community Cloud** – The cloud infrastructure is shared by several organizations and supports a specific community that has shared concerns (eg, mission, objectives, security requirements, policy, and compliance considerations). It may be managed by the organization or a third party, and may exist on-premises or off-premises.

Advantages & Risks of Cloud-Based Service Arrangements

- Advantages

  o **Global accessibility** – Services are available to any location, including remote or home offices.

  o **Uniform deployment** – Users have a uniform experience and have the same version of all cloud-hosted applications.

  o **Centralized administration** – Administration, verification, and access can be controlled from a central location for all users and cloud-hosted applications.

- Risks

  o **Security risks** – Cloud services are designed to be globally accessible and introduce unique identity and access management risks. Cyber threats, such as distributed denial-of-service attacks (DDoS), are also increased.

- o **Deployment risk** – In any cloud services arrangement, there are applications or hardware that the subscriber does not control. Updates and upgrades are controlled by the cloud services vendor.

- o **Service delivery risk** – Reliance on third parties for business processes introduces risks associated with the disruption of those services, which cannot be controlled by the cloud services subscriber.

Other Business Systems

Transaction processing systems focus on relieving humans of the tedious work involved in general recordkeeping and reporting. Management reporting systems assist in the decision-making process within the organization. The most common business systems include:

- **Decision support system** – An interactive system that provides the user with easy access to decision models and data, to support semi-structured decision-making tasks.

- **Customer Relationship Management (CRM)** – CRM is a system that manages an entity's customer relationship data. CRM is generally used by marketing, sales, and business development departments. It manages data regarding past, present, and potential customers to improve profitability and customer service. CRM can be part of an ERP system.

- **Supply Chain Management (SCM)** – SCM is a system that manages an entity's supply chain, which includes the purchasing, conversion, and logistics processes. The supply chain is the flow of goods from suppliers all the way to the customer. Thus, SCM is generally used by the purchasing, manufacturing, warehousing, and shipping departments. SCM can be part of an ERP system.

- **Executive support information system** – These are systems designed specifically to support executive work (eg, nonroutine decisions, such as answering questions regarding competitors and identifying new acquisitions).

- **Analytical processing system** – This is software technology that enables the user to query (ask) the system, retrieve data, and conduct analysis.

- **Expert system** – This type of system uses artificial intelligence. An expert system has a built-in hierarchy of rules, which are acquired from human experts in the appropriate field. Once input is provided, the system should be able to define the nature of the problem and provide recommendations to solve the problem.

Transaction Processing

The processing of transactions can take place in one of two general ways:

- **Online Transaction Processing (OLTP)** or **Online Real-Time (OLRT) processing** – OLTP means that the database is updated as soon as a transaction is received (**immediately**). This produces records that are as up-to-date as possible, but requires the system to be running continually. This is a good method to be used by retail businesses. This is generally the default processing method for most business activities.

- **Batch processing** – This involves gathering information and then entering transactions in a group **periodically**. This allows for greater control over the input process, including more possibility for verifying data entry with control totals and authorization before input. Due to the **delay** between the transactions and the input, accounting records may not accurately reflect the current situation at a particular point in time.

IT Enablement

IT enablement is the use of technology to increase the efficiency of processes while reducing costs and ensuring the accuracy of data. IT enablement is achieved through **business process reengineering (BPR)**. BPR is the redesigning of business processes to take advantage of newer technologies to automate manual tasks and capture important data. Such **digital transformations** improve competitive advantage.

The Internet and other technologies ushered in a paradigm shift from the computer as a number-crunching device to a communication tool. This shift was aided by significant declines in computing costs coupled with dramatic increases in computing power in the last several decades. Since the introduction of smartphones in 2007, technology has driven another shift from desktop computers to mobile devices (ie, **mobile computing**), integrating computers more fully into daily life.

Obviously, businesses are still using the number-crunching aspect of computers. Indeed, **automation** of many tasks once performed by humans is ubiquitous. The communications aspect's applicability to accounting might be less obvious. For example, employees use smartphones to take pictures of paper receipts, which are submitted to a website that "reads" them and requests approval. Once approved, an electronic payment is issued to the employee's bank account.

Other examples of technologies employed to enhance business processes include electronic-commerce (e-commerce), Electronic Data Interchange (EDI), Blockchain, Internet of Things (IoT), Robotic Process Automation (RPA) and artificial intelligence.

E-Commerce

E-commerce is one of the most popular electronic business (e-business) implementations. It is any activity that involves buying and selling products/services over the Internet.

Typically, a website will advertise goods/services, and the buyer will fill in a form on the website to select the items to be purchased and provide delivery and payment details. A website may gather details about customers and offer other items that may be of interest. The cost of physical store locations ("brick-and mortar") is avoided; the savings are often a benefit to the customers, sometimes leading to spectacular growth.

E-commerce uses technology to enhance the processes of transactions among a company, its customers, and business partners. The technology used can include the Internet, multimedia, web browsers, proprietary networks, ATMs, home banking, and the traditional approach to EDI. However, the primary area of growth in e-commerce is through the Internet as an enabling technology.

Electronic Data Interchange

EDI is a type of e-commerce that involves a distributor's computer communicating with manufacturers' and retailers' computers to order and ship products without human intervention.

Whenever a network allows one computer to initiate an action that will affect the other, it is known as a **Value-Added Network (VAN).** Extranets have been established as VANs to enable a process of communication between suppliers and customers (ie, trading partners) known as EDI. This allows a company, for example, to have its inventory program automatically send an order to a supplier when quantities in stock of an item drop below a certain level.

Note that it is also possible to use the Internet rather than a traditional VAN for EDI. The advantage is that this would permit suppliers and customers to use the system without having previously established an extranet with each other.

Electronic Funds Transfer & EDI Considerations

E-commerce often involves electronic funds transfers (EFT), which can significantly reduce transaction costs. There are several special considerations related to EDI:

- **Strict standards** are needed for the form of data, so that it will be understood by the computers at both ends and to ensure **completeness** and **accuracy**. The critical nature of many EDI transactions, such as orders and payments, requires that there be positive assurances that the transmissions were complete.

- **Translation software** is needed by each computer so that it can convert data between the standard used for EDI and the form needed for processing internally. The process of identifying which field on the transmitted form corresponds to each field on the internal form is known as **mapping**.

- **Unauthorized access** to company computers and interception of transmissions are great dangers to EDI and EFT. Thus, EDI and EFT require the following **IT controls**:

  o **Encryption** programs that make stolen data unreadable to someone without knowledge of the coding method

  o **Firewall** programs that prevent access to the network without the explicit permission originating from the company computer

In EDI **cryptography**, a public key certificate (aka, **digital certificate** or **identity certificate**) is an electronic document that uses a **digital signature** to bind together a public key with an identity. Such information may include the name of a person or an organization, their address, and so forth. The certificate can be used to verify that a public key belongs to an individual.

Advantages of EDI

- It eliminates the need for human intervention, which **reduces errors** and **increases efficiency**.

- When inventory is ordered automatically at the reorder point, it eliminates gaps and **shortens the business cycle**.

- Payments are made and received automatically, which **reduces accounts receivable**.

- EDI enables:

o Communication without the use of paper

o EFT and sales over the Internet

o Simplification of the recording process using scanning devices

o Sending information to trading partners as transactions occur

E-Commerce Risk

E-commerce, as is true of any other form of commerce, depends on a level of trust between two parties. Some of the most important **risks** are:

- **Confidentiality** – Potential consumers are concerned about confidentiality of their personal information when providing it to unknown vendors.

- **Data integrity** – Data, both in transit and in storage, could be susceptible to unauthorized alteration or deletion (ie, through hacking or design/configuration problems in the system).

- **Availability** – Business may be conducted 24/7; hence, high availability is important with any system failure becoming immediately apparent to customers and/or business partners.

- **Authentication** – Parties should be in a known and trusted business relationship. This requires that they prove their respective identities before executing the transaction. There is a danger that orders and confirmations might be sent by an imposter (ie, **spoofing**), or transmitted files may be intercepted and altered maliciously by third parties before being sent to their destination. Controls might include:

  o Echoing of transmitted documents back to the claimed sender so they know what the recipient has received in their name

  o **Digital signatures** on files and emails to prove the identity of the sender and to provide assurance that the information was unaltered in transmission

- **Nonrepudiation** – After the transaction is executed, authentication of the transacting parties ensures that neither can deny the validity or terms of the transaction.

- **Power shift to customers** – The Internet gives consumers unparalleled access to market information and generally makes it easier to shift between suppliers.

- **Misuse of information** – E-commerce increases the risk of Improper use of information. Controls might include:

  o Security mechanisms and procedures that, taken together, constitute a security architecture for e-commerce

  o Firewall mechanisms that are in place to mediate between the public network (the Internet) and an organization's private network

  o A process whereby participants in an e-commerce transaction can be identified uniquely and positively

- **Improper distribution of information** – There is also the risk of *improper distribution* of transactions with information being electronically transmitted to an inappropriate company. Controls might include:

  o Routing verification procedures

   o Message acknowledgement procedures
- **Reduction in the paper audit trail** – This creates special challenges to the auditor:

   o Detection risk may not be sufficiently reduced through substantive testing.

   o Control risk must be reduced adequately to achieve an acceptable level of audit risk.

   o Controls must be built into the system to ensure the validity of information captured.

3.05 IT Risks & Controls

Overview

Since the auditor will usually want to rely heavily on the internal control (I/C) structure of a computer-based accounting system, gaining an understanding of the I/C structure is crucial. In addition to **entity-level controls** (previously discussed), the operation of computer systems requires two more broad types of controls:

- **IT General controls** – These relate to the **overall integrity of the system**. Controls include IT governance policies, procedures, and practices (tasks and activities) established by management to provide reasonable assurance that specific objectives will be achieved.

- **Application controls** – These are the policies, procedures, and activities designed to provide reasonable assurance that objectives relevant to a given **automated solution (application)** are achieved. They are designed to ensure that an individual computer application program performs properly, accepting authorized input, processing it correctly, and generating appropriate output.

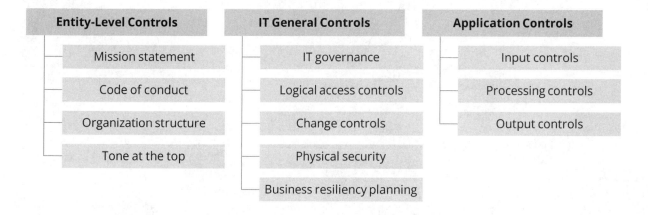

Controls have a function of either **preventing** misstatements (errors or fraud) before they occur (most effective) or **detecting** and **correcting** misstatements that have already occurred. Detecting and correcting is less expensive to implement, but could detect the issue too late.

Initially, the focus of the auditor will be on understanding the general controls that relate to the overall integrity of the system. Later, the auditor may examine application controls that relate to the performance of individual computer programs. If the general controls are poor, it is unlikely that the application controls will be effective, no matter how strong they are.

IT General Controls

IT Governance

IT governance is a formal structure within an entity that is overseen by the board of directors (BOD) and executive management. IT governance helps a business meet strategic goals and objectives through the management and control of IT acquisition, deployment, and use. IT governance provides the **strategies**, **policies**, and **procedures** that are needed to meet IT objectives.

Logical Access Controls & Cybersecurity

Limiting access to an entity's computers and the data they hold is becoming an increasingly challenging problem. Clearly, general controls over **unauthorized access** to computers and files are of great significance in evaluating I/C in an IT environment. **Firewalls** and **user authentication** are particularly important in **networks** since the data are distributed widely; the more points of access there are, the greater the risk.

Furthermore, sensitive data should be **encrypted** to minimize the possible damage (ie, theft, alteration, or destruction of data) should the user authentication process fail. Such controls designed to protect against **cyberattacks** are referred to as **cybersecurity**.

- **Firewalls** – Another tool for establishing security is a **firewall**, which prevents unauthorized users from accessing the system and data. A firewall can be in the form of a computer program (software) or a physical device that blocks the transmission media being used (hardware).

   - A **network firewall** is designed to prevent unauthorized access to the company computers. Network firewalls are easier and cheaper to implement, but if penetrated, leave the computers at severe risk.

   - **Application firewalls** protect individual programs and data. They need to be installed for each program the company wishes to protect, but they allow additional user authentication procedures, making access more difficult.

- **User authentication** – **User IDs** and **passwords** are used to authenticate users (ie, they are who they say they are) and prevent others from accessing the system. Other methods of authentication might include biometrics, smartcards, security tokens, multifactor identification, and multimodal authentication. An auditor can test these procedures by entering invalid user information to see that they are rejected.

   - Passwords should be changed regularly (eg, every 90 days) to make unauthorized access more difficult.

   - Protocols for passwords should encourage the use of random letters, numbers, and symbols, making it more difficult for someone to guess.

   - It is also considered good practice to require that individual users change assigned passwords when new accounts are created.

   - Failure to remove user accounts when an employee leaves a client is a major security risk.

   - A user should be locked out after three failed attempts to access the system.

- **Encryption of data** – There are two types of encryption:

   - **Private key encryption** – Data is encrypted and decrypted using the *same private key*.

   - **Public key encryption** – Data is *encrypted with a public key* and decrypted using a private key.

- **Vulnerability testing** – Systems should be tested periodically for vulnerabilities (ie, weaknesses). This process may be manual or an automated scan.

- **Penetration testing** – This involves IT personnel or an independent consultant attempting to hack the system intentionally.

- **Intrusion detection** – An intrusion-detection program monitors the system to detect network break-ins.

A network should also have **authorization controls.** These controls **limit** (1) **access** to certain files to authorized employees and (2) the **rights** that those individuals should have with respect to the files.

- **Role-based access controls** – This type of access control varies based on an individual's role in the organization. An auditor can test these procedures by verifying that valid passwords only provide compatible access. For example, just as in a manual system, one of the general controls in an IT environment involves segregation of **incompatible duties**:

  - **Authorization** – The development of new programs and changes to existing programs should be performed by **systems analysts, administrators,** and **programmers**. These personnel should not be involved in the supervision of computer operations or the control and review of output. Also, since the **security administrator** controls the access to networks, programs, and data, they should not have any other responsibilities.

  - **Recording** – **Data input clerks** and **computer operators** have the role of entering information into the computer and running the programs. These personnel should not have access to program code that would enable them to modify programs nor should they control the output.

  - **Custody** – **Control clerks** and **librarians** review input procedures, review exception reports indicating incorrect functioning of the computer, send outputs to the proper destinations, and maintain physical storage of data. These personnel should not have the ability to create or alter programs or to operate the computers that generate the information. Also, since the **database administrator** maintains the organization's data, they should not have any programming or other operational responsibilities.

- **Rule-based access controls** – This type of access control can vary based on any set rule. Rules should be set so that:

  - Certain individuals have **read-only access** rights to files.

  - Authorized individuals have the rights to **read, write, or edit** the data in the files.

- These procedures can be tested by verifying that valid passwords provide only compatible access.

There are various types of malicious code (malware) that could infect a system. **Antivirus software** is designed to detect and potentially eliminate malicious code before damage is done and repair or quarantine files that have already been infected. It should be deployed at multiple points in an IT architecture.

Social engineering is the development of a deceptive scenario that tricks an individual into disclosing confidential information for fraudulent purposes (eg, phishing). The best defenses against social engineering are employee **training** and **security policies.**

Change Controls

Change control measures should be implemented to ensure that changes to processing programs and business processes have minimal impact.

- **Systems Development Life Cycle (SDLC) –** SDLC consists of the phases deployed in the development or acquisition of a software system. It is used to plan, design, develop, test, and implement an application system or a major modification to an application system.

- **Change management** – After implementation, a formal change control process manages ad-hoc system changes. This process requires four steps:

  o A **formal change request** that describes the desired change and the plans for implementation should be documented and distributed to stakeholders.

  o The formal change request will be **evaluated** to determine the impact on the project schedule and budget.

  o If the change is **authorized**, it is **implemented**.

  o The change is then **tested** to verify that the desired results have been achieved.

- **Systems documentation** of new programs and alterations to existing programs ensures that IT personnel are aware of the availability and proper use of programs. Also, changes in programming personnel during projects will not interfere with the ability of other employees to understand what has been done previously. Such documentation may also assist the auditor in learning about the system.

Physical Security

Physical security consists of physical access controls and environmental controls.

- Physical access controls can include locks, cameras, badges, biometrics, etc.

- Environmental controls include temperature and humidity control, fire protection without the use of sprinklers, uninterruptable power supply, etc.

Business Resilience Planning

The purpose of business resilience planning is to enable a business to quickly adapt and continue operations while safeguarding assets in the event of a disruption. The following general controls will contribute to a business's ability to return to normalcy as quickly as possible.

- **Identify the business processes of strategic importance** – These are the key processes that are responsible for both the permanent growth of the business and for the fulfillment of the business goals. Based on the key processes, the risk management process should begin with a risk assessment. The risk is directly proportional to the impact on the organization and the probability of occurrence of the perceived threat.

- **Backup controls –** Copies of files and programs should be maintained to allow reconstruction of destroyed or altered files. This may include copies on the same computer, backups to removable storage media, such as disks, and off-premises backups to computers and locations outside the company. Copies may be identical, or the client may use the **grandfather-father-son** retention system.   This involves the periodic saving of data versions to allow the reconstruction of records by starting with an older file and reentering lost data since that time.

The three basic backup strategies, which are commonly used together, are:

- o **Full** – Makes a full backup of the system's data. This complete backup takes the longest and utilizes the most backup media. Usually performed over longer time periods, such as once a week.

- o **Differential** – Copies *only* data that has changed since the last **full** backup. These backups are cumulative until the next full backup is complete and are typically done daily. Differential backups sacrifice completeness for speed, although as the week progresses, they, along with any required data restoration procedures, will take longer.

- o **Incremental** – Copies *only* data that has changed since the last backup of any kind, usually in increments of hours or minutes. These small increments can be restored relatively quickly, but rely on the presence of a full backup. Any restoration must start with the last full backup, then load each incremental backup sequentially.

- **Planned downtime controls** – Since some downtime is inevitable, planned downtime allows maintenance so that unplanned downtime doesn't interrupt system operations.

- **Checkpoints** – This is similar to grandfather-father-son, but at certain "checkpoints," the system makes a copy of the database and this "checkpoint" file is stored on a separate disk or tape. If a problem occurs, the system is restarted at the last checkpoint.

- **Business continuity & disaster recovery** – The company should have plans in place that will allow operations to be restored and continued in the event of physical destruction or disabling of the site of computer operations. The configuration that represents the most complete disaster recovery plan should provide for an alternative processing site, backup and off-site storage procedures, identification of critical applications, and testing of the plan. This can be done by maintaining a(n):

- o **Hot site** – This is an alternate site that has computers and data ready to begin operations immediately in the event of the disaster.

- o **Cold site** – This is an alternate site that has space available for operations but will require setup of computers and loading of data before operations can begin.

- o **Off-site mirrored server** – This is an off-site server that is replicated from a production server in real-time, and can take over operations in a matter of seconds in the event of an outage. This is used to ensure continuous delivery of mission-critical data or services, such as those needed by government and medical applications.

- **Incident response planning** – An important part of business continuity planning is the detection and response to IT security threats. An **incident response plan** is the IT-focused counterpart to the **disaster recovery plan**, which primarily addresses physical disrupters. Incident response plans address a wide variety of IT-specific threats, including service outages, data loss, and intellectual property theft. Robust incident response plans help IT staff detect technology-related threats, and offer a course of action for all significant incidents.

Risks/Threats* – Overall Computer Environment	IT General Controls
Not Meeting IT Objectives	**IT Governance**
• Misalignment of IT strategy with business strategy • IT doesn't deliver the value it should	• Strategic guidance • Direction (setting policies & procedures) • Monitoring
Unauthorized Access	**Access Controls & Cybersecurity**
• Cyberattacks • Theft, alteration, or destruction of data • Malicious code • Social engineering • Misuse of data by employees • Incompatible functions (fraud/error)	• Firewalls & user authentication (lock out after 3 unsuccessful attempts) • Encryption of sensitive data • Antivirus software • Employee training • Authorization controls (limits access/rights to alter data)
Computer Facility Vulnerabilities	**Physical Security**
• Unauthorized access • Theft, physical destruction of IT assets • Environmental hazards • Fire, heat, humidity, electrical outages	• Locks, ID badges, etc. • Cameras • Fire protection (no sprinklers) • Uninteruptable power supply (ie, battery backup) and emergency power supply (ie, generators)
Change Risk	**Change Controls**
• Disruption of operations • Unauthorized system alterations • Uninformed IT staff	• Systems Development Life Cycle (SDLC) • Change management • Systems documentation
Disruption of Operations	**Business Resilience Planning**
• Accidental/intentional destruction or unauthorized alteration • Natural disasters	• Back up controls • Disaster recovery planning • Alternative processing site • Off-site storage procedures • Incident response planning

This is not meant to be an all-inclusive list.

Application Controls

Application controls are those applied to specific business activities within a computerized processing system to achieve financial reporting objectives. Application controls are specific to each cycle and refer to a client's activities. Application controls relate to data input, data processing, and data output. They are designed to ensure the proper recording of transactions and to prevent or detect errors and fraud for transactions within these cycles.

Because application controls are related to specific transactions, audit teams rely extensively on the effectiveness of these controls to mitigate the risk of material misstatement for account balances or classes of transactions.

Input Controls

Input controls are designed to provide reasonable assurance that data received for processing have been **properly authorized** and **accurately entered** or converted for processing. These controls also provide the opportunity for entity personnel to correct and resubmit data initially rejected as erroneous. Errors can be avoided through:

- Observational controls

- Use of point-of-sale devices, such as scanners, to gather and record data automatically

- The use of preprinted recording forms

- Data transcription controls, such as preformatted screens, when converting data to machine-readable form

- Automated log-off of inactive users to prevent unauthorized access to sensitive data

 Historically, many of the controls discussed on the exam involve verifying data that has been input to ensure the program doesn't accept inappropriate information.

As data is being entered, it should be subject to various **forms of verification** (ie, **logic tests**).

- **Field checks** – Data is validated as to the correct length and format. For example, an entry of a license plate might be verified for type (alphanumeric, so that only letters and numbers are acceptable) and length (not longer than 7).

  o **Missing data check** (Completeness check) – Data is validated to make sure that all required fields have values. For example, a timecard entry system would require that the hours worked in a day field contain a value.

- **Validity checks** – Data is compared with a list of acceptable entries to be sure it matches one of them. For example, a field to accept the two-letter state abbreviation will be checked against a file that lists all the acceptable choices, so that an entry of OG for the state will be rejected as invalid.

- **Limit tests** – Numbers are compared to limits that have been set for acceptability. For example, the entry of a pay rate may be compared to the current minimum wage on the lower side and $50 per hour on the upper side to be sure the number entered makes sense.

This is sometimes called a reasonableness test, and is the closest computer equivalent to human judgment in reviewing information.

- **Check digits** – Numbers with no obvious meaning, such as identification numbers, are often designed so that one of the digits is determined by a formula applied to the rest of the number. The computer applies the formula when a number is entered to determine if it is an acceptable one.

This control makes it difficult for someone to invent a fake number if they don't know the formula; the program will recognize a number that isn't designed so that the check digit is correct. The check digit can be either a number or letter, and can be placed in any consistent position in the overall identification.

For example, many states have driver licenses that start with a letter which is derived from a formula applied to the numbers which follow it, and a person trying to create a fictional license will only have a 1 in 26 chance of correctly guessing the letter that should be in the first position based on the numbers.

When using batch processing of data, manual **control totals** can be prepared and compared with computer-generated totals of entered information to ensure accuracy of inputs. These totals include:

- **Record count** – The total number of records entered into the program at that time.

- **Financial total** – The total dollar amount of entries that are financial in nature.

- **Hash total** – The total of values which cannot be meaningfully added together, but which serve as a way to verify the correct entry of these values.

- **Other quantitative total** – The total of some column of numbers, such as check numbers or invoice numbers, that can be used to determine that all transactions have been entered as well as that a sequence has not been broken.

 Assume that the checks written during a particular day are being entered into a checkbook program, and that the data input clerk is working from the following sheet to make the entries:

Check Number	Payee	Amount	Account Code
1001	Philipp Corporation	$500.00	307
1002	Rog Enterprises	$3,000.00	602
1003	Ruiz Company	$600.00	302
3006		$4,100.00	1211

After the data input clerk enters each of the checks, the computer will then indicate:

Checks Entered = 3 (record count)
Check Number total = 3006 (quantitative total)
Amount total = $4,100.00 (financial total)
Account Code total = 1211 (hash total)

The data input clerk would have also determined these numbers by computing them from the input sheet; the agreement of the clerk's totals with those of the program will indicate all lines must have been entered correctly.

A program may also perform **edit checks** on batch-processed data to verify that each individual entry is appropriate; it will then generate a list of rejected transactions for review by the control clerk.

Processing Controls

Once data is input, processing controls are designed to provide reasonable assurance that data processing has been performed accurately without any omission or duplicate processing of transactions. Many processing controls are similar in nature to input controls, but they are used in the processing phases, rather than at the time input is verified.

- **Run-to-run totals** use values in the batch control record to monitor records as they move from one batch process to another batch process. They are calculated at the end of each batch process and compared to the batch control record.

- **Transaction logs** track whether transactions were successfully processed or not.

- **Prenumbered documents** ensure that there are no duplicate or missing records in a batch.

- **Sequence checks** ensure that records in a batch are processed in correct sequential order.

- A **concurrent update control** (concurrency control) helps to address conflicts in a multi-user system. For example, when two people are trying to purchase tickets at the same time, it will lock one user out, so as not to oversell the tickets.

- The most fundamental processing control a client can implement is **periodic system testing and evaluation** of the processing accuracy of its programs. This testing helps ensure that data is being handled or rejected appropriately, and that logical functions are correct and working.

  o Computer programs can be tested using **error testing compilers** to ensure that they do not contain programming language errors.

  o **Test data** exposes the program to one sample of each type of exception condition (ie, an unusual condition) likely to occur during its use.

  o **Systems and software documentation** allows system analysts to verify that processing programs are complete and thorough.

Output Controls

Output controls represent the final check on the results of computerized processing. Output controls are concerned with **detecting errors** rather than preventing errors. These controls should be designed to provide reasonable assurance that only authorized persons receive output or have access to files produced by the system.

Risks/Threats* – Specific Programs	Application Controls	
Inappropriate Inputs	**Input Controls**	
• Invalid data • Poor data quality • Incomplete data • Inaccurate data	• Check digit • Validity check • Edit test • Limit test	• Financial total • Record counts • Hash total • Nonfinancial totals
Compromised Processing Integrity	**Processing Controls**	
• Invalid data • Incomplete data • Inaccurate data • Redundant data	• Run-to-run totals • Transaction logs • Prenumbered documents	• Sequence checks • Concurrency control • Periodic system testing
Ineffective Outputs	**Output Controls**	
• Inaccurate and/or incomplete data • Improper disposal • Improper distribution of information	• System testing • Shredders • Distribution lists	

This is not meant to be an all-inclusive list.

3.06 Business Processes: Revenue Cycle

Overview

The revenue cycle generally consists of the following six business processes, which can be grouped into three main categories:

Sales orders			Sales returns	Collections
Credit checks	Shipping	Billing		

As you cover the following operating cycles, remember that a business process and its control activities are easier to recall when remembering that there is a **SACREd-MAPP** to every process and its components (previously discussed).

Employees & Duties

To properly segregate the incompatible functions of authorization, recording, custody, and comparisons, the business processes may include specific employees with certain duties:

- **Salesclerk** – Accepts orders from customers and prepares written sales orders using internal prenumbered, preprinted forms (PPN) (recording).

- **Credit manager** – Approves customer credit on orders (authorization).

- **Warehouse clerk** – Holds goods in inventory awaiting requests for shipment (custody).

- **Shipping clerk** – Removes items from inventory to ship to customer (custody).

Start (initiation) of a transaction/event

Authorize transaction/event

Complete (execute) transaction/event in accordance with policies/procedures

Record transaction/event

Evaluate defenses (verify)

Matching documents
Authoritative signatures
Prenumbered documents
Periodic reconciliations

- **Billing clerk** – Prepares sales invoices to send to customers (recording).

- **Accounts Receivable (A/R) clerk** – Posts sales and collections to individual customer accounts based on sales invoices and remittance advices, respectively (recording).

- **General ledger (G/L) bookkeeper** – Posts journal entries for sales and collections (recording).

- **Mailroom clerk/receptionist** – Opens mail containing customer checks (or cash) and remittance advices, prepares a prelist of checks (ie, a remittance listing), and directs these items to appropriate parties within the system (custody).

- **Cashier** – Receives checks, prepares deposit slip, and deposits funds at the bank (custody).

- **Cash receipts clerk** – Receives remittance listing and posts to cash receipts journal (recording).

- **Receiving clerk** – Receives all goods that are being returned and returns them to inventory (custody).

- **Treasurer** – Approves credit memos for returns and write-offs of uncollectible accounts (authorization).

- **Controller/Internal Audit** – Bank reconciliations and analyses of past-due accounts receivable should be performed by individuals independent of cash receipts and disbursements (comparison).

A system may not necessarily include all the above employees.

- Sometimes a function may be performed by another employee or one of the above employees identified by a different title. For example, all the clerks involved in **recording** may simply be called **bookkeepers**. Also, periodic reconciliations may be performed by any employee who is not involved in the preparation of either of the two types of records being compared and does not have custody of resources being compared to recorded amounts.

- **Automation** can also affect these processes. It can reduce expenses, increase efficiency, and decrease the incidence of errors in the process. However, when errors do occur in an automated system, there is a risk that they will affect many transactions before being discovered and corrected.

  o For example, if the sales process is automated through the use of **e-commerce** or **electronic data interchange (EDI)**, as previously discussed, several of the positions involved in the sales, billing, and collections processes could be eliminated.

  o Alternatively, if the entity uses a **point-of-sale (POS) system** with **barcode scanners**, a salesclerk would not need to manually take/input an order, reducing the possibility of error.

  o Furthermore, **Robotic Process Automation (RPA)** can repeat a set of tasks normally conducted by an employee using a graphical user interface (GUI). For example, RPA could automate repetitive, rules-based tasks, such as opening an email with a sales order, extracting the data, and then entering that sales order into a computer application.

Documents & Records

Some of the documents and records (paper or electronic) that may be used to capture, distribute, and summarize information within the revenue cycle include the following:

- **Sales order** – The list of goods ordered by the customer along with the prices (from a **price list**) to be charged. Even if a customer has submitted their own purchase order, a sales order will be prepared, since these are prenumbered, making it possible to periodically verify that orders were processed.

- **Pick ticket** – The list used by the warehouse clerk to gather the items ordered for shipping.

- **Packing slip** – The list of all items included in a particular shipment.

- **Bill of lading** – The shipping document that is signed by the courier, often a trucker, accepting goods from the shipping clerk.

- **Shipping log** – List of shipments that can be used to track the status of orders.

- **Sales invoice** – The bill that is prepared and sent to the customer after shipment to request payment. Before preparing a sales invoice, the billing clerk should compare the sales order and bill of lading to ensure they agree.

- **Sales journal** – A special journal in which sales are posted.

- **Subsidiary receivables ledger** – A ledger that lists the outstanding receivables with a separate record for each customer.

- **Receiving log** – List of goods returned in the order they were returned.

- **Receiving report** – Form completed by receiving personnel that indicates the quantity and condition of items returned.

- **Credit memo** – Documents the return of goods and adjusts the customer's account and credit limit.

- **Remittance advice** – The document included in an envelope with the check or other form of payment to indicate the purpose of the check.

- **Remittance listing** – A summary of the money received that day. This may be called a prelist in some cases, and is prepared by the employee first receiving the cash, which is usually the mailroom clerk.

- **Cash receipts journal** – A special journal in which the remittance listings are posted.

- **Deposit slip** – The document signed or stamped by the bank to acknowledge receipt of checks and that is periodically reconciled to postings into the cash receipts journal by an independent employee.

- **Bank reconciliation** – Comparison of the cash balance according to the entity's records to the amount indicated by the bank that it is holding on behalf of the entity.

Control Activities

Ultimately, the reason an auditor cares about the I/C structure is that it relates to whether the **financial statement assertions** (**RACE, CPA-CO, RACOUn**) are achieved by mitigating risks through the implementation of controls (**PIPS-ARCC**). These controls may vary from entity to entity, even within the same industry. The following list includes some of the most common controls in the revenue cycle; however, it is not intended to be all-inclusive.

- Performance reviews – Management compares actual sales performance with forecasted sales and prior year sales to check for unexplained variances.

- Information processing

  - The sequence of **prenumbered documents** can be checked for omitted transactions.

  - **Matching documents** avoids invalid/duplicate transactions, inaccuracies, and period cutoff issues.

- **Physical controls** – Physical access to inventory, cash, and records should be controlled through the use of locks, cameras, passwords, etc.

- **Segregation of duties** – The following incompatible functions should be separated:

- o **Authorizing** sales, issuing (**recording**) credit memos and bad debt write-offs, and **custody** of cash

- o **Authorizing** sales, **recording** accounts receivable, and having **custody** of inventory

- o **Custody** of cash, **recording** of cash receipts, and preparing the bank reconciliations (**comparison**)

- **Authorization** – Sales on account should be authorized prior to executing the transaction to avoid fictitious customers and approve credit limits to avoid possible credit losses. Price lists and price concessions should also be authorized. Similarly, sales returns should be authorized prior to issuing credit.

- **Recording** – Recording of transactions should not occur until obligations have been fulfilled (eg, goods have been shipped). Recorded information should be compared to source documents and all source documents should be retained. Sending customers statements of their account helps detect and correct errors.

- **Custody** – Only certain individuals should have custody of assets (ie, cash and inventory) or access to programs and data to avoid theft or unauthorized alteration/destruction of programs/data. Obtaining **bonds** (insurance and background searches) for employees who handle large amounts of cash is an effective deterrent to theft and fraud since bonding companies often prosecute those accused of dishonest acts.

- **Comparisons – Periodic reconciliations**

  - o Periodic reconciliations of inventory on hand to inventory records can indicate whether inventory has been lost or stolen.

  - o Similarly, monthly reconciliations of deposits to the accounting records should be performed.

In obtaining an understanding, the auditor should consider activities that may occur outside of the entity. For example, the company may direct customers to send payments directly to a bank lockbox instead of to the company itself, thereby eliminating access to cash and checks by any of the employees in the revenue cycle. This obviously strengthens the I/C over cash receipts.

3.07 Business Processes: Spending Cycle

Overview

The spending cycle of a business can generally be broken down into the following six business processes and grouped into three main categories:

Purchase orders			Purchase returns	Cash disbursements
Receiving	Inventory control	Accounts payable		

Employees & Duties

To properly segregate the incompatible functions of authorization, recording, and custody, the activities may include specific employees with each of the following duties:

- **Purchasing manager** – Approves purchase requests before they are processed and negotiates terms with vendors (authorization).

- **Purchasing clerk** – Places orders with vendors (recording).

- **Receiving clerk** – Receives delivery of goods from vendors (custody).

- **Payables clerk** – Prepares payment voucher, which is the basis for authorizing the issuance of a check to the vendor after verifying the accuracy of the vendor invoice and comparing supporting documents (recording).

- **Payables manager** – Oversees the posting of vouchers to appropriate purchase records (recording).

- **Treasurer** – Signs and mails check for payment (custody).

- **Shipping department** – Sends goods back to vendors when goods are nonconforming or a right to cancel an order is being exercised by the company (custody).

Since the spending cycle is essentially the opposite of the revenue cycle, **automation** may affect these processes similarly. For example, if the purchasing process is automated using **e-commerce**, **electronic data interchange (EDI)**, or **robotic process automation (RPA)**, several of the positions involved in purchasing, accounts payable, and cash disbursement processes could be eliminated. Such automation can reduce expenses, increase efficiency, and decrease the incidence of errors in the process.

Documents & Records

The documents and records involved in the spending cycle generally include:

- **Purchase requisition** – The internal request by the department in need for goods to be ordered by the purchasing department.

- **Purchase order** – The external form mailed to the vendor to request that goods be delivered to the company. When the **purchase order** is prepared by the purchasing clerk to send to the vendor, additional copies are sent to the receiving department and the payables department.

  o The receiving department copy is a **blind copy**; that is, it does not include price or quantities to ensure that the receiving department will perform an **independent count** of the goods delivered.

  o The payables clerk compares the purchase order and receiving report with the vendor invoice to ensure they agree before preparing the payment voucher.

- **Packing slip** – The list of all items included in a shipment.

- **Bill of lading** – A shipping document that is signed by the receiving clerk, accepting goods from the courier.

- **Receiving report** – The document prepared in the receiving department to note the quantity and condition of the items received. This report is signed by the courier to acknowledge the goods that have been delivered to the company.

- **Receiving log** – A list of all receipts in the order they were received.

- **Purchase (vendor) invoice** – The document received from the vendor indicating the goods the vendor claims to have shipped. This is the same document that is known as the sales invoice when considered from the vendor's side of the transaction.

- **Invoice register** – A listing of all invoices received from vendors.

- **Payment voucher** – The document prepared by the payables clerk to request that a check be issued for payment to a vendor.

  o The check for payment is usually prepared by a clerk in the treasury department who doesn't have signature authority. They will provide the **unsigned check** along with the **payment voucher** and **supporting document** to the treasurer for signature. The treasurer makes sure the check **agrees** with the voucher and other documents before signing.

  o Immediately after signing, the treasurer **cancels** the **supporting documents** (so that they won't accidentally be processed again), places the check in the envelope, seals it, and arranges for mailing.

- **Purchase journal (or voucher register**) – A listing of all payment vouchers generated by the company.

Control Activities

The following list includes some of the most common control activities (**PIPS-ARCC**) in the spending cycle; however, it is not intended to be all-inclusive.

- **Performance reviews** – Management can compare actual purchases to the budget to check for unexplained variances.

- **Information processing**

  o The sequence of **prenumbered documents** can be checked for omitted transactions.

  o **Matching documents** avoids invalid/duplicate transactions, inaccuracies, and period cutoff issues.

- **Physical controls** – Physical access to inventory, cash, and records should be controlled using locks, cameras, passwords, etc.

- **Segregation of duties** – The following incompatible functions should be separated:

  o **Authorizing** purchases, receiving goods purchased (**custody**), and **recording** the purchase

  o **Authorizing** payment for purchases, **recording** payments, access to checks (**custody**), and reconciliation of the bank account (**comparison**)

  o **Authority** to approve vouchers for payment and access to unused purchase orders (**custody**)

- **Authorization** – Vendors and purchases should be authorized prior to executing the transaction to avoid fictitious vendors, excess purchases, and pricing issues. Similarly, purchase returns and debit memos should be authorized prior to returning items.

- **Recording**– Receiving reports should be prepared for all goods received. Credit memos should be prepared for all returned goods.

- **Custody**– All goods should be received by the receiving department and returns should be shipped by the shipping department.

- **Comparisons** – Periodic reconciliations of inventory on hand to inventory records can provide evidence of lost or stolen inventory, fictitious purchases, unrecorded purchases, or period cutoff issues.

Investing & Financing Cycle

The investing and financing cycle deals with transactions involving acquisition and disposal of assets other than inventory and transactions with creditors and shareholders. Since there are typically very few transactions in these areas in a typical year for a client, an auditor will often find it most efficient to ignore the I/C structure and simply test the few transactions that took place. In this case, the auditor will:

- Not test the controls

- Assess risk of material misstatement (RMM) at the same level as inherent risk, assuming that control risk is at the maximum level, generally resulting in a high RMM

- Reduce detection risk by performing extensive substantive tests

In those less frequent cases where a large number of transactions have occurred, the auditor may find it more efficient to rely on the I/C structure rather than test the numerous transactions that took place. In this case, the auditor will:

- Test the controls to determine their effectiveness

- Reduce RMM based on the results of the tests of controls

- Accept higher detection risk by performing only limited substantive tests

Control Activities

Many of the following control activities will typically be applied by management or other employees at a very high level, reflecting the extremely large value and great danger of fraud in connection with marketable securities. Examples of such control activities generally include:

- **Performance reviews** – Controls should be regularly reviewed by senior management or some independent body. Senior management examines securities on hand to ensure that they are registered in the name of the company or confirms such with custodians of the investments.

- **Physical controls** – The entity maintains physical custody of investments in a secure physical location. Requiring two officers to be involved in access is common.

- **Segregation of duties** – As usual, the incompatible functions of authorization, recording, custody, and comparisons should be separated.

  o **Authorization** – Definitions, limits, and constraints on investment activities should be reviewed regularly. Senior management should authorize investment transactions.

  o **Custody** – It is generally best to have an independent trustee maintain possession of securities so that they are safeguarded from all misappropriation by company employees.

  o **Comparisons**

- Regular reconciliations to control account balances should be performed.

- The internal auditor makes a list of securities in bank safe deposit boxes and compares them with the securities listed in the records.

- The treasurer vouches the agreement of broker advices on purchases with cancelled checks.

- The controller determines that debt securities are classified in the records correctly as trading securities, available-for-sale securities, or held-to-maturity securities, based on management decisions as to the intent of holding them.

- The recorded values of investments are periodically compared to current market prices.

- The investments on hand and held by custodians are periodically reconciled to their recorded amounts.

Fixed Assets

Most testing related to **property, plant, and equipment** transactions concerns itself with the different types of controls that reduce the risk of misstatement. In a good I/C structure, the internal audit staff will periodically inspect physical assets. This cycle includes acquisitions, disposals, and depreciation expense. Among the **objectives** are:

- Verifying the *existence* of recorded assets by vouching from records to the physical assets. This can assist in identifying unrecorded disposals.

- Verifying the completeness of acquisitions by tracing from the physical assets to the records. This can assist in identifying unrecorded acquisitions.

A common problem involves the recording of equipment purchases in expense accounts, especially for repairs and maintenance. Besides the tracing of physical assets to records mentioned above, the internal audit staff may also examine the relevant accounts and compare them with budgeted amounts, since large variances may indicate the expensing of costs that should have been capitalized.

Production & Conversion Cycle

The production and conversion cycle deals primarily with manufacturing operations. It generally consists of the following business processes, which can be grouped into three main categories for our purposes:

Production Planning			Production	Inventory control
Engineering	Capital Budgeting	Scheduling		

Employees, Duties, Documents & Records

The results of **production planning** will determine what, how, when, and how many products will be produced in addition to the resources that will be needed to do so. This can be broken down into the following four processes:

- **Engineering** – In this process, engineers will provide the designs and specifications of products as well as the methods for producing the products. The following documents will also be prepared:

  - **Bill of materials** – A list of materials and parts needed for production of a product.

  - **Operations list** – A list of the processes to perform to produce a product.

- **Capital budgeting** – This process will determine the budget for resources (generally fixed assets) needed for production.

- **Scheduling** – This process determines when production activities will occur while trying to meet customer demand, coordinate with the availability of materials and resources, and minimize down time. The following documents will be prepared:

  - **Production order** (or work order) – This document authorizes the production of a product, which may be initiated by a sales forecast or a sales order.

  - **Production schedule** – This document specifies the timing of a production run.

Production is the process of converting raw materials into finished goods.

  - **Materials requisition** (or routing slip) – This documents the quantity and type of raw materials moved into work-in-progress inventory at the beginning of the production process.

  - **Inventory status** (or move ticket) – This documents the work completed at each stage of production, moving it to the next stage of production.

Inventory control – Acquisition of, and accounting for, raw materials purchased in a manufacturing process is similar to merchandise inventory in a nonmanufacturing entity. While inventory control may be of the most concern to the auditor in this cycle, we won't cover it again here since it is so similar to that which has already been covered in the spending cycle.

Control Activities

Examples of controls related to the management assertions for manufactured inventory include:

- **Performance reviews**

  o Management can compare actual production costs to the budgeted production costs to check for unexplained variances.

  o Allocations of salaries and wages to inventory are reviewed to make certain appropriate amounts are included.

- **Information processing**

  o The sequence of **prenumbered documents** can be checked for omitted transactions (eg, acquisition of raw materials).

  o **Matching documents** avoids invalid/duplicate transactions, inaccuracies, and period cutoff issues.

- **Physical controls** – Physical access to inventory and records should be controlled using locks, cameras, passwords, etc.

- **Segregation of duties** – As usual, the incompatible functions of **Authorization**, **Recording**, and **Custody** should be separated.

- **Comparisons**

  o Perpetual inventory records are regularly **reconciled** to goods in inventory to make certain that recorded amounts are still on hand.

  o Direct labor charged to individual time tickets is compared to the total direct labor charged to work-in-process to ensure direct labor costs have not been charged to manufacturing overhead.

3.09 Business Processes: Personnel & Payroll

Overview

The personnel & payroll cycle can be broken down in three basic categories of business processes:

Hiring	Payroll	Terminations

	Time recording	Cash disbursements	

These processes, however, are normally spread across four different departments to segregate the duties properly.

	Authorize	Recording	Custody	Comparison
Department	Personnel	Accounting	Treasurer	Controller
Duties	Hire & fire	Calculate pay	Signs & distributes payroll	Bank reconciliations
	Salary rates		Custody of cash	

Employees, Duties, Documents & Records

- **Personnel (Human Resources)** – HR is responsible for **authorization**.
    - HR is involved with personnel **records** and all **hiring forms**, including **forms** for payroll **deductions**.
    - HR approves changes in **pay rates**.
    - HR is also involved in the termination process. It is essential that they promptly send employee **termination notices** to the payroll department.
- **Employee** – The employee prepares a **timecard**, and submits it to the supervisor for authorization. The timecard is then sent to the payroll department.
- **Payroll accountant** – Payroll accountants are responsible for **recording**.

- o They examine and then **update records** based on authorization forms for hiring, firing, and pay rates received from personnel.

- o They **calculate payroll** based on timecards and other reports approved by appropriate supervisors. They enter all timecard and wage rate information into the **payroll register**.

- o They also prepare a **payroll cost allocation** based on the timecard information. The payroll cost allocation is used to distribute payroll costs over the various accounts affected.

- o They **prepare vouchers** for payment.

- o Finally, payroll is recorded in the **payroll journal** (or in the **general ledger** for smaller entities).

> **Key Documents & Records**
> - Personnel records
> - Hiring & deduction authorization forms (W-4)
> - Timecards
> - Payroll register
> - Paychecks
> - Payroll cost allocation
> - Bank reconciliations

- **Treasurer** – The treasurer is responsible for **custody**.

  - o The treasurer authorizes electronic payroll distribution.

  - o If actual checks are used, they are submitted to the treasurer for signature and distribution to employees.

  - o Unclaimed checks should *not* be returned to the payroll department. Unclaimed paychecks should be retained until they are either distributed or voided.

  - o If payment of wages is in cash, employees should be required to sign a receipt for the amount received.

- **Controller** – As an overall verification of custody controls over cash, the controller should prepare monthly **bank reconciliations (comparison)** to verify that there were no errors made.

Control Activities

- **Performance reviews** – Management should review payroll documents for unusual information.

- **Information processing**

  - o The sequence of **prenumbered checks** can be checked for omitted transactions (ie, paychecks that were unrecorded).

  - o **Matching** the payroll register with established payrates avoids inaccuracies.

  - o **Batch processing – Control totals** and **hash totals** can be used to verify the appropriate payroll amounts.

- **Physical controls** – Physical access to cash, blank checks, as well as personnel and payroll records should be controlled using locks, cameras, passwords, etc.

- **Segregation of duties** – The following incompatible functions should be separated:

- o **Authorizing** the hiring of personnel, payroll processing (**recording**) and distributing paychecks (**custody**)

- o **Authorizing** payroll rate changes and payroll processing (**recording**)

- o Preparation of paychecks (**recording**) and the signing of the checks (**custody**)

- **Authorization** – Supervisors should review and approve timecards.

- **Comparison** – Periodic bank reconciliations should be performed. Having a separate bank account for payroll will make this process easier.

3.10 Reliance on SOC 1 Reports

Service Organizations

Service organizations are entities that provide services—such as payroll or web-hosting—to other entities. When an entity uses one of these service organizations, AU-C 402[2] provides guidance as to the impact on an audit. It defines a service organization as "an organization or segment of an organization that provides services to user entities that are relevant to those user entities' internal control over financial reporting."

Objectives of the User Auditor

The objectives of the user auditor (ie, the auditor of the client using the services of the service organization) are to:

- Obtain an understanding of the nature and significance of the services provided
- Evaluate their effect on the user entity's I/C to assess the risks of material misstatement
- Design and perform audit procedures responsive to those risks

In some cases, the user auditor will be unable to obtain a sufficient understanding of the nature and significance of the relationship with a service organization using the resources available through the client. In such cases, the auditor will obtain a sufficient understanding by performing one or more of the following:

- Obtaining and reading a SOC 1 Report, as defined below, if available
- Obtaining information from contact with the service organization, through the client
- Applying procedures directly to the operations of the service organization
- Using the work of another auditor applying procedures designed to obtain the necessary information

As part of obtaining an understanding of the internal controls of a client using a service organization, the user auditor should *obtain an understanding* as to *how* the client uses the service organization. The understanding will include:

- The nature of the services provided
- The significance of the services to the user entity
- The effect on the user entity's I/C
- The nature and materiality of transactions that are processed by the service organization
- Interaction between the activities of the user entity and of the service organization
- The nature of the relationship between the entities
- Contractual terms for activities performed by the service organization

---

[2] *Audit Considerations Relating to an Entity Using a Service Organization*

Complementary Controls

The user auditor will also evaluate the internal controls established by the client to administer the relationship with the service organization. The entity may, for example, have controls to verify the accuracy of the output of the service organization. The user auditor will use the understanding of the nature and significance of the services provided by the service organization, along with the entity's related controls, to identify and assess risks of material misstatement that may result.

SOC 1 Reports

Since the user auditor is not able to examine the activities of such an outside organization, they will often need to rely on reports of the auditor of the service organization itself (ie, the **service auditor)**. The service auditor will usually issue a report on the I/C structure that the user auditor may consider in assessing the I/C structure of the client. These are called SOC 1 Reports. Other types of SOC Reports are discussed in a later section.

The SOC 1 report will describe the service auditor's procedures and the services of the organization that are covered by the report. This will enable the user auditor to understand the overall impact of the service organization's work on the I/C structure of the client.

User Auditor's Responsibilities

Before relying on such a report, the auditor should be satisfied as to the:

- Competence and independence of the service auditor
- Adequacy of the standards under which the report was issued

The SOC 1 report will assist the user auditor in gaining an understanding of the I/C structure of the client, to the extent it depends on the service organization's work. This will not, however, be considered a basis for determining the effectiveness of the customer's I/C structure. Thus, the use of the report is **not a division of responsibility**, so there must be **no reference** to the service auditor in the user's audit report on the F/S of the client.

Two Types of SOC 1 Reports

There are *two reports* of SOC 1 reports that the service auditor may issue.

- A **Type 1 report** is a report on management's description of the service organization's system of controls and the suitability of the **design** of the controls. It consists of:
  - Management's description of the system
  - Management's written assertion that, in all material respects, based on appropriate criteria:
    - The description of the system fairly presents the system that was designed and **implemented** as of a specified date.
    - Controls related to objectives stated in management's description were **suitably designed** to achieve those objectives.

- o A report from the service auditor, expressing an opinion in relation to management's written assertions

- A **Type 2 report** is a report on management's description of the service organization's system of controls and the suitability of the **design and the operating effectiveness** of the controls. It consists of:

  - o Management's description of the system

  - o Management's written assertion that, in all material respects, based on appropriate criteria:

    - The description of the system fairly presents the system that was designed and **implemented** throughout the specified period.

    - Controls related to objectives stated in management's description were **suitably designed** to achieve those objectives.

    - The controls related to the specified objectives were **operating effectively** throughout the specified period.

  - o A report from the service auditor expressing an opinion in relation to management's written assertions and describing the **tests of controls** performed and the **results** of those tests

To rely upon a Type 1 or Type 2 report, the user auditor should:

- Determine that the date of a Type 1 report, or the period covered by a Type 2 report is appropriate for the auditor's needs.

- Evaluate whether the evidence provided by the report is appropriate and sufficient for the purpose of obtaining an understanding of the user's I/C.

- Determine if the user entity has developed controls that are complementary to those of the service organization that address risks of material misstatement relating to relevant assertions in the user's F/S.

Relying on Service Organization Controls

When the user auditor intends to rely on the controls at the service organization, they must be subjected to tests of controls, which may be accomplished by one or more of the following:

- Obtaining and reading a Type 2 SOC 1 report

- Applying tests of controls at the service organization

- Using another auditor to perform tests of controls at the service organization

If the user auditor's tests of controls consist of obtaining and reading a type 2 report, the auditor will evaluate the report to determine whether:

- It is for an appropriate period.

- There are **complementary controls** at the user entity identified by the service organization as addressing risks of material misstatement.

  o If so, the user auditor should determine if those controls have been designed and implemented and apply tests of controls to them.

- The time period covered by tests of controls is adequate.

  o The auditor should also evaluate the length of time since testing.

- Tests of controls performed by the service auditor provide sufficient appropriate audit evidence to support the user auditor's risk assessment.

AUD 4
Internal Control
Reports &
Communications

4.01 GAAS Financial Statement Audit

Overview

Engagement Types

Auditors have a responsibility to communicate with management and those charged with their clients' governance regarding certain internal control (I/C) matters. Those responsibilities vary, depending on the nature of the engagement.

Under GAAS

1. An auditor of nonissuers is required to communicate identified weaknesses in I/C. (AU-C 265)

2. An auditor may be engaged to perform an examination of I/C as of a specified date or for a period of time. (AU-C 940)

   o Such an engagement may only be accepted when integrated with an audit of the entity's F/S.

   o As a result of such an engagement, the auditor issues a report on the effectiveness of the entity's I/C.

Under PCAOB

3. An auditor of issuers is required to report on management's assertion regarding the effectiveness of I/C as of a specified date. (AS 2201)

GAAS I/C Reports		PCAOB
1. Financial Statement Audit	2. Integrated Audit	3. PCAOB Audit
GAAS (AU-C 265)	GAAS (AU-C 940) **"Audited** in accordance with GAAS"	PCAOB AS 2201 **"Audited** in accordance with standards of the PCAOB"
Controls → Rely on	All Controls	All Controls
No Opinion → Disclaimer	Opinion → Mgt maintained effective I/C over financial reporting	Opinion → Mgt maintained effective I/C over financial reporting
Letter of Recommendation (LOR)		

GAAS I/C Reports		PCAOB
1. Financial Statement Audit	2. Integrated Audit	3. PCAOB Audit
Purpose of audit = opinion on F/S but not on I/Cs	*Inherent limitations* that I/C may not prevent/detect & correct misstatements *Projection* subject to risks	*Inherent limitations* that I/C may not prevent/detect misstatements *Projection* subject to risks
Definition of significant deficiency & material weakness		
Identify significant deficiency & Material Weaknesses		
Limited use statement (No general public viewing – giving it to management. Limited because you only looked at controls you rely on).	For General Distribution	For General Distribution

GAAS I/C Reports		PCAOB
1. Financial Statement Audit	2. Integrated Audit	3. PCAOB Audit
Written Comm Req'd to Mgt: govn (w/i 60 days)	**To Mgt chrgd governance (by report release date)**	**To Mgt To audit comm (by report release date)**
Control deficiency: YES** NO	YES NO (60 days)	YES NO
Significant deficiency: YES YES	YES YES	YES YES
Material weakness: YES YES	YES YES	YES YES
*** If auditor thinks it warrants attention*		

Internal Control Reports for a F/S Audit under GAAS

The auditor obtains an understanding of a client's I/C as part of the understanding of the entity and its environment, for the purpose of assessing the risk of material misstatement (RMM) of the F/S and to determine the nature, timing, and extent of further audit procedures. During the course of obtaining that understanding, the auditor may become aware of deficiencies in I/C.

AU-C 265 requires the auditor to communicate to those charged with governance and management deficiencies in I/C that, in the auditor's judgment, are sufficiently important to merit their attention.

Control Deficiencies

A deficiency in I/C exists when the *design or operation* of a control does not allow management or employees, in the normal course of performing their assigned functions, to prevent, or detect and correct misstatements on a timely basis.

- A deficiency in **design** occurs when either a needed control has not been put into place, or a control that has been put into place is not designed to mitigate the risk it was intended to address.

- A deficiency in **operation** occurs when either a well-designed control is not operating as designed or the individual responsible for performing the control lacks the authority or ability to perform it effectively.

In addition to deficiencies identified while the auditor is obtaining an understanding of I/C, the auditor may identify control deficiencies during risk assessment. When an auditor assesses RMM as moderate to high for a management assertion, it implies that either:

- Inherent risk is high and of a nature that an effective control could not be designed and effectively put into operation.

- Inherent risk is high and of a nature that an effective control could be designed and effectively put into operation, but that is not the case due to a deficiency in design or operation.

When an auditor becomes aware of deficiencies in I/C, the auditor will evaluate them to determine if they amount to material weaknesses or significant deficiencies.

- A **material weakness** is a deficiency, or combination of deficiencies, in I/C, such that there is a **reasonable possibility** that a **material misstatement** of the entity's F/S will not be prevented, or detected and corrected, on a timely basis.

  o A reasonable possibility exists if the likelihood of an event is either reasonably possible or probable.

- A **significant deficiency** is a deficiency, or combination of deficiencies, in I/C that is less severe than a material weakness yet important enough to merit attention by those charged with governance.

There are **two factors** to consider when evaluating a control deficiency to determine if it is a significant deficiency or a material weakness (see table below):

- The **probability** (likelihood) that a control deficiency will result in a misstatement to the F/S.

- The **magnitude** of a misstatement that might occur as a result of the deficiency.

Evaluation of Control Deficiencies		
Probability of Possible Misstatement	**Magnitude**	
	Immaterial	Material
Remotely possible	Minor control deficiency	Possible significant deficiency*

Reasonably possible	Possible significant deficiency*	Material weakness
Probable		

The auditor must use their judgment in determining whether a control deficiency, individually or in combination with others, is a significant deficiency or material weakness.

If an auditor determines that a deficiency, or combination of deficiencies, is not a material weakness, the auditor should consider if prudent officials, having the same knowledge of the facts and circumstances, would draw the same conclusion.

Material weaknesses are also indicated by:

- Ineffective oversight by those charged with governance

- Restatements of prior years' F/S due to material misstatements due to error or fraud

- Material misstatements that would have not been detected by the company's I/C, but were identified by the auditor

- Fraud by senior management, whether material or immaterial

Communicating I/C Related Matters Identified in an Audit of F/S (Nonissuers)

Although identifying such deficiencies is not an objective of the audit, the auditor must notify the client, management and those charged with governance (board, audit committee), **in writing**, of any significant deficiencies or material weaknesses that come to the auditor's attention. This requirement includes significant deficiencies and material weaknesses that were previously communicated and have not yet been resolved.

The communication is best made by the *report release date*, but should be made no later than **60 days** after the report release date. They may also be communicated during the audit, if the auditor sees fit. The **written communication** should:

- State that the *purpose of the audit* was to report on the F/S and not to provide assurance on the effectiveness of I/C.

- Indicate that the auditor is *not expressing an opinion* on the effectiveness of I/C.

- State that the auditor's consideration of I/C was *not designed to identify all* significant deficiencies or material weaknesses.

- Include the *definition of material weaknesses* and, if applicable, significant deficiencies.

- *Identify* which *matters* are considered significant deficiencies and material weaknesses.

- State that the communication is intended solely for management, those charged with governance, and others within the organization, and is *not* intended for any others (**Limited Use statement**).

A written report indicating that *no material weaknesses* were identified may be issued; however, a written report indicating that *no significant deficiencies* were identified may not be issued.

The auditor is also required to provide the following to an appropriate level of management on a timely basis:

- A written communication indicating significant deficiencies and material weaknesses that the auditor intends to communicate to the audit committee or those charged with governance.

- A written or oral communication indicating other deficiencies in I/C that:

  o Have not been communicated to management by others

  o Are sufficiently important to merit management's attention

Written Communication to Management and Those Charged with Governance
(For communicating I/C-related matters identified in a F/S audit)

INTERNAL CONTROL REPORT

To: Management, the Audit Committee and the Board of Directors (Governance)

(Date: no later than **60 days** after the report release date)

In planning and performing our audit of the financial statements of ABC Company as of and for the year ended December 31, 20XX, in accordance with auditing standards generally accepted in the United States of America, we considered ABC Company's internal control over financial reporting (internal control) as a basis for designing our auditing procedures that are appropriate in the circumstances for the purpose of expressing our opinion on the financial statements, but not for the purpose of expressing an opinion on the effectiveness of the Company's internal control. Accordingly, we do not express an opinion on the effectiveness of the Company's internal control.

Our consideration of internal control was for the limited purpose described in the preceding paragraph and was not designed to identify all deficiencies in internal control that might be significant deficiencies or material weaknesses and therefore, significant deficiencies or material weaknesses may exist that were not identified. However, as discussed below, we identified certain deficiencies in internal control that we consider to be *material weaknesses* [*and other deficiencies that we consider to be* significant deficiencies].

A deficiency in internal control exists when the design or operation of a control does not allow management or employees, in the normal course of performing their assigned functions, to prevent, or detect and correct, misstatements on a timely basis. A material weakness is a deficiency, or a combination of deficiencies, in internal control, such that there is a reasonable possibility that a material misstatement of the entity's financial statements will not be prevented, or detected and corrected, on a timely basis. We consider the following deficiencies to be material weaknesses in internal control:

[Describe the material weaknesses that were identified and an explanation of their potential effects.]

[A significant deficiency is a deficiency, or combinations of deficiencies, in internal control that is less severe than a material weakness, yet important enough to merit attention by those charged with governance. We consider the following deficiencies in the Company's internal control to be significant deficiencies.]

[Describe the significant deficiencies that were identified and an explanation of their potential effects.]

This communication is intended solely for the information and use of management, [identify the body or individuals charged with governance], others within the organization, and [identify any specified governmental authorities to which the auditor is required to report] and is not intended to be, and should not be used by anyone other than these specified parties.

L. Rosenthal, CPA
Santa Monica, CA
April 8, 20XX

4.02 GAAS Integrated Audit

Overview

AU-C 940[1] provides guidance to be applied by the auditor of a **nonissuer** when accepting an engagement to report on the entity's internal control over financial reporting (ICFR). Such an engagement is **optional** for a **nonissuer**; however, PCAOB standards require the auditor of an issuer to perform an *integrated audit* and report on ICFR.

Objectives

The objectives of an audit of ICFR are to:

- Obtain **reasonable assurance** about whether **material weaknesses** exist (as of the date of management's assessment)
  - ICFR cannot be effective if one or more material weaknesses exist.
  - The auditor is not required to search for I/C deficiencies that are not material weaknesses.
  - A material weakness may exist even though the F/S are not materially misstated.
- Express an opinion as to the effectiveness of ICFR
- Communicate the findings to management and those charged with governance

Management's Written Assessment

The auditor must obtain management's written assessment as to the effectiveness of ICFR. In performing the examination, the auditor uses the same criteria management uses in evaluating the effectiveness of ICFR.

The **refusal** to provide such assessment is a **scope limitation** that cannot be overcome. The auditor should **withdraw** from the integrated engagement if allowed to do so by law or regulation. If that is not an option, the auditor will issue a **disclaimer** of opinion.

Timing

The auditor will normally examine the effectiveness of ICFR as of the end of the entity's fiscal year. The examination may be as of a different date, which should correspond to the date of the balance sheet being audited. The examination may be for the period of time covered by the financial statements (F/S) being audited. In all cases, the examination should only be performed in conjunction with the audit of the entity's F/S, and should use of the same measure of materiality.

---

[1] *An Audit of Internal Control Over Financial Reporting (ICFR) that is Integrated with an Audit of Financial Statements*

Performance Requirements

Planning

An integrated audit is planned and performed to meet the objectives of *both* the audit of the entity's F/S and the examination of the entity's ICFR. As a result, tests of controls should be designed to provide sufficient appropriate evidence to support:

- The auditor's opinion on the effectiveness of ICFR (as of the date specified in management's assessment of ICFR).

- The degree to which the auditor has decided to rely on the entity's I/C to reduce the assessed risk of material misstatement.

The planning of the examination considers the auditor's risk assessment, used to identify significant accounts and disclosures, as well as relevant assertions. The auditor should also evaluate whether controls address risks of fraud, including those identified in the discussion among the audit engagement team.

- As is true in the audit, the auditor pays more attention to those areas representing greater risk.

- Controls that, even if deficient, would not cause at least a reasonable possibility of a material misstatement occurring do not need to be tested.

Top-Down Approach

In both the audit of the F/S and the examination of I/C, the auditor uses a top-down approach:

- First, the auditor assesses risk at the **financial statement level.**

  - Incorporates use of the auditor's overall understanding of the risks of material misstatement.

  - Concentrates on **entity level controls,** including controls over:

    - The control environment

    - Management override

    - Company's risk assessment process

    - Monitoring results

    - Assessing business risk

    - Monitoring the activities of the audit committee

    - The period-end financial reporting process

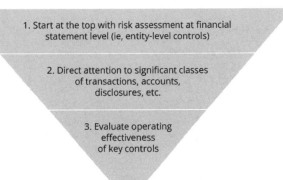

1. Start at the top with risk assessment at financial statement level (ie, entity-level controls)

2. Direct attention to significant classes of transactions, accounts, disclosures, etc.

3. Evaluate operating effectiveness of key controls

- Next, the auditor directs attention to significant classes of transactions, accounts, and disclosures and their **relevant assertions**.

  - Attention is directed to accounts, disclosures, and assertions that present a greater than remote possibility of material misstatement.

- The understanding of risks in the entity's processes is verified, often through the performance of **walkthroughs.** Walkthroughs may include reperformance or recalculation, inquiry, inspection of documents, and observation (**RIIO**).

- From there, the auditor identifies potential deficiencies in the design or operation of key controls that would mitigate the risk that relevant assertions would not be achieved. Therefore, controls that address risks of material misstatement in each of the relevant assertions are selected for testing:

  - The auditor performs tests of the effectiveness of both the design and the operation of controls.

  - Testing is designed to provide evidence that is sufficient and appropriate for the degree of risk represented by a potential deficiency.

  - The auditor evaluates the **severity** of identified deficiencies, which consists of their **magnitude** and **probability:**

    - A material weakness has the potential of causing a **material** misstatement to the F/S.

    - A material weakness indicates at least a **reasonable possibility** that controls will not prevent the misstatement, nor detect and correct it on a timely basis.

Forming an Opinion

The auditor *forms an opinion* on the effectiveness of ICFR through the consideration of various factors, including:

- Tests of controls performed for the examination of ICFR, as well as any additional tests of controls performed in relation to the audit of the F/S

- Misstatements detected during the audit of the F/S

- Deficiencies identified

- Reports issued by internal auditors

- The results of substantive procedures performed in the audit of the F/S, including:

  - The auditor's risk assessment

  - Findings related to noncompliance with applicable laws and regulations

  - Related party transactions and complex or unusual transactions

  - Indications of management bias in the selection of accounting principles or in the development of estimates

  - The nature and extent of misstatements detected

Management's Report and Written Representations

Once the auditor has formed an opinion on the effectiveness of the entity's ICFR, they will evaluate management's report, which will accompany the auditor's report. **Management's report** should contain:

- Acknowledgment of management's responsibility for I/C

- A description of what was examined (eg, controls related to preparing F/S in accordance with GAAP)

- Identification of the criteria used to evaluate I/C, such as those established by the report of the Committed of Sponsoring Organizations of the Treadway Commission (COSO) entitled *Internal Control – Integrated Framework*

- Management's assessment regarding the effectiveness of the entity's I/C

- A description of any material weaknesses

- The date of the assessment

The auditor should also obtain **written representations** from management, some of which will repeat items in the report. Representations will indicate:

- Management's responsibility for I/C

- That management has performed an assessment of the entity's ICFR based on a set of criteria that is identified

- That management's assessment did not incorporate the results of procedures performed by the auditor

- Management's assessment of ICFR as of a specified date

- That management has informed the auditor of all deficiencies in ICFR, whether deficiencies in design or operation, separately indicating significant deficiencies and material weaknesses

- Any fraud either resulting in a material misstatement to the F/S or involving senior management, management, or other employees involved in ICFR, even if the fraud does not result in a material misstatement to the F/S

- Whether significant deficiencies and material weaknesses previously identified have been resolved, identifying those that have not

- Whether any changes were made to ICFR after the date being reported on, including any corrective action taken by management

Communication

At the conclusion of the engagement, the auditor communicates certain matters to management and those charged with governance. The communication includes **all material weaknesses** and **significant deficiencies** identified by the auditor, including those that may have been identified in a previous period but have not yet been corrected. It should be in writing and made by the date on which the auditor's report is released.

The auditor also issues a written report to management within **60 days** of the report release date. It includes all deficiencies, including those that are not material weaknesses or significant deficiencies.

Unmodified Report Requirements

The auditor issues a report on I/C that includes certain elements:

- A title that includes the word "independent"

- An appropriate addressee
- The first section should be titled *"Opinion on Internal Control Over Financial Reporting."* It should contain:
  - The identity of the entity whose ICFR was audited
  - An indication that ICFR has been audited
  - The date as of which the ICFR was assessed
  - The criteria against which ICFR was measured
  - Auditor's opinion on ICFR
- The second section should be titled *"Basis for Opinion."* It should:
  - State that the audit was conducted in accordance with U.S. GAAS
  - Refer to the auditor's responsibility section of the report
  - State that the auditor is required to be independent and meet other relevant ethical requirements
  - State that the auditor believes the audit evidence obtained is sufficient and appropriate to provide a basis for the opinion
- A section with the heading *"Responsibilities of Management for Internal Control Over Financial Reporting"* that indicates management's responsibility for:
  - The design, implementation, and maintenance of effective ICFR
  - Its assessment of the effectiveness of ICFR
  - Providing management's report on ICFR
- A section with the heading "Auditor's Responsibilities for the Audit of Internal Control Over Financial Reporting" that indicates:
  - The objectives of the auditor to obtain reasonable assurance about whether effective ICFR was maintained in all material respects and to express an opinion and report on ICFR
  - That reasonable assurance is a high level of assurance but is not absolute assurance and therefore is not a guarantee that an audit of ICFR conducted in accordance with GAAS will always detect a material weakness when it exists
  - That, in performing an audit of ICFR in accordance with GAAS, the auditor's responsibilities are to:
    - Exercise professional judgment and maintain professional skepticism throughout the audit
    - Obtain an understanding of ICFR, assess the risks that a material weakness exists, and test and evaluate the design and operating effectiveness of ICFR based on the assessed risk
- A section with an appropriate heading such as *"Definition and Inherent Limitations of Internal Control Over Financial Reporting"* that includes the definition of I/C with an indication of its inherent limitations

- The audit firm's signature, the city and state in which the report is issued, and the date of the report, which should be no earlier than the date on which sufficient appropriate audit evidence is obtained

Unmodified Opinion on I/C (Nonissuer)

Independent Auditor's Report

To: Management, the Audit Committee and the Board of Directors

Report on Internal Control Over Financial Reporting

Opinion on Internal Control Over Financial Reporting

We have **audited** Asher Company's internal control over financial reporting as of December 31, 20XX, based on [identify criteria, such as those established in Internal Control—Integrated Framework issued by the Committee of Sponsoring Organizations of the Treadway Commission (COSO)]. In our opinion, Asher Company maintained, in all material respects, effective internal control over financial reporting as of December 21, 20XX, based on [identify criteria].

We also have audited, in accordance with auditing standards generally accepted in the United States of America (GAAS), the [*identify financial statements*] of Asher Company, and our report dated [*date of report, which should be the same as the date of the report on the audit of ICFR*] expressed [*include nature of opinion*].

Basis for Opinion

We conducted our audit in accordance with GAAS. Our responsibilities under those standards are further described in the Auditor's Responsibilities for the Audit of Internal Control Over Financial Reporting section of our report. We are required to be independent of Asher Company and to meet our other ethical responsibilities, in accordance with the relevant ethical requirements relating to our audit. We believe that the audit evidence we have obtained is sufficient and appropriate to provide a basis for our audit opinion.

Responsibilities of Management for Internal Control Over Financial Reporting

Management is responsible for designing, implementing, and maintaining effective internal control over financial reporting, and for its assessment about the effectiveness of internal control over financial reporting, included in the accompanying [*title of management's report*].

Auditor's Responsibilities for the Audit of Internal Control Over Financial Reporting

Our objectives are to obtain reasonable assurance about whether effective internal control over financial reporting was maintained in all material respects and to issue an auditor's report that includes our opinion on internal control over financial reporting. Reasonable assurance is a high level of assurance but is not absolute assurance and therefore is not a guarantee that an audit of internal control over financial reporting conducted in accordance with GAAS will always detect a material weakness when it exists.

In performing an audit of internal control over financial reporting in accordance with GAAS, we:

- Exercise professional judgment and maintain professional skepticism throughout the audit.
- Obtain an understanding of internal control over financial reporting, assess the risks that a material weakness exists, and test and evaluate the design and operating effectiveness of internal control over financial reporting based on the assessed risk.

Definition and Inherent Limitations of Internal Control Over Financial Reporting

An entity's internal control over financial reporting is a process effected by those charged with governance, management, and other personnel, designed to provide reasonable assurance regarding the preparation of reliable financial statements in accordance with [*applicable financial reporting framework, such as accounting principles generally accepted in the United States of America*]. An entity's internal control over financial reporting includes those policies and procedures that (1) pertain to the maintenance of records that, in reasonable detail, accurately and fairly reflect the transactions and dispositions of the assets of the company; (2) provide reasonable assurance that transactions are recorded as necessary to permit preparation of financial statements in accordance with [*the applicable financial reporting framework indicated above*], and that receipts and expenditures of the entity are being made only in accordance with authorizations of management and those charged with governance; and (3) provide reasonable assurance regarding prevention, or timely detection and correction of unauthorized acquisition, use, or disposition of the entity's assets that could have a material effect on the financial statements.

Because of its inherent limitations, internal control over financial reporting may not prevent, or detect and correct misstatements. Also, projections of any assessment of the effectiveness to future periods are subject to the risk that controls may become inadequate because of changes in conditions, or that the degree of compliance with the policies or procedures may deteriorate.

Report on Other Legal and Regulatory Requirements

[*The form and content of this section of the auditor's report would vary depending on the nature of the auditor's other reporting responsibilities.*]

[*Signature of the auditor's firm*]

Combined Unmodified Opinion on I/C and an Unmodified Opinion on F/S (Nonissuer)

Independent Auditor's Report

To: Management, the Audit Committee and the Board of Directors (Governance)

Report on the Financial Statements and Internal Control

Opinions on the Financial Statements and Internal Control Over Financial Reporting

We have **audited the financial statements** of Roger Company, which comprise the balance sheet as of December 31, 20XX, and the related statements of income, changes in stockholders' equity, and cash flows for the year then ended, and the related notes to the financial statements. In our **opinion**, the accompanying financial statements present fairly, in all material respects, the financial position of Roger Company as of December 31, 20XX, and the results of its operations and its cash flows for the year then ended in accordance with accounting principles generally accepted in the United States of America.

We also have **audited Roger Company's internal control over financial reporting** as of December 31, 20XX, based on *[identify criteria]*. In our **opinion**, Roger Company maintained, in all material respects, effective internal control over financial reporting as of December 31, 20XX, based on *[identify criteria]*.

Basis for Opinions

We conducted our audits in accordance with auditing standards generally accepted in the United States of America (GAAS). Our responsibilities under those standards are further described in the Auditor's Responsibilities for the Audits of the Financial Statements and Internal Control Over Financial Reporting section of our report. We are required to be independent of Roger Company and to meet our other ethical responsibilities, in accordance with the relevant ethical requirements relating to our audits. We believe that the audit evidence we have obtained is sufficient and appropriate to provide a basis for our audit opinions.

Responsibilities of Management for the Financial Statements and Internal Control Over Financial Reporting

Management is responsible for the preparation and fair presentation of the financial statements in accordance with accounting principles generally accepted in the United States of America, and for the design, implementation, and maintenance of effective internal control over financial reporting relevant to the preparation and fair presentation of financial statements that are free from material misstatement, whether due to fraud or error. Management is also responsible for its assessment about the effectiveness of internal control over financial reporting, included in the accompanying *[title of management's report]*.

In preparing the financial statements, management is required to evaluate whether there are conditions or events, considered in the aggregate, that raise substantial doubt about Roger Company's ability to continue as a going concern *[insert the time period set by the applicable financial reporting framework]*.

Auditor's Responsibilities for the Audits of the Financial Statements and Internal Control Over Financial Reporting

Our objectives are to obtain reasonable assurance about whether the financial statements as a whole are free from material misstatement, whether due to fraud or error, and about whether effective internal control over financial reporting was maintained in all material respects, and to issue an auditor's report that includes our opinions.

Reasonable assurance is a high level of assurance but is not absolute assurance and therefore is not a guarantee that an audit of financial statements or an audit of internal control over financial reporting conducted in accordance with GAAS will always detect a material misstatement or a material weakness when it exists. The risk of not detecting a material misstatement resulting from fraud is higher than for one resulting from error, as fraud may involve collusion, forgery, intentional omissions, misrepresentations, or the override of internal control. Misstatements are considered to be material if there is a substantial likelihood that, individually or in the aggregate, they would influence the judgment made by a reasonable user based on the financial statements.

In performing an audit of financial statements and an audit of internal control over financial reporting in accordance with GAAS, we:

- Exercise professional judgment and maintain professional skepticism throughout the audits

- Identify and assess the risks of material misstatement of the financial statements, whether due to fraud or error, and design and perform audit procedures responsive to those risks. Such procedures include examining, on a test basis, evidence regarding the amounts and disclosures in the financial statements.
- Obtain an understanding of internal control relevant to the statement audit in order to design audit procedures that are appropriate in the circumstances.
- Obtain an understanding of internal control over financial reporting relevant to the audit of internal control over financial reporting, assess the risks that a material weakness exists, and test and evaluate the design and operating effectiveness of internal control over financial reporting based on the assessed risk.
- Evaluate the appropriateness of accounting policies used and the reasonableness of significant accounting estimates made by management, as well as evaluate the overall presentation of the financial statements.
- Conclude whether, in our judgment, there are conditions or events, considered in the aggregate, that raise substantial doubt about Roger Company's ability to continue as a going concern for a reasonable period of time.

We are required to communicate with those charged with governance regarding, among other matters, the planned scope and timing of the audit, significant audit findings, and certain internal control-related matters that we identified during the financial statement audit.

Definitions and Inherent Limitations of Internal Control Over Financial Reporting

An entity's internal control over financial reporting is a process effected by those charged with governance, management, and other personnel, designed to provide reasonable assurance regarding the preparation of reliable financial statements in accordance with accounting principles generally accepted in the United States of America. An entity's internal control over financial reporting includes those policies and procedures that (1) pertain to the maintenance of records that, in reasonable detail, accurately and fairly reflect the transactions and dispositions of the assets of the entity; (2) provide reasonable assurance that transactions are recorded as necessary to permit preparation of financial statements in accordance with accounting principles generally accepted in the United States of America, and that receipts and expenditures of the entity are being made only in accordance with authorizations of management and those charged with governance; and (3) provide reasonable assurance regarding prevention, or timely detection and correction of unauthorized acquisition, use, or disposition of the entity's assets that could have a material effect on the financial statements.

Because of its inherent limitations, internal control over financial reporting may not prevent, or detect and correct, misstatements. Also, projections of any assessment of effectiveness to future periods are subject to the risk that controls may become inadequate because of changes in conditions, or that the degree of compliance with the policies or procedures may deteriorate.

Report on Other Legal and Regulatory Requirements
[The form and content of this section of the auditor's report would vary depending on the nature of the auditor's other reporting responsibilities.]

[Signature of the auditor's firm]
[City and state where the auditor's report is issued]
[Date of the auditor's report]

Modified Reports

There are several reasons that an auditor's report on ICFR may be modified. Examples include:

- The identification of material weaknesses

- An incomplete or improper management report

- A scope limitation

- Reference to the report of a component auditor

- The inclusion of other information in management's report

Material Weaknesses

Unless there is a limitation on the scope of the engagement, when material weaknesses are identified, the auditor will express an **adverse opinion** on the effectiveness of an entity's ICFR. The report will include a definition of a material weakness and a statement that one or more material weaknesses have been identified.

- The report will also identify material weaknesses described in management's assessment of ICFR.
- When material weaknesses identified by the auditor are not included in management's assessment, the report will be modified to indicate as much.

The auditor will also determine the impact, if any, of the material weakness on the opinion on the F/S. It should be disclosed whether the opinion has been affected in a separate paragraph within the Adverse Opinion on ICFR section of the report.

When one or more material weaknesses exist, the "Basis for Adverse Opinion on Internal Control Over Financial Reporting" section should:

- Define a material weakness
- State that one or more material weaknesses have been identified and an identify the material weaknesses described in management's assessment about ICFR

Incomplete or Incorrect Management Report

Management's report may be missing one or more of the elements required to be included by auditing standards. When this is the case, the auditor will request that management revise the report. If management refuses to do so, the auditor will include an *other-matter* paragraph describing the reason the auditor considers the report deficient.

Scope Limitations

When a scope limitation is imposed on the auditor after acceptance of the engagement, the auditor should either *withdraw* from the engagement or express a *disclaimer of opinion*. If the scope limitation consists of the client's refusal to provide an assertion regarding the effectiveness of ICFR, the auditor is required to withdraw and will only issue a disclaimer if not allowed to withdraw as a result of law or regulation.

Making Reference to the Report of a Component Auditor

When an entity includes one or more components, the ICFR of which was audited by a component auditor, the auditor responsible for the report, the engagement auditor, will use the same criteria in determining whether or not to refer to the report of the component auditor as used when reporting on the audit of group F/S.

Reference should not be made to a component auditor unless the engagement auditor is satisfied that the component auditor conducted an audit in accordance with GAAS, or with the provisions of the PCAOB, if appropriate; and that the component auditor has issued a report on ICFR that is not restricted.

Additional Information in Management's Report

In some circumstances, management's report, or the document containing management's report, will also include additional information. When this is the case, the auditor should:

- Read the additional information to identify material inconsistencies with management's report and remain alert for material misstatements of fact.

- If the auditor becomes aware of a material inconsistency or material misstatement of fact, the auditor should request that management correct the information, and:

  o If management agrees, determine that the correction has been made.

  o If management refuses, communicate the matter to those charged with governance and request that the correction be made. If the correction is still not made, the auditor should:

    - Consider the implications for the auditor's report and communicate to those charged with governance about how the auditor plans to address the material inconsistency or material misstatement of fact

    - Withhold the auditor's report

    - Withdraw from the engagement, if possible

    - When the additional information is included in management's report and no material inconsistencies or material misstatements of fact are identified, the auditor should disclaim an opinion, in an other-matter paragraph, on the additional information.

4.03 PCAOB Audit

Overview

When auditing the financial statements (F/S) of entities that report to the SEC under the 1934 act (issuers) and are subject to the requirements of the Public Company Accounting Oversight Board (**PCAOB**), the auditor will have to also perform an audit of internal control over financial reporting (**ICFR**) that is *Integrated* with an audit of F/S in order to determine that management has complied with Rules 404a & b of the Sarbanes-Oxley Act of 2002. (AS 2201)

- Rule 404a requires the annual report to include a report on internal control (I/C) indicating management's responsibility for I/C and management's assessment of I/C's effectiveness.

- Rule 404b requires the auditor to report on management's assessment of I/C.

  - The auditor does not report on the efficiency or the effectiveness of I/C but reports on management's assessment of it.

  - The Act does not specify a date by which the auditor's report is to be submitted.

The standards for audits of ICFR under AU-C 940 were written to apply the guidance in PCAOB AS 2201 to nonissuers. The requirements and guidance are almost identical and, as a result, the information provided will reflect only those **differences** between AS 2201 and AU-C 940.

One major difference is that AS 2201 is a *requirement* and auditors of issuers are required to perform an examination of I/C that is integrated with a financial statement audit, which expresses an opinion as of the date of the F/S. An examination under GAAS, however, is performed only if the auditor is engaged to do so.

While most requirements are the same, under AS 2201, an auditor has greater responsibilities for the **communication** of I/C deficiencies:

- **Material weaknesses** must be communicated to management and the audit committee in writing prior to the issuance of the auditor's report on ICFR.

- **Significant deficiencies** identified by the auditor must also be communicated in writing to the audit committee prior to the issuance of the auditor's report on I/C.

- The auditor should also communicate **control deficiencies** that are not significant deficiencies or material weaknesses to management in writing on a timely basis, prior to the issuance of the audit report on I/C.

AS 2201 also provides slightly different definitions of control deficiencies and material weaknesses.

- AS 2201 indicates that a control deficiency "exists when the design or operation of a control does not allow management or employees, in the normal course of performing their assigned functions, to prevent or detect misstatements on a timely basis," while GAAS indicates a control deficiency as existing "when the design or operation of a control does not allow management or employees, in the normal course of performing their assigned functions, to prevent, or detect **and correct**, misstatements on a timely basis."

- The definition of a *material weakness* is also different for the same reason.

Unqualified Opinion on ICFR
(Used when separate reports are issued on F/S and I/C in a PCAOB audit.)

REPORT OF INDEPENDENT REGISTERED PUBLIC ACCOUNTING FIRM ON
INTERNAL CONTROL OVER FINANCIAL REPORTING

To the shareholders and the board of directors of ABC, Inc.

Opinion on Internal Control over Financial Reporting

We have **audited** ABC, Inc.'s internal control over financial reporting **as of** January 31, 20X8, based on criteria established in *Internal Control–Integrated Framework* issued by the Committee of Sponsoring Organizations of the Treadway Commission (the COSO criteria). In our opinion, the Company maintained, in all material respects, effective internal control over financial reporting as of December 31, 20X8, based on the COSO criteria.

We also have audited, in accordance with the standards of the Public Company Accounting Oversight Board (United States) ("PCAOB"), the consolidated balance sheets of ABC, Inc. as of January 31, 20X8 and 20X7, and the related consolidated statements of income, shareholders' equity, and cash flows for each of the three years in the period ended January 31, 20X8 and our report dated March 26, 20X8 expressed an unqualified opinion thereon.

Basis for Opinion

ABC Inc.'s management is responsible for maintaining effective internal control over financial reporting, and for its assessment of the effectiveness of internal control over financial reporting, included in the accompanying [*title of management's report*]. Our responsibility is to express an opinion on the Company's internal control over financial reporting based on our audit. We are a public accounting firm registered with the Public Company Accounting Oversight Board (United States) ("PCAOB") and are required to be independent with respect to the Company in accordance with the U.S. federal securities laws and the applicable rules and regulations of the Securities and Exchange Commission and the PCAOB.

We conducted our audit in accordance with the standards of the PCAOB. Those standards require that we plan and perform the audit to obtain reasonable assurance about whether effective internal control over financial reporting was maintained in all material respects.

Our audit of internal control over financial reporting included obtaining an understanding of internal control over financial reporting, assessing the risk that a material weakness exists, and testing and evaluating the design and operating effectiveness of internal control based on the assessed risk. Our audit also included performing such other procedures as we considered necessary in the circumstances. We believe that our audit provides a reasonable basis for our opinion.

Definition and Limitations of Internal Control Over Financial Reporting

A company's internal control over financial reporting is a process designed to provide reasonable assurance regarding the reliability of financial reporting and the preparation of financial statements for external purposes in accordance with generally accepted accounting principles. A company's internal control over financial reporting includes those policies and procedures that (1) pertain to the maintenance of records that, in reasonable detail, accurately and fairly reflect the transactions and dispositions of the assets of the company; (2) provide reasonable assurance that transactions are recorded as necessary to permit preparation of financial statements in accordance with generally accepted accounting principles, and that receipts and expenditures of the company are being made only in accordance with authorizations of management and directors of the company; and (3) provide reasonable assurance regarding prevention or timely detection of unauthorized acquisition, use, or disposition of the company's assets that could have a material effect on the financial statements.

Because of its inherent limitations, internal control over financial reporting may not prevent or detect misstatements. Also, projections of any evaluation of effectiveness to future periods are subject to the risk that controls may become inadequate because of changes in conditions, or that the degree of compliance with the policies or procedures may deteriorate.

W. Philipp, CPAs
SF, CA
March 26, 20X8

Combined Unmodified Audit Report on F/S and Unqualified I/C opinion (Issuer)

REPORT OF INDEPENDENT REGISTERED PUBLIC ACCOUNTING FIRM

To the shareholders and the board of directors of Roger Company

Opinions on the Financial Statements and Internal Control over Financial Reporting

We have **audited** the accompanying balance sheets of Roger Company (the "Company") as of December 31, 20X8 and 20X7, and the related statements of income, stockholders' equity and comprehensive income, and cash flows for each of the years in the three-year period ended December 31, 20X8, and the related notes [*and schedules*] (collectively referred to as the "financial statements"). **We also have audited the Company's internal control over financial reporting as of December 31, 20X8, based on criteria established in Internal Control – Integrated Framework issued by COSO.**

In our opinion, the financial statements referred to above present fairly, in all material respects, the financial position of the Company as of December 31, 20X8 and 20X7, and the results of its operations and its cash flows for each of the years in the three-year period ended December 31, 20X8 in conformity with accounting principles generally accepted in the United States of America. **Also in our opinion, the Company maintained, in all material respects, effective internal control over financial reporting as of December 31, 20X8, based on criteria established in Internal Control – Integrated Framework issued by COSO.**

Basis for Opinion

The Company's management is responsible for these financial statements, **for maintaining effective internal control over financial reporting, and for its assessment of the effectiveness of internal control over financial reporting, included in the accompanying [*title of management's report*].** Our responsibility is to express an opinion on the Company's financial statements **and an opinion on the Company's internal control over financial reporting based on our audits.** We are a public accounting firm registered with the Public Company Accounting Oversight Board (United States) ("PCAOB") and are required to be independent with respect to the Company in accordance with the U.S. federal securities laws and the applicable rules and regulations of the Securities and Exchange Commission and the PCAOB.

We conducted our audits in accordance with the standards of the PCAOB. Those standards require that we plan and perform the audits to obtain reasonable assurance about whether the financial statements are free of material misstatement, whether due to error or fraud, **and whether effective internal control over financial reporting was maintained in all material respects.**

Our audits of the financial statements included performing procedures to assess the risks of material misstatement of the financial statements, whether due to error or fraud, and performing procedures that respond to those risks. Such procedures included examining, on a test basis, evidence regarding the amounts and disclosures in the financial statements. Our audits also included evaluating the accounting principles used and significant estimates made by management, as well as evaluating the overall presentation of the financial statements. *Our audit of internal control over financial reporting included obtaining an understanding of internal control over financial reporting, assessing the risk that a material weakness exists, and testing and evaluating the design and operating effectiveness of internal control based on the assessed risk. Our audits also included performing such other procedures as we considered necessary in the circumstances.* We believe that our audits provide a reasonable basis for our opinions.

Definition and Limitations of Internal Control Over Financial Reporting

A company's internal control over financial reporting is a process designed to provide reasonable assurance regarding the reliability of financial reporting and the preparation of financial statements for external purposes in accordance with generally accepted accounting principles. A company's internal control over financial reporting includes those policies and procedures that (1) pertain to the maintenance of records that, in reasonable detail, accurately and fairly reflect the transactions and dispositions of the assets of the company; (2) provide reasonable assurance that transactions are recorded as necessary to permit preparation of financial statements in accordance with generally accepted accounting principles, and that receipts and expenditures of the company are being made only in accordance with authorizations of management and directors of the company; and (3) provide reasonable assurance regarding prevention or timely detection of unauthorized acquisition, use, or disposition of the company's assets that could have a material effect on the financial statements.

Because of its inherent limitations, internal control over financial reporting may not prevent or detect misstatements. Also, projections of any evaluation of effectiveness to future periods are subject to the risk that controls may become inadequate because of changes in conditions, or that the degree of compliance with the policies or procedures may deteriorate.

Critical Audit Matters [if applicable]

[Include critical audit matters]

Aaron & Co. CPAs
We have served as the Company's auditor since 20X1.
San Francisco, California, United States of America
February 20X9

Previously Reported Weaknesses under AS 6115

Under PCAOB AS 6115, the auditor of an issuer may be engaged to report on whether a previously reported *I/C weakness* continues to exist. In such an engagement, the auditor obtains reasonable assurance about whether the weakness continues to exist as of a date specified by management and issues a report to that effect.

The standards for such an engagement involve:

- Planning the engagement.

- Obtaining an understanding of ICFR.

- Testing and evaluating whether a material weakness continues to exist.

- Form an opinion on whether a previously reported material weakness continues to exist.

AUD 5
Obtaining Sufficient Appropriate Audit Evidence

5.01 Audit Evidence

Overview

Steps in an Audit

| Prepare for the audit | Obtain understanding of client, its environment & I/C | Assess RMM & design further procedures | Perform tests of controls | **Perform substantive procedures** | Form opinion | Issue report |

| **Management's Assertions (U-PERCV)** | Audit Objectives | **Audit Procedures (I-CORRIIA)** | Audit Evidence |

Understandibility & Classification		Inquiry	
Presentation & Disclosure		Confirmation	
Existence or Occurrence		Observation	
Rights & Obligations		Recalculation	
Completeness & Cutoff		Reperformance	
Valuation, Allocation, & Accuracy		Inspection of Tangible Assets	
		Inspection of Records & Documents	
		Analytical Procedures	

AU-C 330, *Performing Audit Procedures in Response to Assessed Risks and Evaluating the Audit Evidence Obtained*, requires the auditor to obtain **sufficient appropriate audit evidence** by designing and performing audit procedures to address the assessed risks of material misstatement (RMM). This should be done in a manner that is not biased toward obtaining evidence that is corraborative over evidence that is contradictory.

AU-C 500, *Audit Evidence*, helps the auditor to determine whether the audit evidence obtained is, in their professional judgment, sufficient and appropriate. As a basis for this conclusion, the auditor will consider the results of the audit procedures performed. The nature, extent, and timing (NET) of such procedures will affect the **persuasiveness** of the audit evidence.

Persuasiveness of Audit Evidence			
	Measure of:	**Affected by:**	**Relationship to testing:**
Sufficiency	*Quantity* of evidence	• Risks of material misstatement (RMM)* • Quality of audit evidence obtained	• Extent
Appropriateness	*Quality* of evidence	• *Relevance* and *reliability* of audit evidence	• Nature • Timing **

As RMM increases, the acceptable level of DR decreases, thus, substantive testing must be increased.

**For example, testing at year-end may provide stronger evidence than testing at an interim date.*

The auditor uses **professional judgment** to evaluate both the sufficiency and appropriateness of audit evidence. Generally, though, the lower the acceptable level of detection risk (DR), the the higher the level of persuasiveness needed to reduce the chances of a material misstatement going undetected.

Acceptable level of DR

Persuasiveness of audit evidence

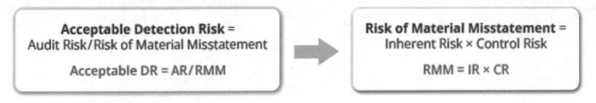

Acceptable Detection Risk =
Audit Risk/Risk of Material Misstatement

Acceptable DR = AR/RMM

Risk of Material Misstatement =
Inherent Risk × Control Risk

RMM = IR × CR

Audit Evidence Defined

Audit evidence is any information to which audit procedures have been applied and is used by the auditor to develop their opinion. Such evidence will either support (ie, corroborate) or contradict management's financial statement (F/S) assertions. This can include:

Accounting Records. For example, checks, invoices, contracts, the general and subsidiary ledgers, journal entries and other adjustments, worksheets, spreadsheets, and other records that support cost allocations, computations, reconciliations, and disclosures

Note: Underlying accounting data alone is not sufficient appropriate evidence upon which to base the auditor's opinion.

Other Information. For example, minutes of board of directors' meetings; confirmations; information obtained from *external information sources* in developing an understanding of the entity and its environment (eg, comparable data about competitors to use for benchmarking purposes); information prepared by *management's specialist*; and information obtained through the performance of audit procedures (eg, inquiry, observation, etc.)

- **External information source** – This is an external party that provides information that is either used by the entity in preparing the F/S or the auditor as audit evidence, when such information is suitable for use by a broad range of users. It does not include a party acting as a specialist or service organization with respect to that information.

- **Management's specialist** – This is an external party with expertise in a field other than accounting or auditing (eg, engineering or actuarial services) that is used by the entity to assist in preparing the F/S.

Evaluating Audit Evidence

The auditor should evaluate information to be used as audit evidence by considering:

- The **relevance** and **reliability** of the information, including the source from which it was obtained

- Whether the information **corroborates** or **contradicts** F/S assertions

Such evaluation should include:

- Determining whether the information is **sufficiently precise** and **detailed** for the auditor's purposes

- Obtaining evidence regarding the **accuracy** and **completeness** of the information, if necessary

Information to be used as audit evidence may come in different forms: oral (inquiries), visual (observation), paper documents, and electronic documents or data. The form of the information will determine the procedures necessary to evaluate the information.

Relevance and Reliability of Audit Evidence

Appropriateness of audit evidence relates to the **quality** of the audit evidence, including its relevance and reliability in providing support for the conclusions on which the auditor's opinion is based.

Relevance. Information to be used as audit evidence is relevant if it is **timely** and **supports** or **contradicts** a relevant assertion (**U-PERCV**). For example, an audit data analytic (ADA) can use commodity pricing data to assess recorded revenue, but the time periods for the data and the revenue must be aligned.

Reliability. The reliability of audit evidence is directly related to the **nature** of the audit evidence, the **source** from which it is obtained, the **conditions** under which it is developed and acquired, and its **form**. The reliability of information is affected by its **accuracy**, **completeness**, **authenticity**, and susceptibiltity to **management bias**.

Audit evidence, ranking from the most reliable to the least, may come from the following sources.

- **Auditor developed** – The auditor may develop information to be used as audit evidence (eg, the auditor may have accumulated data on industry trends). The auditor may use a specialist to assist in developing audit evidence. The auditor may also produce audit evidence using automated tools and techniques to analyze information provided by management or external parties.

- Audit evidence obtained directly by the auditor (eg, observing a control being applied) is more reliable than evidence obtained indirectly or by inference (eg, inquiring about the application of a control).

- **External information sources and other external parties (Outside)** – Information obtained directly from independent sources outside the entity (eg, data, confirmations received from banks) is less susceptible to management bias and is, therefore, generally more reliable than evidence received from inside the entity. Keep in mind that such evidence received from outsiders can be compromised due to collusion.

  - Note also that other types of information from external sources may be used by management or the auditor (eg, information used as inputs to forecasts or models used to prepare accounting estimates).

  - The reliability of an external information source is affected by the **nature** and **credibility** of the source, the assessed RMM to which the information is relevant, and the extent to which the information is related to the reasons for the assessed RMM.

  - External information is less likely to be subject to bias if it is provided to the public for free or is available to a wide range of users for a fee.

- **Management** – Management may provide information obtained from the financial reporting process as well as information obtained from outside of the accounting records (eg, risk management system). This information may be stored within the IT systems or in a remote server. Management may also have a specialist provide information that will be used as audit evidence.

  - **Outside/Inside** – Evidence that **originated outside** the entity but is provided **from inside** the entity (eg, a bank statement provided by the client) is more reliable than information that is both received from the entity and prepared by the entity. This evidence is less reliable than evidence received directly from outsiders since management or other employees may have the ability to alter external documents within the client's control.

  - **Inside** – **Internally generated** audit evidence is less reliable than evidence obtained directly by the auditor or received from outsiders since such documents are the most susceptible to alteration by the client.

    - **Original documents** are **more reliable** than audit evidence transformed into electronic form (eg, photocopies, facsimiles, etc.). Further audit procedures may be necessary to determine the reliability of such information. This may include verifying the authenticity of the documents or testing the controls over the document's transformation and maintenance.

    - **Documents**, whether paper or electronic, are **more reliable than oral** evidence.

    - The **reliability** of internally generated documents **depends** on the operating effectiveness of the **controls** over their preparation and maintenance.

When the source of information is a combination of management and external parties (eg, many parties may contribute to the information contained in a distributed ledger), the auditor must use professional judgment to evaluate the relevance and reliability of the information.

Reliability of Audit Evidence		
Category	**Source**	**Example**
1. Auditor developed	Directly obtained by auditor	Inventory observation
2. Outside	Obtained directly from outsider	Bank confirmations
3. Outside/Inside	Prepared by outsider but obtained from client	Bank statements
4. Inside	Prepared by client	Client sales invoices

Persuasiveness ↑

No audit can rely entirely on client-prepared accounting data. Keep in mind, however, that the auditor may rely in part on evidence obtained with any level of persuasiveness. The representation letter, for example, is obtained in every audit even though it represents the lowest level of persuasiveness due to the absence of effective I/C over management.

Summary

The auditor uses **professional judgment** to evaluate both the sufficiency and appropriateness of audit evidence. In doing so, the auditor should also consider:

- Previous audit experience

- The auditor's understanding of the entity and its environment

- The significance and likelihood of potential misstatements

- The effectiveness of management's responses and controls

- Whether any instances of fraud or error were identified

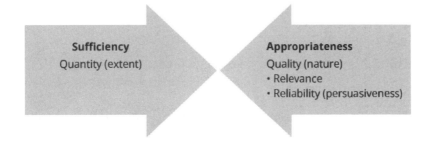

Sufficiency
Quantity (extent)

Appropriateness
Quality (nature)
• Relevance
• Reliability (persuasiveness)

5.02 Audit Risk, F/S Level, and Assertion Level

Overview – Responding to RMM

The purpose of obtaining an understanding of the entity and its environment is to identify and assess risks of material misstatement (RMM), whether due to fraud or error, at the **financial statement level** and **relevant assertion level.** This assessment provides the basis for designing and implementing responses at both levels. (AU-C 315)

Remember, to keep audit risk (**AR**) to an acceptably low level, detection risk (DR) levels must be lowered as RMM increases; thus, the extent of substantive procedures (**SUB**) must increase as RMM increases.

- DR = Probability that substantive tests will not detect material misstatements (TD × AP)

    o **TD** = Risk associated with tests of details

    o **AP** = Risk associated with analytical procedures

- IR = Inherent risk

- CR = Control risk

Audit Risk
$AR = DR \times \underbrace{CR \times IR}_{RMM}$
Rely↓ RMM↑ DR↓ SUB↑
Rely↑ RMM↓ DR↑ SUB↓

Financial Statement Level

At the financial statement level, the auditor will **consider** the **users** of the F/S and the **purpose** for which they will be used to determine if management may have an incentive to overstate or understate results of operations (I/S) and financial position (B/S). In addition, the auditor will consider the following in determining if there is an increased or decreased risk that the entity may issue materially misstated F/S:

- The economic and industry conditions

- Management compensation arrangements

- Financing arrangements and the state of the capital markets

- Changes in entity management or other key personnel

- A variety of other relevant factors

To address the RMM at the financial statement level, some of the **auditor's responses to reduce audit risk** to an acceptably low level may include:

- Increasing professional skepticism

- Assigning more experienced audit staff with specialized skills or even using specialists

- Increasing staff supervision

- Incorporating more unpredictability into audit procedures

- Adjusting the nature, timing, and extent of further audit procedures when the control environment is weak (eg, shifting interim substantive testing to year-end substantive testing)

Relevant Assertion Level

The auditor should design and perform further audit procedures whose **nature, timing, and extent** are responsive to the assessed RMM at the relevant assertion level. The auditor should consider:

- The significance and probability that a material misstatement will occur

- The characteristics of the class of transactions, account balance or disclosure involved

- The nature of the controls used (manual vs. automated)

- Whether the auditor expects to test the operating effectiveness of controls in preventing or detecting material misstatements

The **nature** of audit procedures (appropriateness) includes both its **purpose** (tests of controls vs. substantive procedures) and its **type** (I-CORRIIA). This is the *most important* consideration in responding to assessed risks.

- The higher the auditor's assessment of RMM, the lower the acceptable level of DR.

- A lower level of DR is achieved by obtaining audit evidence that is more *relevant and reliable*.

The **timing** of audit procedures refers to *when* the audit procedures are performed as well as the period or date for which the audit evidence is applicable.

- Tests may be performed at an interim date or at period end.

- The higher the auditor's assessment of RMM, the closer to period-end that substantive procedures should be performed.

The **extent** of audit procedures (sufficiency) refers to the *quantity* of a specific audit procedure to be performed. This is based on the auditor's judgment, and the auditor should consider the tolerable misstatement level, the assessed RMM, and the degree of assurance that is sought.

- The higher the auditor's assessment of RMM, the greater the extent of audit procedures.

- This may mean more procedures or larger sample sizes to which procedures are applied.

Purpose of Audit Procedures

As previously mentioned, the auditor may use either a **substantive approach**, in which substantive procedures are emphasized, or a **combined approach**, in which both tests of controls and substantive procedures are used.

- For certain relevant assertions and risks, **only substantive procedures** will be performed. This may occur because either there are no effective controls or because it would *not be efficient* (cost/benefit) to test the operating effectiveness of controls.

    o Substantive procedures should be performed for each material transaction class, account balance, and disclosure item.

- In other situations, **both tests of controls and substantive procedures** are used. Typically, if controls are operating effectively, less assurance will be required from substantive procedures.

- o The auditor will generally perform tests of controls to obtain evidence as to whether controls are functioning effectively as designed.

    - If controls are found to be effective, the auditor can reduce the amount of substantive testing, which generally increases the efficiency of the audit.

    - If controls are found to be ineffective, the auditor will not be able to rely on them and will not be able to reduce the amount of substantive testing, resulting in a less efficient audit.

- o Tests of controls are required in circumstances when **substantive testing alone cannot provide sufficient evidence** to adequately address the RMM.

    - In situations where a significant amount of information is initiated, authorized, recorded, processed, or reported electronically, there may not be documentary evidence to support transactions due to the highly automated nature of the client's IT system. Therefore, the auditor must test the IT controls to determine whether the transactions are being recorded properly.

Types of Audit Procedures

To address risk at the assertion level, the auditor will consider the individual elements of financial reporting. Operating items and account balances will be scrutinized to determine if they represent RMM and, if so, the type of likely misstatement. This then allows the auditor to determine which **assertions** are most affected (ie, at risk) and what **procedures** will be most effective in obtaining evidence that either will or will not support the assertion.

Assets like inventory may represent risk if they are susceptible to theft, in which case the auditor will concentrate on the *existence assertion.*

- The auditor will determine if there are control procedures in place that can be relied upon and that, if operating as designed, would effectively prevent theft.

- The auditor may apply substantive procedures, such as comparing physical observations of inventory to recorded amounts and performing analytical procedures to determine if the relationships among inventory, cost of sales, and gross profits are reasonable.

- Assets like inventory may represent risk if they are susceptible to theft, in which case the auditor will concentrate on the existence assertion.

Transactions like sales may be misstated due to the use of numerous shipping arrangements under various shipping terms, increasing the likelihood that a sale will be recognized on an inappropriate date. In this case, the auditor will concentrate effort on the *cutoff assertion*.

- The auditor will determine if there are control procedures in place that can be relied upon and that, if operating as designed, would assure that sales are recognized in the appropriate period.

- The auditor may apply substantive procedures such as tracing recorded sales transactions surrounding the end of the period to shipping documents while evaluating shipping terms and tracing shipping documents surrounding the end of the period to the journals to determine if related sales were reported in the appropriate period.

- Transactions like sales may be misstated due to the use of numerous shipping arrangements under various shipping terms, increasing the likelihood that a sale will be recognized on an inappropriate date. In this case, the auditor will concentrate effort on the cutoff assertion.

Management assertions and types of audit procedures are discussed in more detail in the next lecture.

5.03 Management's Assertions & Audit Procedures

Management's Assertions

Management's Assertions (AU-C 315) are representations made by management in the financial statements (F/S) being audited.

Management makes implicit or explicit assertions regarding the recognition, measurement, presentation, and disclosure of information in the F/S and related disclosures. All the procedures applied in an audit are directed toward the eventual goal of expressing an opinion on the F/S. The auditor should always keep in mind the **management assertions** that are represented in the F/S. These assertions can be summarized as follows (**COCA-CURVE**):

- Completenes**s**

  o All transactions and events that should have been recorded have been recorded.

  o All assets, liabilities, and equity interests that should have been recorded have been recorded.

  o All disclosures that should have been included in the F/S have been included.

- Occurrence

  o Transactions and events that have been recorded have occurred and pertain to the entity.

  o Disclosed events, transactions, and other matters have occurred and pertain to the entity.

- Cutoff

  o Transactions and events have been recorded in the correct accounting period.

- Accuracy

  o Amounts and other data relating to recorded transactions and events have been recorded appropriately.

  o Financial and other information is disclosed fairly and in appropriate amounts.

- Classification

  o Transactions and events have been recorded in the proper accounts.

  o Financial information is appropriately presented and described.

- Understandability

  o Disclosures are clearly expressed.

- Rights & Obligations

Management Assertions
Understandability & Classification
Presentation & Disclosure
Existence or Occurrence
Rights & Obligations
Completeness & Cutoff
Valuation, Allocation & Accuracy
OR
Completeness
Occurrence
Cutoff
Accuracy
Classification
Understandability
Rights & Obligations
Valuation & Allocation
Existence

- o The entity holds or controls the rights to assets, and liabilities are the obligations of the entity.
  - o Disclosed events, transactions, and other matters pertain to the entity.
- Valuation & Allocation
  - o Assets, liabilities, and equity interests are included in the F/S at appropriate amounts, and any resulting valuation or allocation adjustments are appropriately recorded.
  - o Financial and other information is disclosed fairly and in appropriate amounts.
- Existence
  - o Assets, liabilities, and equity interests exist.

The auditor should use relevant assertions in assessing risks by considering the different types of potential misstatements that may occur, and then designing further audit procedures that are responsive to the assessed risks. To identify relevant assertions, the auditor should determine the *source* of likely potential misstatements in each significant class of transactions, account balance, and presentation and disclosure.

In determining whether a particular assertion is relevant, the auditor should evaluate:

- The nature of the assertion
- The volume of transactions or data related to the assertion
- The nature and complexity of the systems used to process information supporting the assertion

Management assertions are grouped within **three main categories**:

- Assertions about classes of *transactions and events* for the period under audit (income statement) (CPA-CO).
- Assertions about *account balances* at the period end (balance sheet) (RACE).
- Assertions about *presentation and disclosure* in the F/S (RACOUn).

Classes of Transactions & Events (CPA-CO)	Account Balances at Year-end (RACE)	Presentation & Disclosures (RACOUn)
Completeness	**R**ights & Obligations	**R**ights & Obligations
Period Cutoff	**A**llocation & Valuation	**A**ccuracy & Valuation
Accuracy	**C**ompleteness	**C**ompleteness
Classification	**E**xistence	**O**ccurrence
Occurrence		**Un**derstandability & Classification

When solving CPA exam questions that call for lists of procedures, the most efficient approach may be to group the 11 objectives into six groups. These six groups can then be applied to any area. They are **U-PERCV**, as follows:

- **Understandability & Classification** – Management asserts that information is presented and described clearly, and transactions and events have been recorded in the Proper Accounts.

- **Presentation & Disclosure** – Management asserts that all accounts are presented in the proper sections of the F/S and that all necessary informative disclosures have been made.

- **Existence or Occurrence** – Management asserts that all assets, liabilities, and equity interests listed on the balance sheet exist, and disclosed transactions and events that have been recorded have occurred and pertain to the entity.

- **Rights & Obligations** – Management asserts that it is the legal owner of all assets listed on the F/S, and that the liabilities represent legal obligations of the entity. Also, that all disclosed events pertain to the entity.

- **Completeness & Cutoff** – Management asserts that ALL assets, liabilities, equity interests, transactions and events have been recorded and ALL disclosures that should have been included have been included. Transactions and events have been recorded in the Correct accounting period (CUTOFF).

- **Valuation, Allocation & Accuracy** – Management asserts that amounts are valued using a method in accordance with generally accepted accounting principles, and that revenues and expenses are allocated to the proper periods. Recorded transactions and disclosures have been recorded appropriately.

Audit Objectives

The auditor develops specific audit objectives to substantiate assertions that are material to the F/S.

Audit Procedures

Purpose of Audit Procedures

Audit procedures are used by an auditor for **three main purposes**. By performing such audit procedures, the auditor should obtain evidence to draw reasonable conclusions on which to base an opinion.

- **Risk assessment procedures** are performed to obtain an understanding of the entity and its environment, including its internal control, and to assess the risk of material misstatement (RMM) at the financial statement and relevant assertion levels. They do not provide a sufficient basis for the auditor's opinion.

- **Tests of controls** are performed to test the *operating effectiveness* of controls in preventing or detecting material misstatements at the relevant assertion level. They are necessary when the auditor's risk assessment presumes controls are operating effectively or if substantive procedures alone do not provide sufficient appropriate audit evidence.

- **Substantive procedures** should be used to detect material misstatements through tests of details and analytical procedures for all relevant assertions related to each material class of transactions, account balance, and disclosure. Substantive procedures are **required** for each material transaction class, account balance, and disclosure item. There are two categories of substantive tests:

- o **Test of details** (**TD** = Test of Details risk) – No audit can be performed without including substantive tests of details. These are tests designed to verify:

  - Transactions and events

  - Account balances

  - Presentation and disclosures

- o **Analytical procedures** (**AP** = Analytical Procedures risk) – These are tests designed to examine the relationship between different numbers and nonfinancial information to identify unusual relationships, which may indicate misstated amounts.

Types of Audit Procedures

- *Inquiry* (eg, written inquiries and oral inquiries) – The auditor can make inquiries of management and others, including those external to the entity (note that this does not constitute a confirmation). Inquiries may be written or oral and may be used to learn about:

> A nice way to remember the **audit procedures** is that I love to travel the world, and **I** have even been to **Korea** (**I-CORRIIA**).

  - o The entity and its environment, including its internal control

  - o Accounting policies and procedures, such as capitalization policies and how estimates are developed

  - o How balances were derived, including the sources used for developing measurements or the methodology for determining balances

  - o Any other matters that the auditor believes a response to which will provide audit evidence

- **Confirmation** (eg, accounts receivable) – Audit evidence in the form of a written response obtained directly from parties outside the entity, whether paper or electronic (discussed in more detail later).

- *O*bservation (eg, observation of inventory count, observation of control activities) – The auditor can observe activities physically or remotely with the use of technology (eg, a drone). This might include observing the performance of processes to determine if internal controls have been implemented and are being applied effectively. The auditor can also observe the physical count of inventory to both obtain evidence about the existence of inventory and to verify the accuracy of the counts.

- **Recalculation** (eg, checking the mathematical accuracy of documents or records) – The auditor may recalculate information included in the F/S, manually or using generalized audit software (more on this later). An example would be recalculating depreciation expense and accumulated depreciation to compare it to the client's amounts.

- **Reperformance** (eg, reperforming the aging of accounts receivable) – The auditor can reperform processes to determine the outcome and compare that outcome to information provided by the client. For example, the auditor can reperform an internal control procedure to determine if the procedure would be effective in preventing a material misstatement from occurring or detecting it so that it can be corrected on a timely basis.

- **Inspection of tangible assets** (eg, inventory items) – The auditor can inspect assets (physically or remotely) to verify that they are in appropriate condition and that they are the same as described by the entity.

- **Inspection (Examination) of records or documents** (eg, invoice for an equipment purchase transaction) – The auditor can inspect electronic and paper documents (manually or with automated techniques) to determine if they have been interpreted and recorded properly.

  - **Tracing (Completeness)** – The information on the document may be traced from the source document into the books and records to check for completeness, such as tracing the inventory quantity from a count sheet directly into the books and records.

  - **Vouching (Existence or Occurrence)** – Performing the test in the other direction is called *vouching*. This occurs when the information is vouched from the books back to the source documents, to check for existence or occurrence. An example would be vouching the inventory quantity from the books back to the inventory count sheets.

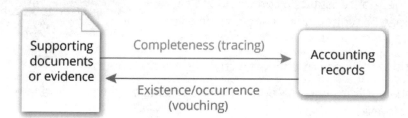

 The examiners sometimes use the word *trace* for inspection procedures in both directions. Don't let it confuse you; know the assertions that differentiate the tests.

- **Analytical Procedures** (eg, ratio analysis) – This is the study of data comparisons and relationships based on the expectation and anticipation theory. This may be performed manually or using audit data analytics, which we will discuss in greater detail in a later section.

Tests of Details

The objective of tests of details is to detect material misstatements in the F/S.

Selection of Procedures

The decision by the auditor as to what tests of details to apply will depend on the **level of detection risk** that is acceptable and the availability of appropriate evidence. For example, observation may not be possible for an intangible asset (eg, goodwill). Observation may also not be necessary when the RMM is low and the auditor is willing to accept evidence obtained from other sources.

In selecting appropriate audit procedures, the auditor may consider the relationship between **cost and usefulness**. However, in situations where there is no appropriate alternative procedure, difficulty or expense are *not* valid reasons for choosing to omit necessary audit procedures.

Timing of Procedures

Since the balances at the F/S date often depend heavily on transactions occurring near the end of the year, the auditor must be careful about the decision to perform **substantive tests at interim dates**. This can **increase incremental audit risk** and should be avoided unless the acceptable level of detection risk is relatively high or the accounts are such that year-end balances are reasonably predictable.

Factors influencing interim substantive testing include:

- Effectiveness of internal controls

- Availability of needed information at year end

  - Some electronic information may only be available for a certain amount of time; thus, the auditor may need to ask for that information to be retained for the performance of audit procedures.

- Purpose of the test

- Assessed risk of material misstatement

- Type of account or transactions

- Cost and ability to control audit risk between interim and year end

- Predictability of year end balances after interim testing

In some cases, tests of details **cannot** be performed until after the close of the fiscal year under audit. Examples include the search for unrecorded liabilities (since the auditor must know what was recorded to perform the search) and obtaining a management representation letter (since it must be dated as of the audit completion date). Other tests must be performed as close to the balance sheet date as possible (eg, counts of inventory and marketable securities on hand).

5.04 Analytical Procedures

Overview

Analytical procedures (eg, scanning numbers for reasonableness, calculating ratios) are audit procedures that involve the auditor developing an **expectation** based on knowledge that may have been obtained from a variety of sources. This expectation is then **compared to client representations.** The degree to which they match will provide the auditor with evidence as to the reliability of management's representation. (AU-C 520)

The **reliability of the expectation** is generally a **function of the source** of information used by the auditor to develop it. The reliability and precision of the expectation determine the reliability of the evidence obtained.

Performing an analytical procedure

Develop expectation of amount based on other information (eg, prior year results)

↓

Compare with expectation to recorded amounts and consider whether differences are reasonable

↓

Investigate significant differences

When to Perform

Analytical procedures may be performed at three different times during an audit:

- During planning (required)
- Substantive testing (optional)
- The overall review (required)

Planning

Analytical procedures are **required** to be used during the planning phase of the audit as risk assessment procedures. Since the auditor has not yet begun to examine the details of the client's information, the procedures will be applied to data that are aggregated at a high level.

The application of analytical procedures to the interim financial data can help the auditor **gain a basic understanding of** the **client's business** and **identify unusual relationships** between data. Unusual relationships may suggest the need for greater amounts of testing of certain accounts.

Substantive Testing

Using analytical procedures as substantive tests to reduce detection risk in the audit is **optional**. For certain assertions, using these procedures to **verify the reasonableness of accounts/assertions** may be sufficient to satisfy the requirements of the audit, eliminating the need to perform tests of details of those transactions and accounts. The decision to use analytical procedures instead of tests of details is made based on the auditor's judgment as to the relative efficiency and effectiveness of the two types of substantive tests.

When using analytical procedures in **substantive testing**, the auditor should complete the following steps:

1. Determine the suitability of particular substantive analytical procedures for given assertions.

2. Evaluate the reliability of data from which the auditor's expectations are developed.

3. Develop an expectation for a recorded amount or ratio that is based on recorded amounts.

4. Evaluate whether the expectation is sufficiently precise to identify a misstatement that may cause the F/S to be materially misstated.

5. Determine the amount of discrepancy between the recorded amount or ratio and the auditor's expectation that would not require further investigation.

6. Compare the recorded amounts or ratios with the expectations.

7. Investigate any significant differences from the expectations.

Overall Review

At the conclusion of the audit, analytical procedures are **required** to be applied to the data to identify relationships that were not identified earlier in the audit engagement. This assists the auditor in assessing conclusions reached and in evaluating the overall financial statement presentations.

If these procedures suggest the presence of misstated account balances, the auditor may need to perform additional tests of details to satisfactorily complete the engagement.

- These analytical procedures should be performed by the manager or partner with overall knowledge of the client's business and industry.

- The ultimate purpose of these analytical procedures is to form an overall conclusion as to whether the F/S are consistent with the auditor's understanding of the entity.

Using Analytical Procedures		
Planning (risk assessment)	Required	• To enhance understanding of the entity • To identify high risk accounts/assertions
Substantive testing	Optional	• Verify reasonableness of accounts/assertions
Overall review	Required	• Confirm that F/S are consistent with overall understanding of entity • Ensure all unexpected amounts/relationships have been explained

Five Basic Types of Comparisons

There are five basic types of comparisons that may be performed as analytical procedures (**CRAFT**):

- **Client vs. Industry** – A client's financial data can be expected to have some plausible relationship to industry averages. A client's sales, for example, may tend to rise and fall at the same time the revenues of competitors in the industry change.

- **Related Accounts** – Certain accounts are closely associated with each other and have a range of expected relationships. Interest expense, for example, should approximate the weighted average of liabilities for the period to the weighted average effective interest rate paid by the entity.

- **Actual vs. Budget** – Results during the year should have a plausible relationship to budgets, allowing for the inevitable variances. Actual payroll expenses, for example, should be reasonably close to budgets for payroll, given the control management has over the level of hiring.

- **Financial vs. Nonfinancial** – Certain nonfinancial measures are clearly associated with dollars of revenues or costs. Number of passenger miles flown during the year, for example, should have a predictable relationship to airline revenues.

- **This year vs. Prior** – In the absence of extreme changes in the company and with appropriate adjustments for normal growth and changes to the entity's environment, income statement amounts for the current period should be closely associated with those from previous years of the company. Rent expense, for example, will be similar to the previous year in the absence of major changes in company size or alteration of the ratio of purchased to leased assets.

> The mnemonic **CRAFT** will remind the auditor to craft different types of analytical procedures to achieve the objectives of the audit.

In general, relationships involving **income statement accounts** are **more predictable** than those involving only balance sheet accounts. For example, there isn't any relationship between *equipment* and *accumulated depreciation* on equipment (except that the accumulated depreciation won't exceed the total cost); but there should be a predictable relationship between *equipment* and *depreciation expense* on equipment (I/S) that reflects the average useful life of the assets, since that is a basis for the calculation of annual expense.

Most Popular Ratios

Some of the most popular ratios that are the basis for analytical procedures include:

- **Current ratio** – Current assets divided by current liabilities.

- **Quick or acid test ratio** – Quick assets (cash + marketable securities + accounts receivable) divided by current liabilities.

- **Receivables turnover** – Net credit sales divided by the average level of accounts receivable.

- **Inventory turnover** – Cost of goods sold divided by the average level of inventory.

- **Debt-to-equity ratio** – Total liabilities divided by stockholders' equity.

These ratios can be compared with comparable ratios for prior years, budgets, industry averages, or other benchmarks to identify data that may be materially misstated. In addition, these ratios may be useful in making other determinations necessary in an audit.

 For example:

- A current ratio of less than 1 may indicate an upcoming inability to pay debts as they come due within the current year. This may lead the auditor to have substantial doubt as to the client's ability to continue as a going concern for a reasonable period of time.

- A very low inventory turnover ratio may indicate slow-moving or obsolete inventory that needs to be written down or off in the valuation of ending inventory.

It is very important to understand the ratios and the Purpose or Use for the ratios. Some of the frequently tested ratios include:

Ratio	Formula	Purpose or Use
Liquidity – Measures of the company's short-term ability to pay its maturing obligations.		
1. Working Capital	Current assets – Current liabilities	Measures ability to meet current expenses
2. Current ratio	Current assets / Current liabilities	Measures short-term debt-paying ability
3. Quick or acid-test ratio	[Cash, marketable securities, and receivables (net)] / Current liabilities	Measures immediate short-term liquidity
4. Current cash debt coverage ratio	(Net cash provided by operating activities) / Average current liabilities	Measures a company's ability to pay off its current liabilities in a given year from its operations

Ratio	Formula	Purpose or Use
Activity – Measures how effectively the company uses its assets		
5. Receivables turnover	Net credit sales / Average trade receivables	Measures liquidity of receivables
6. Inventory turnover	Cost of goods sold / Average inventory	Measures liquidity of inventory
7. Asset turnover	Net sales / Average total assets	Measures how efficiently assets are used to generate sales
8. Number of days' supply in average inventory	= 365* / Inventory Turnover **or** = Average (ending) inventory / Average daily cost of goods sold	Measures number of days required to sell inventory
9. Number of days' sales in average receivables	= 365* / Receivables Turnover	Measures number of days required to collect receivables
Profitability – Measures of the degree of success or failure of a given company or division for a given period of time.		
10. Profit margin on sales (Gross margin)	Net income / Net sales	Measures net income generated by each dollar of sales
11. Rate of return on assets	Net income / Average total assets	Measures overall profitability of assets
12. Rate of return on common stock equity (Return on equity)	(Net income –preferred dividends) / (Average common stockholders' equity)	Measures profitability of owners' investment
13. Earnings per share	(Net income minus preferred dividends) / (Weighted shares outstanding)	Measures net income earned on each share of common stock
14. Price-earnings ratio	Market price of stock / Earnings per share	Measures the ratio of the market price per share to earnings per share
15. Payout ratio	Cash dividends / Net income	Measures percentage of earnings distributed in the form of cash dividends

Ratio	Formula	Purpose or Use
Coverage – Measures of the degree of protection for long-term creditors and investors.		
16. Debt to equity	Total liabilities / Stockholders' equity	Shows creditors the corporation's ability to sustain losses
17. Debt to total assets	Total debt / Total assets	Measures the percentage of total assets provided by creditors
18. Times interest earned	(Income before interest expense and taxes) / Interest expense	Measures ability to meet interest payments as they come due
19. Cash debt coverage ratio	(Net cash provided by operating activities) / (Average total liabilities)	Measures a company's ability to repay its total liabilities in a given year from its operations
20. Book value per share	(Common stockholders' equity) / Outstanding shares	Measures the amount each share would receive if the company were liquidated at the amounts reported on the balance sheet

Candidates should use 365 days unless told to assume 360 days.

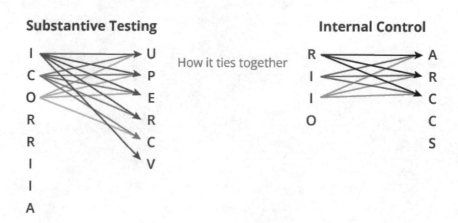

To understand the application of the assertions to the audit of individual accounts, let's look at an example involving **inventory (RACE):**

- *R*ights & obligations
  - The auditor may determine that the entity has adequate controls to reasonably assure that only inventory to which the entity has rights is recorded, in which case the auditor will perform tests of controls to make certain that the controls are operating as designed.
  - The auditor may obtain evidence about the entity's rights to inventory by tracing inventory purchases to supporting documentation.

- *A*llocation & valuation
  - The auditor may determine that the entity's procedures for measuring and recording inventory reasonably assure that inventory is fairly measured and valued in accordance with GAAP, in which case the auditor will perform tests of controls to make certain that procedures are being followed as designed.
  - The auditor may obtain evidence that inventory is appropriately reported at the lower of cost or net realizable value by performing tests involving recalculation to determine if the client has made appropriate calculations.
  - The auditor may perform substantive analytical procedures to obtain satisfaction that inventory is fairly stated by comparing amounts reported as inventory and cost of sales, as well as the relationships to sales and accounts payable to expectations.

- *C*ompleteness
  - The auditor may determine that the entity has adequate controls to reasonably assure that all inventories to which the entity has rights are recorded, in which case the auditor will perform tests of controls to make certain that the controls are operating as designed.

- o The auditor may obtain evidence that all inventory that is owned is recorded by tracing items in inventory to the accounting records to make certain that they have been recorded.

- *Existence*

  - o The auditor may determine that recorded inventory actually exists by observing the physical inventory.

  - o The auditor may obtain evidence that recorded inventories exist by obtaining written confirmations from warehouses storing inventory on behalf of the entity.

Applying the **U-PERCV** approach:

- **Understandability & Classification** – To verify that transactions and events have been recorded in the proper accounts and are clearly described, the auditor would read the F/S and trace purchases into the purchases journal.

- **Presentation & Disclosure** – To verify that all necessary disclosures have been made and that inventory is classified properly, the auditor will read the F/S and notes.

- **Existence or Occurrence** – To verify that the inventory exists, the auditor will observe the physical count of inventory.

- **Rights and obligations** – To verify that the client owns the inventory, the auditor will examine vendor invoices.

- **Completeness & Cutoff** – To verify that that the client has included all inventory owned by them at year-end, the auditor will perform cutoff tests of receiving and shipping occurring in the days surrounding the balance sheet date.

- **Valuation, Allocation & Accuracy** – To verify that the client is properly accounting for the inventory at the lower of cost or net realizable value, the auditor will review supplier catalogs in order to estimate the replacement cost of the inventory on hand.

With respect to income accounts, such as sales and purchases, the auditor will examine and compare documents related to the transactions. In general, documents will be traced through the system in the **normal order** of processing to verify **completeness** and will be vouched in **reverse order** to determine **existence or occurrence**.

For example, comparing shipping documents to sales invoices verifies that all shipments have been billed (completeness) and comparing sales invoices to shipping documents verifies that all bills are for goods actually shipped (existence or occurrence).

Two Different Audit Approaches

- Test of Balances (Balance Sheet)

  - o Many transactions, small dollar amounts

    - Cash, A/R, Inventory, A/P

- Test of Transactions (Income Statement)

  - o Few transactions, large dollar amounts

    - Investments, PP&E, Bonds, N/P, stockholders' equity

Audit Program / Audit Plan

An audit program is **required** for every GAAS audit. It is a step-by-step list of audit procedures that emphasizes account balances. It is designed so that:

- The procedures will achieve specific audit objectives, which relate to management's assertions.

- It supports the auditor's conclusion.

AU-C 330[1] indicates that an auditor is required to design and perform substantive procedures for all relevant assertions related to each material class of transaction, account balance, and disclosure. This means that even when inherent risk (IR) and control risk (CR) are low enough to result in an audit risk (AR) below the level considered necessary, the auditor is still required to design and perform substantive procedures in relation to that relevant assertion.

How to Draft an Audit Program / Audit Plan

Audit programs can be developed on an assertion-by-assertion basis using a process like the following:

1. Identify a material class of transaction (eg, sales), account balance (eg, inventory), **or disclosure**.

   o The auditor develops audit programs using a cumulative top-down basis.

   o This is accomplished by beginning with the class of transaction, account balance, or disclosure that represents the highest RMM.

2. *Identify the relevant assertions* based on whether the auditor is concerned about intentional overstatements or understatements, or misstatements due to error, which could be over or understatements.

   o If the auditor believes that the client may intentionally overstate sales, for example, the assertion related to occurrence would clearly be relevant as the client may record sales that did not actually occur.

   o If the auditor believes that the client may intentionally overstate inventory, the assertion related to rights and obligations would clearly be relevant as the client may include on the balance sheet inventory that it may be holding on consignment or does not own for some other reason.

3. *Identify all control activities* that pertain to the relevant assertion and evaluate whether they appear to be sufficient to prevent or detect and correct a material misstatement.

---

[1] AU-C 330, *Performing Audit Procedures in Response to Assessed Risks and Evaluating the Audit Evidence Obtained*

- o The auditor will evaluate all of the control activities that were identified to determine if the identified controls would be sufficient to prevent a sale that did not actually occur from being recorded, or to detect such a misstatement and correct it on a timely basis, assuming the controls are in place and operating effectively.

- o If the auditor determines internal controls are sufficient:

  - The auditor may decide to perform tests of controls and modify the planned nature, timing, and extent of further audit procedures based on the results; or

  - The auditor may decide to ignore controls, assess CR at maximum, and perform substantive procedures that will adequately reduce DR as if there are no internal controls to prevent the recording of a sale that did not occur.

- o If the auditor determines that internal controls are not sufficient:

  - The auditor will inquire of the client if there might be additional controls that the auditor did not identify. If so, the auditor may determine that controls are sufficient.

  - If there are not sufficient mitigating controls, the auditor will assess CR at maximum and design and perform substantive tests accordingly.

4. *Decide on the procedure(s)* that will provide sufficient appropriate evidence to support the assertion being evaluated.

   - o To determine if all sales that were recorded actually occurred, the auditor may select a sample of all recorded sales and trace them to supporting documentation, including customer purchase orders and shipping documents, to verify that the sale actually occurred.

   - o To determine if the entity owns all of the inventory that it is reporting on its balance sheet, the auditor may select a sample of items that are included in inventory and trace them to purchase documents.

5. *Evaluate the evidence* obtained through the performance of the procedure to determine if it supports other relevant assertions related to the same class of transactions, account balance, or disclosure, or related to a different one.

   - o In addition to providing evidence that sales occurred, tracing sales to supporting documents may provide some evidence regarding the existence and the rights and obligations assertions related to accounts receivable.

   - o In addition to providing evidence that inventory is owned by the entity, tracing items in inventory to purchase documents may provide evidence about the existence and valuation and allocation assertions related to accounts payable.

6. *Prepare audit programs* on an incremental basis for assertions that represent lower risks, evaluating the additional procedures required to obtain sufficient appropriate audit evidence to support the assertion.

   - o The auditor will determine what additional procedures, if any, are necessary to obtain evidence about the assertion related to the existence of accounts receivable, for example, if the auditor has traced a sample of sales to supporting documents and there were no significant exceptions.

The auditor will determine what additional procedures, if any, are necessary to obtain evidence to support the assertion related to the existence of accounts payable if a sample of items in inventory were traced to purchase documents and there were no significant exceptions.

 If on the exam you must prepare a list of substantive tests to be performed, use the following simplified approach:

- Procedures – Attempt to identify one procedure for each of the categories in I-CORRIIA (observation may not be possible if the account is not a tangible asset).
- Assertions – Ensure that there is at least one test related to each of the financial statement assertions in U-PERCV (unless the problem explicitly is limited to one or two assertions).
- Related accounts – Include at least one procedure for each account that is related to the one being addressed (eg, when preparing a list for receivables, include tests of credit loss accounts).
- Certain tests are applicable to almost every account:
  o Read F/S and notes.
  o Review minutes of board and shareholder meetings.
  o Obtain representations from management.
  o Reconcile the trial balance to supporting records.

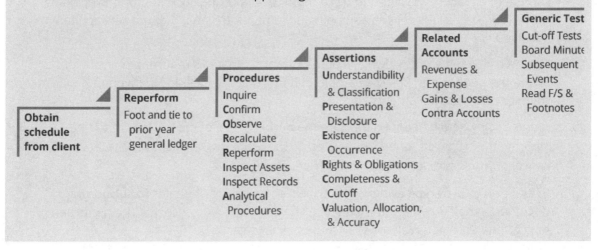

Audit Documentation (Workpapers)

Financial Statements

X Company Balance Sheet	
Cash	65,000
Accounts receivable	XXX

Rounded from Trial Balance

Working Trial Balance

Sched	Acct	Beg bal.	Reclassifications & Adjustments	End bal.
A	Cash	65,124	0	65,124

Tied to Lead Schedule

Cash Lead Schedule		Sched A
Cash in Bank:		$49,318
General Acct	A-1	15,806
Payroll Acct	A-3	65,124
Total		To Trial Bal

Sched A-1

$49,318

To Lead Sched A

Bank Reconciliations, Confirmations, and Supporting Documents

 The exam occasionally addresses **deficiencies** (weaknesses) in audit workpapers. Look for the following possible deficiencies when a working paper is presented on the exam for analysis (**Foot CCHIT**):

- **Comment on Exceptions** – Comments in the body of the working paper or tickmark legend may refer to unusual circumstances or indications of a problem. Make sure each exceptional item has been resolved and that the resolution has been documented.

- **Conclusions** – Closing comments at the bottom of the working paper should be reviewed to ensure they are consistent with the information in the audit documentation. They are usually wrong.

- **Heading** – The name of the client, title of the working paper (such as the account being analyzed), and audit year should all be included.

- **Initials** – Each person who prepares or reviews a working paper should initial it.

- **Tickmarks** (symbols) – Amounts on the working paper are often verified arithmetically or by comparison with other accounts. Symbols may be created as needed to place next to these amounts with a legend at the bottom of the paper explaining what each symbol means (ie, how the working paper amount was verified).

- **Foot** – Check the mathematical accuracy of the schedule.

- **Working Trial Balance** – A listing of ledger accounts with columns for current year-end balances (as well as last year's ending balances), adjusting and reclassifying entries, and final current year-end adjusted balances. Typically, both balance sheet and income statement accounts are included.

- **Lead Schedules** – Schedules that summarize like accounts, the total of which is typically transferred to the working trial balance. For example, a client's various cash accounts may be summarized on a lead schedule with only the total cash amount transferred to the working trial balance.

Audit Documentation Requirements

AU-C 230 requires audit documentation (ie, working papers) to be sufficient to enable an experienced auditor, having no previous connection with the audit, to understand:

- The nature, timing, and extent of the audit procedures performed to comply with GAAS and applicable legal and regulatory requirements

- The results of the audit procedures performed and the audit evidence obtained

- Significant findings or issues arising during the audit, the conclusions reached thereon, and significant professional judgments made in reaching those conclusions

Audit documentation serves as a basis for:

- The auditor's conclusion as to whether the objective of the audit (ie, to obtain sufficient appropriate audit evidence to support the auditor's opinion) has been achieved

- Evidence that the auditor has planned and performed the engagement in accordance with GAAS and other regulatory requirements, if applicable

In addition, audit documentation should:

- Assist in the planning and performance of the engagement.

- Enable engagement team members with supervision and review responsibilities to understand the evidence obtained and the nature, timing, extent and results of auditing procedures performed.

- Indicate the engagement team members *who performed* and reviewed the work.

- Include a written audit program (or set of audit programs) for every audit.

- Be **completed** no later than **60 days** following the report release date.

- Be **retained** at least **five years** from the report release date (longer if legal and regulatory requirements so require).

- Be kept confidential as the property of the auditor.

- Document procedures performed, evidence examined, and conclusions reached.

- Provide a means of preserving information that may be relevant to future engagements.

- Enable the performance of quality control reviews and inspections, as well as external inspections or peer reviews.

- Assist successor auditors when they request to review the predecessor's working papers.

- Enhance an auditor's understanding of work performed in prior periods and its potential effect on the current period's engagement.

While it is not necessary to document every matter considered during an audit, oral explanations alone (absent working paper documentation) are not sufficient to support the work of the auditor.

Confidentiality

The accountant, not the client, owns the working papers and any other documentation that the accountant creates during an engagement. Nevertheless, the accountant must maintain confidentiality, and cannot provide the working papers or other information obtained during engagements to other parties without the permission of the client.

Client confidentiality does not, however, prevent a CPA from providing access to other members of the auditor's firm. Other **exceptions** to confidentiality, include:

- A valid subpoena

- An IRS administrative subpoena

- A **court order**, except in those few states that have a privilege statute

- A **quality control peer review**, providing access to other accountants and the PCAOB in connection with a valid program of peer review

Common law does not recognize the concept of **privilege**, which would allow the accountant to refuse to honor a court subpoena. A small number of states have enacted privilege statutes, and the federal government now recognizes working papers developed in connection with the preparation of a tax return to be privileged in certain circumstances.

Nevertheless, privilege may not be used if the accountant has already provided some of the information requested in a subpoena. The purpose of privilege is to protect the client, not the accountant, so the accountant may not assert privilege even where privilege statutes exist if the client waives the privilege.

Significant Contracts, Agreements, Findings & Discussions

When audit procedures include the inspection of significant contracts or agreements, copies or extracts of those documents should be included in the working papers. In addition, documentation should indicate discussions with management, those charged with governance, or others regarding significant findings or other issues and should include the nature of the items discussed and identification of who was involved in the discussions.

When an auditor has identified information that is inconsistent with the auditor's final conclusion in relation to the F/S, documentation should include an indication as to how the issue was addressed.

Departure from Mandatory Requirements

There are two levels of requirements that apply to an audit performed in accordance with GAAS, PCAOB standards, and governmental audits:

- An **unconditional requirement** must be complied with for the auditor to complete an engagement in accordance with GAAS. An unconditional requirement will always include the word "must" or the phrase "is required to" in every circumstance to which it applies.

- A **presumptively mandatory requirement** is one that the auditor is also expected to comply with in every circumstance to which it applies. A presumptively mandatory requirement will always include the word "should."

In rare circumstances, an auditor may find it necessary to depart from a presumptively mandatory requirement and apply alternative procedures. When this is the case, the auditor must document the reason for the departure and an indication of how the alternative procedures performed achieved the objectives of the presumptively mandatory requirement.

Assembly, Retention and Modifying the Workpapers

Working papers will indicate the report release date and should be assembled on a timely basis, no later than **60 days** after that date. Once complete, the auditor may not delete or discard any documentation until the retention period expires. The retention period is established by the auditor's firm but must be at least equal to **5 years** or the period required by law or regulation, whichever is longer.

If the auditor determines it is necessary to modify existing documentation or add additional working papers, the auditor should document:

- The reasons for the changes

- Who made the changes, who reviewed them, when the changes were made, and when they were reviewed

After the report's release date, the auditor may perform new or additional procedures or draw new conclusions. If so, the auditor will document:

- The circumstances causing the modification

- The new or additional procedures performed, evidence obtained, and conclusions reached

- The effect on the audit report

- Who made the changes, who they were reviewed by, when they were made, and when they were reviewed

Nature & Extent of Workpapers

Six factors must be considered in determining the nature and extent of documentation for a particular audit area or procedure:

1. The RMM associated with the assertion being examined

2. The extent of judgment the auditor exercises in performing the work

3. The nature of the auditing procedures performed

4. The significance of the evidence obtained

5. The nature and extent of exceptions identified, if any

6. The need to document a conclusion or basis for conclusion that is not evident from the other documentation

Among the specific **types of audit documentation** that must be included are the following:

- Abstracts or copies of significant contracts or agreements

- Identification of the items that were selected for tests of the operating effectiveness of controls and substantive tests of details that involve inspection or confirmation

  o Identification should be specific enough so that another audit team member would be able to determine which documents and record items were actually tested.

  o An example of identification is a list of the invoice numbers selected in a sample.

The auditor is required to document significant **audit findings and issues** including:

- Matters involving the selection of accounting principles and related disclosures

- Results of procedures that indicate the possibility of material misstatements and require modification of the auditing procedures

- Circumstances that caused the auditor significant difficulty in applying audit procedures

- Other findings that could result in modification of the auditor's report

Audit documentation is the principal support for the auditor's report. At a minimum, the audit documentation must **always** include:

- Reconciliation of the accounting records with the F/S.

- An audit program that details the procedures to be performed during the engagement.

- Documentation of the auditor's understanding of the internal control structure.

- Documentation of the assessed level of control risk.

- Proof the sufficient evidence was obtained to support the auditor's opinion on the F/S.

- A client representation letter (obtained from management at the conclusion of fieldwork).

In addition, several factors will affect the **quantity, type, and content** of the audit documentation for a particular engagement. These factors include:

- The condition of the client's **accounting records** – Audit documentation may have to be prepared to complete the records in some cases.

- The RMM.

- The **type of report** being issued by the auditor – A qualified or adverse opinion will require working paper discussion of the reasons.

- **Staff disagreements** – If a member of the audit team doesn't agree with a decision made that has an impact on the fieldwork or conclusions, the audit documentation should document the disagreement.

The audit documentation generated during an audit may go into either the **current** file (if they only relate to that year's engagement) or the **permanent** file (if they're related to more than one year).

- Examples of items that will be included in the **current** file are:

  o **Audit program** – Each audit is unique, so a program will only be relevant to documenting the work of that particular year.

  o **Working trial balance** – This is a trial balance pulled from the client's records, which provides additional columns for reclassifications and adjustments. The final column is the adjusted balances of the accounts, which should agree with the F/S that are issued that year.

  o **Lead schedules** – These summarize all the major components that determine an amount appearing in the F/S or notes, and serve as a form of table of contents referencing individual audit documentation that support the components listed. A separate lead schedule will normally be needed for each material account balance.

  o **Responses to information requests** – These include confirmations, the attorney's letter, and the client representation letter.

  o **Reconciliations and analyses by the auditor** – These refer to evidence directly obtained by the auditor to support amounts in the current F/S or notes.

- Examples of items that will be included in the **permanent** file are:

  o **Organization documents** – These include the articles of incorporation and bylaws.

  o **Minutes** – Board of director and shareholder meetings often discuss items of long-term significance.

  o **Flowcharts of the internal control structure** – Though changes occur over the year, the general internal control structure will be similar enough that a flowchart will be useful for many years.

  o **Debt agreements** – Contracts for long-term liabilities are, by their nature, relevant to many years. This category includes note, bond, lease, and pension agreements.

  o **Analyses of equity accounts** – Capital stock and related accounts change rarely, so evidence is valid for many years.

  o Depreciation schedules

PCAOB Audit Documentation

For audits of public companies reporting to the SEC, the PCAOB has established standards for audit documentation. (AS 1215) Most are identical to those required by GAAS (AU-C 230), but AS 1215 specifically added the requirement of the preparation of an **engagement completion document.** This document will identify all significant findings and issues and be sufficiently specific for a reviewer to obtain a thorough understanding of them. It may include either:

- All information necessary to understand the significant findings and issues

- Cross-references, as appropriate, to other available supporting documentation

- The documentation must:

- Demonstrate that the engagement complied with PCAOB standards

- Be completed within **45 days** (not 60 days) following the report release date

- Be retained for **7 years** (rather than 5 years) from the report release date, or the period required by law, if longer

Evaluation of Misstatements Identified During the Audit

AU-C 450 requires the auditor to accumulate misstatements, other than those that are clearly trivial, for the purpose of determining the effect, if any, on the overall audit strategy and the audit plan.

- **Misstatements** are any difference between the way an amount, classification, presentation, or disclosure is presented on or with the F/S and how it should be presented on or with the F/S in order to be fairly presented in accordance with the applicable financial reporting framework (AFRF). Omissions of elements of financial reporting or required disclosures are also considered misstatements.

Revision to the overall audit strategy and audit plan will be called for if identified misstatements either:

- Indicate that other misstatements may occur, such as when errors are caused by a flaw in an aspect of the accounting system, the cumulative effect of which could be material when considered along with other misstatements identified during the engagement; or

- The aggregate effect of all misstatements identified during the audit approach the auditor's measurement of materiality.

In determining if misstatements are material, the auditor will consider both *quantitative and qualitative* factors. Some **qualitative factors** the auditor will consider will include whether:

- Misstatements affect trends of profitability

- Misstatements change losses into income, or vice versa

- Misstatements affect segment information

- Misstatements affect compliance with legal and contractual requirements

The auditor will request that management correct those misstatements that have been identified by the auditor. Upon correction by the client, the auditor will apply procedures to obtain evidence as to whether the misstatements have been properly corrected. If the client does not correct the F/S for identified misstatements, the auditor will:

- Obtain an understanding of the client's reasons for not correcting the misstatements

- Consider the effects when evaluating whether the F/S taken as a whole are free of material misstatement

Before determining if uncorrected misstatements result in material misstatement to the F/S, the auditor will reevaluate materiality considering revisions to financial statement amounts. The determination of whether F/S are materially misstated will be based on the aggregate of all uncorrected misstatements. Consideration will be in relation to the F/S taken as a whole as well as the particular account balances, classes of transactions, or disclosures affected. The auditor will consider:

- The size and nature of the uncorrected misstatements

- The effect of uncorrected misstatements in relation to prior periods

5.07 Management Representation Letter & Attorney Letter

Management Rep. Letter/Client Rep. Letter (Required)

The auditor is **required** to obtain a letter from the client's management reaffirming in writing some of the information that was provided to the auditor during the audit and confirming other matters (eg, that all appropriate information was made available to the auditor). (AU-C 580)

- U-PERCV is included in the letter
- Dated no earlier than audit report date
- From CEO/CFO/Governance
- Scope limitation if not received

The representations are made in the form of a letter written to the auditor. It should be signed by the chief executive officer and chief financial officer of the client, or, in some circumstances, those charged with governance. The letter of representations is:

- Dated as of the *audit report date*, which is the date on which the auditor has determined that sufficient appropriate audit evidence has been obtained, generally the final day of fieldwork
- Required to cover all of the F/S and periods referred to in the audit report

Though the representations made in the letter are not audited further, requiring management to provide such a letter is a mandatory audit procedure. The failure to receive such a letter is considered a **scope limitation** sufficient to preclude the expression of an unmodified/unqualified opinion on the F/S. In most circumstances, in fact, a disclaimer of opinion will need to be issued in the absence of such a letter.

An important purpose of this letter is to emphasize management's responsibility for the F/S. Another is to provide the auditor with some assurance that management is not deliberately concealing any information that might have affected the auditor's opinion. Should the auditor have some evidence of intentional misbehavior by management, the auditor will, of course, place less reliance on the representations made by management in the letter.

The content of the letter will, to some extent, depend on what has taken place during the audit prior to that point. In addition, the management representation letter clearly cannot have an impact on the gathering of evidence by the auditor during the audit, since it is obtained after the planning and performance of all other tests. Certain representations, however, will be present in all such letters.

- Management is responsible for:
  - The preparation and fair presentation of the F/S in accordance with the AFRF
  - The design, implementation, and maintenance (**DIM**) of internal controls relevant to the preparation and fair presentation of F/S so that they are free from material misstatement, whether due to fraud or error

- An indication by management that:

  o Management is **unaware** of any **errors or fraud** that would have a **material effect** on the F/S.

  o There have been no acts of fraud or noncompliance (illegal acts) of any kind (even immaterial ones) by management or other key employees responsible for the internal control structure.

  o Minutes of all board of director and shareholder meetings are complete and have been made available to the auditor.

  o All financial records that exist have been made available to the auditor.

  o There are no pending legal matters with a material impact on the F/S that have not been disclosed to the auditor (such as legal restrictions on assets or pending lawsuits or government investigations).

  o Management believes all estimates are reasonable.

  o All related parties and related-party transactions have been identified to the auditor and properly accounted for and disclosed.

  o Subsequent events have been properly accounted for and disclosed.

Management **cannot** make a representation that there have been no errors or fraud committed by any employees. They only represent to be unaware of any and to have not committed any fraud themselves.

In some cases, the auditor will be expressing an opinion on *supplementary information* included with the F/S. When this is the case, the auditor is also required to obtain **written representations** indicating:

- Management's acknowledgement of its responsibility for the preparation and fair presentation of the supplementary information in accordance with applicable criteria.

- Management's belief that the supplementary information is fairly presented in accordance with applicable criteria, including both its form and content.

- That measurement and presentation methods either have not changed from the prior period or, if they have, the reasons for the changes.

- Any significant assumptions or interpretations that affected the measurement or presentation of the supplementary information.

- If the supplementary information is presented without the audited F/S in the same document, that management will make the audited F/S readily available to the users of the supplementary information.

Management (Client) Representation Letter

(Date of the Auditor's Report)

(To Independent Auditor)

This representation letter is provided in connection with your audit of the financial statements of ABC Company, which comprise the balance sheet as of December 31, 20XX, and the related statements of income, changes in stockholders' equity, and cash flows for the year then ended, and the related notes to the financial statements, for the purpose of expressing an opinion on whether the financial statements are presented fairly, in all material respects, in accordance with accounting principles generally accepted in the United States (U.S. GAAP).

Certain representations in this letter are described as being limited to matters that are **material**. Items are considered material, regardless of size, if they involve an omission or misstatement of accounting information that, in the light of surrounding circumstances, makes it probable that the judgment of a reasonable person relying on the information would be changed or influenced by the omission or misstatement.

Except where otherwise stated below, immaterial matters less than $XXX collectively are not considered to be exceptions that require disclosure for the purpose of the following representations. This amount is not necessarily indicative of amounts that would require adjustment to or disclosure in the financial statements.

We confirm, to the best of our knowledge and belief, having made such inquiries as we considered necessary for the purpose of appropriately informing ourselves as of [*the date of the auditor's report*]:

Financial Statements

1. We have fulfilled our responsibilities, as set out in the terms of the engagement dated [insert date], for the *preparation and fair presentation of the financial statements in accordance with U.S. GAAP*.

2. We acknowledge our responsibility for the design, implementation, and maintenance (DIM) of internal control relevant to the preparation and fair presentation of financial statements that are free from material misstatement, whether due to fraud or error.

3. We acknowledge our responsibility for the design, implementation, and maintenance of internal control *to prevent and detect fraud*.

4. Significant assumptions used by us in making accounting estimates, including those measured at fair value, are reasonable.

5. Related party relationships and transactions have been appropriately accounted for and disclosed in accordance with the requirements of U.S. GAAP.

6. All events **subsequent to** the date of the financial statements and for which U.S. GAAP requires adjustment or disclosure have been adjusted or disclosed.

7. The effects of uncorrected misstatements are immaterial, both individually and in the aggregate, to the financial statements as a whole. A list of the uncorrected misstatements is attached to the representation letter.

8. The effects of all known actual or possible litigation and claims have been accounted for and disclosed in accordance with U.S. GAAP.

Information Provided

9. We have provided you with:

   a. Access to all information, of which we are aware that is relevant to the preparation and fair presentation of the financial statements such as records, documentation and other matters;

   b. Additional information that you have requested for the purpose of the audit; and

   c. Unrestricted access to persons within the entity from whom you determined it necessary to obtain audit evidence.

10. All transactions have been recorded in the accounting records and are reflected in the financial statements.

11. We have disclosed to you the results of our assessment of the risk that the financial statements may be materially misstated as a result of fraud.

12. We have [no knowledge of any] [disclosed to you all information that we are aware of regarding] fraud or suspected fraud that affects the entity and involves:

    a.   Management;

    b.   Employees who have significant roles in internal control; or

    c.   Others when the fraud could have a material effect on the financial statements.

13. We have [no knowledge of any] [disclosed to you all information that we are aware of regarding] allegations of fraud, or suspected fraud, affecting the entity's financial statements communicated by employees, former employees, analysts, regulators or others.

14. We have disclosed to you all known instances of noncompliance with laws and regulations whose effects should be considered when preparing financial statements.

15. We [have disclosed to you all known actual or possible] [are not aware of any pending or threatened] litigation, claims, and assessments whose effects should be considered when preparing the financial statements.

16. We have disclosed to you the identity of the entity's related parties and all related party relationships and transactions of which we are aware.

[Any other matters that the auditor may consider necessary]

(Name of Chief Executive Officer and Title)   (Name of Chief Financial Officer and Title)

Attorney's letter (Letter of Audit Inquiry)

The auditor will also obtain a letter from each attorney engaged by the client to help address any **litigation, claims, or assessments**. (AU-C 501)

- **Corroborates info** from management.

- If attorney's letter is not received, it is considered a **scope limitation**.

- Management requests the inquiry, but the letter should be physically mailed by the auditor.

The primary source of evidence about litigation, claims, and assessments is the **management** of the client. Even though legal counsel will be involved, attorney-client privilege prevents the attorney from directly providing the auditor with information about legal matters.

Instead, the auditor will discuss with management how legal issues with a material effect on the F/S can be identified. Management will meet with legal counsel and then report to the auditor matters that should be communicated. Management will eventually provide assurance in the **management representation letter** that all litigation, claims, and assessments with a material effect on the F/S have been disclosed to the auditor.

The auditor will then prepare and arrange for management to sign a **letter of inquiry** to the attorney to obtain **corroborating evidence**. Management requests the inquiry, but the letter should be physically mailed by the auditor. The letter will identify those matters about which the auditor was informed by management, and request that the attorney corroborate information about the likelihood of losses and, where appropriate, estimates of the amount of losses.

- For losses with only a remote chance of occurring, no further information is needed.

- If the attorney's response indicates that a loss is reasonably possible or probable, clarification of the estimated loss may be needed to determine the appropriate disclosures and accruals.

- If the attorney **refuses to respond** to the letter of inquiry, or if management refuses to give the auditor permission to communicate with the entity's external legal counsel, it is considered a **scope limitation** and may require a qualified opinion or disclaimer of opinion.

- If the attorney is uncertain about the possible resolution of certain issues, this **uncertainty** may result in an **emphasis-of-matter paragraph** in the auditor's report without requiring any modification of the opinion.

- If a client's lawyer resigns shortly after the receipt of an attorney's letter which indicated no significant disagreements with the client's assessment of contingent liabilities, the auditor should inquire as to the reason for the resignation, as this may indicate a problem.

 Attorney's Letter for Financial Audits (Letter of Audit Inquiry)

(Entity Letterhead)
(Date)
(Legal Service Provider's Name and Address)

Dear (Name):

In connection with an audit of our financial statements as of (Balance Sheet date) and for the (period) then ended, management of (name of entity) has prepared, and furnished to auditors (name and address of auditors) a description and evaluation of certain contingencies, including those set forth below involving matters with respect to which you have been engaged and to which you have devoted substantive attention on behalf of (name of entity) in the form of legal consultation or representation. These contingencies are regarded by management as material for this purpose ($ amount). Your response should include all matters that existed at (balance sheet date) and during the period from that date to the date of your response.

[Alternative wording will be used when management requests the lawyer to prepare the list that describes and evaluates pending or threatened litigation, claims, and assessments.]

List of Pending or Threatened Litigation (excluding unasserted claims)

[Ordinarily, management's information would include (1) the nature of the litigation, (2) the progress of the case to date, (3) how management is responding or intends to respond to the litigation (for example, to contest the case vigorously or to seek an out-of-court settlement), (4) an evaluation of the likelihood of an unfavorable outcome, and (5) an estimate of the amount or range of potential loss.] This letter will serve as our consent for you to furnish to our auditor all the information requested herein. Accordingly, please furnish to our auditors such explanation, if any, that you consider necessary to supplement the foregoing information, including an explanation of those matter as to which your views may differ from those stated and an identification of the omission of any pending or threatened litigation, claims and assessments or a statement that the list of such matter is complete.

[Alternative wording will be used when management requests the lawyer to prepare the list that describes and evaluates pending or threatened litigation, claims, and assessments.]

List of Unasserted Claims and Assessments
(Considered by management to be probable of assertion, and that, if asserted, would have at least a reasonable possibility of an unfavorable outcome)

[Ordinarily, management's information would include (1) the nature of the matter, (2) how management intends to respond if the claim is asserted, (3) an evaluation of the likelihood of an unfavorable outcome, and (4) an estimate of the amount or range of potential loss.] Please furnish to the auditors such explanation, if any, that you consider necessary to supplement the foregoing information, including an explanation of those matters as to which your views may differ from those stated.

We understand that whenever, in the course of performing legal services for us with respect to a matter recognized to involve an unasserted possible claim or assessment that may call for financial statement disclosure, if you have formed a professional conclusion that we should disclose or consider disclosure concerning such possible claim or assessment, as a matter of professional responsibility to us, you will so advise us and will consult with us concerning the question of such disclosure and the applicable requirements of Financial Accounting Standards Board (FASB) *Accounting Standards Codification* (ASC) 450, *Contingencies*. Please specifically confirm to our auditors that our understanding is correct.

[Alternative wording will be used when management requests the lawyer to prepare the list that describes and evaluates pending or threatened litigation, claims, and assessments.]

Please specifically identify the nature of and reasons for any limitation on your response.

[The auditor may request the client to inquire about additional matters, for example, unpaid or unbilled charges or specified information on certain contractually assumed obligations of the company, such as guarantees of indebtedness of others.]

Please respond directly to the auditors at the above address by (date), with a specified effective date no earlier than (date).

Sincerely,
(Signature and title of Management's Representative)

5.08 Related Party Transactions

Overview

GAAP requires that material transactions with **related parties** (eg, owners, management, affiliates) and all parties who control or are controlled by the entity be identified. **Related party transactions,** such as sales, borrowings, and the provision of services, commonly occur in the normal course of business.

When a company has engaged in significant transactions with related parties, the auditor's primary concern is to ensure the users of the F/S are made aware of them through proper **disclosure and presentation.** Information regarding such transactions is useful in comparing an entity's F/S with those of prior periods and other entities.

In some circumstances, management may not be aware of certain related parties and information systems may be ineffective at identifying such transactions. Thus, the auditor must remain alert when inspecting the accounting records and performing other audit procedures for **transactions that suggest involvement** with related parties, including:

- Loans at zero or unusually low interest rates

- Sales at prices far above or below fair market value

- Nonmonetary exchanges of property

- Loans with no repayment terms

> An **arm's length transaction** is one in which the terms and conditions reflect a willing buyer and willing seller who are un-related, act independently, and pursue their own best interests.

There also may be a desire to conceal related party transactions from the auditor, as such relationships may present a **greater opportunity for fraud** (eg, collusion, concealment, or manipulation) by management. Thus, related party transactions may represent a **higher risk of material misstatement** than arm's length transactions. (AU-C 550)

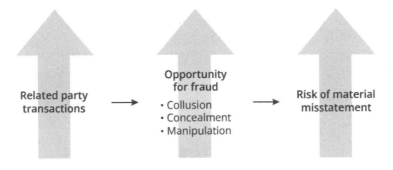

The auditor's objectives, therefore, are to:

- Gain an understanding of the entity's related party relationships and transactions through **risk assessment procedures** (eg, to recognize fraud risk), and

- Obtain sufficient appropriate audit evidence through **further audit procedures** about whether such relationships/transactions are appropriately identified, accounted for, and disclosed.

Risk Assessment Procedures

To obtain information that will help in identifying the risks of material misstatement associated with related party relationships and transactions, the following procedures should be performed.

- The engagement team should consider, as part of their **brainstorming session**, the types of fraud and error that might occur due to such relationships/transactions.

- The auditor should **inquire of management** and others regarding:

  - The identities of the related parties, including changes from the prior period

  - The nature of the relationships (eg, ownership structure)

  - The business purpose for entering a transaction with a related party versus an unrelated party

  - Whether the entity entered, modified, or terminated any transactions with related parties during the period and, if so, the type and purpose of the transactions

- The auditor should inquire* of management and others and perform other risk assessment procedures necessary to **obtain an understanding of the controls** established to:

  - Identify, record, and disclose related party relationships and transactions

  - Authorize and approve significant related party transactions and arrangements as well as **significant unusual transactions** and arrangements outside the normal course of business

Inquiries should include asking about transactions (1) that were not properly authorized according to established policies and (2) for which exceptions were granted, along with the reasons for such exceptions.

- The auditor should **inquire of those charged with governance** (or the audit committee) about:

  - Their understanding of the entity's significant related-party relationships and transactions

  - The substance of any concerns they may have regarding any related party relationships/ transactions

- While the auditor should remain alert when inspecting *any* records/documents for information that indicates the existence of undisclosed related party relationships/transactions, **special attention** should be paid to the following:

  - Bank and legal confirmations

  - Minutes and summaries of board meetings with shareholders

  - Other records/documents the auditor deems necessary

- If **significant unusual transactions** have been identified, the auditor should inquire of management regarding the nature of such transactions and whether related parties may be involved.

Identifying & Assessing Risks

When identifying and assessing the risks of material misstatement, the auditor should determine whether any of the risks identified with respect to related parties are **significant risks**. Note that all **significant unusual transactions** involving related parties should be considered significant risks.

If **fraud risk factors** associated with related parties are identified, they should be considered along with all other fraud risk factors when assessing the risks of material misstatement due to fraud[2]. An example of such a fraud risk factor would be a related party with *dominant influence* over the entity.

Further Audit Procedures

To respond to the risks identified, further audit procedures must be designed to **obtain sufficient appropriate evidence** to conclude that the F/S are fairly presented. This should include the following procedures.

- The auditor should **evaluate** whether the entity has identified its related parties properly. This will include an assessment of the entity's **process** for such identification as well as testing the **accuracy** and **completeness** of identified instances.

- The auditor should **test** the **balances** of affiliated entities.

- If evidence suggests there are other related party relationships/transactions that were previously unidentified by management, the auditor should confirm whether those instances are in fact related party relationships/transactions. If these instances are confirmed, the auditor should:

  o Inform the rest of the engagement team

  o Request that management identify all transactions with such parties

  o Inquire as to why relevant controls failed to identify these instances

  o Perform substantive audit procedures with respect to the newly identified parties and any significant transactions with them

  o Reconsider the risk that there may be other related party relationships and significant transactions that are still unidentified, and perform additional procedures as necessary

  o Evaluate the implications for the audit if the nondisclosure appears intentional (ie, it could be a fraud risk factor)

- For any significant related party transactions that are determined to be significant risks or are otherwise required to be disclosed in the F/S, the auditor should:

  o Read underlying contracts/agreements and evaluate whether:

    ▪ There is a business purpose, or lack thereof, that suggests the transactions were entered into for fraudulent purposes

    ▪ The terms of the transactions are consistent with management's' explanations

    ▪ The transactions have been accounted for and disclosed properly

---

[2] *AU-C 240, Consideration of Fraud in a Financial Statement Audit*

- Obtain evidence that the transactions were authorized and approved properly

- If management asserts in the F/S that a related party transaction was made on terms equivalent to an arm's length transaction, the auditor should obtain sufficient appropriate evidence regarding the assertion. Such assertions are difficult to substantiate, as there is no practical way to determine if such transactions would have taken place in the absence of the relationship, or if the terms would have been the same in an arm's-length transaction.

5.09 Accounting Estimates

Auditing Accounting Estimates, Including Fair Value

With respect to estimates that are used in the financial statements (such as the allowance for credit losses and estimated warranty liability accounts), the auditor's main concern is to determine the **reasonableness** of the estimates made by management. In evaluating the reasonableness of estimates, auditors normally concentrate on assumptions that are subjective and therefore susceptible to bias.

An accounting estimate is an approximation of a financial statement element, item or account.

Many items that are required to be reported or disclosed in the F/S may not be susceptible to precise measurement as of the F/S date. As a result, these items require the use of an accounting estimate. AU-C 540 provides guidance and requirements relative to the auditor's responsibility for such accounting estimates, including fair value measurements.

Examples of Accounting Estimates	
Involving fair value	**NOT involving fair value**
<ul><li>Values of complex financial instruments that are not actively traded</li><li>Share-based payments</li><li>Assets held for disposal</li><li>Assets/liabilities acquired in a business combination, identifiable intangibles and goodwill</li><li>Nonmonetary exchanges</li></ul>	<ul><li>Allowance for credit losses (ie, bad debts)</li><li>Inventory obsolescence</li><li>Warranty obligations</li><li>Depreciation methods, salvage values, and useful lives</li><li>Allowances recognizing the uncertainty of recoverability of certain investments</li><li>Results of long-term contracts</li><li>Financial effects of litigation</li></ul>

When auditing accounting estimates, a combination of approaches may be used, including:

- Reviewing and testing management's process, including the method of measurement, assumptions made, and the data used
- Developing an estimate Independently.
- Reviewing subsequent events up to the date of the auditor's report
- Testing the effectiveness of internal controls related to accounting estimates

Auditor's Objective

The auditor's main concern is to **determine** the **reasonableness** of the **estimates** and the related **disclosures** made by management. In evaluating the reasonableness of estimates, auditors normally concentrate on assumptions that are subjective and, therefore, more susceptible to bias (and fraud).

Understanding Management's Process

The auditor's initial step is to understand the process used by management to prepare significant estimates. Thus, the auditor will consider estimates when performing risk assessment procedures to understand the entity and its environment. In doing so, the auditor will obtain an understanding of:

- The requirements of the AFRF

- How management determines when estimates are necessary

- How management develops accounting estimates and the data upon which they are based

Assessing the Risks of Material Misstatement

Based on the understanding, the auditor will evaluate the RMM of estimates. All accounting estimates are subject to a degree of estimation uncertainty, which results in RMM. The degree of that estimation uncertainty depends upon:

- The nature of the estimate

- The subjectivity of assumptions used

- The availability of a generally accepted method or model to arrive at the estimate

Examples	
Lower-risk estimates	**Higher-risk estimates**
<ul><li>Estimates related to transactions and activities that are *not complex*</li><li>Estimates related to *routine* transactions</li><li>Estimates based on *readily available, reliable data* (eg, published market values)</li><li>Fair value estimates measured:<ul><li>Using *simple* and easily applied approaches</li><li>Under generally accepted models that use *observable inputs/assumptions*</li></ul></li></ul>	<ul><li>Estimates involving the outcome of litigation</li><li>Estimates of fair value for securities that are not publicly traded</li><li>Fair value estimates formulated:<ul><li>Using a *complex* or sophisticated model</li><li>Involving assumptions or inputs that are *not observable*</li></ul></li></ul>

Procedures to Respond to RMM

Based on the assessed RMM with respect to estimates, the auditor will undertake one or more of the following **procedures**, considering the nature of the accounting estimate:

- Determine whether events up to the date of the auditor's report provide evidence regarding the estimate.

- Test the methods and assumptions used by management and the data upon which they are based.

- Test the operating effectiveness of controls over the development of accounting estimates.

- Develop an expectation in the form of a point or range of estimates to use as a basis for evaluating management's estimate.

- Reperform or recompute estimates using the same information and method used by management.

When estimates represent **significant RMM**, the auditor will apply **additional procedures**:

- Address the effects of estimation uncertainty, including whether management has considered alternative assumptions and whether management's assumptions are reasonable

- Evaluate management's decision to recognize or not recognize accounting estimates and the basis used for measurement

Evaluation of Evidence, Disclosures and Management Bias

Based on the evidence obtained, the auditor must:

- Determine whether the accounting estimates are reasonable in relation to the AFRF or are misstated

- Determine if disclosures are in compliance with the AFRF

- Evaluate management's decisions and judgments for potential management bias

Management bias is inherent in subjective decisions and may be intentional or unintentional. Professional skepticism will be very important in evaluating any of the following indicators of possible management bias:

- Arbitrary changes in estimates or methods.

- Changes in estimates or methods were changed based on a subjective assessment that circumstances have changed.

- Events indicate that an estimate is misstated.

- The auditor believes the efforts of management to address the effects of estimation uncertainty are inadequate.

- Fair value estimates are inconsistent with observable market assumptions.

- Significant assumptions are selected or constructed to yield an estimate that favors management objectives.

- Estimates indicate a pattern of optimism or pessimism.

Documentation

The auditor should document the basis for the auditor's conclusions about:

- The reasonableness of estimates giving rise to significant risks

- Indicators of possible management bias

Guidelines for Auditing Fair Value Estimates

Fair value estimates are not given any special consideration other than the fact that the auditor needs to be aware that fair value estimates may be particularly susceptible to misstatement, depending on the availability of reliable information to measure fair value. Comparable to other estimates:

- Management is responsible for making the fair value measurements and disclosures included in the financial statements as well as identifying the significant assumptions underlying fair value measurements and disclosures.

- The auditor evaluates whether fair value measurements and disclosures, as determined by management, including the allocation of the acquisition cost relating to a business combination, are in conformity with the guidance in accounting technical literature.

- The auditor should gain an understanding of:

  - How management develops its fair value measurements and disclosures, including:

    - The experience of the personnel involved in the measurements

    - The significant assumptions used to develop the estimates

    - The relevant market information used to develop these assumptions (eg, stock price quotations and official commodity price indexes)

    - The procedures used to monitor changes in the assumptions and estimates

    - The extent to which management used outside specialists to develop the estimates

  - Procedures for estimating fair values in accordance with GAAP include:

    - The market approach, using observable market price data

    - The revenue or cash flow approach, using discounted cash flow methods

    - The cost approach, using the replacement cost of the asset

  - Risks associated with the use of estimates that could result in misstatement, based on the number, significance, and subjectivity of assumptions used to make the estimates

5.10 Subsequent Events & Subsequently Discovered Facts

Subsequent Events

An audit cannot be completed until after the balance sheet (B/S) date, and often is not completed until several weeks or more after year-end. Subsequent events are events occurring during the time interval between the B/S date but before the report is issued. Such events may have an impact in one of **two ways** (AU-C 560):

- **Type 1** – Some events provide evidence of **conditions existing** at the B/S date that are **recognized** and require **adjustment**.

    o The filing of bankruptcy by a customer early in the period subsequent to year-end may indicate that a receivable from that customer was not collectible as of the end of the period and should be written off.

    o Another example might be the settlement of litigation for an amount different than the amount that had been accrued.

- **Type 2** – Some events do not affect the B/S, as the **condition did not exist** at the B/S date, but still represent important information that should not be recognized by adjusting the F/S but should be **disclosed** to assist users of the F/S.

    o A fire that destroys the company's main warehouse shortly after the end of the period does not affect either the inventory balance or the amount reported as property, plant, and equipment at year end, but would affect the significance of those assets and may suggest possible future difficulties.

    o Other examples include sale of bonds or issuance of stock, a purchase of a business, or a loss due to flood.

Subsequent events must be evaluated by nonpublic entities (nonissuers) through either the *date of issuance of the F/S* or the *date that the F/S are available to be issued*. In the case of issuers, however, subsequent events are evaluated through the date of issuance of the F/S. The date on which F/S are available to be issued is the date the auditor signs the audit report. The client may issue their F/S on that date or at some later date, but the responsibility for subsequent events does not extend beyond that date.

The auditor's responsibility is to make certain that management has properly identified, evaluated, and recognized or disclosed, as appropriate, subsequent events up through the date of the auditor's report. There are several audit procedures occurring **after the B/S date** that may reveal evidence of subsequent events:

- Read minutes of meetings of the board of directors and other appropriate committees occurring after year-end to determine if there is discussion of major events occurring in the subsequent period

- Make inquiries of the client's legal counsel to determine if there is litigation, or if there are claims or assessments arising or being settled after the B/S date

- Read interim reports prepared by management in the subsequent period to determine if they show unusual transactions occurring after year-end

- Make inquiries of the client and obtain a management representation letter to determine if there were unusual transactions or major events occurring in the subsequent period

- Evaluate changes in long-term debt after year-end to determine if there were major financial transactions occurring after the B/S date that affect the classification of liabilities and require adjustment of the B/S or may need to be disclosed to users

The search for subsequent events does **not** refer to **all audit procedures** applied after the B/S date, **only** those that are designed to identify **events occurring after the B/S date**. Confirmations of receivables reported by the client at the B/S date are sent to customers after year-end and responses are received after year-end. This is **not**, however, a part of the search for subsequent events since it is verification of transactions and activities occurring on or before the B/S date. The examination of write-offs of customer receivables after year-end, however, is used to determine either the need to adjust the B/S or make disclosures for a subsequent event, since the write-offs were events occurring after year-end.

Once the audit report has been issued, the auditor normally has no ongoing responsibility to update the report for events occurring after that, including the resolution of lawsuits that were properly disclosed. The subsequent event's period refers only to the period between the B/S date and the date of the auditor's report, so the auditor's responsibility for subsequent events does not indicate a responsibility for events occurring after the report date.

A problem arises if there was a transaction or **event occurring before the report date** that the auditor **discovers after the report** has been issued. This would **not** be limited to the subsequent events period between the B/S and report dates, but could include events that occurred during the year under audit which were not identified by the auditor before the report was issued. Such discovery may affect the ability of the auditor to support the opinion expressed in the report, but only if it represented information that should have been available at the report date.

Assume that the audit of a client's calendar-year 20X0 F/S is completed and a report dated March 5, 20X1 is issued, expressing an unmodified/unqualified opinion on the 20X0 statements. On May 28, 20X1, the auditor discovers that the client had recently suffered major losses due to the destruction by fire of a public warehouse which was storing major assets of the client. This information was previously unknown to the auditor.

- If the fire occurred on December 15, 20X0, then the F/S for the year ended December 31, 20X0 require adjustment.

- If the fire occurred on February 15, 20X1, then the 20X0 F/S should have included a disclosure of this subsequent event.

- If the fire occurred on April 15, 20X1, then the auditor has no responsibility for the new information, since it did not represent information existing at the March 5, 20X1 report date.

In the first two cases, the auditor should determine if there are parties relying on the March 5, 20X1 report who would find this information important. If so, the auditor must ensure that those parties are notified that the audit report can no longer be relied on.

Omitted Procedures (or Subsequent Discovery of Facts)

After the report is issued, the auditor will occasionally discover that they omitted procedures (AU-C 585) (or subsequent discovery of facts – AU-C 560) that were believed to be important at the time of the audit. This could result from a miscommunication among the audit staff or the failure to note an item in the audit program. When this occurs, the auditor should:

- Assess the importance of the omitted procedure

- Determine tests to compensate for the omitted procedure (eg, subsequent receipts test for A/R)

- Perform tests

- Determine if there is a need to minimize reliance on the F/S

  - If so, notify the client, regulatory agencies and anyone relying on the statements.

Notice that this discovery does not automatically indicate that the audit was deficient or that there were misstatements in the F/S or notes. The auditor should first consider the actual importance of the omitted procedure to the auditor's opinion. The auditor may decide that the omitted procedure wasn't significant enough to impair their ability to support their opinion or that other tests applied during the engagement provided sufficient competent evidential matter to support the opinion, so that no further action is necessary.

If the auditor decides that the omitted procedure is needed to support the opinion, then the client should be contacted and the procedure performed. Once completed, there is no need to notify parties relying on the report, since the auditor will once again feel they can support their opinion. Only if the client refuses to permit the auditor to perform the omitted procedure will it be necessary to withdraw the report and notify parties that they may not rely on it.

If the procedure leads to information affecting the statements and/or notes, this will be treated as a subsequent discovery of facts and handled in the manner discussed earlier in this section.

5.11 Using the Work of Others

Overview

There are times that an auditor will use the work of others in an audit to help perform audit procedures and gather evidence. This might include:

- **Component auditors** in the case of a group financial audit

- **Internal auditors** of the client to provide audit evidence or direct assistance

- **Specialists** to provide a certain expertise that the auditor does not possess

- **IT auditors** to evaluate the client's IT system

Using the work of others comes with certain responsibilities for the **direction** and **supervision** of such individuals. There are also factors for the auditor to consider, such as their competence, objectivity, the nature and scope of their work, documentation, and reporting requirements.

Component Auditors & Group Financial Audits

If the client has a major investment in another company requiring the use of the equity method of accounting, the F/S of the client may be materially impacted by the investee's results. If the F/S of the investee company are audited by another accounting firm, a responsibility issue arises for the group engagement auditor. The **group engagement auditor** is the accounting firm that has examined the company with the largest impact on the overall report. (AU-C 600)

 Most questions on the CPA exam involve a group engagement partner who is the auditor of a parent corporation that needs to rely on the work of component auditors who audited one or more subsidiaries.

The group engagement auditor must **evaluate component auditors**, taking into consideration:

- The component auditor's understanding and willingness to comply with ethical requirements, including independence

- The component auditor's competence

- The extent to which the group engagement team will be involved in the work of the component auditor

- Whether the group engagement team will be able to obtain necessary consolidating information from the component auditor

- Whether the component auditor operates in an environment with appropriate oversight

The group engagement auditor should obtain sufficient appropriate audit evidence regarding the component without using any of the work of the component auditor when:

- The component auditor does not meet independence requirements, or

- The group engagement auditor has reservations about other matters.

Reporting Requirements

In preparing the audit report, the group auditor may decide to **assume responsibility** for the work of a component auditor and make **no reference** to the component auditor. If, however, the group auditor determines that it will **refer** to the component auditor as a means of indicating a **division of responsibility**:

- The component auditor must have complied with GAAS.

- The component auditor's report cannot be restricted.

- The group auditor should:

  o Obtain the component auditor's express permission.

  o Clearly indicate in the report that the component was not audited by the group auditor but the component auditor. Such indication should include the magnitude of the portion of the F/S audited by the component auditor.

  o Present the component auditor's report together with the report on the group F/S.

  o Consider whether modifications to the component auditor's report may necessitate modifications to the group auditor's report.

If the F/S of a component were prepared in accordance with a financial reporting framework (FRF) that is different from the FRF applicable to the group F/S, no reference should be made unless:

- The measurement, recognition, presentation, and disclosure criteria incorporated into the FRF used for the component are similar to those applicable to the FRF applied to the group F/S; and

- The group auditor has obtained evidence indicating that adjustments made to convert the component's F/S to the FRF used in the group F/S are appropriate.

Internal Auditors

AU-C 610 requires the auditor to obtain an understanding of the role of the internal audit function while obtaining an understanding of the entity and its environment, including its internal controls. Based on that understanding, the auditor may conclude that the work of the internal audit function may provide audit evidence. In addition, members of the internal audit function may be used to directly assist the external auditor in performing audit procedures.

The internal auditor can assist the external auditor in a variety of areas which include:

- Gaining an **understanding of the internal control** structure – The internal auditor will be a useful source of information about the structure.

- **Testing controls** – The internal auditor can obtain evidence for review by the external auditor.

- **Substantive testing** – The internal auditor can pull appropriate documents and assist the external auditor in locating assets to prove their **existence**.

To use the work of internal auditors, the auditor will need to evaluate:

- The **objectivity and competence** of internal auditors and the internal audit function

- Whether the internal audit function applies a **systematic and disciplined approach** that includes quality control in the performance of its responsibilities

Objectivity

In evaluating the objectivity of **internal auditors,** the external auditor will determine whether internal auditors are:

- Free of bias or conflicts of interests

- Subject to the undue influence of others such that the professional judgment of internal auditors may be overridden or otherwise affected

When performing an evaluation of the objectivity of the internal audit function and of individual internal auditors, the external auditor should keep in mind that neither can be independent in relation to the entity. There are several other **factors** that affect the objectivity of internal auditors and the internal audit function.

- The level of authority to which internal auditors report will significantly affect objectivity.

  - Objectivity is *enhanced* when internal auditors report to those charged with governance or an officer with appropriate authority.

  - Objectivity is *impaired* when internal auditors report to management, although this can be mitigated if the internal auditors have access to those charged with governance.

- Other responsibilities of internal auditors, such as participation in management or operations, may impair objectivity as internal auditors may be responsible for drawing conclusions about their own performance.

- Constraints or restrictions on internal auditors, such as restrictions on communications with the external auditors, impairs objectivity.

- The level at which employment and remuneration decisions related to internal auditors is made also affects objectivity. Conclusions based on internal audit procedures applied to those responsible for such decisions may be affected.

- Objectivity is enhanced when internal auditors participate in professional associations that impose professional standards related to objectivity on their members or when the entity's internal policies are designed to achieve comparable objectives.

Competence

The auditor will evaluate the **knowledge** and **skills** of the internal audit function and individual internal auditors to determine if they are sufficient to enable them to perform with the appropriate level of quality. There are several **factors** that enhance such competency.

- Resources (eg, money, staff, etc.) available to the internal audit function, relative to the size of the entity and the nature of its operations.

- Policies related to the hiring, training, and matching of internal auditors with engagements.

- Availability of technical training and experience.

- Achievement of professional designations (eg, Certified Internal Auditor) based on established professional standards.

- Demonstrated knowledge of the entity's AFRF and knowledge specific to the industry and the entity's financial reporting.

- Membership in professional associations establishing relevant professional standards and requirements for the continuing education of its members.

A deficiency in objectivity cannot be compensated for by strength in competency, nor vice versa. To judge both **competence and objectivity**, the external auditor may also consider:

- Entity policies and procedures, along with the status of internal audit within the organization

- The quality of internal audit documentation

- Discussions with management

- The external auditor's previous dealings with the internal auditor

- The internal auditor's compliance with professional internal auditing standards

Applying a Systematic & Disciplined Approach

When considering using the work of the internal audit function in obtaining audit evidence, it is essential that the work is performed applying a systematic and disciplined approach that includes an element of quality control. When such an approach is not applied, neither a high level of competence nor the strong support of the internal audit function's objectivity can compensate.

Internal audit activities that do not apply a systematic and disciplined approach are considered to be a monitoring component of the entity's internal control structure. Each of the following factors will enhance the auditor's perception that a systematic and disciplined approach is being applied:

- Documentation of internal audit procedures or guidance covering areas such as risk assessment, audit procedures and programs, documentation, and reporting

- The existence of quality control procedures, such as those related to leadership, human resources, and engagement performance

- Adherence to quality control requirements established by professional associations

Matters Requiring the Auditor's Judgment

Regardless of the level of objectivity, competence, or the application of a systematic and disciplined approach, the external auditor will not rely on the internal audit function or internal auditors in relation to any matters that require the application of the **auditor's judgment**. This includes significant judgments, such as:

- Assessing the RMM.

- Evaluating the sufficiency of tests performed.

- Evaluating management's assumptions as to substantial doubt as to whether the entity is a going concern.

- Evaluating significant estimates.

- Evaluating the adequacy of disclosures or any other issues that may affect the external auditor's report on the F/S.

Using the Work of the Internal Audit Function to Obtain Audit Evidence

Once the external auditor has determined that the internal audit function maintains appropriate levels of objectivity and competence, and that it applies a systematic and disciplined approach to the performance of its activities, the auditor will determine if the work of the internal audit function is relevant to the audit strategy and audit plan that has been established for the engagement.

- Based on the auditor's assessed RMM at the assertion level, the external auditor determines the nature, timing, and extent of further audit procedures that are responsive to that assessment.

- Further audit procedures may include some combination of tests of controls and substantive audit procedures, some of which may be similar to, or the same as, procedures performed by the internal audit function.

- When this is the case, the external auditor may decide to modify the nature or timing of, or reduce the extent of, further audit procedures that will be performed directly by the external auditor.

The work of the internal audit function may:

- Include **tests of controls** and/or **substantive tests**. The external auditor may be able to use the results of such tests to modify the nature or timing, or to reduce the extent, of the respective tests that the auditor had planned to perform.

- Be applied to a **component of a group** for which the external auditor is the group auditor. The external auditor may be able to use the results of those procedures, for example, to reduce the number of components to which audit procedures are applied.

- Be used to obtain evidence regarding the tracing of transactions through the **accounting information system** to determine if information is being properly and accurately captured and summarized for reporting purposes and regarding compliance with regulatory requirements.

Before relying on the work of the internal audit function, the auditor will perform certain procedures to determine that:

- The work was properly planned, performed, supervised, reviewed, and documented.

- Sufficient appropriate evidence was obtained to support any conclusions drawn.

- Conclusions that were reached were appropriate under the circumstances.

The external auditor will evaluate the overall quality of the work and the objectivity with which the work was performed through:

- Making inquiries

- Observing procedures

- Reviewing work programs and documentation

- Reperform some of the procedures performed by the internal audit function as a whole

- o **Reperformance** provides more persuasive evidence than other procedures that might be applied.

- o The external auditor will generally focus on areas requiring a greater degree of judgment.

Using Internal Auditors to Provide Direct Assistance in Performing Audit Procedures

When the external auditor decides to use internal auditors to provide direct assistance in the performance of audit procedures, it will be under the *direction, supervision, and review of the external auditor*. Before making such a decision, however, the external auditor must evaluate threats to the objectivity and level of competence of the internal auditors providing the assistance.

Prior to using internal auditors to provide direct assistance in the performance of audit procedures, the external auditor will obtain **written representation** from management or those charged with governance *indicating* that:

- The internal auditors will be allowed to follow the instructions of the external auditor; and

- The entity will not intervene in the work performed for the external auditor by the internal auditors.

The amount of direction, supervision, and review will be based on the external auditor's evaluation of the objectivity and competence of the internal auditors.

- Review procedures will include testing some of the work performed by the internal auditor.

- The external auditor will instruct internal auditors to bring identified accounting and auditing issues to their attention.

- The auditor should remain alert to any indications that prior evaluations of the internal auditor's objectivity or competence are no longer appropriate.

Documentation

The auditor will document the results of the evaluation of:

- The objectivity of the internal audit function and the internal auditors, including its status within the organization and entity policies and procedures that support objectivity.

- The competence of the internal audit function and the internal auditors.

- The application of a systematic and disciplined approach by the internal audit function, including quality control, but only if using the work of the internal audit function to obtain audit evidence.

When using the work of the internal audit function to obtain audit evidence, the external auditor will document the:

- Nature and extent of the work used and the basis for the decision to use it.

- Period covered by the work performed by the internal audit function and the results of the work.

- Procedures performed to evaluate the adequacy of the work of the internal audit function, including procedures applied in reperforming some of the work.

- Basis for concluding that the external auditor was adequately involved in the engagement.

When using internal auditors to provide direct assistance to the external auditor in performing audit procedures, documentation will include:

- Threats to the objectivity of the internal auditors and safeguards that eliminated the threats or reduced them to an acceptable level.

- The level of competence of the internal auditors providing direct assistance.

- The basis for deciding on the nature and extent of work to be performed by internal auditors.

- The nature and extent of the review performed by the external auditor in relation to work performed by internal auditors.

- Working papers prepared by internal auditors providing direct assistance to the external audit in the performance of audit procedures.

- The basis for concluding that the external auditor was adequately involved in the engagement.

Specialists

Circumstances sometimes arise in an audit when the work of a **specialist** is needed[3]. For example:

- In an audit of a jewelry store, the auditor will likely require the services of an expert gemologist to verify the **valuation** of items during the inventory count.

- A land surveyor might be needed to help gauge the **quantity** of property owned by the client.

- An actuary may be needed to provide interpretation of a pension agreement and determine the client's liability.

AU-C 620 establishes the auditor's responsibilities when using the work of a specialist. When using a specialist, the auditor should keep in mind that the audit opinion is solely the responsibility of the auditor and the findings of a specialist constitute audit evidence to be evaluated by the auditor.

Although the specialist will often be performing tasks that the auditor is not personally capable of performing, the **auditor must understand** the **methods** and **assumptions** underlying the specialist's work, and must be able to **evaluate** the **results** of that work. The specialist, in turn, must understand the way the auditor will be utilizing the specialist's work to provide **corroborative evidence** to support the auditor's opinion. These understandings should be documented.

In evaluating the timing, nature, and extent of audit procedures that will be applied to the work of a specialist, the auditor will consider:

- The nature of the subject matter the specialist will address

- The RMM associated with the subject matter

---

[3] *An internal auditor is not considered to be a specialist.*

- The significance of the specialist's work in the context of the audit

- The auditor's knowledge of, and previous experience with, the work of the specialist

- Whether the specialist is subject to the auditor's firm's quality control policies and procedures

The auditor should carefully consider the specialist's **competence and objectivity.**

- Competence may be demonstrated by licenses, reputation, and the quality of written reports.

- Objectivity depends on the specialist not having any relationship with the client that would impair the specialist's independence.

- An auditor may still utilize the work of a specialist who lacks objectivity but must consider the situation in gauging the level of persuasiveness of the evidence received from the specialist.

The auditor will evaluate the adequacy of the work of the specialist, including:

- The relevance and reasonableness of the specialist's findings and conclusions and their consistency with the audit evidence

- The specialist's use of significant assumptions and methods, which the auditor should understand and evaluate

- The specialist's use of source data, in which case the auditor will evaluate its relevance, accuracy, and completeness

The auditor must be cautious about references to the work of the specialist in the audit report. Since it is not appropriate to divide responsibility for the opinion with someone who is not also an auditor, the auditor must **not refer** to the specialist in the audit report if it contains an **unmodified/unqualified** opinion.

The auditor may refer to the work of a specialist if it is relevant to the understanding of a modification to the auditor's opinion. When referring to the work of a specialist, the auditor should indicate in the report that the reference does not reduce the auditor's responsibility for the opinion.

IT Auditors

IT auditors can bring vital skills to an engagement. For example, they can:

- Perform tests to determine whether automated processes and systems run accurately, efficiently, securely and in compliance with applicable laws

- Test networks, software solutions, programs, communication systems, security systems and any other services that rely on the company's technological infrastructure

- Evaluate automated internal controls and processes to determine whether data is accurate, timely, and secure from external or internal threats

- Review the client's system change process, ensuring that controls are in place to prevent unauthorized or untested changes

- Evaluate the security of client information processed by a vendor or stored in a vendor location (eg, in the cloud)

An auditor may need to consider using an IT auditor in planning the audit and/or in the performance of audit procedures when the client's IT system:

- Is complicated (eg, the client uses custom applications rather than packaged software)

- Is newly implemented or has undergone substantial changes

- Shares data across many applications

- Includes sophisticated e-commerce components

- Processes its financial information with relatively new technology

- Produces most of the client's audit evidence in electronic form rather than paper (ie, the auditor cannot "audit around the computer")

IT auditors can play an important role in the achievement of the objectives of an audit. For example, an IT auditor can assist the auditor with:

- Obtaining an **understanding** of the **IT system**, including its general and application controls, and the effect on the audit

- Identifying and assessing IT risks as well as control deficiencies

- Designing and performing **tests of IT controls** and **substantive tests** through the computer using computer-assisted auditing techniques (**CAATs**)

- Determining the effect of outsourced IT activities and evaluating controls that mitigate any associated risks

- Preparing system audit documentation (ie, system flowcharts, data flow diagrams, process diagrams, etc.)

IT auditors may be employed by the audit firm or the client as part of the internal audit function, or they may be external specialists that are called upon to assist in select audit situations.

- If they are part of the audit firm, they would be viewed as part of the **audit staff** performing an engagement.

- If the IT auditor is employed by the client as part of the internal audit function, any resulting work they perform would be subject to the same evaluation as that of an **internal auditor** as described above.

- If the IT auditor is an external **specialist**, any resulting work they perform would be subject to the same evaluation as that of a specialist as described above.

5.12 Audit Data Analytics & Other CAATs

Computer-Assisted Auditing Techniques

Generalized Audit Software

When examining a company in an IT environment, the auditor can check the client's data for quality, completeness, accuracy, and consistency with the help of generalized audit software. This software enables the auditor to use **computer-assisted auditing techniques (CAATs)** for both tests of IT controls and substantive testing. Software packages generally include programs for the following purposes.

Extraction of client files for analysis – Such programs access and import *read-only* client files that can be manipulated for further analysis. For example, the auditor's program may access computerized inventory files to determine the location of inventory and perform audit data analytics (ADAs) to analyze dates of last purchase and sale to identify obsolete or slow-moving inventory. See the chart below for more examples of software features the auditor can use to manipulate and analyze data.

Generalized Audit Software Features			
Manipulation of data		**Analysis**	
• Join/merge files • Compare files • Perform queries	• Split tables/columns • Sort data • Filter data	• Summarization of data • Statistical analysis • Ratio calculation	• Aging • Stratification • Outlier analysis

This is not intended to be an all-inclusive list.

- **Parallel simulation** – These programs duplicate common functions of client software that can be used to test the processing integrity of their system. In a parallel simulation, the auditor inputs **client data** into the **auditor's program** to see if it produces the same results as the client's program. For example, the auditor might obtain the raw data for an actual payroll period and run it through a payroll program to see if the checks and payroll records produced are identical to the checks and records generated by the client's program.

- **Other automated tools** – Other tools can increase overall audit efficiency and effectiveness by automating various functions, such as:

  o **Gap & duplicate detection** – Generalized audit software can quickly identify gaps in prenumbered documents (eg, checks) as well as duplicate data (eg, duplicate invoices).

  o **Recalculating balances** – The auditor can set up a calculated field that recalculates certain amounts based on other data within a file (eg, net pay can be recalculated by subtracting withholdings from gross pay).

o **Sampling** – This may include, for example, creating and evaluating random samples, stratified random samples, or monetary unit samples.

o **Generating confirmations** – For example, customer contact information can be exported to a word processing program to create multiple confirmations at once with the help of the "mail merge" function.

o **Detection of fraud/errors using Benford's Law** – Benford's Law provides that certain numbers are more likely to naturally occur as the first digit in an amount than others. For example, the first digit of a number is 1 about 30% of the time, and the frequency of occurrence decreases for each succeeding number. Benford's Law generally holds true for large data sets. Thus, any deviations from Benford's Law in such circumstances may need further investigation.

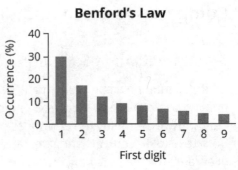

o **Automation of audit procedures** – Scripts can be programmed to reperform the same procedures later.

o **Managing workpapers** – All procedures performed and their results are logged automatically (aka, an audit log).

Source Code Comparison Programs

Source code comparison programs can detect unauthorized changes made by the client in programs that the auditor is testing. For example, after the auditor has verified the proper functioning of a copy of the payroll program provided to them by the client for testing, a source code comparison program would match the tested program with the one being used by the client to process an actual payroll period to be sure the files are identical.

Test Data

When the client has a program that the auditor wishes to verify and for which there is no appropriate equivalent program available to the auditor, techniques involving the direct use of the client program are required. One approach is known as the test data approach, in which the auditor will develop **simulated data** to enter into the **client's program**. Characteristics of this approach include:

- Entry of both **valid and invalid audit data** to verify that the program processes appropriate data correctly and rejects inappropriate data.

- **Simulated data** designed for only those valid and invalid conditions that interest the auditor.

- Only **one example** of each valid and invalid condition, since computer programs are consistent in the way they handle items, making this an efficient method of testing.

- Auditor compares actual test results with expected results to verify that the application is processing transactions correctly.

Continuous Auditing Techniques

While the following continuous auditing techniques have been around for some time, continuous auditing is increasing in popularity. This is due to the increase in data, the emergence of better data analytic technologies, and the decrease in the cost of IT (eg, ERP systems), among other things.

- **Program tracing & transaction tagging** – Program tracing requires the auditor to walk-through the application's internal logic contained in the source code. With tracing, the auditor first creates test transactions with electronic "tags" and then examines how the application's logic processes those transactions.

- **Integrated test facility (ITF)** – While the test data method tests application processing at a point in time, ITF supports continuous monitoring of controls. ITF involves creating audit modules in the **client's application** during **normal processing.** The auditor will include **test data** in an ITF, mixing **simulated data** (fictitious transactions) in with actual data during a program run. For example, the auditor may add simulated payroll data to actual data for a pay period so that testing occurs during the normal processing of payroll.

- **Embedded audit modules (EAM)** – These programs are implanted in the client's processing system to perform audit procedures on a **continuous, real-time basis**. EAMs are designed to extract transactions that meet certain conditions. For example, the auditor could use an EAM to extract all invoices greater than $25,000 to a separate audit file. The auditor can then follow-up on these invoices in the audit file.

Controlled Reprocessing

If it isn't practical to use an ITF, the auditor may use controlled reprocessing. In this approach, the auditor supervises the entry of **actual client data** into the client program to reproduce the results of a previous run of the program by the client. After verifying that the results are identical to the previous run, the auditor knows that the program is the actual one used, and can enter the test data into it at a separate time.

CAATs Summary

It is important to remember that computer software cannot replace the judgment of the auditor. The responsibility for determining the acceptable level of audit risk and assessing the component risks remains with the auditor.

	Actual Client Data	Simulated Data
Actual Client Program	Controlled Reprocessing	Test Data (Integrated Test Facility)
Auditor's Program	Parallel Simulation	No relevance to audit of client

Approach	Data	Program
Test Data (Phony data)	Auditor's	Client's
Controlled Reprocessing	Client's	Client's (but Auditor's computer)
Integrated Test Facility (ITF) (Dummy Division or file & Fictitious transactions)	Auditor & Client's	Client's
Program Tracing & Transaction Tagging	Client's information with a Tag	Client's
Parallel Simulation	Client's	Auditor's (Going around their system)

Benefits of Data Analytics

The proliferation of "big data", advances in storage technology, and data modeling and visualization software allow for better decisions using data analytics. Data can be extracted, both *internally and externally*, for every facet of operations to gain insights that are then used to strategize and drive an organization's decisions to meet its goals and solve its problems.

Much of the same data and tools used to drive client decisions are valuable resources to the auditor as well. The auditor can mine an entity's data (as well as external data) to **discover relevant patterns** and **anomalies** and **analyze** such information **through modeling** and **visualization** to gain a deeper understanding of the business and its environment, assess the risks, and plan the audit accordingly. Auditors can also use different data analytic techniques throughout the audit to perform tests of controls, tests of details, and substantive analytical procedures, as well as in the conclusion of the audit.

Audit data analytics (ADAs) are having a profound effect on the audit from beginning to end. For example, instead of sampling, auditors can test entire populations of data efficiently and effectively, thereby increasing the possibility of detecting material misstatements. To top it all off, ADAs and the use of visualizations also improve the auditor's ability to communicate effectively with those charged with governance.

AICPA's 5-Step Process for ADAs

Note that there is no authoritative guidance with respect to the use of ADAs specifically. To help auditors through this transition of using more ADAs throughout the audit, the AICPA has published a nonauthoritative *Guide to Audit Data Analytics*. Among the useful information contained within the guide are ideas for effectively using and streamlining ADAs, including examples and illustrations, as well as connections to the existing generally accepted auditing standards (GAAS) that apply. [4] The guide also suggests the following 5-step process for auditors to follow:

1. **Plan the ADA.**

   o Overall purpose of the ADA?

   o Specific objective(s) of the ADA?

     ▪ Items/assertions being analyzed.

   o Data population to be used?

   o ADA techniques, tools, visualizations, etc. to be used?

2. **Access and prepare the data for purposes of the ADA.**

   o Extract the data from the system it lives in.

   o Transform the data into a format the auditor can use.

   o Load the data into the analysis software.

3. **Consider the relevance and reliability of the data used.**

   o Nature of the data?

   o Source?

   o Process used to produce the data?

   o Should procedures be performed to verify that the data is sufficiently reliable?

4. **Perform the ADA.**

   o Does the ADA need to be revised and reperformed?

   o If not, and the ADA has identified items that need further investigation, plan and perform additional procedures on those items that are consistent with the purpose and specific objectives of the ADA.

5. **Evaluate the results.**

   o Were the purpose and specific objectives of performing the ADA achieved?

   o If not, plan and perform other procedures to achieve the objectives.

Types of Data

- **Structured** – Data contained in fields within records or files (eg, databases and spreadsheets). ADAs are typically focused here.

- **Unstructured** – Raw data not contained within a database/spreadsheet (eg, text, video, audio, photos, etc.).

---

[4] *We appreciate the AICPA's permission to provide you with some highlights of their work and a few of their examples and illustrations within this lecture.*

- **Semi-structured** – Data that has information associated (ie, metadata or tags) that makes it easier to process than unstructured data (eg, HTML tagged text).

Examples of Data Sources			
Internal*		**External**	
• Accounting data • Customer data • Employee data	• Marketing data • Supplier data • Shipping data	• Industry data • Government data	• Census data • Social media

Consideration should be given to whether internal data is obtained from within the financial accounting reporting system or outside that system (ie, not controlled by the accounting department).

Examples of Data Characteristics/Attributes			
Nature			
• Financial • Nonfinancial • Descriptive	• Process-related • Control-related • Regulatory	• Demographic • Economic • Geographic	• Historical • Prospective • Time-sensitivity
Timing		**Extent**	
• Point in time or over a period of time • The rate at which the data changes		• Volume of data • Variety of subject matter (ie, scope)	
Basis of Aggregation			
• By database file, table, or field. • By frequency (eg, annually, monthly, daily, etc.) • At F/S item level, account balance, or part of an account balance. • At the consolidated entity level, or by segment, division, location, etc.			

Types of Data Analytics, Techniques, Tools & Visualizations

Types of Data Analytics

There are four main types of data analytics. An auditor, however, would generally be focused on the first three here:

- **Descriptive Analytics** focuses on *what has happened*.

- **Diagnostic Analytics** aims to tell you *why something happened*.

- **Predictive Analytics** tell you *what should happen* based on past patterns and trends.

- **Prescriptive Analytics** use the other three types of analytics to tell you *what to do* to get to the results desired.

While there are four main approaches to data analytics, there are many different techniques, tools (ie, software), and visualization options to choose from. We've listed some examples of each below.

Examples of Techniques

- **Sorting** – A simple categorizing of data to identify outliers.

- **Cluster analysis** – Grouping data by similarities in a way that shows the structure/relationships between the data.

- **Matching** – Comparing data from various sources (eg, electronic documents) to identify unexpected differences.

- **Process mining** – Identifying deviations from a specified process.

- **Comparative analysis** – Comparing the relationships between variables (eg, financial statement items) over two or more periods.

- **Trend analysis** – Analyzing changes in data (eg, account balances) over time to look for trends (a type of comparative analysis).

- **Ratio analysis** – Calculating ratios to discover relationships among financial and nonfinancial data.

- **Predictive modeling** – Comparing expectations to actual data to identify deviations (aka, reasonableness test).

- **Regression analysis** – Using a statistical analysis to examine the relationship between one or more independent variables (ie, predictors) and a dependent variable.

- **Time-series regression analysis** – A regression analysis that uses data from *more than one past periods* to make predictions for future periods.

- **Cross-sectional regression analysis** – A regression analysis that uses data from *one period of time or a point in time* to make predictions.

Tools	
• Excel (smaller amounts of data)	• ACL™
• Python™	• Tableau™
• IDEA™	• MySQL™
• R™	• SAS™

Visualizations

Data visualization boils down to four basic presentation types: *comparison, composition, distribution, and relationship*. Some techniques, such as regression analysis, are generally associated with certain visualizations, like a scatterplot, which shows both distribution and relationship, but most visualizations are a matter of professional judgment as to which options to use and combine to best communicate the results of an ADA.

The auditor will need to find the right balance of information to present in each graphic; that is, the information presented in a visualization should be neither too scant nor too crowded. The user should be able to figure out what the graphic is trying to communicate without needing to read too much. The following are some great examples of the use of visualizations from the AICPA's ADA Guide. [5]

Examples of Visualizations

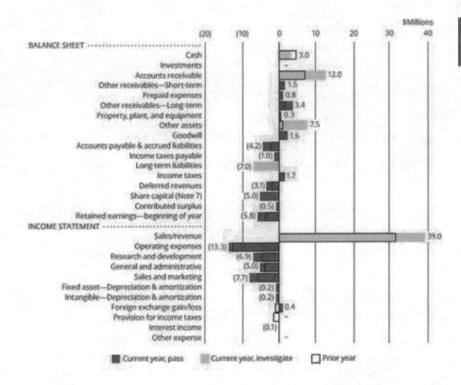

Comparative Analysis

Divergent bar charts show data that have both positive and negative values.

Graphic Source: AICPA ADA Guide, Exhibit A-4

Trend Analysis

Stacked column charts show how the parts make up the whole, and the *trend lines* show how the parts have changed over time.

Graphic Source: AICPA ADA Guide, Exhibit A-5

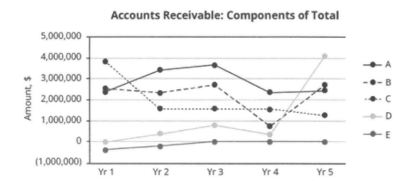

Trend Analysis

Multiple-line charts compare the trends in data over time.

Graphic Source: AICPA ADA Guide, Exhibit A-5

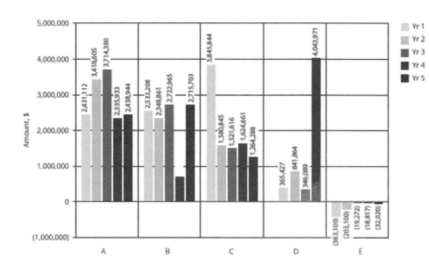

Trend Analysis

Grouped column charts compare different categories of different groups of data.

Graphic Source: AICPA ADA Guide, Exhibit A-5

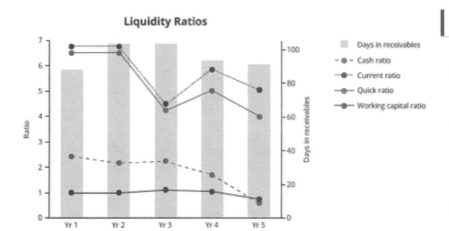

Ratio Analysis

Column & line charts (ie, dual-axis charts) can be combined to show the correlation over time between variables with different scales of measurement.

Graphic Source: AICPA ADA Guide, Exhibit A-6

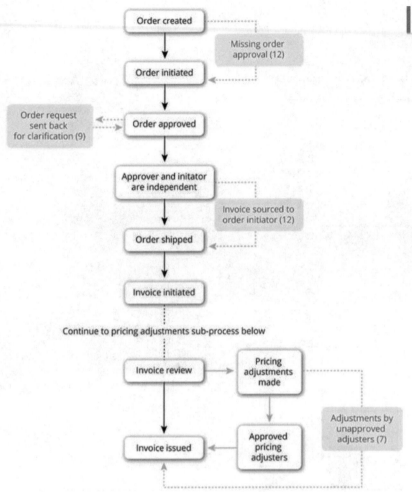

Process Mining

Flow charts are essential for showing the steps in a process and the variances from that standard process.

Graphic Source: AICPA ADA Guide, Exhibit A-16

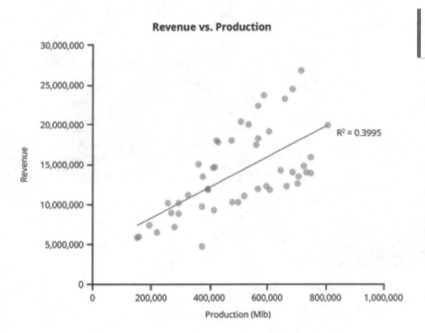

Regression Analysis

Scatterplots and *regression lines* show the correlation (R^2) between two variables. The closer R^2 is to 1, the stronger the correlation and the more precise a prediction of the dependent variable (Y) based on the independent variable (X) will be. Here, R^2 means that only 39.95% of the variance in Revenue can be explained by the regression model in relation to Production (ie, a weak correlation).

Graphic Source: AICPA ADA Guide, Exhibit B-4

Access & Preparation of Data

Sometimes referred to as **Extract, Transform** and **Load (ETL)**, the process of accessing and preparing the data to be analyzed can be the most complicated part of using an ADA. There are two key issues regarding access to data:

- Gaining access to the data in a format the auditor can use

- Maintaining security, confidentiality, and integrity of the data (eg, the entity may be concerned that the auditor could corrupt the data).

Preparation of the data includes "cleaning" or "scrubbing" the data. This is the process of identifying and removing errors in the data (eg, empty fields, numeric fields that contain text, etc.) so that it can be analyzed properly. Such issues could indicate that controls are not working properly, and in some cases, the data may not be auditable until the entity addresses the cause(s) and corrects the problem(s).

Data preparation may also require merging the format of a field from different systems into one. For example, the format of dates could be different—MM/DD/YYYY vs. DD/MM/YYYY.

Audit Data Standards (ADS)

To make the ETL process easier, the AICPA has developed voluntary Audit Data Standards (ADS). The ADS provide:

- **A uniform data model** – If implemented by an entity, the ADS help standardize the formatting of essential audit data in files and fields to avoid the time-consuming processes mentioned above. Even if the entity has not implemented the ADS, the auditor can map the entity's data to the ADS and automate the standardization of subsequent data extractions.

- **Standards for data requests** – The ADS provide questionnaires for the entity to answer each time data is provided. The answers to the questions will help the auditor understand the data and any exceptions to the ADS that may exist.

- **Automated data validation procedures** – Such procedures help the auditor evaluate the completeness and integrity of data extracted and received. These tests include, for example:

  o Checking that all **files** and data **fields** requested have been received.

  o Checking the range of **dates** on the data to be sure the data is for the dates requested.

  o Checking **control totals** (eg, record counts, financial totals, hash totals) to determine whether all data requested have been received.

  o Counting the number of **blank values** by field.

  o Counting the records that contain fields with **incorrect formatting**.

Relevance & Reliability of Data

AU-C 500, *Audit Evidence*, requires the auditor to consider whether information used as audit evidence is relevant and sufficiently reliable. This topic was covered in another section, so we'll stick to the basics for ADAs here.

- **Relevance** – Relevant data has a logical connection with the purpose of the audit procedure and the assertion being considered.

- **Reliability** – The auditor should evaluate the **accuracy** and **completeness** of the data in determining whether it will be sufficiently reliable to meet the objectives of the particular procedure.

  o The reliability of audit evidence is influenced by its **source** and **nature**, as well as the **circumstances in which it is obtained**. For example, the reliability of data obtained from a system with adequate controls over the preparation and maintenance of such data would be more reliable than data obtained from a system with weak controls.

  o The auditor might also consider the following in assessing the reliability of data:

    - The **ADA's purpose** (eg, test of controls, test of details, etc.) and the specific *objective* of the procedure. Data should be sufficiently *precise* and *detailed* for the auditor's purposes. For example, data used for a substantive analytical procedure ADA may need to be more persuasive than data used in a risk assessment ADA.

    - The **risk assessment** of the account and/or assertion being audited.

    - The **extent of other procedures** performed with regard to the account/assertion being audited. That is, if other audit procedures are performed with respect to the account/assertion, the reliability of the data used for the ADA may already be somewhat vetted.

    - **Performing procedures** to assess data reliability (eg, verifying the continuity of invoice numbers and the absence of duplicates). In determining the nature, timing, and extent of such procedures, the auditor might consider other factors, such as the **characteristics** of the data and the **availability** of relevant and reliable sources of audit evidence. For example, it may be difficult to obtain evidence regarding the reliability of certain external data sources.

Items Requiring Further Consideration

When testing very large populations (eg, 100 percent), an ADA may produce too many items for an auditor to address individually. While some of the items found can indicate real problems (eg, unidentified risks, control deficiencies, or misstatements), an ADA is likely to highlight many nonissues, or "false positives" as well. As a result, the auditor may need to consider:

- Reperforming the ADA after narrowing down the analyzed data with more specific criteria (ie, characteristics/attributes of data that are indicative of issues that actually require an audit response).

- Breaking the population down further into groups and applying additional procedures to each group. These procedures could produce evidence that the group as a whole is, or is not, problematic (ie, needs further consideration).

- Applying another ADA or other procedure.

GAAS Requirements & ADA Examples for Different Types of Procedures

The most important overarching GAAS requirements to remember with respect to planning, performing, and evaluating the results of ADAs are the auditor's requirements to use **professional judgment** and maintain an attitude of **professional skepticism** throughout the audit.[6] Since these requirements were discussed at length in a previous section, we won't go into all the specifics again here.

Risk Assessment Procedures

AU-C 315[7] defines risk assessment procedures as "[t]he audit procedures performed to obtain an understanding of the entity and its environment, including the entity's internal control, to identify and assess the risks of material misstatement, whether due to fraud or error, at the financial statement and relevant assertion levels." Some of these procedures are required to be analytical procedures, so ADAs may be a perfect fit for identifying and assessing risks of material misstatement (RMM). Note that some risk assessment ADAs could provide audit evidence that fulfills other purposes as well (eg, tests of details, tests of controls, etc.).

In planning a risk assessment ADA, the specific objectives might be affected by the requirements in AU-C 315 to obtain an understanding of:

- Relevant industry, regulatory, and other external factors

- The nature of the entity, including its operations; its ownership and governance structures; its investments; and the way the entity is structured and financed

- The entity's selection and application of accounting policies

- The entity's objectives and strategies and those related business risks that may result in RMM

- The measurement and review of the entity's financial performance

- Relevant internal controls

Performing an ADA is an iterative process. Once the auditor has decided that the ADA no longer needs to be revised and reperformed, the auditor should evaluate the results. As previously mentioned, large populations can sometimes produce a large number of items to address, so the auditor may want to sort and filter the items into groups; for example, here it might make sense to group items by common characteristics that indicate a particular risk at the relevant assertion level.

Also, after excluding any false positives that do not require further consideration, the auditor can group the remaining "notable items" from a risk assessment procedure into the following categories:

- Items that represent previously unidentified risks (ie, new risks)

- Items that represent risks that are higher than originally assessed

---

[6] AU-C 200, *Overall Objectives of the Independent Auditor and the Conduct of an Audit in Accordance with Generally Accepted Auditing Standards*

[7] AU-C 315, *Understanding the Entity and Its Environment and Assessing the Risks of Material Misstatement*

- Items that provide information to better design further audit procedures to address the RMM (ie, items that are consistent with the original assessment of risk)

If the number of notable items found is too large to address manually, the auditor may need to design further risk assessment ADAs to obtain more information about the items.

 If you are an auditor of a small printer manufacturer and you're assessing the RMM and you want to know if there were any unusual changes or trends in sales this year compared to prior years, how might you design an ADA to achieve this objective? In doing so, what else might you learn from this ADA?

Additional information:

- Annual sales are generally about $25 million.
- Your firm has audited the financial statements of the client for the last three years (ie, 2012 – 2014).
- There was a labor strike at one of the company's plants for more than half of the current year. It ended in the third quarter.
- A new advanced printer (Type H) was introduced early this year (2015) and quickly became the best-selling product.
- The company began operations in Q2 of 2012.
- Inquiries of management indicate that there were no sales of the Type D printer in the current year since production was discontinued last year.

Based on this information, what would you expect to see in the ADA results?

1. Plan the ADA.

- Overall purpose of the ADA?	- To identify and assess RMM related to sales

- Specific objective(s) of the ADA?
 	
   o Items/assertions being analyzed?
	- Determine if there were any unusual changes or trends in sales this year.
	- ADA should provide information relevant to assessing and responding to RMM with regard to the following assertions:
	
	   o Revenue–
	
	      ▪ Occurrence
	
	      ▪ Completeness
	
	      ▪ Accuracy
	
	   o Other–
	
	      ▪ Adequacy of allowance for obsolete stock (ie, inventory valuation)
	
	      ▪ Completeness of warranty provisions

- Data population to be used?	- Amounts recorded in general ledger for sales of printers for the current and last 3 years

	• Quarterly sales data for current year
	• Units sold for each type of printer from company database
• ADA techniques, tools, visualizations, etc. to be used?	• Trend analysis
	o A chart showing quarterly sales over each year to expose any trends in sales revenue
	o A chart showing trends in sales with regard to the different types of printers

2. Access and prepare the data for purposes of the ADA.

3. Consider the relevance and reliability of the data used.

4. Perform the ADA.

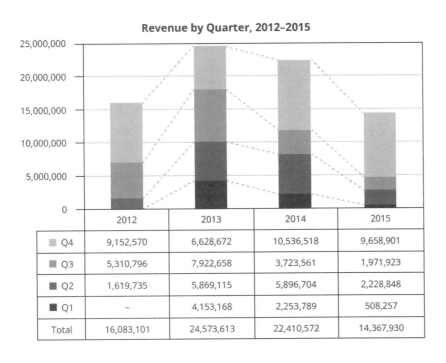

Revenue by Quarter, 2012–2015

	2012	2013	2014	2015
▦ Q4	9,152,570	6,628,672	10,536,518	9,658,901
▦ Q3	5,310,796	7,922,658	3,723,561	1,971,923
▦ Q2	1,619,735	5,869,115	5,896,704	2,228,848
▦ Q1	–	4,153,168	2,253,789	508,257
Total	16,083,101	24,573,613	22,410,572	14,367,930

Trend Analysis

Are the results consistent with expectations?

Yes; due to the strike, sales for 2015 are less than the prior year and they start to recover by the last quarter of the year.

Graphic Source: AICPA ADA Guide, Exhibit A-1

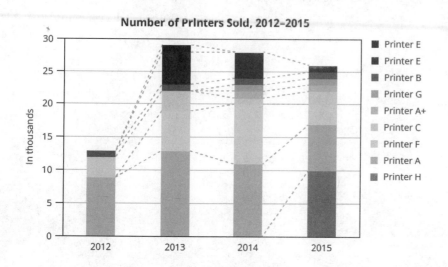

Trend Analysis

Are the results consistent with expectations?

Yes; there is a significant amount of Type H printer sales to the detriment of other printer types in 2015.

Yes; there are no sales of the Type D printer in the current year since they were discontinued in a prior year.

Graphic Source: AICPA ADA Guide, Exhibit A-2

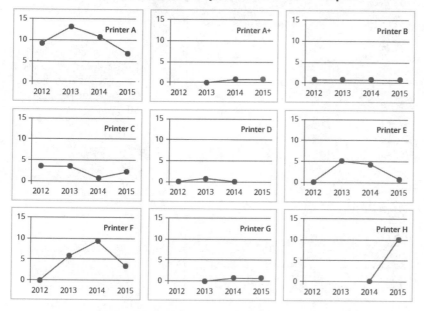

Trend Analysis

In this alternative graphic it is a little easier to see which printer sales decreased (primarily Printer F) as a result of introducing Printer H in 2014. Printer H may have also affected the sales of Printers A and E but sales for those printers were already on their way down.

Graphic Source: AICPA ADA Guide, Exhibit A-3

5. Evaluate the results.

• Were the purpose and specific objectives of performing the ADA achieved?
 	
 • If not, plan and perform other procedures to achieve the objectives.
	• **Overall purpose**: *Achieved*
	 • **Specific Objective:** Achieved; no unusual trends.
	
	    o Auditor's original risk assessments regarding revenue:
	
	      ▪ Occurrence – Confirmed; no change.
	      ▪ Completeness – Confirmed; no change.
	      ▪ Accuracy – Confirmed; no change.
	
	    o Other:
	
	      ▪ Adequacy of allowance for obsolete stock – *Confirmed expected higher risk; no change.*
	
	      ▪ Completeness of warranty provisions – ADA did not identify a need to modify planned procedures.

Tests of Controls

While ADAs can be used to test controls, the AICPA's ADA Guide does not cover this topic and the CPA Exam Blueprints also do not mention that such ADAs will be tested.

Tests of Details

AU-C 330, *Performing Audit Procedures in Response to Assessed Risks and Evaluating the Audit Evidence Obtained*, provides the requirements for substantive procedures. Substantive procedures consist of tests of details and substantive analytical procedures. The suggested steps in applying an ADA for tests of details are essentially the same as those suggested for risk assessment ADAs, so let's just focus on the performance stage to see how the process is a little different:

4. Perform the ADA. Does the ADA need to be revised and reperformed? If not, and the ADA has identified items that need further investigation, plan and perform additional procedures on those items that are consistent with the purpose and specific objectives of the ADA.

- When a test of details ADA produces a large number of notable items, grouping/filtering the results by the following categories will help sort out the issues that need further investigation versus those that do not:

  o Items with common characteristics (eg, size, nature, or circumstances)

  o False positives

  o Possible misstatements

  o Inconsequential items

  o Possible misstatements that are NOT clearly inconsequential (This category needs further investigation.)

- AU-C 450, *Evaluation of Misstatements Identified During the Audit*, requires the auditor to determine whether uncorrected misstatements are material, individually or in the aggregate. To decide, the auditor should consider the *size* and *nature* of the misstatements *in relation to particular classes of transactions, account balances, or disclosure* and the *financial statements as a whole*, as well as the *particular circumstances* of their occurrence.

- When misstatements are found, the auditor should determine if such misstatements were a result of a deficiency in internal control. If it is determined that a *material* misstatement would not have been detected by the entity's internal control, such deficiency is generally an indication of a *material weakness*.

 If you are an auditor of a medium-sized manufacturer of furniture and you need to test for evidence of occurrence and accuracy of sales, how might you design an ADA to achieve this objective?

Additional information:

- The client generally has about 60,000 sales transactions per year.
- Revenue is recognized when goods are shipped to the customer on an FOB basis.
- There are two main product lines: residential furniture sold to retailers and commercial furniture sold to companies for their own use.
- There are about 80 different types of products that fall into seven groups of products (eg, couches, chairs, desks, etc.)
- There are thousands of product variations based on fabric, color, material, etc.
- Each product style has its own stock keeping unit (SKU) number and a different price.
- There are six premium customers who receive a price discount due to high purchase order volumes. Sales representatives are authorized to give a discount up to 15% off of the prices in the master price list to these customers. Deeper discounts must be approved by the VP of Sales.
- Evidence has also been obtained from tests of controls and other audit procedures, such as confirmation of accounts receivable and verification of cash.

As required by AU-C 240[8,] procedures have been performed to respond to the presumption that risks of fraud exist in revenue recognition.

1. Plan the ADA.

• Overall purpose of the ADA?	• Test of Details
• Specific objective(s) of the ADA? • Items/assertions being analyzed?	• To provide evidence regarding *occurrence* and *accuracy* of sales transactions (Revenue)

[8] *Consideration of Fraud in a Financial Statement Audit*

• Data population to be used?	• Customer orders
	• Sales invoices
	• Shipping documents
	• Master Price List
	• Files regarding the contract process
	• Data from company's database, including:
	   o Customer account identification
	   o Sales order identification, product identification, quantity, and unit price
	   o Shipment identification, product identification, quantity, unit of measure and unit price
	   o Invoice identification, product identification, and amount
	   o Discount percentage
	• Date of entry

• ADA techniques, tools, visualizations, etc. to be used?	• Comparison (ie, matching) of customer orders (including prices) with the related invoices and shipping documents. • Using two three-way matches of: o The quantity sold per sales invoice, shipping document, and internal sales order. • The price on the sales invoice, the purchase order or similar documentation, and the master price list.

2. Access and prepare the data for purposes of the ADA.

3. Consider the relevance and reliability of the data used.

4. Perform the ADA.

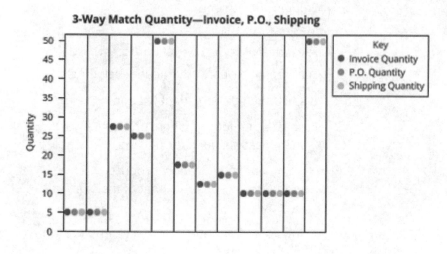

Matching

This grouped chart shows that there are no mismatches between the different data sources.

Note that a graphic summarizing only mismatches would be more appropriate for a large number of invoices.

Graphic Source: AICPA ADA Guide, Exhibit C-3

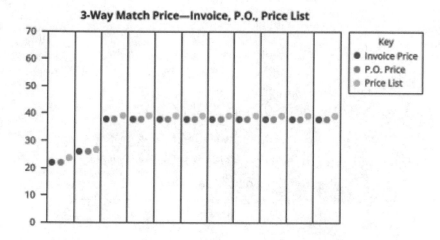

Matching

Many pricing differences. The auditor responded to the pricing differences by using another ADA to see if the mismatches showed a pattern of common attributes that would help identify the circumstances in they which they occurred. This showed that the mismatches were due to the ADA process not taking into account discounts.

Graphic Source: AICPA ADA Guide, Exhibit C-4

• Does the ADA need to be revised and reperformed?	• Yes; ADA redesigned to test whether any customer, other than a premium customer, received a discount and whether any premium customer received a discount larger than 15%.
• If not, and the ADA has identified items that need further investigation, plan and perform additional procedures on those items that are consistent with the purpose and specific objectives of the ADA.	• No further items to investigate.

5. Evaluate the results.	
• Were the purpose and specific objectives of performing the ADA achieved? • If not, plan and perform other procedures to achieve the objectives.	• Achieved; the client's invoicing process regarding quantities and pricing is consistent with customer orders, providing evidence of the occurrence and accuracy of sales transactions for the year.

Substantive Analytical Procedures

While AU-C 330, *Performing Audit Procedures in Response to Assessed Risks and Evaluating the Audit Evidence Obtained*, provides the requirements for substantive procedures in general, AU-C 520, *Analytical Procedures*, builds on that to provide requirements specific to substantive analytical procedures. AU-C 520 states that the auditor should:

- **Determine** the **suitability of** such **procedures** for given assertions, considering the assessed RMM and any tests of details applied.

- **Evaluate** the **reliability of data** from which the auditor's expectations of amounts are to be developed, considering the source, comparability, nature and relevance as well as the controls over its preparation.

- **Develop** an **expectation** of recorded amounts/ratios and evaluate whether the expectation is sufficiently precise to identify a misstatement that, individually or when aggregated with other misstatements, may cause the financial statements to be materially misstated.

- **Determine** the **difference** between recorded amounts and expected values that is **acceptable** without further investigation and **compare** the recorded amounts (or ratios) with expectations.

You might notice that these requirements make ADAs used for substantive analytical procedures more involved and detailed than ADAs used for assessing risks or forming overall conclusions near the end of the audit. Typically, *ratio analysis, trend analysis, nonstatistical predictive modeling,* and *regression analysis* are used for these purposes. Let's take a look at the general 5-step process again to see the extra steps that go into using an ADA as a substantive analytical procedure.

1. Plan the ADA.

   o Overall purpose of the ADA?

      ▪ What assessed RMM does the procedure intend to address?

      ▪ What is the desired level of assurance?

         • The level of assurance is the degree to which the procedure reduces audit risk.

   o Specific objective(s) of the ADA?

      ▪ Items/assertions being analyzed?

   o What is the nature of the auditor's expectation?

      ▪ Independent variables (ie, predictors)?

      ▪ Sources of data for those variables?

- Level of data disaggregation (eg, annual data broken down by month)?
  - What is the desired precision of the auditor's expectation?
    - Higher level of assurance = more precision.
  - What amount of difference from the expectation is acceptable without further investigation?
    - Acceptable difference is influenced by materiality and desired level of assurance.
    - Acceptable difference must decrease as the desired level of persuasive evidence increases due to the assessed level of risk.
  - ADA techniques, tools, visualizations, etc. to be used?

2. Access and prepare the data for purposes of the ADA.

3. Consider the relevance and reliability of the data used.

4. Perform the ADA.
   - Based on the data collected, what is the auditor's **expectation** of the recorded amount or ratio?
   - Is the expectation sufficiently **precise**? If not, what can be done to increase the precision?
     - Precision is affected by the type of expectation, the reliability/characteristics of the data, and the nature of the account/assertion (ie, its *predictability*). For example, interest income would be easy to predict as it is pretty objective compared to an account that is subjective in nature (eg, allowance for credit losses). Also, income statement accounts/relationships are generally easier to predict than balance sheet accounts/relationships because they occur over a period of time as opposed to a point in time. Other factors that may affect predictability include the stability of the economic environment in which the entity operates and management's discretion in making estimates or other judgments.
     - Precision of the auditor's expectation could likely be increased by:
       - Using data on a more disaggregated level (eg, monthly vs. annual)
       - Considering other information available such any significant events, accounting changes, business/industry factors, market/economic factors, management incentives, etc.
   - **Compare** the auditor's expectation to the recorded amount or ratio.

5. Evaluate the results.
   - Is the difference between the expectation and the recorded amount significant?
   - Investigate significant differences and the possible/probable causes.
     - Inquire of management and obtain appropriate audit evidence.
     - Perform other procedures as necessary.
   - Has a misstatement been identified? If so, how bad is it?
   - Were the purpose and specific objectives of performing the ADA achieved?
     - If not, plan and perform other procedures to achieve the objectives.

Assume you are auditing the financial statements of a small, privately-owned company that owns and manages 10 residential apartment buildings with a total of 1,200 units of varying size. The buildings are located in different parts of the same city. Annual rental revenue from these units have averaged about $14 million per year over the past few years.

Additional information:

- Procedures were performed with respect to the entity's control environment and they did not indicate any incentives or inclinations of the owners or managers to deliberately misstate rental revenue.

- Procedures with respect to the design and implementation of the company's controls over rental revenue were performed.

- Other procedures, such as verification of cash receipts from tenants, confirmation requests sent to tenants, and terms of lease agreements, also provide audit evidence both directly and indirectly with regard to rental revenues.

1. Plan the ADA.

• Overall purpose of the ADA?
 	
   o What assessed RMM does the procedure intend to address?
 	
   o What is the desired level of assurance?
	• Substantive analytical procedure
	
	   o To respond to moderate RMM in revenue recognition due to fraud[9].
	
	   o Moderate – affected by the results of other procedures performed.

• Specific objective(s) of the ADA?
• Items/assertions being analyzed?
	• To provide audit evidence regarding rental revenue.
	• Assertions addressed:
	
	   o Occurrence
	
	   o Completeness
	
	   o Accuracy
	
	   o Cutoff

[9] AU-C 240, Consideration of Fraud in a Financial Statement Audit, requires the auditor to address the RMM due to fraud in revenue recognition based on the presumption that risks of fraud exist in revenue recognition.

• Nature of the auditor's expectation?
 	
    o Independent variables?
 	
    o Data sources for variables?
 	
    o Level of data disaggregation?
	• Estimates of rental revenue for each month, combined to get an estimate for the year
	
	    o Internal data source outside financial reporting system
	
	    o # of units in each building
	
	    o Sq. footage and # of rooms in units
	
	    o Lease expiration dates for current year
	
	    o External data source
	
	        ▪ Market avg. rental rates (monthly)
	
	        ▪ Market avg. vacancy rates (monthly)

• Desired precision of the expectation?	• Performance materiality (ie, materiality at the account level)
• Amount of difference from expectation that is acceptable without further investigation?	• A difference small enough that when combined with other misstatements, performance materiality is not exceeded.

• ADA techniques, tools, visualizations, etc. to be used?	• ADA technique – A nonstatistical predictive model that groups rental units by size and # of rooms, then multiplies the # of units in each group by the avg. mkt rental rate for the type of unit. Adjustments to be made for vacancy rates and expiration dates. Final amounts to be aggregated to get monthly and annual revenue estimates/expectations.
	
	• Tool – Spreadsheet program
	
	• Visualizations
	
	    o A comparison or total expected revenue with total actual rental revenue by month
	
	    o A comparison or total expected revenue with total actual rental revenue by year for each building

2. Access and prepare the data for purposes of the ADA.

3. Consider the relevance and reliability of the data used.

4. Perform the ADA.

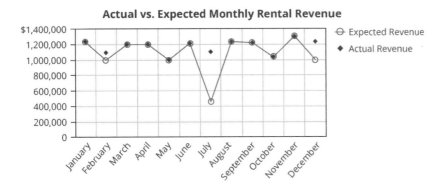

Predictive Modeling

February, July and December show higher rental revenues than expected.

Graphic Source: AICPA ADA Guide, Exhibit B-1

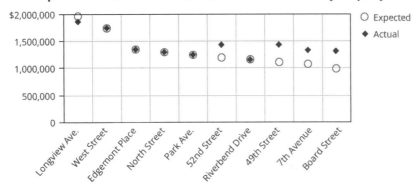

Predictive Modeling

Longview Ave., 52nd St., 49th St., 7th Ave., and Board St. show higher rental revenues than expected.

Graphic Source: AICPA ADA Guide,

5. Evaluate the results.

• Is the difference between the expectation and the recorded amount significant?	• All differences were considered significant in this case.
• Investigate significant differences and the possible/probable causes. • Inquire of management and obtain appropriate audit evidence. • Perform other procedures as necessary.	• The model expected that revenue would dip in July due to the expiration of a large number of leases and the likelihood that it would take at least 2 weeks to replace the tenant; however, management inquiries reveal that certain areas of the city had recently been revitalized. This helped to replace tenants faster and increase the rental rates that could be charged in those areas. New leases can be checked to verify this understanding.

• Has a misstatement been identified? If so, how bad is it?	• No
• Were the purpose and specific objectives of performing the ADA achieved? • If not, plan and perform other procedures to achieve the objectives.	• Yes

Audit Completion Procedures

ADAs can be used to meet the requirement in AU-C 520, *Analytical Procedures,* to "design and perform analytical procedures near the end of the audit that assist the auditor when forming an overall conclusion about whether the financial statements are consistent with the auditor's understanding of the entity." ADAs for this purpose would be very similar to those performed with regard to risk assessment, except that at the end of the audit the auditor should have a slightly different perspective and may also possess new information that might have changed those earlier risk assessments.

Documenting an ADA

In accordance with AU-C 230, *Audit Documentation,* the auditor's workpapers should be sufficient to enable an experienced auditor, with no previous connection with the audit, to understand the nature, timing, and extent of the procedures performed; the results of the procedures and the evidence obtained; as well as any significant findings, the conclusions reached, and significant professional judgments made in reaching such conclusions. In satisfying these requirements with respect to ADAs, the auditor might consider including information regarding:

- The ADA, tools, and techniques used.
- The objectives of the ADA and the RMM the ADA intended to address.
- Sources of the data used and the reasoning behind the determination that it is sufficient and appropriate.
- Tables/graphics used and how they were produced.
- How the data was accessed, extracted, and transformed as well as the system from which it was obtained.
- The evaluation of issues identified and actions taken with respect to such issues.
- The specific characteristics of items tested.
- Who performed the work and the date completed.
- Who reviewed the work and the date and extent of the review.

Keep in mind that, if an ADA is used as a substantive analytical procedure, AU-C 520 adds documentation requirements with regard to:

- The auditor's expectation and the factors considered in developing it

- The results of the comparison of expectations with recorded amounts, or ratios developed from recorded amounts

- Additional procedures performed to investigate significant unexpected discrepancies, including the results of such procedures

AUD 6
Auditing Specific
Financial Statement
Accounts

AUD 6: Auditing Specific Financial Statement Accounts

6.01 Cash & Cash Equivalents

Overview: Auditing Financial Statement Accounts

To develop an audit plan for specific items on the financial statements (F/S), the auditor will determine which **assertions (U-PERCV)** apply, based on whether the item being examined is a **class of transactions (CPA-CO)**, an **account balance (RACE)**, or a **disclosure** or presentation-related item **(RACOUn)**. The auditor will also identify which assertions are relevant assertions in that a misrepresentation could result in a material misstatement to the F/S. For each relevant assertion:

Management Assertions
Understandability & Classification
Presentation & Disclosure
Existence or Occurrence
Rights & Obligations
Completeness & Cutoff
Valuation, Allocation & Accuracy

- **RELY** – If the auditor is planning to **test controls**, the auditor will identify the controls that support the assertion, determine how to test them, and determine what substantive procedures will be performed if controls prove to be reliable.

- **NOT Rely** – If the auditor is not planning to test controls, the auditor will determine the **substantive procedures** that will provide evidence that will support that assertion.

Audit Procedures
Inquiry
Confirmation
Observation
Recalculation
Reperformance
Inspection of tangible assets
Inspection of records/documents
Analytical procedures

Misappropriation of Cash

Of all fraud schemes, **misappropriation of assets** is the most common, and the asset that is most frequently misappropriated is cash. This is done in a variety of ways.

- Cash may be stolen as it is received. This is evaluated as part of the understanding of the internal controls in the revenues and cash receipts systems.

- Cash may be stolen from cash registers, petty cash accounts, or other areas where accessible. The entity's policies regarding access to cash will be evaluated to determine the entity's susceptibility.

- Employees may steal cash by causing the entity to make inappropriate cash disbursements in the form of overpayments, payments without the receipt of goods or services, payments to phantom entities or employees, etc. The auditor evaluates these in the various tests related to cash disbursements as part of the audit of expenses and the handling of other expenditures.

- Management may overstate cash using some technique, such as kiting (discussed below), to hide the overstatement.

Auditing Cash & Cash Equivalents: Overview

Objectives

- Adequate I/C
- **R**ights & obligations – Cash is not restricted.
- **A**llocation & valuation – Cash is recorded in the appropriate amount.
- **C**ompleteness – All cash is included.
- **E**xistence – Cash balances actually exist.

Analytical Procedures

The auditor will first evaluate whether there is reason to believe that cash is misstated at the financial statement element or account balance level. The auditor will consider the amount reported as cash and apply analytical procedures to determine if the amount seems reasonable considering, for example:

- The normal pattern of expenditures experienced by the entity
- The entity's policies for maintaining minimum and maximum balances in cash, and for cash reserves, along with the means of maintaining balances within that range
- The entity's policies for authorizing expenditures

Forms of Evidence

There are various forms of evidence the auditor may use in the audit of cash and cash equivalents (collectively referred to as "cash" below). Some will be obtained from the client, some directly from outside sources, and some may result from the direct actions of the auditor.

- **Bank statements** received by the client and provided to the auditor, including statements related to accounts closed during the period
- **Bank cutoff statements** received directly by the auditor
  - o These are bank statements for a relatively short period (eg, a couple weeks) beginning with the first transaction after the last bank statement at year end.
  - o The cutoff statement helps ensure that outstanding checks and deposits in transit have cleared within a reasonable period of time.
- **Bank reconciliations** prepared by the client ⟶

  > Balance per bank
  > + Deposits in transit
  > − Outstanding checks
  > Balance per book – G/L

- **Bank confirmations** obtained directly by the auditor from all institutions with which the entity (1) has accounts and (2) had accounts that were closed
  - o The information that will be provided includes:
    - ▪ Balances in all deposit accounts as of the B/S date
    - ▪ Outstanding loan balances at that date

- Collateral agreements on loans (including agreements to maintain compensating balances in cash accounts)

  o The bank will only send such a confirmation at the request of the client. Since the information is provided directly to the auditor by the bank, it has a higher level of persuasiveness than bank statements and other information examined by the auditor at the client's premises.

  o One concern is that the specific bank employee preparing the form may not be aware of all the financial relationships the client has with the bank; thus, the information provided may be incomplete.

- **Observation** of cash on hand at the B/S date

- **Minutes** of meetings of those responsible for governance to identify authorization for opening, closing, or encumbering cash

- Since the **statement of cash flows** is derived entirely from transactions affecting the B/S and income statement (I/S), one of the auditor's responsibilities is to **reconcile** the amounts on the statement of cash flows to the information on the two source statements.

Interbank transfer schedule prepared by the auditor (discussed below)

Interbank Transfer Schedule

Special attention must be paid to transfers made by the client between different bank accounts around the B/S date. The auditor will prepare an interbank transfer schedule (aka, intercompany bank transfer schedule) that includes all checks written from one of the client's accounts to another for the few days surrounding year end. It might look as follows:

	Bank Accounts		Disbursement Date		Receipt Date	
Check No.	From	To	Per books	Per bank	Per books	Per bank
576	East Bank	West Bank	Dec 30	Jan 4	Dec 30	Jan 3
583	West Bank	East Bank	Jan 3	Jan 2	Dec 30	Dec 31

The auditor will examine each transfer with the intention of identifying:

- **Deposits in transit at B/S date** – This occurs when the disbursement per books occurred before year end but the receipt per bank occurred after year end.

  o Normally, the check will be written from the disbursing account and posted to the cash disbursements journal (or check register) on that date. Thus, the **disbursement date per books** should be the **earliest date**. The check may then be transmitted to another location for deposit, which will cause a delay in the deposit of the check at the receiving bank.

○ The auditor wants to make sure that deposits in transit are listed on the **bank reconciliation** in determining the correct balance of the receiving account. This ensures that the total cash in the bank is not understated.

- **Kiting** – This is an attempt by the client to overstate total cash in the bank by reporting a receipt in the current period without reporting the equivalent disbursement. Kiting occurs when the **disbursement per books** occurred **after year end** but the **receipt** (per books and/or per bank) occurred **before year-end** (see Check #583 above).

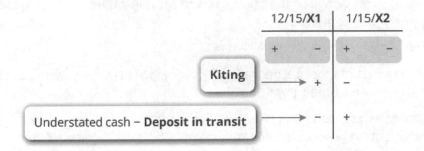

RACE Approach to Audit Procedures for Cash

Rights & Obligations

The accounts containing cash are owned by the entity and are not encumbered or otherwise restricted by parties outside the entity. In seeking evidence to support this assertion, the auditor will determine if there are appropriate **controls** in place, such as:

- Policies established for limiting the authority to encumber (restrict) cash

- Instructions to banks to inform governance of any encumbrances placed on cash accounts

- Accounting policies that require the reclassification of encumbered cash accounts into another asset category as appropriate

Substantive procedures may include:

- **Confirming** cash accounts to verify that there are no encumbrances affecting the accounts

- **Inquiring** as to whether there are any encumbrances on any accounts

- **Inspecting** the minutes of meetings of those charged with governance to determine if the encumbrance of any cash accounts have been authorized

Allocation & Valuation

The amounts reported as cash are accurately measured (ie, they are not overstated or understated). In seeking evidence to support this assertion, the auditor will determine if there are appropriate **controls** in place, such as:

- Periodic reconciliation of reported cash balances to bank statements or other statements of account received from other account holders

- Periodic test counts of petty cash

Substantive procedures may include:

- **Confirming** accounts and comparing the year-end balance to the bank reconciliation

- **Inspecting** bank reconciliations to determine that all amounts are correct and agree with amounts in the trial balance and on the F/S

- Preparing a summary of all cash and trace the amount to the trial balance and, ultimately, to the amount reported on the F/S **(recalculation)**

- Obtaining bank cutoff statements and reconciling to verify that deposits in transit, outstanding checks, and other issues either cleared the account or were otherwise resolved **(recalculation)**

- **Observing** cash on hand at the B/S date

- Verifying the conversion of foreign currency balances into the reporting currency **(recalculation)**

Completeness

All cash on account or on hand is included in the reported balance. In seeking evidence to support this assertion, the auditor will determine if there are appropriate **controls** in place, such as:

- Policies and procedures related to the receipt and depositing of cash to make certain that it is deposited into accounts that are owned and reported by the entity

- Periodic high-level reviews by management of cash receipts and disbursements to determine if reported amounts are reasonable in relation to expected and known levels of entity activity

Substantive procedures may include:

- Comparing the amounts and the volume of transactions to the auditor's expectations **(analytical procedures)**

- **Confirming** accounts that were closed during the period

- **Inquiring** as to whether there are any cash accounts that have not been reported

Existence

The amount reported as cash represents cash that is either on hand or on account (ie, it actually exists). In seeking evidence to support this assertion, the auditor will determine if there are appropriate **controls** in place, such as:

- Periodic reconciliation of reported cash balances to bank statements or other statements of account received from account holders

- Periodic test counts of petty cash both on prescribed dates, such as at the end of each month, and on randomly selected dates to enhance the possibility of detecting fraudulent use

Substantive procedures may include:

- **Confirming** accounts and obtaining bank cutoff statements directly from institutions to verify that the reported accounts actually exist

- **Observing** cash on hand at the B/S date

- **Inspecting** bank reconciliations prepared by the entity, matching bank statements to each reported account to verify existence

Summary of Alternative Approaches for Cash*	
RACE	**PERCV**
Rights & obligations - Bank confirmations to verify accounts and identify restrictions *Allocation & valuation* - Bank confirmations to verify balance - Review bank reconciliations to corroborate amounts - Reconcile summary schedules to general ledger (G/L) - Obtain bank cutoff statement to verify items on bank reconciliation - Observe cash on hand at B/S date - Test translation of foreign currency balances *Completeness* - Analytical procedures (do amounts & volume of transactions match expectations?) - Bank confirmations for accounts that were closed (unreported balances?) *Existence* - Bank confirmations - Observe cash on hand at B/S date	*Presentation & disclosure* - Review disclosures for GAAP compliance - Inquire about compensating balance requirements & restrictions *Existence or occurrence* - Confirmation/observation - Count cash on hand - Prepare bank transfer schedule *Rights & obligations* - Review cutoffs (receipts & reimbursements) - Review passbooks, bank statements *Completeness & cutoff* - Analytical procedures - Review bank reconciliation - Obtain bank cutoff statement to verify items on bank reconciliation *Valuation, allocation & accuracy* - Foot (adding) summary schedules - Reconcile summary schedules to G/L - Test translation to any foreign currencies

These lists are not intended to be all-inclusive.

6.02 Receivables

Auditing Receivables: Overview

Objectives

- Adequate I/C
- **R**ights & obligations – The entity has a legitimate claim to receivables.
- **A**llocation & valuation – Receivables are presented at net realizable value (NRV).
- **C**ompleteness – All receivables are reported.
- **E**xistence – Receivables actually exist.

Analytical Procedures

The auditor will first evaluate whether there is reason to believe that receivables are misstated at the financial statement element or account balance level. The auditor will consider the amount reported as accounts receivable (A/R) and apply analytical procedures to determine if the amount seems reasonable. Based on the auditor's knowledge of the client's collection policies and the strictness with which they are enforced, the auditor will develop an expectation for the number of days' sales in A/R.

The auditor may also apply an analytical procedure to the allowance for credit losses (ie, doubtful accounts) if the relationship between A/R and the allowance is predictable. This will also depend, to a degree, on how strictly the entity enforces its collection policies and the degree to which it is systematic in determining when accounts will be written off, turned over to collection, etc.

Forms of Evidence

There are various forms of evidence the auditor may use in the audit of receivables. Some will be obtained from the client, some directly from outside sources, and some may result from the direct actions of the auditor.

- Sequential order of prenumbered sales invoices, shipping reports, and documents related to the selection of merchandise from inventory prepared internally by the entity
- Customer purchase orders (PO) provided to the auditor by the entity
- Aged analyses of A/R used as a basis for determining the appropriate balance in the allowance for credit losses
- Correspondence between the entity and the customer regarding a receivable
- Periodic statements sent by the entity to its customers
- **Confirmations** sent directly from the customer to the auditor (discussed further below)

RACE Approach to Audit Procedures for Receivables

Rights & Obligations

The entity is entitled to the proceeds from the collections of the receivables. A misrepresentation might occur if the entity was acting as an agent in the sale of goods and is, therefore, not entitled to the proceeds or if receivables have been used as collateral. In seeking evidence to support this assertion, the auditor will determine if there are appropriate **controls** in place, such as:

- Policies established by those responsible for governance limiting the authority to borrow using receivables as collateral

- Factoring policies established by those responsible for governance

  o Factoring is a financial transaction where the entity sells receivables for an agreed-upon amount of cash. The purchaser of the receivables becomes responsible for collection and is entitled to the proceeds from collection.

  o The entity would no longer have the right to collect factored receivables.

- Information processing controls requiring that supporting documents that evidence a sale are evaluated and matched before recognizing receivables

Substantive procedures may include:

- **Inspecting** the documentation that supports a receivable, including the customer PO, entity sales order, shipping documents, documents requesting that the goods be moved from inventory to shipping, and sales invoices to verify that the transactions creating the receivables were satisfied by the entity

- Tracing receivables to subsequent collections **(observation)**

- Obtaining **confirmations** directly from customers to verify that reported amounts are actually owed to the entity

Allocation & Valuation

The amounts reported as receivables are accurately measured. A misrepresentation might occur if receivables are overstated, perhaps because of misappropriated cash receipts or understated due to an unrecorded sale. In seeking evidence to support this assertion, the auditor will determine if there are appropriate **controls** in place, such as:

- Regular evaluation of receivables to determine if accounts should be written down or off

- Investigation of discrepancies reported by customers on a timely and thorough basis

- Periodic high-level reviews by management to determine if receivables seem reasonable in relation to the entity's volume of activity

Substantive procedures may include:

- Obtaining **confirmations** directly from customers verifying the amounts that are owed to the entity

- Obtaining an aged analysis of the client's receivables and **recalculating** an estimated amount for the allowance for credit losses to be compared to the client's balance; or **inspecting** the client's aged analysis to determine if the allowance was properly calculated and reported

- Tracing amounts reported as receivables to subsequent collections **(observation)**

Completeness

All receivables to which the entity is entitled to the proceeds from collection are recorded. In seeking evidence to support this assertion, the auditor will determine if there are appropriate **controls** in place, such as:

- Using prenumbered forms for all transactions and accounting for all numbers missing from a particular sequence

- Periodic high-level reviews by management of receivable balances in relation to sales to determine if reported amounts are reasonable in relation to expected and known levels of activity experienced by the entity

Substantive procedures may include:

- Obtaining **confirmations** directly from customers to verify that all amounts owed to the entity are reported

- Accounting for the sequence of all prenumbered documents that are used in the process to make and record sales on account

- Tracing shipping documents for transactions occurring near the end of the period to the accounting records to make certain that there is a proper cutoff and that all sales and receivables were recognized in the appropriate period **(observation)**

  o The auditor may account for the numerical sequence of all shipping documents to make certain that all shipments are accounted for.

  o The auditor may trace shipping documents to sales invoices to make certain that all goods shipped have been billed to the customer.

  o The auditor may account for the numerical sequence of all sales invoices to make certain that all sales are accounted for.

  o The auditor may trace sales invoices to the sales journal to make certain that all sales have been recorded.

- Comparing amounts reported as receivables to the auditor's expectations that are based on the auditor's knowledge of the entity's receivable policies and its reported sales for the period **(analytical procedures)**

Existence

The amount reported as receivables represents claims for cash or other financial instruments that are enforceable against other parties (ie, all sales on account actually occurred). In seeking evidence to support this assertion, the auditor will determine if there are appropriate **controls** in place, such as:

- Information processing controls requiring that supporting documents evidencing a sale are evaluated and matched before recognizing receivables
- Periodic evaluations by management to verify that past-due accounts and write-offs were due to existing customers

Substantive procedures may include:

- **Inspecting** documents that support a receivable, including the customer PO, entity sales order, shipping documents, documents requesting that the goods be moved from inventory to shipping, and sales invoices to verify that the transactions creating the receivables actually occurred
- Tracing receivables to subsequent collections **(observation)**
- Obtaining **confirmations** directly from customers to verify that reported amounts are actually owed to the entity

Summary of Alternative Approaches for Receivables*	
RACE	**PERCV**
Rights & obligations • Confirm A/R • Trace receivables to documentation of sales transactions	*Presentation & disclosure* • Review disclosures for GAAP compliance • Inquire about pledging, discounting • Review loan agreements for pledging, factoring
Allocation & valuation • Confirm A/R • Trace receivables to subsequent collections • Review process for estimating credit loss allowance • Analytical procedures to evaluate the reasonableness of receivables	*Existence or occurrence* • Confirmation • Inspect notes • Vouch (examine shipping documents, invoices, credit memos)
Completeness • Trace sales transactions to recorded A/R • Analytical procedures to evaluate the reasonableness of receivables	*Rights & obligations* • Review cutoffs (sales, cash receipts, sales returns) • Inquire about factoring of receivables
Existence • Confirm A/R • Trace receivables to documentation of sales transactions • Trace receivables to subsequent collections	*Completeness & cutoff* • Analytical procedures *Valuation, allocation & accuracy* • Foot subsidiary ledger • Reconcile subsidiary ledger to G/L • Examine subsequent cash receipts • Age receivables to test adequacy of credit loss allowance • Discuss adequacy of credit loss allowance with management & compare to historical experience

These lists are not intended to be all-inclusive.

External Confirmations

External confirmations (AU-C 505) are considered one of the more reliable sources of audit evidence because they are:

- Obtained directly from parties outside the entity.

- In documentary form, which is more reliable than evidence obtained orally.

External confirmations may be used for a variety of audit purposes, including confirmations to:

- Banks regarding bank balances and related transactions

- Customers to verify A/R amounts and terms

- Vendors to verify accounts payable amounts and terms

- Warehouses to verify existence of inventories or other assets being held for the entity

- Brokers or investment firms to verify existence and balances of investment securities held on behalf of the entity

- Lenders to verify amounts due and terms

The auditor is required to use external confirmations for A/R, unless:

- The overall A/R balance is not material.

- The use of external confirmations is not expected to be effective.

- RMM at the relevant assertion level is low and the auditor can address the assessed risk through the use of other planned substantive procedures.

When using external confirmations, the auditor is required to maintain control over various aspects of the confirmation process. Specifically, the auditor should:

- Determine the information to be confirmed or requested

- Select the appropriate party to whom to address the confirmation

- Design the confirmation requests to make certain:

  o They are addressed to the appropriate responding party.

  o Responses are provided directly to the auditor.

- Send the requests, including follow-up requests

Three Types of Confirmations

- **Negative** – The customer is asked to respond only if the amount is incorrect.

  o There is no need to respond.

  o The auditor does not expect the request to be ignored.

  o A low exception rate is expected.

  o No news is good news.

  o They are most applicable for small balances.

  o They provide *implicit evidence*.

$$RMM \downarrow (CR \downarrow)$$

- **Positive** (RSVP) – The customer is asked to verify the correctness of the amount on the confirmation.

  o They require a response.

  o They are most applicable for large balances.

  o They provide **explicit evidence**.

  > RMM ↑ (CR↑)

  o One problem with the use of positive confirmations is that some parties may not respond or may do so, but not on a timely basis. Methods that *encourage a higher response* may include:

    ▪ The use of clear language on the confirmation.

    ▪ Sending the confirmation to a specific individual.

    ▪ Identifying the entity being audited.

    ▪ Having the client sign the confirmation request by hand.

    ▪ Setting a deadline for a response.

    ▪ Sending second requests.

    ▪ Calling addressees to obtain oral confirmation and request a response to the written confirmation.

  o When an addressee **does not respond** to a positive confirmation, there are various actions an auditor may take, including:

    ▪ Sending second confirmation requests.

    ▪ Asking the client to contact the addressee to request a response.

    ▪ Reviewing related transactions in subsequent periods, such as cash receipts in relation to A/R.

    ▪ Inspecting supporting documents, such as a customer's PO and shipping documents.

    ▪ Examining correspondence between the addressee and the client.

    ▪ Considering an audit adjustment.

- **Blank** – This is a special form of *positive confirmation*, in which the customer is asked to provide an amount without being told the value on the client's records.

Factors Suggesting Need for Positive or Blank Confirmations

- A large balance

- An active account

- Delinquency

- High assessed level of RMM

- The expectation that the customer will not pay attention to a negative confirmation

Other Issues

AU-C 505 also suggests that when reconciliation of aggregate balances to positive or blank confirmation requests proves difficult, confirmation of single transactions, such as individual invoices, may be a suitable alternative.

If management refuses to allow the auditor to perform external confirmation procedures, the auditor should seek evidence to determine if management's reasons are valid and reasonable.

- If so, the auditor will evaluate the effect on the RMM and apply alternative audit procedures.
- If not, or if the auditor is not able to obtain sufficient appropriate audit evidence applying alternative audit procedures, the auditor should:
  - Communicate with those in charge of governance.
  - Evaluate the implications on the audit and on the auditor's report.

6.03 Investments in Securities

Auditing Investments in Securities: Overview

Objectives

- Adequate I/C
- **R**ights & obligations – The entity owns the investments.
- **A**llocation & valuation - Investments are reported at appropriate amounts.
- **C**ompleteness – All investments are reported.
- **E**xistence – All investments actually exist.

Analytical Procedures

In obtaining evidence about investments in securities, the auditor will first evaluate whether there is reason to believe that investments are misstated at the financial statement element or account balance level.

- The auditor will consider the entity's policies for retaining and investing working capital, for accumulating funds for long-term or short-term investment purposes, and related to distributions to shareholders.
- The auditor may also look at investment-related income to determine if it seems reasonable in relation to the level of investment reported by the entity. (AU-C 501)

Forms of Evidence

There are various *forms of evidence* the auditor may use in the audit of investments in securities. Some will be obtained from the client, some directly from outside sources, and some may result from the direct actions of the auditor.

- Stock certificates and bonds held by the entity
- Communications between the entity and third parties holding investment securities on behalf of the entity
- Minutes of meetings of those charged with governance authorizing activities involving investments in securities
- Management's analyses used to determine if investments, other than those reported at fair value, have been impaired
- Client schedules of investments and investment activity
- Bank statements and cancelled checks evidencing payments for purchases and deposits from sales of investments in securities

- **Confirmations** sent directly from issuers of investment securities and custodians of securities on behalf of the entity

RACE Approach to Audit Procedures for Investments

Rights & Obligations

The entity owns the investments that are reported. In seeking evidence that supports this assertion, the auditor will determine if there are appropriate **controls** in place, such as:

- Policies established for limiting the authority to borrow using investments as collateral

- Periodic evaluation of the reasonableness of investment income in relation to the investments owned

Substantive procedures may include:

- **Inspecting** stock certificates, bonds, and other securities maintained in the entity's possession

- **Inspecting** the documentation that supports transactions occurring near the year end to ensure that the cutoff is appropriate and all transactions were reported in the appropriate period

- Obtaining **confirmations** from holders (custodians) of investment securities on behalf of the client

- Performing **analytical procedures** to evaluate the reasonableness of investment income in relation to the entity's investment activity

Allocation & Valuation

The amounts reported as investments are accurately measured. In seeking evidence to support this assertion, the auditor will determine if there are appropriate **controls** in place, such as:

- Policies and procedures for obtaining information about fair value for those investments reported at fair value

- Policies for measuring fair value when level 1 inputs are not available, including means of determining adjustments to fair values for investments whose fair value is measured using level 2 inputs and the valuation techniques applied for investments whose fair value is measured using level 3 inputs

Substantive procedures may include:

- **Recalculating** market value for investments in trading securities, AFS securities, and other investments reported at fair value

- **Inspecting** the audited F/S of investees accounted for under the equity method to verify the amount of earnings and adjustments to the investment reported by the entity

- **Inspecting** statements from financial institutions to verify fair value

- Footing (ie, adding amounts in a column) and cross footing (ie, adding amounts across columns) schedules of investments maintained by the client and tracing balances to the G/L and the F/S **(recalculation)**

- **Recalculating** interest and dividend income that should have been earned on investments reported by the entity and compare to amounts received and reported

- Performing **analytical procedures** to evaluate the relationship between investment income and amounts reported as investments to determine if it seems reasonable

For investment securities valued at **fair value**, AU-C 501[1] also requires the auditor to:

- Evaluate whether methods used for determining fair value are consistent with requirements, if any, of the AFRF

- Determine if methods used by brokers or dealers are appropriate when values are obtained from such sources

- Obtain evidence to support management's assertions about fair value determined using a valuation model, when appropriate

- Evaluate management's conclusions regarding whether investments have been impaired

- Obtain evidence supporting any impairment adjustment reported, including a determination of whether the requirements of the AFRF have been appropriately applied

Completeness

All investments in securities owned by the entity are included in the B/S (ie, no investments were excluded). In seeking evidence to support this assertion, the auditor will determine if there are appropriate **controls** in place, such as:

- Periodic reconciliation of investment securities held to amounts reported on the F/S

- Tracing dividends, interest, or other investment income received to investment securities

Substantive procedures may include:

- Obtaining **confirmations** directly from third parties holding securities on behalf of the entity and closely held issuers of securities owned by the entity

- Performing **analytical procedures** to evaluate the reasonableness of interest, dividends, and other investment income in relation to the investments held

- **Inspecting** the client's schedule reconciling beginning balances in investment accounts to ending balances, tracing increases and decreases to supporting documents

- **Inspecting** minutes of meetings of management and those charged with governance authorizing transactions involving investments

[1] *Audit Evidence – Specific Considerations for Selected items*

Existence

The amount reported as investments in securities are actual investments in the custody of the entity or in the custody of a third party on behalf of the entity. In seeking evidence to support this assertion, the auditor will determine if there are appropriate **controls** in place, such as:

- Controls requiring that all securities remain in the custody of the treasurer's department or, when in the custody of a third party, only the treasurer's department can authorize purchase or sale transactions

- Keeping security instruments in a secure location

Substantive procedures may include:

- Obtaining **confirmations** directly from third parties holding investment securities on behalf of the entity from issuers of investment securities held by the entity.

- **Inspecting** the investment securities that are in custody of the client

- Tracing recorded investments to purchase documents, evidence of payment, and authorizations from those charged with governance **(reperformance)**

Summary of Alternative Approaches for Investments*

RACE	PERCV
Rights & obligations • Inspect underlying agreements • Trace to documentation supporting acquisition • Confirm significant terms with counterparties & holders • Review bank confirmations for evidence of use as collateral **Allocation & valuation** • Confirm significant terms with counterparties & holders • Compare to market values for financial instruments with observable market data • Test amortization of discount/premium • Review F/S of major investees **Completeness** • Reconcile dividends received to publicly available information • Obtain confirmations from counterparties regarding the absence of side agreements • Confirm holdings with 3rd party custodians **Existence** • Confirm with 3rd party custodians • Reconcile to interest/dividends received • Observe securities in the client's custody • Trace to acquisition documents	**Presentation & disclosure** • Review disclosures for GAAP compliance • Inquire about pledging • Review loan agreements for pledging • Review management's classification of securities **Existence or occurrence** • Confirmation of securities held by third parties • Inspect/count stock certificates/bonds • Vouch (to available documentation) **Rights & obligations** • Review cutoffs (examine transactions near year end) • Confirm significant terms with holders • Inspect underlying agreements • Consider findings from other procedures **Completeness & cutoff** • Analytical procedures • Reconcile dividends received to published records • Confirm with holders concerning existence of undisclosed side-agreements • Test existence of undisclosed instruments • Compare beginning account detail with ending account detail • Review board minutes **Valuation, allocation & accuracy** • Foot summary schedules • Reconcile summary schedules to G/L • Test amortization of premiums/discounts • Determine market value for trading & AFS securities • Review audited F/S of major investees

These lists are not intended to be all-inclusive.

Auditing Accounting Estimates, Including Fair Value Estimates, & Related Disclosures

GAAP requires companies to use **fair value** for measuring, presenting, and disclosing various accounts, such as:

- Investments in trading or AFS securities

- Assets and liabilities acquired in a business combination

- Assets and liabilities exchanged in nonmonetary transactions

- Derivatives

- Impaired assets

- Financial instruments for which the entity has elected the fair value option

Fair value is generally considered to be the amount at which an asset could be sold in a current transaction between willing parties, or the amount that would have to be paid to transfer a liability. Auditing fair values is similar to that of other estimates in that a combination of three approaches is often used (AU-C 540):

- Review and test management's process

- Independently develop an estimate

- Review subsequent events

The auditor will consider estimates when performing risk assessment procedures by obtaining an understanding of:

- Requirements of the applicable financial reporting framework (AFRF) regarding estimates

- How management determines when estimates are necessary for the recognition or disclosure of items in the financial statements

- How management develops accounting estimates and the data upon which they are based

Based on the understanding, the auditor will evaluate the risk of material misstatement of estimates and will undertake one or more of the following procedures, considering the nature of the accounting estimate:

- Determine whether events up to the report date provide evidence regarding the estimate.

- Test the methods and assumptions used by management and the data on which they are based

- Test the operating effectiveness of controls over the development of accounting estimates.

- Develop an expectation in the form of a point or range of estimates to use as a basis for evaluating management's estimate

In addition, when estimates represent significant risks of material misstatement to the financial statements, the auditor will apply additional procedures:

- Address the effects of **estimation uncertainty**, including whether management has considered alternative assumptions and whether management's assumptions are reasonable

- Evaluate management's decision to recognize or not recognize accounting estimates and the basis used for measurement

- Evaluate the reasonableness of the accounting estimates

- Determine if disclosures comply with the AFRF

- Review decisions and estimates to evaluate for potential management bias

The auditor will also document the basis for the auditor's conclusions about the reasonableness of estimates giving rise to significant risks and indicators of possible management bias.

Using the Work of Management's Specialist

When the work of a management's specialist is to be used as audit evidence, AU-C 501 requires the auditor to consider the significance of that work to the audit and perform the following procedures, as necessary:

- Assess the competence, capabilities, and objectivity of the specialist

- Obtain an understanding of the specialist's work

- Determine whether the specialist's work is appropriate audit evidence for the relevant assertion

With regard to the **reliability** of any information produced by the specialist, it is important to assess any entity controls over the specialist's work in addition to their competence, capabilities, and objectivity.

6.04 Inventories

Auditing Inventories: Overview

Objectives

- Adequate I/C
- **R**ights & obligations – Inventory is owned by entity.
- **A**llocation & valuation – Quantities are correct and properly priced.
- **C**ompleteness – All inventory is included.
- **E**xistence – Inventory actually exists.

Analytical Procedures

In obtaining evidence about inventories, the auditor will first evaluate whether there is reason to believe that inventories are misstated at the financial statement element or account balance level. The auditor will consider the amount reported as inventory and apply analytical procedures to determine if the amount seems reasonable.

Based on the auditor's knowledge of the client's inventory policies (eg, reorder points, shelf lives, inventory turnover), the auditor will establish an expectation for the amount of inventory the client should have on hand. This amount will be compared to the amount reported by the client. (AU-C 501)

Forms of Evidence

There are various *forms of evidence* the auditor may use in the audit of inventories. Some will be obtained from the client, some directly from outside sources, and some may result from the direct actions of the auditor.

- POs and receiving reports indicating that the inventory was ordered and received
- Reconciliations of perpetual inventory records to periodic physical counts taken by the client
- Agreements with consignees and consignors
- Confirmations from warehouses, consignees, and others that may be holding inventory on behalf of the entity
- Client inventory count sheets
- Bank confirmations indicating whether there are any collateral arrangements involving the entity's inventories
- The auditor's personal observation of inventory
- Invoices for purchases of inventory
- Sales prices for inventory and costs associated with disposal

- Sequential prenumbered materials requisitions

- Correspondence between the entity warehouses, consignees, and other third parties holding the entity's inventories

RACE Approach to Audit Procedures for Inventory

Rights & Obligations

The entity owns the inventories. A misrepresentation might occur if either of the following are included on the B/S: inventory held on consignment on behalf of another entity or purchased inventory in transit shipped under a destination contract. In seeking evidence to support this assertion, the auditor will determine if there are appropriate **controls** in place, such as:

- Policies established by those responsible for governance limiting the authority to borrow using inventory as collateral

- Information processing controls requiring that entries to the perpetual inventory records be supported by appropriate documentation, including POs and receiving reports

Substantive procedures may include:

- **Inspecting** the documentation that supports an inventory purchase, including materials requisitions, POs, and receiving reports

- **Inspecting** agreements and documents related to transactions with consignors and consignees to verify that inventory sent out on consignment is included and that inventory received on consignment is not included

- **Inspecting** UCC (Universal Commercial Code) filings and public records that may indicate a secured interest in the entity's inventories

- Obtain **confirmations** from financial institutions, providing information as to whether inventory has been pledged as collateral for a financing arrangement

- **Inspecting** vendor invoices and other evidence of the purchase of the goods by the client.

- **Inspecting loan agreements** to determine if any inventory has been pledged as collateral for a loan or assigned to a creditor for value.

  - Since any such actions require disclosure in the F/S or notes, this procedure also contributes to verifying the assertions related to **presentation and disclosure**.

Allocation & Valuation

The amounts reported as inventory are accurately measured. In seeking evidence that supports this assertion, the auditor will determine if there are appropriate **controls** in place such as:

- Adequate review and supervision of the data entry process to provide assurance that amounts are being input accurately

- Periodic evaluations of inventory to identify slow moving, damaged, or obsolete inventories.

- Periodic comparisons to net realizable value to verify that inventories are properly reported.

Substantive procedures may include:

- Tracing amounts reported in inventory to invoices from suppliers to verify cost **(observation)**

- Using information about sales prices and costs of disposition to **recalculate** NRV and compare it to cost to determine if the entity has reported inventory at the lower of cost or NRV

- Comparing the relationship of sales to cost of sales and cost of sales to inventories to the auditor's expectations based on knowledge of the client's inventory policies to determine if the amount reported as inventory seems reasonable **(analytical procedures)**

- For manufactured inventory, examining standard cost rates (especially for overhead that is applied to inventory costs)

- Examining *inventory turnover rates* to identify slow-moving and obsolete inventory that may need to be written off or written down to NRV

Completeness

All inventory owned by the entity and held for sale in the ordinary course of business is included in the amount reported on the B/S. In seeking evidence to support this assertion, the auditor will determine if there are appropriate **controls** in place, such as:

- Performing periodic counts of inventory and verifying that all items counted are included in the inventory records

- Instructions for tagging and counting inventories to make certain all items are counted

- Use of prenumbered receiving reports with a reconciliation to identify any receiving reports that did not result in an entry to inventory

Substantive procedures may include:

- Obtaining **confirmations** directly from warehouses, consignees, and other third parties holding the entity's inventory

- Accounting for the sequence of all prenumbered documents that are used in the processes related to the purchases and sales of inventory to make certain all are included in the accounting records **(recalculation)**

- **Inspecting** purchases and sales of inventory near the end of the period, including shipping terms, to determine if it is appropriately included in, or excluded from, inventory

- **Inspecting** inventory held by employees

- **Observing** the counting of inventory, performing test counts, and verifying that all items counted are included in the inventory records.

- Tracing inventory tags to the inventory records **(inspection)**

- Perform **cutoff** tests for receiving and shipping that occurred around the B/S date

Existence

The amounts reported as inventories are existing goods held for sale in the ordinary course of business. A misrepresentation might be the inclusion on the B/S of inventory that has already been sold or goods in transit that are not yet, or no longer, the property of the entity. In seeking evidence that supports this assertion, the auditor will determine if there are appropriate **controls** in place, such as:

- Limited access to inventory to prevent inventory theft

- Information processing procedures that provide assurance that all inventory recorded in perpetual inventory records has been purchased and title and risk of loss has transferred to the entity

- Periodic counts by the entity to verify that amounts included in the inventory records continue to exist

- Procedures indicating what items have been counted to avoid counting the same inventory multiple times

Substantive procedures may include:

- **Observing** the entity's physical count of inventory and performing test counts

  - If the client has a strong **perpetual** inventory system, this count can be performed at various dates and different batches of inventory can be counted at different times.

  - When RMM with respect to inventory is high, especially when the client uses a **periodic** inventory system, the count must be made at the B/S date, or as close to it as possible.

  - During the count, the auditor should examine items that are in the listed inventory count and, on a test basis, trace those amounts to the inventory tags on actual goods.

- Tracing recorded inventory items to materials requisitions, POs, and receiving reports **(inspection)**

- **Inspecting** purchases and sales of inventory near the end of the period, including shipping terms, to determine if it is appropriately included in, or excluded from, inventory

- Obtaining **confirmations** directly from warehouses, consignees, and others having possession of the entity's inventory

Summary of Alternative Approaches for Inventory*	
RACE	**PERCV**
Rights & obligations	*Presentation & disclosure*
• Trace inventories to purchase documents	• Review disclosures for GAAP compliance
• Perform search & obtain bank confirmations to determine if inventory is pledged as security	• Inquire about pledging
• Review consignment agreements to identify inventory not owned	• Review purchase commitments
Allocation & valuation	*Existence or occurrence*
• Evaluate entity's procedures for valuing inventory	• Confirm consigned inventory & inventory in warehouses
• Verify that inventory counts match quantities in the accounting records	• Observe inventory count
• Evaluate obsolete & slow-moving inventory for potential adjustment	*Rights & obligations*
• Perform analytical procedures to evaluate reasonableness of inventories & relationships to A/P & cost of sales	• Review cutoffs (sales, sales returns, purchases, purchase returns)
Completeness	*Completeness & cutoff*
• Evaluate inventory counting procedures to make certain that all inventory is counted	• Perform test counts and compare with client's counts/summary
• Trace inventory counts to accounting records	• Inquire about consigned inventory
• Identify inventory held by employees, consignees, & warehouses	• Perform analytical procedures
• Perform analytical procedures to evaluate the reasonableness of receivables	• Account for all inventory tags and count sheets
Existence	*Valuation, allocation & accuracy*
• Observe physical count of inventories	• Foot & extend summary schedules
• Confirm with warehouses & consignees with custody of entity's inventories	• Reconcile summary schedules to G/L
	• Test inventory costing method
	• Examine inventory quality (salable condition)
	• Test inventory obsolescence
	• Determine whether the periodic vs. perpetual inventory system is used for valuation

These lists are not intended to be all-inclusive.

Specific Considerations – Inventory

When **inventory is material**, AU-C 501[2] requires the auditor to attend the physical inventory count for the purpose of obtaining evidence regarding the existence of inventory and its condition. While attending the physical inventory count, the auditor should:

[2] *Audit Evidence – Specific Considerations for Selected Items*

- Evaluate instructions and procedures

- Observe the performance of count procedures

- Inspect inventory

- Perform test counts

Having obtained evidence about the accuracy of the inventory count, the auditor will also perform procedures to determine if the physical counts are accurately reported in the accounting records. If the count is performed on a date other than the date of the F/S, the auditor will also obtain evidence to determine that changes between the count date and the date of the F/S have been properly reflected.

When the auditor is unable to attend the physical count, alternate procedures should be applied including the performance of test counts on alternate dates and applying audit procedures to transactions occurring between the count date and the date of the F/S.

When inventory that is in the custody of third parties is material, AU-C 501 requires the auditor to request confirmations from the third parties, perform an inspection of the inventory, or perform other procedures as the auditor considers appropriate under the circumstances.

Goods in Transit

When a company buys or sells goods, the shipping terms will determine whether they are included in that entity's inventory while the goods are in transit. Although there are numerous factors that differentiate shipping contracts, most fall into one of two categories:

- **Shipping contracts, FAS** (free alongside), **shipping point, or FOB** (free on board), in which title transfers from the seller to the buyer when goods are delivered by the seller to a common carrier.

- **Destination contracts, FAS destination or FOB destination**, in which title transfers from the seller to the buyer when goods are delivered by a common carrier to the buyer.

Seller
FOB* Shipping point
(Shipped)

12/31
Whose inventory is it
if cut-off is here?

Buyer
FOB* Destination
(Received)

FOB = Free on Board

FOB Shipping Point

- Title passes to the buyer when the seller delivers the goods to a common carrier (shipped).
- Included in buyer's books at year-end.

FOB Destination

- Title passes to the buyer when the buyer receives the goods from the common carrier.
- Included in seller's books until received by buyer.

6.05 PP&E & Current Liabilities

Auditing Fixed Assets: Overview

Objectives

- Adequate I/C
- **R**ights & obligations – Fixed assets are owned by the entity.
- **A**llocation & valuation – Assets are properly valued, including proper capitalization of costs, depreciation or amortization, and impairments.
- **C**ompleteness – All fixed assets are included.
- **E**xistence – Fixed assets actually exist.

Analytical Procedures

In obtaining evidence about **property, plant, and equipment and identifiable intangibles***
(eg, software), the auditor will first evaluate whether there is reason to believe that fixed assets
are misstated at the financial statement element or account balance level.

Collectively referred to as "fixed assets."

Based on the auditor's knowledge of the entity and its industry, the auditor will determine
whether:

- There has been a change in capacity, indicating an increase or decrease in the overall fixed assets held by the entity
- Any fixed assets were near the end of their useful lives
- Disposals and replacements have occurred
- Depreciation and accumulated depreciation seem appropriate

Forms of Evidence

There are various forms of evidence the auditor may use in the audit of fixed assets. Some will
be obtained from the client, some directly from outside sources, and some may result from the
direct actions of the auditor.

- Legal documents, state filings, and contracts that evidence rights represented by identifiable intangible assets
- Invoices, purchase agreements, shipping records, and other documents related to the acquisition of fixed assets
- Sales agreements, escrow statements, and closing statements related to the disposal of fixed assets

- Client schedules reporting fixed asset holdings along with related depreciation and amortization

- Property tax bills and insurance policies

- Minutes of meetings of management or those charged with governance authorizing acquisitions or disposals of fixed assets

- Bank confirmations indicating whether fixed assets have been used as collateral for loans

Test of Transactions Approach for Fixed Assets

Since there are generally relatively few transactions involving fixed assets and identifiable intangibles, the auditor will often use a **test of transactions** approach in which the emphasis is on changes during the year.

Additions

With respect to reported additions of fixed assets during the year, the auditor will inspect purchase documents that support these additions to verify **valuation**, then observe the actual fixed assets to verify **existence**.

Beginning Balance

\+ Additions

– Dispositions

Ending Balance

In the case of real property, deeds generally consist of a legal conveyance of rights, but sales price and related mortgage acquisition costs are rarely specified. As to **completeness**, the auditor will examine repairs and maintenance accounts to determine if any expenditures for property and equipment were incorrectly expensed.

Dispositions

With respect to retirements, the auditor is primarily concerned with **existence**, and will obtain listings of property and then try to locate the actual assets to be certain there are no unrecorded retirements of assets. The auditor will also examine the journal entries made for retirements to ensure that the correct amounts were removed from relevant accounts, supporting the **valuation** assertion. This is one of the few entries that results in a debit to accumulated depreciation. Such a debit can only result from one of the following:

- Removal of accumulated depreciation upon retirement or sale of an asset

- Correction of an excessive entry for depreciation expense made previously

- Costs incurred to extend the useful life of the asset

Depreciation, Amortization & Impairment

For assets that were owned for the entire year, the auditor's main concern will be with depreciation. The auditor will review the computations of depreciation expense and consider the appropriateness of the useful lives and methods to verify **allocation and valuation**. The auditor will then review the posting of these amounts to the proper categories in order to verify **presentation and disclosure**.

When auditing intangible assets, verification of **rights and obligations** is achieved through the inspection of records for those that were purchased as well as those that resulted from expenditures to acquire or defend legal intangibles, such as patents. Of course, these inspections also provide evidence of **valuation**.

In addition, **amortization** entries will be reviewed for mathematical accuracy, and the auditor will consider evidence that intangibles may have been impaired in value and need to be written off. This also relates to **valuation**.

For **goodwill**, the auditor is concerned with **existence or occurrence**, since only goodwill purchased as part of the acquisition of a business may be recorded. The auditor is also concerned with **allocation and valuation** as it relates to the computation of goodwill and impairment.

RACE Approach to Audit Procedures for Fixed Assets

Rights & Obligations

The entity owns the fixed assets that are reported. In seeking evidence to support this assertion, the auditor will determine if there are **controls** in place that would provide assurance that the entity has not used fixed assets as collateral or is not entitled to the rights associated with identifiable intangibles.

Substantive procedures may include:

- **Inspecting** purchase documents, including escrow or closing statements, as appropriate
- **Inspecting** insurance policies and property tax bills to determine if fixed assets are properly included
- Obtaining **confirmations** from financial institutions requesting information about fixed assets that may have been used as collateral
- Performing a UCC search to determine if any fixed assets have been encumbered with any other parties **(inspection)**

Allocation & Valuation

The amounts reported as fixed assets are accurately measured. A misrepresentation might occur if fixed assets are not being depreciated appropriately or costs that should have been capitalized (eg, delivery, installation) have been expensed. In seeking evidence to support this assertion, the auditor will determine if there are **controls** in place, such as:

- Appropriate policies for determining when expenditures will be reported as repairs and maintenance expense and when they should be capitalized
- Evaluation and periodic re-evaluation of useful lives, salvage values, and allocation methods applicable to depreciable fixed assets and amortizable identifiable intangibles
- Policies and procedures appropriate to identify events and circumstances that may indicate that an asset has been impaired

Substantive procedures may include:

- **Recalculating** depreciation and amortization expense for the period

- **Inspecting** purchase documents, escrow or closing statements, and other documents to determine if amounts were properly capitalized

- **Inspecting** charges to repairs and maintenance expense to determine if amounts that should have been capitalized have been expensed

- **Observing** fixed assets to determine if they appear to be working as intended to ensure that impairment losses are not required to be recognized

- Footing and cross footing schedules of fixed assets, depreciation expense, and accumulated depreciation and recalculate amounts included on the schedules **(recalculation)**

- Evaluating whether amounts recorded for the acquisition of fixed assets approximate the auditor's expectations for such items **(analytical procedures)**

Completeness

All fixed assets owned by the entity are reported on the B/S. A misrepresentation might occur if the entity held fixed assets that were recorded as repairs and maintenance expense. In seeking evidence to support this assertion, the auditor will determine if there are appropriate **controls** in place, such as:

- Capitalization policies that are communicated and enforced to make certain that all capital expenditures are reported as such instead of being expensed

- Policies requiring appropriate approval for removal of fixed assets from fixed asset schedules

- Periodic comparisons of fixed assets to schedules of fixed assets and amounts reported on the F/S

Substantive procedures may include:

- **Observing** fixed assets and trace them to fixed asset schedules and to the F/S

- Evaluating the reasonableness of fixed assets, considering the entity's volume of activity **(analytical procedure)**

- **Inspecting** insurance policies and property tax statements to make certain that all fixed assets listed are reported on the F/S

- **Inspecting** amounts reported as repairs and maintenance expense to verify that no amounts that should have been capitalized have been recognized as expense

Existence

The amount reported as fixed assets are actual assets in the custody of the entity. A misrepresentation might occur if fixed assets that were sold are included, an expenditure that should have been expensed is capitalized, or an acquisition that did not occur is recorded. In seeking evidence to support this assertion, the auditor will determine if there are appropriate **controls** in place, such as:

- Policies and procedures requiring all disposals of fixed assets to be approved

- Policies limiting access to fixed assets to appropriate parties

- Means of anchoring or otherwise securing fixed assets to prevent theft
- Periodic reconciliation of schedules of fixed assets maintained by the entity to actual observations of fixed assets

Substantive procedures may include:

- **Observing** fixed assets to ascertain their existence
- Obtaining **confirmations** directly from warehousemen who may be holding inventory or fixed assets for the entity
- **Inspecting** purchase documents for items purchased during the period
- **Inspecting** insurance policies and property tax bills to make certain that reported fixed assets are listed when appropriate
- **Inspecting** agreements between the entity and others granting the entity rights associated with identifiable intangible assets
- Tracing cash receipts that are from sources other than revenues to verify that all sales of fixed assets have been properly recorded **(inspection)**

Summary of Alternative Approaches for Fixed Assets*	
RACE	PERCV
Rights & obligations • Trace additions to purchase documents • Perform search & obtain bank confirmations to determine if fixed assets are pledged as security *Allocation & valuation* • Evaluate the entity's procedures for capitalizing costs • Determine if there is an indication of impairment & whether the assets have been appropriately evaluated • Test depreciation & amortization calculations *Completeness* • Observe fixed assets & trace additions to accounting records • Perform analytical procedures to determine reasonableness of fixed assets *Existence* • Observe fixed assets	*Presentation & disclosure* • Review disclosures for GAAP compliance • Inquire about liens & restrictions • Review loan agreements for liens & restrictions *Existence or occurrence* • Inspect/vouch additions • Review leases for proper accounting • Perform search for unrecorded retirements *Rights & obligations* • Review minutes for approval of additions *Completeness & cutoff* • Perform analytical procedures • Vouch major entries to repairs & maintenance expense *Valuation, allocation & accuracy* • Foot summary schedules • Reconcile summary schedules to G/L • Recalculate deprecation

These lists are not intended to be all-inclusive.

Auditing Current Liabilities: Overview

Current liabilities consist primarily of **accounts payable (A/P)** and **accrued expenses**, including **payroll.** The current portion of long-term debt is generally examined as part of the audit of long-term debt.

Objectives

- Adequate I/C

- Rights & obligations – Payables are legitimate obligations of the entity.

- Allocation & valuation – Payables reported in appropriate amounts.

- Completeness – There are no unrecorded liabilities.

- Existence – Payables actually exist.

Analytical Procedures

In obtaining evidence about current liabilities, the auditor will first evaluate whether there is reason to believe that current liabilities are misstated at the financial statement element or account balance level. Based on the auditor's knowledge of the entity's purchasing and payment policies, the auditor should evaluate:

- The relationship between A/P and inventories

- The relationship between accrued expenses and the entity's regular monthly expenses that are generally paid in cash

Forms of Evidence

There are various forms of evidence the auditor may use in the audit of current liabilities. Some will be obtained from the client, some directly from outside sources, and some may result from the direct actions of the auditor.

- Invoices from suppliers

- Timecards, payroll summaries, payroll tax bills, and other internally generated schedules related to payroll

- Leases; agreements for regular services (eg, janitorial); and bills from service providers, such as utility companies

RACE Approach to Audit Procedures for Current Liabilities

Rights & Obligations

The entity received the goods or services creating the current liabilities making them the obligations of the entity. A misrepresentation would occur if a liability belonging to a member of management was included in the B/S. In seeking evidence to support this assertion, the auditor will determine if there are appropriate **controls** in place, such as:

- Information processing controls that require that all recorded A/P be supported by properly authorized requisitions, POs, and evidence of receipt of the ordered goods or services
- Policies that require comparisons to budgeted amounts as a requirement for recognizing expenses
- Policies requiring authorizations for expenses not budgeted

Substantive procedures may include:

- Tracing recorded payables for inventory (in A/P) and expenses (in accrued expenses) to supporting documentation **(inspection)**
- Comparing expenses for the period to the auditor's expectations **(analytical procedures)**

Allocation & Valuation

The amounts reported as current liabilities are accurately measured. A misrepresentation would occur, for example, if the entity accrued expenses like rent or utilities in amounts that did not reflect a reasonable estimate of the actual amount. In seeking evidence to support this assertion, the auditor will determine if there are appropriate **controls** in place, such as:

- Policies requiring that expenses be compared to budgeted amounts with variances investigated
- Timely reconciliation of statements received from vendors to amounts reported as liabilities

Substantive procedures may include:

- Comparing the relationship of A/P to inventories to the auditor's expectations **(analytical procedures)**
- Comparing the relationship between of accrued expenses and the entity's monthly payments to determine if accruals align with the auditor 's expectations **(analytical procedures)**
- Tracing payments made during a reasonable time after year end to supporting documents to identify those that were for goods or services received during the period and trace those amounts to recorded liabilities **(inspection)**
- **Inspecting** documents for purchased goods in transit to determine if those shipped under shipping contracts have been included in A/P when the entity owned the items during shipping
- Comparing the amount accrued for payroll and payroll-related expenses, such as payroll taxes, to the auditor's expectation **(analytical procedures)**
- **Inspecting** receiving reports that have not been matched to other documents to determine if amounts are included in A/P when appropriate
- **Inspecting** leases and other arrangements, such as service agreements, calling for regular payments to determine if amounts accrued are appropriate
- Comparing the amount reported as accrued expenses in the current period to amounts reported in prior periods, accounting for changes in the makeup or amount of various items **(analytical procedures)**

- Obtaining **confirmations** directly from vendors and suppliers to verify that all amounts owed are properly reported

- **Recalculating** payroll accruals and comparing calculations with source information, such as timecards to verify hours worked and personnel records to verify pay rates

Completeness

All current liabilities that are the obligations of the entity are included in the amounts reported on the B/S. A misrepresentation might occur, for example, if the entity neglects to record a payable for the purchase of goods that have already been received by the entity. In seeking evidence to support this assertion, the auditor will determine if there are appropriate **controls** in place such as:

- Policies requiring that expenses be compared to budgeted amounts with variances investigated

- Timely reconciliation of statements received from vendors to amounts reported as liabilities

- Policies requiring that invoices received during a reasonable time after the end of the period be evaluated to determine if they should be included in the period-end accrual

Substantive procedures may include:

- Comparing the relationship of A/P to inventories to the auditor's expectations **(analytical procedures)**

- Comparing the relationship between accrued expenses and the entity's monthly payments to determine if accruals align with the auditor's expectations **(analytical procedures)**

- Tracing payments made during a reasonable time after year end to supporting documents to identify those that were for goods or services received during the year and trace those amounts to recorded liabilities **(inspection)**

- **Inspecting** documents for purchased goods in transit to determine if those shipped under shipping contracts have been included in A/P when the entity owned the items during shipping

- Comparing the amount accrued for payroll and payroll-related expenses (eg, payroll taxes) to the auditor's expectation **(analytical procedures)**

- **Inspecting** receiving reports that have not been matched to other documents to determine if amounts are included in A/P when appropriate

- **Inspecting** leases and other arrangements (eg, service agreements) calling for regular payments to determine if amounts accrued are appropriate

- Comparing the amounts reported as accrued expenses in the current period to amounts reported in prior periods **(analytical procedures)**

- Obtaining **confirmations** directly from vendors and suppliers to verify that all amounts owed are properly reported

Existence

The amount reported as current liabilities are legitimate claims for payment for goods or services that were delivered. A misrepresentation might result, for example, from recording a liability for the purchase of merchandise that has not yet been transferred to the entity. In seeking evidence to support this assertion, the auditor will determine if there are appropriate controls in place such as:

- Policies requiring that purchase requisitions, POs, and receiving reports be matched before a liability is recorded
- Policies requiring vendor names to be compared to lists of approved payees
- Policies requiring accrued expenses to be compared to budgets

Substantive procedures may include:

- Obtaining **confirmations** directly from suppliers verifying amounts payable
- Tracing recorded amounts to supplier invoices, receiving reports, POs, and materials requisitions **(inspection)**
- Determining the length of time between the last date for which employees were paid and the end of the period to determine if accrued payroll liabilities seem legitimate **(analytical procedures)**
- Comparing a listing of items included in accrued expenses to budgets for monthly expenses and amounts incurred in previous periods **(analytical procedures)**
- **Inspecting** leases and service contracts involving regular payments, such as for janitorial or maintenance and bills from service providers

Summary of Alternative Approaches for Current Liabilities*	
RACE	**PERCV**
Rights & obligations • Trace to transaction documents *Allocation & valuation* • Trace to transaction documents • Trace to subsequent payment *Completeness* • Trace subsequent payments to payables • Perform analytical procedures to determine reasonableness *Existence* • Trace to transaction documents • Trace subsequent payments	*Presentation & disclosure* • Review disclosures for GAAP compliance • Review purchase commitments *Existence or occurrence* • Request confirmation from vendors • Inspect copies of notes and note agreements • Vouch A/P (examine POs, receiving reports, invoices) *Rights & obligations* • Review cutoffs (purchases, purchase returns, disbursements) *Completeness & cutoff* • Analytical procedures • Search for unrecorded payables (unrecorded invoices, receiving reports, POs) *Valuation, allocation & accuracy* • Foot subsidiary ledger and reconcile to G/L • Recalculate interest expense, if any • For payroll, review year-end accrual • Recalculate other accrued liabilities

These lists are not intended to be all-inclusive.

When auditing A/P, the management assertion of **completeness** is often considered the most important since the auditor's primary concern is **understatement** of liabilities.

The procedure that is most effective in identifying *unrecorded liabilities* (**"Search for unrecorded liabilities"**) is the examination of cash disbursements after the B/S date. In the case of A/P, these payments should be vouched to the related POs and receiving reports to identify those payables that were owed as of the B/S date. Since most A/P are paid within 30 days of invoicing, subsequent payments provide very persuasive evidence as to the completeness of A/P.

Another method of determining completeness is to **trace receiving reports** to postings of purchases to ensure that all received items have been recorded. The auditor may also **vouch recorded liabilities** back to the supporting documents but, in this case, the emphasis is on the management assertions of **existence and valuation** rather than completeness.

The auditor may choose to **confirm** payables. Because of the emphasis on understatement, however, the bases for selection of payables to confirm will not be identical to those for receivables. In particular, the auditor will choose from the entire population of vendors with whom the client did business during the year, and may confirm with vendors showing low or zero balances owed at the B/S date.

When auditing payroll, the auditor is often able to place reliance on the internal control (I/C) structure of the payroll cycle and assess RMM at a low level, thereby permitting higher detection risk and limiting the necessary substantive testing. Since payroll is generally more predictable than other costs, the auditor should perform **analytical procedures** involving the comparison of actual payroll costs with budgeted or standard costs to determine **completeness** of payroll records.

Contingent Liabilities

Contingencies represent gains or losses that may or may not occur in the future as a result of an event that has already occurred or an existing condition. Contingencies may result from asserted lawsuits as well as conditions that may result in a future lawsuit. If, for example, an entity is aware that it has sold a defective product, a condition exists that may result in future lawsuits and a future liability as purchasers become aware of the defects.

Contingnent gains may not be accrued and are not required to be disclosed. As a result, the auditor is only required to determine if those disclosures regarding gain contingencies that the entity has decided to include with its F/S are appropriate. Contingent liabilities, on the other hand, are required to be accrued and disclosed when they are probable and estimable; disclosed without accrual if either they are probable but not subject to reasonable estimation or if they are reasonably possible; and neither accrued nor disclosed if remote.

In order to make certain that all such accruals and disclosures have been properly made, AU-C 501, *Audit Evidence – Specific Considerations for Selected Items*, requires the auditor to perform audit procedures to determine if there are contingencies and, if so, if they are properly accounted for and disclosed. Procedures designed to identify contingent liabilities, including litigation, claims, and assessments, include:

- Making inquiries of management and others within the entity, such as in-house counsel.

- Obtaining from management a list of all litigation, claims, and assessments both existing at the date of the F/S or during the period between the date of the F/S and the date of the list, with a description and evaluation of each.

- Reviewing minutes of meetings of the board of directors and others.

- Reviewing documents regarding litigation, claims, and assessments received from management, including correspondence between the entity and its legal counsel.

- Reviewing legal expenses and invoices for legal services.

The auditor may determine that no actual or potential litigation, claims, or assessments exist that require accrual or disclosure in the F/S. If this is not the case, however, the auditor is required to seek direct communication with the entity's legal counsel. The auditor will also obtain a letter from each attorney with which the client did business relevant to any litigation, claims, or assessments involving the client.

Loss Contingencies			
	Probabillity of Occuring	**Disclose?**	**Accrue?**
Remote	Slight chance	No	No
Reasonably Possible	More than Remote, less than Probable	Yes Full Disclosure	No Fair presentation
Probable & Estimable	Likely to occur	Yes	**Yes***
Probable & Not Estimable			No

Conservatism / Matching

6.06 L/T Debt, Stockholders' Equity & Payroll

Auditing Long-Term Debt: Overview

Long-term debt consists of **notes payable, bonds payable,** and **lease obligations**. Transactions involving long-term debt tend to be well documented, including authorization from the board of directors or others who are charged with governance, formal agreements between the lender and the entity, and scheduled payments. When payments are made on a timely basis, all amounts, including interest expense, the ending balance of the long-term liability, and the current portion are all readily determinable.

Due to the nature of long-term debt, including the fact that transactions tend to be infrequent, material, and well documented, the auditor will frequently rely heavily on substantive testing.

Objectives

- Adequate I/C
- **R**ights & obligations – Debt is obligation of entity.
- **A**llocation & valuation – Debt is recorded in appropriate amount.
- **C**ompleteness – All debt recorded.
- **E**xistence – Debt actually exists.

Forms of Evidence

There are various forms of evidence the auditor may use in the audit of long-term debt. Some will be obtained from the client, some directly from outside sources, and some may result from the direct actions of the auditor.

- Copies of notes and loans payable and long-term leases
- Spreadsheets and other schedules prepared by the client to recognize principal and interest allocations, determine the current portion of long-term debt, and to keep track of long-term liabilities
- Confirmations from creditors

RACE Approach to Audit Procedures for Long-Term Debt

Rights & Obligations

The entity borrowed the money represented by long-term debt and is obligated on the liability. A misrepresentation might occur, for example, if a liability of a member of management was recorded as a liability of the entity.

Substantive procedures may include:

- Tracing recorded liabilities to supporting documentation **(inspection)**
- Verifying that transactions in which long-term debt was recorded resulted in a deposit of cash for the proceeds **(inspection)**
- Obtaining **confirmation** from creditors

Allocation & Valuation

The amounts reported in long-term debt are accurately measured. A misrepresentation might occur, for example, if the entity incorrectly allocated payments between principal and interest, overstating or understating the principal balance.

Substantive procedures may include:

- Comparing the ending balances reported for long-term debt to the auditor's expectations developed from reviewing loan documents and from repayment schedules **(analytical procedures)**
- Obtaining **confirmation** of ending balances directly from creditors
- **Recalculating** the current portion of long-term debt to verify that the amount reported by the entity is accurate
- **Recalculating** allocations between principal and interest to determine that periodic payments have been properly reported

Completeness

All long-term debt consists of liabilities that are the obligations of the entity and are included in the amounts reported on the B/S. A misrepresentation might occur, for example, if the entity were to record proceeds from a borrowing transaction as revenue or as a capital contribution.

Substantive procedures may include:

- Comparing the relationship between interest expense and the average balance in long-term debt to determine if the relationship is reasonable based on the auditor's knowledge of terms the entity would be subject to **(analytical procedures)**
- Obtaining **confirmations** directly from creditors, including a standard bank confirmation, requesting information about all liabilities owed by the entity to make certain that there are no exclusions
- **Inspecting** the cash receipts journal and tracing significant deposits to source documents to determine if any represent liabilities that have not been recorded as such

Existence

The amount reported as long-term debt represents legitimate obligations that resulted from borrowing transactions that actually occurred.

Substantive procedures may include:

- Obtaining **confirmations** directly from creditors verifying amounts payable and terms of the liabilities

- **Inspecting** long-term leases, notes and loans payable, and other agreements documenting long-term debt arrangements
- Tracing proceeds from borrowing transactions recorded in the cash receipts journal to supporting documents providing evidence of the existence of long-term liabilities **(inspection)**
- **Inspecting** minutes from board of director meetings or meetings of those charged with governance to verify that borrowing transactions have been authorized

Summary of Alternative Approaches for Long-Term Debt*	
RACE	**PERCV**
Rights & obligations • Trace liabilities to loan documents *Allocation & valuation* • Trace liabilities to transaction documents • Trace liabilities to subsequent payment • Confirm amounts with creditors *Completeness* • Evaluate subsequent disbursements • Confirm amounts with creditors • Review minutes for debt authorizations • Obtain letter from attorney • Analytical procedures *Existence* • Trace to loan documents • Trace subsequent payments	*Presentation & disclosure* • Review disclosures for GAAP compliance • Inquire about pledging of assets • Review debt agreements for pledging & events causing default *Existence or occurrence* • Confirm terms & balances with creditors • Inspect copies of notes & note agreements • Trace receipt of funds (& payment) to bank account and cash receipts journal *Rights & obligations* • Review cutoffs • Review minutes for proper authorization (& completeness) *Completeness & cutoff* • Analytical procedures • Inquire of management as to completeness • Review bank confirmations for unrecorded debt *Valuation, allocation & accuracy* • Foot summary schedules and reconcile to G/L • Vouch entries to account • Recalculate interest expense & accrued interest payable

These lists are not intended to be all-inclusive.

The audit of long-term debt is normally quite limited since, by its nature, long-term debt is likely to involve few transactions during a typical year, except for interest payments. As a result, the verification of interest expense and accrued interest payable are the most common objectives, with analytical procedures comparing interest expense to the related debt being the most useful. Confirmation of long-term debt with payees, trustees and other appropriate third parties, may be used to verify any applicable sinking fund transactions. The auditor may also examine legal agreements in connection with such obligations.

Though there is little likelihood of notes and bonds payable going unrecorded, proper **classification** on the B/S is an important issue in connection with the assertion of **disclosure and presentation**. In particular, if a current note is renewed shortly after year-end, the auditor needs to ensure that the note is classified as a long-term debt rather than a current one.

Going Concern

Although not required in some special purpose financial reporting frameworks, when F/S are prepared in accordance with GAAP, ASC 205, Subtopic 40, requires management to evaluate whether the entity has the ability to continue as a going concern for a reasonable time. The ability to continue as a going concern implies that the entity will be able to meet its obligations as they come due. A reasonable period of time is considered one year from the date on which the F/S are issued, or, when appropriate, one year from the date on which they are available to be issued.

Even when the AFRF does not require management to perform such an evaluation, if characteristics of the financial reporting framework according to which the F/S are being prepared incorporate a going concern assumption, the preparation of the F/S requires management to assess the entity's ability to continue as a going concern. The framework in use can indicate such an assumption when receivables are written down to amounts expected to be received, payments for assets are capitalized and amortized instead of being expensed when incurred, and other accounts with long-term implications are handled in a similar manner.

Unless F/S are prepared in accordance with the cash basis or a comparable basis, they are likely being prepared in accordance with a going concern assumption. As a result, preparing the F/S requires management to assess the entity's ability to continue as a going concern even when the AFRF does not explicitly require it.

During the performance of the risk assessment procedures applied by the auditor in obtaining an understanding of the entity and its environment, including its internal control, the auditor should determine if management has made a preliminary evaluation of whether events or conditions exist that raise doubts.

- If management has performed such an evaluation, the auditor should discuss it with management and, if management has identified events or conditions that raise substantial doubt, the auditor should understand management's plans to address them.

- If management has not performed such an evaluation, the auditor should inquire of management whether such events or conditions exist.

The auditor's evaluation should address management's evaluation, covering the same period of time, and should consider whether management has evaluated all events and conditions of which the auditor is aware.

When events or conditions have been identified, the auditor is required to obtain sufficient appropriate audit evidence as to whether they, when considered in the aggregate, raise a substantial doubt about the entity's ability to continue as a going concern for a reasonable period of time, as well as any mitigating factors. The auditor's procedures will include:

- Requesting management to make an evaluation if one has not already been made .

- Evaluating management's plans in relation to the events and conditions to determine if it is probable that they can be implemented effectively and would mitigate the events and conditions that raise the doubt.

- Evaluating a cash flow forecast and analysis, if one was prepared by management, including the reliability of the underlying data and determining if there is adequate support for assumptions made.

- Considering whether additional facts or information have become available based on which management made its evaluation.

If, before considering management's plans, the auditor believes that substantial doubt exists as to the entity's ability to continue as a going concern, the auditor should request written representations from management. They should:

- Describe management's plans intended to mitigate the adverse effects of events or conditions contributing to the substantial doubt, including the probability that they can be implemented effectively.

- Indicate that all relevant matters of which management is aware have been disclosed, including significant conditions and events, and also including management's plans.

Based on the results of the audit procedures applied, the auditor will conclude that either management's plans do, or do not, alleviate the adverse effects of events and conditions causing the substantial doubt as to the entity's ability to continue as a going concern. Based on that conclusion, the auditor will determine if disclosure is adequate.

- If management's plans are expected to mitigate the adverse effects, indicating that there is no longer substantial doubt as to the entity's ability to continue as a going concern, the disclosure should describe the events and conditions that created the doubt, management's evaluation of their significance, and management's plans that mitigated the adverse effects.

- If management's plans are not expected to mitigate the adverse claims to the extent that they remove the doubt, the disclosure will be similar, except it will also indicate that there is substantial doubt. In addition, it will refer to management's plans that are intended to mitigate the effects, rather than indicate that the effects have been mitigated.

Auditing Stockholders' Equity

Stockholders' equity consists of **common** and **preferred stock, additional paid-in capital (APIC), treasury stock, retained earnings,** and **accumulated other comprehensive income (AOCI)**. Transactions involving stockholders' equity are generally limited to issuances or reacquisitions of stock, which are relatively rare; paying **dividends**; and closing net income or loss and other comprehensive income or loss into retained earnings and AOCI, respectively.

- Transactions involving issuance or reacquisition of stock or the payment of dividends tend to be well documented and require authorization by the board of directors or those others who are charged with governance.

- Since the auditor is applying auditing procedures to obtain evidence to support the components of, and amounts reported as, net income and OCI, the auditor will need to determine that the amounts have been appropriately recognized in retained earnings and AOCI.

Due to the nature of stockholders' equity, including the fact that transactions tend to be infrequent, material, and well documented, the auditor will frequently rely heavily on substantive testing.

Objectives

- Adequacy of I/C over stock transactions
- Transactions properly authorized and comply with regulations
- Transactions recorded in conformity with GAAP
- Adequately disclosed in F/S

Forms of Evidence

There are various forms of evidence the auditor may use in the audit of stockholders' equity. Some will be obtained from the client, some directly from outside sources, and some may result from the direct actions of the auditor.

- Copies of minutes of meetings of the board of directors or those charged with governance authorizing the issuance or reacquisition of equity shares or the payment of dividends
- Confirmations from transfer agents or registrars indicating any transactions involving equity shares
- Stock certificate books for entities that do not use transfer agents

RACE Approach to Audit Procedures for Stockholders' Equity

Rights & Obligations

Stockholders' equity represents ownership interests in the entity. A misrepresentation might be the inclusion a hybrid instrument that is more like debt than equity in the stockholders' equity section of the B/S.

Substantive procedures may include:

- **Inspecting** minutes of board of director meetings or meetings of those charged with governance to verify that transactions recognized in stockholders' equity accounts have been authorized
- **Inquiring** of the entity's attorneys to determine if there are any legal issues affecting equity interests
- **Inspecting** the articles of incorporation or other corporate documents to determine if there are restrictions on equity ownership and if all issuances of stock are authorized

Allocation & Valuation

The amounts reported in stockholders' equity are accurately measured. A misrepresentation might occur if the entity incorrectly allocated proceeds from the issuance of stock or amounts paid to reacquire stock between common stock or treasury stock and additional paid-in capital.

Substantive procedures may include:

- Tracing dividend payments to supporting authorizations by those charged with governance and to entries to retained earnings to determine that they have been recognized properly as reductions to retained earnings **(inspection)**

- Tracing the closing of net income into retained earnings and OCI into AOCI **(inspection)**

- **Recalculating** the adjustments that result from treasury stock transactions to verify the accuracy of their recording

- Tracing entries to stockholders' equity accounts to the related cash receipts, for issuances, or disbursements, for reacquisitions, to determine that all have been properly reported **(inspection)**

- Tracing all remaining transactions increasing or decreasing stockholders' equity accounts to supporting documentation to verify that they have been reported accurately **(inspection)**

Completeness

All equity interests in the entity are included in the stockholders' equity amounts reported on the B/S. A misrepresentation might occur if the entity were to record proceeds from the issuance of stock as a borrowing transaction.

Substantive procedures may include:

- **Inspecting** the cash receipts journal and trace significant deposits to source documents to determine if any represent issuances of equity securities that have not been recorded as such

- **Inspecting** minutes of board of director meetings or meetings of those charged with governance to determine if there are any authorizations for the issuance of equity securities that did not result in increases in the amounts reported

- **Inquiring** of management and others as to whether there was an issuance of equity securities during the period

- **Inspecting** the stock certificate book, if applicable, to make certain that all certificates have been accounted for

- Obtaining **confirmations** from transfer agents or registrars, if applicable, to determine if equity securities have been issued during the period but not recorded

Existence

The amount reported as stockholders' equity represents legitimate ownership claims to the entity. A misrepresentation might result from recording money borrowed as proceeds from the issuance of equity or unrecorded reacquisitions of shares.

Substantive procedures may include:

- Obtaining **confirmations** directly from the entity's stock registrar or transfer agent, if applicable

- **Inspecting** the stock certificate book in the custody of the entity if the entity does not use a transfer agent

- Tracing entries made in the stockholders' equity accounts to underlying supporting documents (**inspection**)
- **Inspecting** minutes from board of director meetings or meetings of those charged with governance to verify that transactions recognized in stockholders' equity accounts have been authorized

Alternative Approaches to Audit Procedures for Stockholders' Equity*	
RACE	**PERCV**
Rights & obligations • Review minutes for proper authorization • Inquire of legal counsel on legal issues • Review Articles of Incorporation and bylaws for propriety of equity securities *Allocation & valuation* • Agree amounts to the G/L • Vouch dividend payments • Vouch all entries to retained earnings • Recalculate treasury stock transactions *Completeness* • Analytical procedures • Inspect treasury stock certificates *Existence* • Confirm with registrar and transfer agent • Inspect stock certificate book (when no registrar or transfer agent) • Vouch capital stock entries	*Presentation & disclosure* • Review disclosures for GAAP compliance • Review information on stock options, dividend restrictions *Existence or occurrence* • Confirm with registrar and transfer agent • Inspect stock certificate book (when no registrar or transfer agent) • Vouch capital stock entries *Rights & obligations* • Review minutes for proper authorization • Inquire of legal counsel on legal issues • Review Articles of Incorporation and bylaws for propriety of equity securities *Completeness & cutoff* • Analytical procedures • Inspect treasury stock certificates *Valuation, allocation & accuracy* • Agree amounts to the G/L • Vouch dividend payments • Vouch all entries to retained earnings • Recalculate treasury stock transactions

These lists are not intended to be all-inclusive.

There are generally very few transactions involving the stockholders' equity section, so audit procedures in this area are quite limited. With respect to capital stock and other securities, the auditor will verify that all issuances are approved by the board of directors and consistent with the articles of incorporation. A registrar is normally responsible for executing such transactions, so **confirmation** is an appropriate procedure along with **review of the minutes** of board meetings and inspection of corporate documents.

The primary concern with respect to retained earnings is that any **restrictions** on the use of it for the payment of dividends are disclosed on the face of the statement or in the notes to the F/S.

Dividends

Important Dates

The auditor should be familiar with three important dates related to the declaration and payment of dividends to make certain that they are reported in the appropriate periods.

- **Declaration date** – The date on which the board of directors commits to the dividend, determining the amount of the dividend to be distributed, at which time a liability has been incurred and is recorded.

- **Record date** – The date that is used to determine which shareholders will receive the dividend, which will be those who have legal rights to the shares on that date.

- **Payment date** – The date on which the distribution is made to the shareholders of record.

Types of Dividends

Dividends may be distributed in a variety of different forms:

- **Cash** dividends are the most common.

- **Property** dividends result when the entity distributes assets other than cash to shareholders, at which time a gain or loss is recognized as if the asset were sold for its fair market value, with that amount being reported as a liability.

- **Scrip** dividends are interest-bearing notes given to shareholders to be paid in the future, which are used when an entity wishes to declare a dividend but it does not have the cash to pay it.

- **Liquidating** dividends are distributions of the entity's cash and assets to shareholders during the process of liquidating the company, reported by shareholders as a return of their capital.

- **Stock** dividends involve the entity issuing shares of stock instead of cash.

Stock dividends involve the distribution of additional shares to existing shareholders in lieu of a cash dividend.

- A stock dividend may be considered a *small* stock dividend, usually when the distribution is 20% or less of the outstanding stock. In this case, retained earnings is reduced by the fair value of the shares issued, and the stock is recorded as if issued for that amount.

- A stock dividend may be a *large* stock dividend, usually when the distribution is 25% or more of the outstanding stock. In this case, retained earnings is decreased, and common stock is increased for the par or stated value of shares issued.

- Stock dividends that are for between 20 and 25% of the shares outstanding may be considered large or small stock dividends, depending on the surrounding circumstances.

A **stock split** occurs when the entity issues additional shares to stockholders by decreasing the par or stated value per share and issuing a proportionate number of shares. A stock split does not generally require a journal entry as the amount reported in the common stock account will remain the same. A notation will be made for disclosure purposes, however, as the number of shares will increase and the par or stated value per share will decrease.

Note: All dividends reduce Stockholders' Equity except for stock dividends and stock splits.

Cash Dividend	Scrip—Give dividend but no money	Stock Dividend
RE　　　25 　　Cash　　25	RE　　　　　25 　　Note payable　　25	**Small < 20–25% – FMV** RE　　　　　　25 　　CS　　　　20 　　APIC　　　5
	Partial Liquidating Dividend RE　　　　15 APIC　　　10 　　Cash　　25	**Large > 20–25% – Par** RE　　　　　20 　　CS　　　　20
Property (FMV) RE　　　25 　　Asset　　20 　　Gain　　5	**Person receiving Liq Div** Cash　　　25 　　Div income　　15 　　Investment　　10	**Stock Splits: Double shares, half par** CS (10(10))　　100 　　CS (20(5))　　100

Net effect on Stockholders' Equity = 20

Revenue & Expenses

Revenue and expense transactions make up the core of the operations of many entities and, in many cases, the auditor will obtain the majority of evidence regarding revenues and expenses through the testing of controls applied to the operating systems. The auditor will first determine if there is reason to believe that revenues or expenses are materially misstated by applying analytical procedures. The auditor may compare recorded amounts to expectations developed independently by the auditor, to budgets prepared by the entity, or by comparison to prior periods.

Evidence supporting amounts reported as revenues and expenses is also obtained through the audit of other areas. The audit of A/R provides evidence regarding revenues, and the audit of current liabilities provides evidence regarding many expenses. In addition, expenses like depreciation and amortization are generally audited at the same time as the related assets are examined.

A large portion of the amount reported as expenses results from cash disbursements made on a routine basis in the ordinary course of business. In performing tests of cash disbursements, including tests of controls, the auditor will generally verify that disbursements for expenses are properly reported. In addition, expenses may be put into *three broad categories*, each of which may be examined differently.

- Some expenses, such as depreciation and amortization, are determined on the basis of applying a formula. The auditor will often rely most heavily on *recalculation* or similar procedures to obtain satisfaction that they are not materially misstated.

- Some expenses, such as rent, interest expense, utilities, and other expenses incurred on a routine basis are subject to a high degree of predictability enabling the auditor to develop expectations as to the amounts that should be reported. Payroll-related expenses also often fall into this category. For those expenses for which expectations can be developed that are adequately precise and adequately reliable, the auditor will rely most heavily on *analytical procedures*.

- Many of the remaining expenses are incurred as circumstances create needs and are not subject to developing meaningful expectations. These expenses may be subjected to various substantive procedures, including *tracing items* to underlying supporting documentation, as considered appropriate by the auditor.

Auditors will often rely more heavily on internal controls when obtaining evidence about revenues and expenses than when auditing B/S accounts. The auditor will determine, based on the required understanding, if the systems are designed to record revenues and expenses in appropriate amounts that are fairly presented.

If the auditor concludes that the systems are potentially effective, the auditor will perform tests of controls to make certain that the systems were in place and operating effectively during the period under audit. Satisfactory results to the tests of controls will allow the auditor to limit the nature, timing, and extent of further audit procedures applied to revenue and expenses.

Many revenue and expense (I/S) accounts are verified when tests of controls are performed over the various functions, such as cash receipts and disbursements, purchases, and sales. In addition, they are verified in conjunction with the audit of related asset or liability (B/S) accounts.

B/S Account	I/S Account
Accounts receivable	Sales, credit loss expense
Inventories & A/P	Purchases, cost of goods sold, manufacturing payroll
Investments	Interest, dividends, gains & losses on sales
Property, Plant & Equipment	Rent, gains & losses on sales, depreciation, epairs & maintenance expense
Notes Receivable	Interest
Accrued liabilities & prepaid expenses	Warranty expense, commissions, fees insurance expense, & various expenses

Revenues and expenses are *I/S accounts* and, as a result, the assertions related to **classes of transactions (CPA-CO)** apply.

- **Completeness** – All transactions giving rise to revenues or expenses that relate to the entity are recognized. A misrepresentation in relation to completeness might include capitalizing costs that should be recognized as expenses or neglecting to record a sale with the proceeds being misappropriated.

- **Period Cutoff** – All revenues and expenses are reported in the appropriate period. A misrepresentation in relation to cutoff may include recognizing a sale while goods shipped under a destination contract and are still in transit or neglecting to accrue an expense that had been incurred as of the end of the year but had not yet been paid for.

- **Accuracy** (Amounts) – All revenues and expenses have been reported in appropriate amounts. A misrepresentation in relation to accuracy may involve a revenue transaction being reported at an amount lower than the actual sale, or an expense being reported at a higher amount, with the difference being misappropriated.

- **Classification** – All revenues and expenses are appropriately categorized on the F/S. A misrepresentation in relation to classification may involve reporting the proceeds from the sale of an operating asset, such as a machine used in the manufacturing process, as revenues rather than reporting the difference between the proceeds and the carrying value as a gain or loss on sale.

- **Occurrence** – The transaction giving rise to the recorded revenue or expense did occur and pertains to the entity. A misrepresentation in relation to occurrence might result from recording a sale that no customer has approved or recognizing an expense that was incurred on behalf of a member of management but paid for by the entity.

There are various *forms of evidence* the auditor may use in the audit of revenues and expenses. Some will be obtained from the client, some directly from outside sources, and some may result from the direct actions of the auditor. Evidence the auditor may use includes:

- Copies of POs received from customers, sales orders, vendor invoices, requisitions, receiving reports, and various other documents supporting specific transactions.

- Leases, service agreements, and other contracts related to the incurring of regular expenses.

- Spreadsheets and schedules calculating deprecation or amortization expense, interest expense, or other items requiring allocation or otherwise requiring analysis for proper reporting.

- Approvals from management or those charged with governance, as appropriate, for unusual and nonrecurring expenses.

- Budgets and other analyses providing management's expectations as to revenues expected to be earned during the period and expenses expected to be incurred.

CPA-CO Approach to Audit Procedures for Revenues & Expenses

Completeness

In seeking evidence that all revenue and expense transactions that occurred and pertained to the entity were recorded, the auditor will determine if there are appropriate **controls** in place, such as:

- The use of prenumbered sales invoices and the accounting for all numbers within a sequence
- Comparisons of expenses to budgeted amounts are made on a regular basis with any variances investigated on a timely basis

Substantive procedures may include:

- Comparing recorded revenues and various expenses to the auditor's expectations **(analytical procedures)**
- Tracing a sample of receiving reports and trace them to related transactions recognizing revenue **(inspection)**
- **Recalculation** – The auditor may analyze documents related to purchases of fixed assets to determine if costs that should have been recognized as an expense in the period were capitalized to the cost of the asset.

Period Cutoff

In seeking evidence that all revenue and expense transactions are recorded in the appropriate periods, the auditor will determine if there are **controls** in place, such as:

- Policies requiring that expenses be compared to budgeted amounts with variances investigated
- Policies requiring that invoices received during a reasonable time after the end of the period be evaluated to determine if they should be included in the period-end accrual

Substantive procedures may include:

- Comparing the relationship between accrued expenses and the entity's monthly payments for expenses to the auditor's expectations to make certain that expenses incurred near the end of the year are reported **(analytical procedures)**
- Tracing payments made during a reasonable time after the end of the period to supporting documents to identify those that were for goods or services received during the period and verify that those amounts are recognized as expenses in the appropriate period **(inspection)**
- Comparing the amount accrued for payroll and payroll-related expenses (eg, payroll taxes) to the auditor's expectation **(analytical procedures)**
- **Inspecting** leases and other arrangements (eg, service agreements) calling for regular payments to determine if all amounts related to the current period have been accounted for

Accuracy (Amounts)

In seeking evidence that all revenue and expense transactions are recorded in appropriate amounts, the auditor will determine if there are appropriate **controls** in place, such as:

- Policies requiring that expenses be compared to budgeted amounts with variances investigated
- Timely reconciliation of statements received from vendors to amounts reported as expenses

Substantive procedures may include:

- Comparing recorded revenues and expenses to the auditor's expectations **(analytical procedures)**

- Tracing a sample of amounts recorded as expenses to supporting documentation to determine if expenses were recorded in correct amounts **(inspection)**

- Tracing a sample of recorded sales transactions to supporting documentation to verify that they were recorded in correct amounts **(inspection)**

- Comparing amounts recorded for interest to estimates computed on the basis of average debt and the entity's borrowing rate **(analytical procedures)**

- Comparing payroll and payroll-related expenses (eg, payroll taxes) to auditor estimates based on the auditor's understanding of the number of employees retained by the entity and pay rates **(analytical procedures)**

- **Inspecting** leases and other arrangements (eg, service agreements) calling for regular payments to determine if amounts are appropriate

- Comparing the amounts reported as expenses in the current period to amounts reported in prior periods **(analytical procedures)**

Classification

In seeking evidence that all revenue and expense transactions are classified into appropriate categories, the auditor will determine if there are appropriate **controls** in place, such as:

- Maintenance of a list of regular vendors, such as utility companies, indicating the category that should be used to classify payments made to them

- A review of the coding of disbursements by the individual signing checks and cancelling the voucher package

- Policies requiring that all transactions recorded as revenues be supported by a customer PO, an appropriate prenumbered sales order form, a sales invoice, and a shipping report

Substantive procedures may include:

- Tracing a sample of transactions recorded as sales to supporting documentation to verify that they represent sales of goods or services in the ordinary course of business **(inspection)**

- Tracing a sample of transactions recorded in various expense categories to supporting documentation to verify that the expense category in which they were recorded is appropriate **(inspection)**

Occurrence

In seeking evidence that revenue and expense transactions actually occurred, the auditor will determine if there are appropriate **controls** in place, such as:

- Policies requiring that all regular expenses, such as rents, utilities, and various other expenses be compared to budget as part of the recording process with variances investigated on a timely basis

- Policies requiring matching documentation including customer POs, sales orders, shipping documents, and sales invoices for all revenue-related transactions before the recording of revenues

- Policies requiring appropriate approvals for all unscheduled expenses

- Policies requiring comparisons of payees, including vendors and employees, to approved vendor lists and lists of active employees maintained by human resources

Substantive procedures may include:

- Tracing a sample of recorded revenue transactions to supporting documentation, including a customer PO, a sales order, a shipping report, and an invoice **(inspection)**

- Tracing a sample of recorded expense transactions to supporting documentation, which may include receiving reports, authorized requests, and vendor invoices **(inspection)**

- **Inspecting** leases to determine if recorded rents are for the use of assets being used by the entity

Payroll

When auditing payroll, the auditor is often able to place reliance on the I/C structure of the payroll cycle and assess RMM at a low level, thereby permitting higher detection risk and limiting the necessary substantive testing. Since payroll is generally more predictable than other costs, the auditor should perform **analytical procedures** involving the comparison of actual payroll costs with budgeted or standard costs to determine **completeness** of payroll accruals.

To support the assertion of **valuation**, the auditor should recalculate payroll accruals and compare calculations with source information, such as timecards to verify hours worked and personnel records to verify pay rates.

Objectives

- I/C over payroll

- Employees actually exist (existence).

- Payroll computations are correct (valuation).

- Disclosure is adequate.

AUD 7
Audit
Sampling

7.01 Audit Sampling

Overview

AU-C 530, *Audit Sampling,* refers to the examination of **less than 100%** of a population and using the results as a basis for drawing a **general conclusion** on the entire population. While audit data analytics (ADAs) can be used to test entire populations of data efficiently and effectively, there are still instances in which the use of sampling is essential. Keep in mind that most sampling processes can also be automated with generalized audit software, as previously discussed.

Audit Risk

- Risk of Material Misstatement (RMM)
  - Inherent Risk (IR)
  - Control Risk (CR)
- Detection Risk (DR)
  - Test of Details Risk (TD)
  - Substantive Analytical Procedures Risk (AP)
  - **Nonsampling Risk** (Human error, misinterpreting audit test results, not recognizing misstatements in documents audited)
    - The risk that test results will be misinterpreted due to human error, such as not recognizing a misstatement in items being audited. Nonsampling error is reduced by using qualified staff and through adequate supervision and review.
  - **Sampling Risk** (Bad Sample, Sample is not representative of population) – Risk of drawing wrong conclusion.
    - The risk that a sample will not be representative of the population, causing the auditor to draw an invalid conclusion on the basis of the test results.
    - Type I – Efficiency Error (Alpha risk)
      - Population is okay but based on the sample, don't rely.
        - **Under-rely** on internal control = assess **RMM** ↑
        - **Incorrectly reject** an account balance for substantive testing purposes (less efficient audit).
        - A type I risk, or alpha risk, is the risk that the sample will have disproportionately more errors than the population. This may cause the auditor to perform additional procedures to obtain sufficient appropriate evidence that the assertion is not misrepresented, or may cause the auditor to reject the assertion, potentially affecting the auditor's report.
    - Type II – Less Effective (Beta risk)

- Population is bad but based on the sample, the auditor believes everything is correct.
    - **Over-rely** on internal control = assess **RMM↓**
    - **Incorrectly accept** an account balance for substantive testing purposes (less effective audit).
    - A type II risk, or beta risk, is the risk that the sample will have disproportionately fewer errors than the population. This may cause the auditor to accept a control as effective even though it is not or accept an assertion that is actually misrepresented. The result may be an ineffective engagement with the issuance of an unmodified report despite a material misstatement to the financial statements (F/S).

Sampling is used both in the tests of controls and in substantive testing:

1. During the **internal control phase** of the audit, the auditor will perform **tests of controls** on a sample basis to determine the operating effectiveness of controls they plan to rely on.

2. During the **substantive testing phase** of the audit, the auditor will perform **tests of details** of transactions, accounts, and disclosures on a sample basis to obtain sufficient appropriate audit evidence to support management assertions.

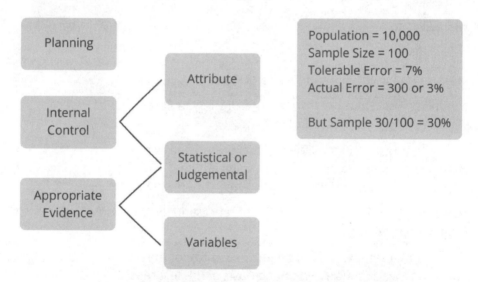

Sampling is **not** practical for all parts of the audit. In **gaining an understanding of the internal control structure** and **documenting the understanding**, the auditor cannot simply look at a part of the structure and use that as a basis for claiming understanding of the entirety. During substantive testing, the application of **analytical procedures** to some accounts cannot be considered evidence applicable to all the accounts.

The primary risk in sampling is that you may draw a conclusion from the sample that is different from the conclusion you would have drawn if you had examined the entire population (Risk of drawing the incorrect conclusion).

In the case of **tests of controls**, the auditor will be examining the implementation of a control activity in order to ensure that the client doesn't deviate from the control more often than the auditor considers tolerable. The auditor will apply judgment in establishing a **tolerable deviation rate**, which is the percentage of times a control not being applied that would not cause the auditor to consider the control ineffective. This will be compared to the actual percentage of items examined in the sample to which the control was not being properly applied, the **true deviation rate**.

- If the **true deviation rate** of the population is **lower** than the **tolerable deviation rate**, then the auditor will want to rely on the control, **reducing the assessed RMM** and increasing the acceptable level of DR. This will result in the auditor not performing as many substantive tests in drawing an audit conclusion in relation to the control's effectiveness.

- If the **true deviation rate** is **higher** than the **tolerable deviation rate**, then the auditor will not want to rely on the control, **increasing the assessed RMM** and reducing the acceptable level of DR. This will result in the auditor performing a greater amount of substantive testing before drawing an audit conclusion as to the effectiveness of the control.

The sampling technique normally applied to tests of controls is called **attribute sampling**. There are **two** different sampling risks associated with attribute sampling:

- The auditor may conclude from the sample that the deviation rate is lower than the tolerable rate, but the overall population has a true deviation rate that is higher than the tolerable rate. Based on the sample, the auditor will improperly rely on the control. This is known as the risk of **assessing the Risk of Material Misstatements too low**. The consequence of this risk is that the auditor will not do a sufficient amount of substantive testing, and may fail to uncover material misstatements in the F/S under audit. This means the audit will be **ineffective** and not achieve its goals.

- The auditor may conclude from the sample that the deviation rate is higher than the tolerable rate, but the overall population has a true deviation rate that is lower than the tolerable rate. Based on the sample, the auditor will improperly choose not to rely on the control. This is known as the risk of **assessing the Risk of Material Misstatements too high**. The consequence of this risk is that the auditor will do more substantive testing than was necessary for the audit conclusions. The audit will be effective, but the unnecessary additional substantive means the audit will be **inefficient**.

Actual Population

		Good	Bad
Sample Results	**Good**	Appropriately Rely	Accounting
	Bad	Under-rely	Appropriately Don't Rely

During substantive **tests of details** of transactions and accounts, the auditor is attempting to determine if an account balance is materially correct. The form of sampling normally used is called **variable estimation sampling.** The two sampling risks are:

- Based on the sample, the auditor may estimate an amount that is close enough to the recorded amount for the auditor to conclude that the number is materially correct, when the amount is actually materially misstated. This is known as the risk of **incorrect acceptance**. The result will be that the auditor draws an inappropriate conclusion, so that the audit is **ineffective**.

- Based on the sample, the auditor may estimate an amount that is different enough from the recorded amount for the auditor to decide that the number is materially misstated, when the amount is actually materially correct. This is known as the risk of **incorrect rejection**. The result will be that the auditor performs a large amount of additional substantive tests on the amount, finally determining that the recorded amount was, in fact, correct. The result will be that the auditor's conclusion is correct, but an unnecessary amount of additional substantive testing takes place, so that the audit is **inefficient.**

The technique known as **statistical sampling** refers to the use of quantitative measures of the risks the auditor is taking in the use of sampling. Formulas are used to determine the sample size necessary to achieve a specified level of risk of the sample results not being consistent with the entire population. The auditor will still have to **use judgment** to determine what level of risk is acceptable.

An auditor using **nonstatistical sampling** (Judgmental sampling) will determine the appropriate sample size by deciding what makes them comfortable that their conclusions are correct. In practice, the lack of mathematical certainty as to the appropriate sample size causes auditors using nonstatistical sampling to overestimate the needed sample size in order to feel comfortable with the conclusions. This means the audit will still be effective, but not as efficient as it might have been using statistical techniques to determine a sufficient sample size.

In both approaches, however, the same sampling risks exist.

Sampling Risk		
Consequences to Audit	Internal Control (Tests of Controls) Attribute Sampling	Substantive Testing (Tests of Details) Variables Estimation Sampling
Ineffective	Assessing RMM Too Low	Incorrect Acceptance
Inefficient	Assessing RMM Too High	Incorrect Rejection

Naturally, an auditor is more concerned about an audit being ineffective than inefficient. In particular, when the cost of additional testing is low, the auditor will often allow higher risks of assessing control risk too high and incorrect rejection.

7.02 Attribute Sampling

The risks associated with attribute sampling are the risk of assessing RMM too high, which will result in an *inefficient* engagement, and the risk of assessing RMM too low, which will result in an *ineffective* engagement. The risk of an ineffective engagement is greater since that means that users will rely on financial statements (F/S) that should not be relied upon. As a result, the auditor will seek to reduce the risk of assessing RMM too low by making certain that the sample size is appropriate.

Factors affecting sample size in an attribute sample include:

- The **tolerable rate of error**, which has an **inverse** relationship to sample size. When a control is not significant and, as a result, the auditor is not as concerned about whether or not it is being followed properly, the auditor will use a smaller sample size, which is less likely to be representative of the population.

- The **expected rate of error**, which has a **direct** relationship to sample size. When the auditor expects that a control is not operating as intended, the auditor will seek a sample size that is adequately large to make certain that there are likely to be a representative number of exceptions in the sample to reflect the error rate in the population.

- The **acceptable risk** of assessing RMM too low, which has an **inverse** relationship to sample size. When a high assessment of RMM is acceptable, the auditor is not concerned about errors that will result from the control not being applied properly and is less likely to be concerned about an accurate measure of the degree to which it is not being complied with.

- To summarize:
  - Internal control – tests of controls
  - Two risks
    - Assessing Risk of Material Misstatement too low – audit ineffective
    - Assessing Risk of Material Misstatement too high – audit inefficient
  - Factors affecting **sample size**
    - Tolerable rate – Inverse effect
    - Expected rate – Direct effect
    - Acceptable risk – Inverse effect
  - Evaluation of sample results
    - Sample rate plus allowance for sampling risk
    - Must not exceed tolerable rate or else auditor must modify planned reliance

There are various types of attribute sampling. These include:

- **Attribute sampling,** or fixed sample-size attribute sampling, used to estimate the rate of deviations in the population.

- **Stop-or-go sampling (Sequential sampling)** is a special type of attribute sampling which allows the auditor to stop when sufficient data is gathered. It is appropriate when the expected deviation rate is low and may provide the auditor with the most efficient sample size in an attribute sampling plan. The sample is selected in several steps and each step relies on the results of the previous step. By selecting sequential samples, the auditor may stop sampling if no deviations are found.

- **Discovery sampling** is also a special type of attribute sampling and is used when the expected deviation rate is very low, near zero. The sample size in this method is usually large enough to find at least one deviation if it exists. Discovery sample sizes and discovery sampling tables are designed to measure the probability of at least one error occurring in a sample if the error rate in the population exceeds the tolerable rate.

When performing tests of controls, the form of sampling that is typically used is **attribute sampling**, which refers to examining a sample of items from a population to determine what percentage of them contain a specific attribute. Notice that attribute sampling cannot be used to verify a quantity or dollar amount, since it only provides information on the presence or absence of something, not its size.

Sampling applies to tests of controls when the auditor needs to decide whether a rate of deviation is equal to or less than a tolerable rate. However, sampling does not apply to risk assessment procedures performed to obtain an understanding of internal control. Furthermore, sampling concepts may not apply to some tests of controls, such as the following: (1) tests of automated application; (2) analyses of controls for determining appropriate segregation of duties or other analyses that do not examine documentary evidence of performance; (3) tests of certain documented controls or analyses of the effectiveness of security and access controls; or (4) tests directed toward obtaining audit evidence about the operation of the control environment or accounting system.

The **"attribute"** or **characteristic** that the auditor is looking to find is a deviation from the proper application of the internal control activity being tested. For example, the auditor, while gaining an understanding of the internal control structure, might have identified a control activity requiring the authorization by an officer of all purchase requisitions. If the auditor considers this a potential strength and wants to rely on the control, it must be tested to determine its operating effectiveness. The auditor will pull a sample from the population of purchase requisitions, and see how many in the sample did not include proper authorization. Failure to authorize is the attribute or **deviation**, being sought.

A few items should be considered when performing attribute sampling:

- It is considered a deviation when the client cannot provide the document the auditor wishes to examine, as well as when the document fails to demonstrate the application of the control being tested.

- For each deviation that is identified, the auditor should consider the **qualitative** issues as well as quantitative. If a deviation gives evidence of **fraud** committed by an employee, the auditor must consider the **broader implications** of that employee's impact on company operations and financial information as a whole, not limited to the specific control being tested.

- When a deviation from control is identified, this doesn't mean there is a misstatement in the F/S as a result. For example, the failure of a purchase to be properly authorized does not mean it wasn't correctly processed and accounted for in the financial records. **Deviation** at a particular **rate** will usually result in actual **misstatements** at a much **lower rate**.

Attribute sampling is appropriate for tests involving **reperformance** or **inspection**, where there is an identifiable population of documents or records from which the auditor can select a sample, but is **not** normally appropriate for tests involving **inquiry** or **observation,** since each inquiry usually is made only once, and sample observations can rarely be performed randomly through the year so as to be representative of the entire year.

In order to determine the appropriate **sample size**, the auditor using attribute sampling will consider three different key factors (**TEA**):

1. **Tolerable deviation rate** – This refers to the percentage of time a control can be violated but still lead the auditor to believe it is operating effectively. It is rarely a problem if a control is not followed on occasion, and since the auditor treats the inability to locate a document as a deviation (which might not be a true violation of the control but simply a problem with the ability of the client personnel to locate the evidence for the auditor), some deviations are normally considered acceptable. The auditor's decision as to the tolerable rate is based on the importance of the control being tested and the impact that each deviation could have on the accuracy of the financial statement assertions.

   o Tolerable deviation rate has an inverse effect on sample size.

   o If the auditor is willing to tolerate a large number of deviations, a smaller sample will be able to satisfy the auditor that the true deviation rate is within these high acceptable limits.

2. **Expected deviation rate** – This refers to the percentage of time the auditor expects the control to have been violated. Clearly, the true deviation rate must be lower than the tolerable rate in order for the auditor to rely on a control. If the deviation rate in a sample is only **slightly** lower than the tolerable rate, though, the auditor will have a problem due to the lack of precision of results.

   o If, for example, in a sample size of 10 items, there is 1 deviation, the deviation rate in the sample is 10%.

   o Based on such a small sample size, the auditor might conclude that the deviation rate in the population is approximately 10%, but could not conclude that the deviation rate in the population is approximately 10%.

     ▪ If the tolerable rate is close to 10%, such as 11%, the auditor may conclude that the potential deviation rate in the population is too high and will decide not to rely on the control.

     ▪ If the tolerable rate is considerably higher than 10%, such as 15%, the auditor may conclude that it is likely, based on that sample, that the actual deviation rate in the population is likely to be below that rate and the auditor may decide to rely on the control.

   o The **expected deviation rate has a direct effect on sample size**. The closer the expected rate gets to the tolerable limit, the larger the sample size the auditor will need to provide results that are precise enough.

3. **Allowable risk of assessing risk of material misstatement (RMM) too low** – This refers to the risk the auditor is taking that the sample will cause them to rely on the control when the true deviation rate of the population was high enough that they should not have relied. There is always a possibility that the sample results are so unrepresentative of the population that a sample which appears to suggest few deviations was drawn from a population in which there were many.

> **TEA** is a mnemonic to remind you that if statistical sampling is your cup of tea, you'll need to know what factors to put into the calculation of sample size.

   o The allowable risk of assessing RMM too low has an inverse effect on sample size.

   o if the auditor is willing to accept a large risk of drawing the wrong conclusion, they can reduce the size of the sample.

In determining sample size, the auditor does **not** need to know the size of the population. Although an increase in the population size would seem to suggest the need for a larger sample, the effect is actually minimal, and the auditor can simplify the calculations by simply assuming a population of infinite size. In political polling, people are often surprised that the results of polling only a few hundred people can often produce estimates about the sentiment of voters throughout the nation that prove extremely accurate. Similarly, if you flipped a coin 1,000 times and it came up heads around 500 times, you'd probably feel comfortable that it was an honest coin, and not think that flipping it 1,000,000 times would make the slightest difference.

Many populations of items, such as invoices, that the auditor is sampling from may number in the thousands. This is sufficiently large such that the appropriate sample size for that population will be about the same as the sample size needed out for a population of many times as many transactions, even if they number in the billions or more. As a result, there is no need to know the population size to determine an adequate sample size in the audit.

Once a sample is taken, the evaluation of the results must be performed carefully. Even if the deviation rate in the sample is lower than the tolerable deviation rate, the results of a sample are not likely to be identical to the true deviation rate of the entire population. If a sample of 50 invoices resulted in 5 deviations (a sample deviation rate of 10%), it would not be unusual for another sample of 50 invoices from the same population to result in 6 or 4 deviations.

The fact that the results of a sample are not precise requires the addition of an **allowance for sampling risk** to the results of the sample, to be more certain that the true deviation rate of the population does not exceed the tolerable rate. The allowance for sampling risk is the amount that is both added to and subtracted from the rate in the sample to determine the actual anticipated range of error in the population. This is similar to the "plus-or-minus" that is mentioned in polling results. Since the auditor is primarily concerned about relying on a control that is not effective, the focus is on the upper end of the range, which is the maximum expected rate in the population, and which is compared to the tolerable rate.

To evaluate the results of a sample, the auditor will:

1. Calculate the sample deviation rate (number of deviations found divided by sample size).

2. Determine the allowance for sampling risk (always provided in CPA exam problems), which is based solely on the sample size.

3. Add the two figures together to obtain the maximum deviation rate.

4. Compare the maximum deviation rate to the tolerable deviation rate.

5. If the maximum rate is higher than the tolerable rate, the auditor will modify their original intention to rely on the control, because it does not appear to be operating effectively. This will increase the assessed level of control risk.

6. If the maximum rate is lower than the tolerable rate, the auditor will accept the results as a valid basis for relying on the control. This will allow them to maintain the lower assessed level of control risk from their preliminary determination based on the controls that were placed into operation.

 For example, if an auditor's sample of 50 invoices found 5 deviations, the tolerable deviation rate was 11%, and the allowance for sampling risk was 2%, the auditor will calculate a sample deviation rate of 5 / 50 = 10% with a maximum deviation rate of 10% + 2% = 12%. Since this is higher than the tolerable rate of 11%, the auditor must modify their original plan to rely on the control.

Effect on Sample Size	
Tolerable Rate ↓	Sample Size ↑
Confidence Level (Reliability) ↑	Sample Size ↑
Deviation Rate ↑	Sample Size ↑
Population size ↑	Sample Size ↑
Allowance (Precision) (More Accurate) ↓	Sample Size ↑

To **develop an Attribute Sampling Plan**, the following steps should be followed:

Step 1 - Determine the audit objective, the control that is being tested. (What testing for?)

Step 2 - Determine the **tolerable rate,** also referred to as the *tolerable deviation rate* or *tolerable rate of deviation*. This represents the greatest error rate the auditor is willing to tolerate and still conclude that the control is operating effectively (accept the population).

Step 3 - Determine **reliability** or the *level of confidence* which represents the degree of sampling risk the auditor is willing to accept. A 98% reliability indicates that the auditor is willing to accept the risk that there is a 2% risk of drawing an incorrect conclusion based on the sample.

Step 4 - Determine the **expected population deviation rate,** also referred to as the *expected rate of deviation used in planning the sample*, the *population expected error rate*, or the *expected deviation rate*. The auditor may use prior experience and knowledge to determine the deviation rate expected in the population.

Step 5 - Determine the method for selecting the sample *(random, systematic, block or cluster sampling)*.

Step 6 - Calculate the sample size. The auditor determines the sample size based on the tolerable rate, the allowable risk of assessing control risk too low, and the expected deviation rate.

Step 7 - Select and test the sample.

Step 8 - Calculate the sample deviation rate as:

$$\frac{\text{Number of Deviations}}{\text{Sample Size}}$$

- Using the number of deviations and the acceptable risk of assessing control risk too low (risk of overreliance), the auditor calculates the **upper precision limit**. The upper precision limit is a statistical measure of the maximum rate of deviations that exist within a population. The upper precision limit can be calculated as follows:

$$\text{Sample Deviation Rate} + \text{Allowance for Sampling Risk} = \text{Upper Precision Limit}$$

Step 9 - Compare the upper precision limit to the tolerable rate to reach conclusions and document the results.

Sampling Methodologies

A sample, by definition, should be representative of the population under consideration. For a sampling method to be valid, all items in the population should have an equal opportunity to be selected. Such methods include:

- **Random-Number Sampling**: Numbered documents or transactions are selected through the use of random number tables or computer software.

- **Systematic Sampling**: Every "nth" item is selected from a randomly distributed population from a randomly selected starting point.

- **Haphazard Sampling**: A sample consisting of units selected without any conscious bias— again assuming the random distribution of the population.

- **Block Sampling** (or Cluster sampling): A sample consisting of contiguous units; for example, a selection of three blocks of ten vouchers each. While this method eases sample selection, its major disadvantage is that the samples selected may not be representative, and thus is regarded as the least desirable method.

All of these methods are forms of random sampling.   When all items are randomly selected for the sample, as in random number sampling, it is considered simple random sampling. Systematic sampling with a random starting point, haphazard sampling without known bias, and block sampling with blocks randomly selected are all forms of random sampling, referred to as systematic random sampling.

7.03 Variables Sampling

Classical Variables Sampling

The risks associated with variables sampling are concluding that:

- An item contains a misstatement when it does not—**the risk of incorrect rejection**—which will result in an **inefficient** engagement, and

- An item does not contain a misstatement despite the fact that it does—**the risk of incorrect acceptance**—which will result in an **ineffective** engagement.

The risk of an ineffective engagement is greater since that means that users will rely on financial statements (F/S) that should not be relied upon. As a result, the auditor will seek to reduce the risk of incorrect acceptance by making certain that the sample size is appropriate.

Factors affecting **sample size** for a variables sample include:

- Tolerable misstatement, which has an inverse relationship;

- Acceptable risk, which has an inverse relationship;

- Population size, which has a direct relationship;

- Expected misstatement, which has a direct relationship;

- Standard deviation, which has a direct relationship; and

- Risk of Material Misstatement (RMM), which has a *direct* relationship.

Tolerable misstatement should usually be set for a particular audit procedure at less than financial statement materiality so that when the results of all audit procedures are aggregated, the required overall assurance will be attained.

Classical Variables Sampling Approaches

Variables sampling is used to estimate an amount, or the amount of a misstatement.

- It is used to estimate an amount, using an approach referred to as **mean-per-unit estimation**, by measuring the value of items in a sample to determine an average value and applying that average to the number of items in the population.

- It can be used to estimate the amount of a misstatement, using an approach referred to as **difference estimation**, by comparing the recorded amounts to the actual amounts for a sample of items, estimating an average error per item, and projecting that error to the population.

- **Ratio estimation**, where the relationship between items in a sample is projected to the population, may be used to estimate an amount or the amount of a misstatement.

When items within a population vary widely, the auditor may increase the efficiency and the effectiveness of sampling by using **stratified sampling**. Under this approach:

- The population is divided into groups or strata, with all items within each group having similar characteristics.

- The groups may be based on quantitative factors, such as putting expensive items in one group and inexpensive items in another, or some other characteristic, such as the profit margin.

- The groups may also be based on other factors such as putting transactions with a higher likelihood of error in one group and those with a lower likelihood in another group.

- A sample is drawn from each group, resulting in a smaller total sample size.

During the substantive testing phase, the auditor will be testing the details of transactions and accounts in order to determine if the individual account balances are materially correct. To do so, they must use sampling to estimate the numerical value of the account balance, and this is known as **variables estimation sampling** or **sampling for variables**.

Of course, the estimate resulting from sampling for variables is not going to exactly equal the account balance, so the estimate will be expressed with an amount to be added and subtracted to determine the range of amounts within which the value of the population is likely to fall. This is known as the **precision** of the results or the precision range. As long as the account balance is within the acceptable precision range, the auditor will consider the sample to support the account balance.

The normal sampling unit for a population of documents is each individual document. When the dollar values on the various documents are widely different from each other, the auditor may **stratify** the sample by dividing the documents into different groups based on approximate values, using larger sample sizes for the more important large documents and smaller sample sizes for the documents with smaller dollar amounts, since they are less significant in determining whether the account being audited is materially correct.

Another method of dealing with widely varying document values is to abandon classical sampling for variables and use **Probability in Proportion to Size Sampling**, or **PPS sampling**, which treats each dollar as a sampling unit.

Four factors enter into the determination of **sample size**: three of them parallel factors used in attribute sampling, and the fourth is specific to sampling for variables. The factors are:

1. **Tolerable misstatement** – This refers to the amount by which an account can differ from the recorded value without being considered materially misstated. It is based on the auditor's determination of the materiality level. The larger the tolerable misstatement, the smaller the sample size.

   o Tolerable misstatement combined for all audit tests should not exceed financial statement materiality.

   o Tolerable misstatement for any specific audit procedure will generally be less than financial statement materiality.

2. **Expected misstatement** – This is the amount by which the auditor expects the account to be misstated. It is based on previous audits as well as information gathered while obtaining an understanding of internal control structure. The larger the expected misstatement, the larger the sample size.

3. **Allowable risk of incorrect acceptance** – This refers to the risk the auditor is willing to take of accepting the account value as materially correct and have it be materially misstated. It is

based on the auditor's overall willingness to accept audit risk as well as the assessed level of risk of material misstatement, since the auditor may be willing to accept greater detection risk when RMM is low. The larger the allowable risk of incorrect acceptance, the smaller the sample size.

4. **Standard deviation –** This is the variability of the dollar values of the individual items in the population. It is usually based on previous audits or a tiny sample of the items in the current population. The larger the standard deviation, the larger the sample size (as discussed earlier, when standard deviation is extremely high, it may be appropriate to stratify the sample or use PPS sampling instead).

> Since we used TEA as the mnemonic for attribute sampling, using **TEAS** for variables estimation sampling makes sense: since substantive testing is the second phase of fieldwork, TEAS can be considered tea for two.

Types of Classical Variables Sampling

Evaluating a sample for variables is normally a matter of determining the average value of the items in the sample and then multiplying this average by the number of items in the population to estimate the total numerical value of the population. This is known as **mean-per-unit estimation**. Occasionally, other methods are used to evaluate a sample. If there is a consistent bias in the book amounts, the auditor may use difference estimation or ratio estimation:

- **Difference estimation –** The auditor determines the average dollar amount by which the audited amounts exceed the book amounts in the sample (or vice versa), and assumes this average difference applies to the entire population, so that the difference per item is multiplied by the number of items in the population, and the result is added to (or subtracted from) the total book amount.

- **Ratio estimation –** The auditor determines the ratio of the audited amounts to the book amounts in the sample (audited amount divided by book amount), and then multiplies the total book amount by this ratio.

For example, assume that 3 invoices are pulled from a population of 100 invoices (with a total account balance of $3,000 on the books). The 3 invoices have recorded amounts of $40, $20, and $27, respectively, but when the auditor examines the support, they find the correct values are $42, $24, and $27, respectively. The evaluation under the 3 methods would be as follows:

- **Mean-per-unit estimation –** $42 + $24 + $27 = $93 / 3 = $31. With a mean-per-unit of $31, the population of 100 invoices is estimated at $31 × 100 = $3,100.
- **Difference estimation –** $2 + $4 + $0 = $6 / 3 = $2. With an average excess of audited over book amount of $2, the population of 100 invoices should be increased by $2 × 100 = $200, estimating the population at $3,000 + $200 = $3,200.
- **Ratio estimation –** 1.05 + 1.20 + 1.00 = 3.25 / 3 = 1.08 (rounded). With an average ratio of audited amount to book amount of 1.08, the population is estimated to have a value of $3,000 × 1.08 = $3,240

Misstatements

The AICPA has created a specific definition of misstatements and discussed the need to identify likely misstatements as well as known misstatements (the primary points being that misstatements in a sample create the likelihood of greater misstatements in the total population, and that the use of estimates increases likely misstatements). The *definition of a misstatement* is:

- A difference between the amount, classification, or presentation of a reported financial statement element, account, or item and the amount, classification or presentation that would have been reported under GAAP.

- The omission of a financial statement element, account, or item.

- A financial statement disclosure that is not presented in accordance with GAAP.

- The omission of information required to be disclosed in accordance with GAAP.

In addition, misstatements should be evaluated **qualitatively**, such as:

- Misstatements that affect trends of profitability.

- Misstatements that change losses into income.

- Misstatements that affect segment information.

Misstatements that affect compliance with legal and contractual requirements.

7.04 Probability Proportional to Size Sampling (PPS)

PPS sampling is a form of sampling for variables in which the sampling unit is each dollar in a population. For this reason, it is also known as **dollar-unit sampling (DUS) or cumulative monetary amount (CMA) sampling**. Under PPS sampling, a **sampling interval** is determined and used to pick out the documents to be examined.

The method for determining the interval amount is complicated, but is based on tolerable misstatement, expected number of misstatements, and allowable risk of incorrect acceptance. The sample size is approximately equal to the dollar value of the population divided by the sampling interval. Beginning with the first item in the population, the dollar amount is counted until the interval is reached and the item containing that amount becomes part of the sample. When items are so large that they include more than one interval, the sample size will be smaller.

- **Probability-Proportional-to-Size** (PPS) or Dollar-unit sampling (DUS)
  - Substantive testing – tests of details
  - **Advantages** over classical variables sampling:
    - Standard deviation not needed
    - Stratifies sample automatically
    - Smaller sample usually results if few errors expected
    - Start sampling without having entire population available
  - **Disadvantages:**
    - Large sample results if many errors expected
    - Zero and negative balances require special handling
    - Not useful to detect understatement
  - **Calculations needed:**
    - **Sampling interval (SI)** = Tolerable misstatement / Reliability factor (from table) or Population amount / sample size
    - **Sample size** = Population amount / SI
    - To determine projected misstatement:
      - Misstatement = Book amount – Audited amount
      - Tainting factor (TF) = Misstatement / Book amount
      - Projected misstatement:
        - If SI > book amount then
          - PM = TF * SI
        - If SI <= book amount then
          - PM = Misstatement from step

For example, assume the auditor is examining an account with a total recorded amount of $100,000, and that the auditor has determined the sampling interval ought to be $10,000. A random number between $1 and $10,000 is selected: let's say the number chosen is $3,112. If the account is represented by 63 invoices, the auditor might obtain a ledger that lists each invoice and then reports the running total of the invoices, such as:

Invoice #	Amount	Cumulative
1	$2,000	$2,000
2	6,500	8,500
3	4,000	12,500
4	1,000	13,500
5	11,000	24,500
....	....	....
63	2,700	100,000

The auditor will examine the invoices that brought the cumulative amount to $3,112 (#2), $13,112 (#4), $23,112 (#5), $33,112, $43,112, $53,112, $63,112, $73,112, $83,112, and $93,112. The total number of invoices selected to examine should be $100,000 / $10,000 = 10, unless an invoice exceeding $10,000 individually was large enough to cross over 2 or more thresholds.

Once the documents have been examined, any misstatements that are found are applied to the entire interval by the calculation of **projected misstatement** (or projected error). This is determined by calculating the misstatement in a document as a percentage of the recorded amount, then applying this percentage to the interval. However, if the document selected is larger than the interval, the actual misstatement in the document is also the projected misstatement.

Assume that 2 of the documents in the example contain errors, as follows:

Invoice #	Recorded Amount	Audited Amount
4	$1,000	$800
5	11,000	10,300

In the example, the sampling interval was $10,000 so that the misstatement in invoice #4 will have to be projected to the entire interval, while the misstatement in invoice #5 will be accepted without adjustment, as follows:

Invoice #	Recorded	Audited	Misstatement	Tainting %	Sampling Interval	Projected Misstatement
4	$1,000	$800	$200	20%	$10,000	$2,000
5	11,000	10,300	700	--	----	$700

The total projected misstatement is $2,700, and this will be compared with the tolerable misstatement to determine whether to accept the account balance as being materially correct.

Some of the **advantages of PPS** sampling over classical variables estimation sampling are:

- Larger accounts automatically have a greater chance of being selected, and individual accounts exceeding the sampling interval are always selected, so the method **automatically stratifies** the population.

- The method accommodates populations with items that vary widely in value **without** any need to compute **standard deviation**.

- A sample can be designed more easily and sample selection can begin before the final and full population is available.

Some of the **disadvantages** of the method are:

- The method is **not useful** in detecting **understated** accounts, since smaller accounts have a proportionately smaller chance of being selected.

- Special methods must be used in order to deal with **zero or negative accounts**, since they will ordinarily never be selected under this approach.

- Identified understatements require special consideration and large understatements may lead to invalid projections or conclusions.

- Larger anticipated misstatements require larger sample sizes, often making classical variables sampling more efficient.

PPS sampling is more conservative than classical variables sampling and is more likely to reject an account balance. This is particularly the case for a population that contains several misstatements. As a result, this method is best for populations that are not believed to contain a large number of misstatements.

This type of sampling is particularly useful for:

- Confirming accounts receivable or loans receivable

- Tests of pricing of investments securities or inventory

- Tests of fixed-asset additions where existence is the primary risk

This type of sampling is generally NOT appropriate for:

- Confirming accounts receivable when there are a large number of unapplied credits

- Inventory test counts and price tests when the auditor anticipates a significant number of misstatements that could be overstatements or understatements

- Converting inventory from FIFO to LIFO

- Populations without individual recorded amounts

- Any application in which the primary objective is to estimate an amount

AUD 8
Audit
Reports

AUD 8: Audit Reports

8.01 Standard Unmodified Opinion

Overview

In this section, we'll be focusing on the **GAAS requirements** for issuing a standard unmodified audit report for a **nonissuer/nonpublic company** (ie, AU-C 700). Before we do that, let's take a brief look at where we are in the audit and all the different types of audit opinions/reports that may be issued.

Steps in an Audit

Prepare for the audit	Obtain understanding of client, its environment & I/C	Assess RMM & design further procedures	Perform tests of controls	Perform substantive procedures	**Form opinion**	**Issue report**

4 Types of Opinions		Will be expressed if ...	Key Report Language
Unmodified* opinions	Standard "clean" opinion	F/S are fairly presented	"... [F/S] present fairly, in all material respects, ... in accordance with [GAAP]."
Modified opinions**	Qualified opinion	F/S are fairly presented, except for...	"... except for ..., the [F/S] present fairly...."
	Adverse opinion	F/S are materially misstated	"... [F/S] do not present fairly..."
	Disclaimer of opinion	Sufficient appropriate audit evidence could not be obtained to conclude that F/S are fairly presented	"We do not express an opinion..."

*Note that GAAS uses the term "unmodified" while the PCAOB standards (discussed later) use the term "unqualified."

**Modified opinions are discussed in further detail in a later section.

Forming an Opinion

The auditor must form an opinion as to whether the F/S are *presented fairly*, *in all material respects*, in accordance with the applicable financial reporting framework (AFRF). To do so, one must determine whether *reasonable assurance* has been obtained that the F/S, taken as a whole, are *free of material misstatement*, whether caused by error or fraud. To arrive at this conclusion, *all* of the following should be considered:

- Has **sufficient appropriate audit evidence** been obtained? (previously discussed)

- **Are uncorrected misstatements material**, either individually or when combined?

- Have the **F/S** been **prepared**, in all material respects (quantitatively and qualitatively), **in accordance with the AFRF** (eg, GAAP)? This includes considering whether:

  o Management's judgments are biased (lack neutrality). For example, did management correct misstatements that increase earnings and disregard those that decrease earnings?

  o Accounting estimates are reasonable.

  o Accounting policies applied are appropriate.

  o The F/S appropriately disclose significant accounting policies.

  o Disclosures are adequate to allow F/S users to understand the effect of material transactions/events.

  o Information in the F/S is relevant, reliable, comparable, understandable, and complete.

  o F/S titles and terminology are appropriate.

  o The overall F/S presentation, structure, and content is appropriate. For example:

    ▪ Does the presentation obscure useful information or result in misleading information?

    ▪ Is the presentation consistent with industry practices?

  o The F/S adequately refer to or describe the AFRF.

When the auditor determines that the F/S are **not fairly presented**, the auditor should discuss the matter with management. If the issue(s) cannot be resolved, the auditor must **modify the opinion**. Such modifications will be discussed in more detail in a later section.

Basic Elements of an Unmodified GAAS Audit Report

Title

The title of the report must clearly indicate that it is the report of an **independent** auditor. Such a title as "Independent Auditor's Report" also emphasizes that the other pages of the annual report were prepared by the client, not the auditor.

Addressees

The addressees depend on the circumstances of the engagement, but generally the report is addressed to the party to which the auditor is reporting.

- This may be the entity, those charged with governance (eg, board of directors) or, in the case of an unincorporated entity, the owners. If a third party hired the auditor to audit an entity, the addressee may be that third-party client.

- It is not acceptable to address the report to members of the management team, since management is the party the auditor is reporting on.

Four Required Sections

An unmodified report will consist of at least four sections, each of which has certain requirements, including a specific title.

- **Opinion** (must be first section) – Should include:

  o The *name of the company* whose F/S were audited

  o A statement indicating that the F/S *were audited* and the *titles* of those F/S

  o The *date* of, or *period covered* by, each F/S

  o A *reference* to the F/S *notes*

  o An opinion that the *F/S present fairly, in all material respects*, the following in *accordance with* [the AFRF]:

    ▪ Financial position of [the company] as of [the B/S date]

    ▪ Results of its operations and its cash flows for the year then ended

Unmodified GAAS Report
1. Opinion
2. Basis for Opinion
• Management Responsibilities*
• Auditor's Responsibilities*
Shortened heading

- **Basis for Opinion** (must be second section) – Should include:

  o A statement that the audit was conducted in accordance with U.S. GAAS

  o A reference to the auditor's responsibility section of the report

  o A statement that the auditor is required to be independent and meet other relevant ethical requirements

  o A statement that the auditor believes the audit evidence obtained is sufficient and appropriate to provide a basis for the opinion

- **Responsibilities of Management for the Financial Statements** – Should include descriptions of management's responsibility for the:

  o Preparation and fair presentation of the F/S in accordance with the AFRF

  o Design, implementation, and maintenance (DIM) of relevant internal controls (I/C)

  o Evaluation of the entity's ability to continue as a going concern, if required by the AFRF

Note that this section should NOT reference any statements made by management regarding their responsibilities.

- Auditor's Responsibilities for the Audit of the Financial Statements – Should include:

  o The auditor's objectives to:

    ▪ Obtain reasonable assurance about whether the F/S as a whole are free of material misstatement, whether due to error or fraud

    ▪ Issue a report that includes the auditor's opinion

- A statement that:

  - Reasonable assurance is a high level of assurance but is not absolute assurance and therefore is not a guarantee that an audit conducted in accordance with GAAS will always detect a material misstatement when it exists

  - The risk of not detecting a material misstatement resulting from fraud is higher than for one resulting from error, as fraud may involve collusion, forgery, intentional omissions, misrepresentations, or the override of I/C

  - Misstatements are considered material if there is a substantial likelihood that, individually or in the aggregate, they influence the judgment made by a reasonable user based on the F/S

  - The auditor is required to communicate with those charged with governance regarding, among other matters, the planned scope and timing of the audit, significant audit findings, and certain I/C–related matters identified during the audit

- A description of the auditor's responsibilities in performing an audit to:

  - Exercise *professional judgment* and maintain *professional skepticism* throughout the audit.

  - Identify and assess the risks of material misstatement of the F/S, whether due to fraud or error, and design and perform audit procedures responsive to those risks. Such procedures include examining, on a test basis, evidence regarding the amounts and disclosures in the F/S.

  - Evaluate the appropriateness of accounting policies used and the reasonableness of significant accounting estimates made by management, as well as evaluate the overall presentation of the F/S.

  - Conclude whether there are conditions or events that raise substantial doubt about the entity's ability to continue as a going concern for a reasonable period of time.

  - Obtain an understanding of I/C to design appropriate audit procedures, *but not for the purpose of expressing an opinion on the effectiveness of the entity's I/C and no such opinion is expressed.* The part in italics is not included, of course, if the auditor is engaged to express an opinion on I/C.

Signature, Location, and Date

- The signature of the auditor's firm may be printed or manual.

- The city and state should be listed for the issuing office (or city and country for a non-U.S. auditor).

- The date of the report should be no earlier than the date on which the auditor has obtained sufficient appropriate audit evidence on which to base the opinion. This includes evidence that:

  - All F/S and disclosures have been prepared.

  - Management has taken responsibility for the F/S.

CPA candidates could be asked to prepare this type of report on the exam starting with a report example, such as the one that follows. This does not mean you need to memorize the reports; just be familiar with the differences in the reports.

Standard Unmodified Opinion (GAAS)

INDEPENDENT AUDITOR'S REPORT

To: The Board of Directors of X Company (Those charged with Governance)

Opinion

We have audited the financial statements of ABC Company, which comprise the balance sheet as of December 31, 20X1, and the related statements of income, changes in stockholders' equity, and cash flows for the year then ended, and the related notes to the financial statements.

In our opinion, the accompanying financial statements present fairly, in all material respects, the financial position of ABC Company as of December 31, 20X1, and the results of its operations and its cash flows for the year then ended in accordance with accounting principles generally accepted in the United States of America.

Basis for Opinion

We conducted our audit in accordance with auditing standards generally accepted in the United States of America (GAAS). Our responsibilities under those standards are further described in the Auditor's Responsibilities for the Audit of the Financial Statements section of our report. We are required to be independent of ABC Company and to meet our other ethical responsibilities, in accordance with the relevant ethical requirements relating to our audit. We believe that the audit evidence we have obtained is sufficient and appropriate to provide a basis for our audit opinion.

Responsibilities of Management for the Financial Statements

Management is responsible for the preparation and fair presentation of the financial statements in accordance with accounting principles generally accepted in the United States of America, and for the design, implementation, and maintenance of internal control relevant to the preparation and fair presentation of financial statements that are free from material misstatement, whether due to fraud or error.

In preparing the financial statements, management is required to evaluate whether there are conditions or events, considered in the aggregate, that raise substantial doubt about ABC Company's ability to continue as a going concern for [insert the time period set by the applicable financial reporting framework].

Auditor's Responsibilities for the Audit of the Financial Statements

Our objectives are to obtain reasonable assurance about whether the financial statements as a whole are free from material misstatement, whether due to fraud or error, and to issue an auditor's report that includes our opinion. Reasonable assurance is a high level of assurance but is not absolute assurance and therefore is not a guarantee that an audit conducted in accordance with GAAS will always detect a material misstatement when it exists. The risk of not detecting a material misstatement resulting from fraud is higher than for one resulting from error, as fraud may involve collusion, forgery, intentional omissions, misrepresentations, or the override of internal control. Misstatements are considered material if there is a substantial likelihood that, individually or in the aggregate, they would influence the judgment made by a reasonable user based on the financial statements.

In performing an audit in accordance with GAAS, we:

- Exercise professional judgment and maintain professional skepticism throughout the audit.

- Identify and assess the risks of material misstatement of the financial statements, whether due to fraud or error, and design and perform audit procedures responsive to those risks. Such procedures include examining, on a test basis, evidence regarding the amounts and disclosures in the financial statements.

- Obtain an understanding of internal control relevant to the audit in order to design audit procedures that are appropriate in the circumstances, but not for the purpose of expressing an opinion on the effectiveness of ABC Company's internal control. Accordingly, no such opinion is expressed.

- Evaluate the appropriateness of accounting policies used and the reasonableness of significant accounting estimates made by management, as well as evaluate the overall presentation of the financial statements.

- Conclude whether, in our judgment, there are conditions or events, considered in the aggregate, that raise substantial doubt about ABC Company's ability to continue as a going concern for a reasonable period of time.

We are required to communicate with those charged with governance regarding, among other matters, the planned scope and timing of the audit, significant audit findings, and certain internal control–related matters that we identified during the audit.

[Auditor's signature]
[Auditor's city and state]
[Date of the auditor's report]

8.02 Additional Sections & Explanatory Language

Overview

Now that we know the basic elements of a standard unmodified report, let's take a look at the additional sections and explanatory language that may be added to an unmodified audit report under GAAS. Note that these additional sections/paragraphs are *not* considered modifications of the report, and in some cases, also apply to other types of reports as well (see table below).

	Additional Section/Paragraph	Specified Title?	Will be added if the auditor...	Applicable Reports
Additional Sections	Substantial Doubt About the Entity's Ability to Continue as a Going Concern	Yes	Has such substantial doubt, which has *not* been alleviated	Unmodified
	Key Audit Matters	Yes	Is engaged to communicate such matters	Unmodified Qualified
	Other Information (OI)*	No	Has to read OI that is included in an annual report for inconsistencies with the F/S	Unmodified Qualified Adverse
	Supplemental Information (SI)*	No	Has to been engaged to audit SI that is presented with the F/S	Any type
	Required Supplemental Information (RSI)*	No	Has to apply limited procedures to determine whether RSI is complete and correct	Any type
	Report on Other Legal and Regulatory Requirements	No	Has reporting responsibilities in addition to those under GAAS	Any type

Additional Section/Paragraph		Specified Title?	Will be added if the auditor...	Applicable Reports
Explanatory Paragraphs	Emphasis of Matter	No	Needs to draw attention to a matter that is *fundamental* to users' understanding of F/S	Unmodified Qualified
	Other Matter	No	Needs to draw attention to matters *other than those presented/disclosed* in F/S that are *relevant* to users' under-standing of the audit, auditor's responsibilities, or report	Unmodified Qualified

Discussed in another chapter.

Substantial Doubt About the Entity's Ability to Continue as a Going Concern

This section is required only if there is such substantial doubt that has not been alleviated.*
It should:

- Draw attention to the F/S notes that disclose:

  o The conditions/events identified and management's plans to deal with these conditions/events

  o That these conditions/events indicate substantial doubt exists about the entity's ability to continue as a going concern for a reasonable period of time

- State that the opinion is not modified with respect to the matter

- Be presented directly after the Basis for Opinion section

- Be titled "Substantial Doubt About the Entity's Ability to Continue as a Going Concern"

When substantial doubt has been alleviated, the auditor may include an emphasis-of-matter paragraph instead.

Key Audit Matters

Section Requirements

This section is required only if the auditor is engaged to communicate key audit matters (KAMs).*

It should:

- Define what a KAM is

- State that these matters were addressed in the context of the F/S audit and a *separate opinion is not expressed* on the KAMs

- Include each KAM to be reported with:

  o An appropriate subheading

  o Reference to any related disclosures

  o A description of *why* the matter is a KAM

  o A description of *how* the matter was *addressed* in the audit

- Be titled "Key Audit Matters"

> KAMs are *matters communicated with those charged with governance* and, in the auditor's professional judgment, were of *most significance in the audit* of the current period F/S.

* *Unless required by law, the KAM section is prohibited when the auditor must issue an adverse opinion or disclaimer of opinion. (AU-C 701)*

Determining KAMs

In determining which matters to report as KAMs, the auditor must choose the most significant of all **items requiring significant auditor attention**, including:

- **Significant risks**, or areas of higher assessed risk of material misstatement (RMM)—eg, the risk of fraud in revenue recognition

- **Areas involving significant management judgment**, which in turn require *significant auditor judgment*, including accounting estimates with high estimation uncertainty

- **Significant events/transactions** occurring during the period and their effect on the audit

KAMs Not Included in KAM Section

Certain KAMs should not be included in the KAM section when *any* of the following circumstances apply.

- Laws/regulations prohibit disclosure.

- The adverse consequences of disclosure (eg, harm to the entity's competitive position) are likely to outweigh the benefits to the public.

- The KAM is described in another section of the report and a reference to that section is appropriate. For example, one should:

  o Reference the Basis for Qualified Opinion section when the matter results in a qualified opinion

  o Reference the Going Concern section when there is substantial doubt about the entity's ability to continue as a going concern

If either or both of the above are the only KAMs to report, or there are no KAMs to report, the KAM section will be modified to say: "[*Except for the matter described in the Basis for Qualified Opinion section or Going Concern section*,] We have determined that there are no [*other*] key audit matters to communicate in our report."

Documentation

Audit documentation should include *all* of the following:

- All matters that required significant auditor attention

- Rationale for why each matter is a KAM or not

- If applicable, the rationale for determining that there are no KAMs to report, or no KAMs other than those required to be reported in the Basis for Qualified Opinion or Going Concern sections

- If applicable, the rationale for determining not to include a KAM in the report due to possible adverse consequences

Report on Other Legal and Regulatory Requirements

This section is required if the auditor has *other reporting responsibilities* in addition to those under GAAS. When this section is required, it should be:

- Titled appropriately, such as "Report on Other Legal and Regulatory Requirements"

- Segmented from the rest of the report by adding "Report on the Audit of the Financial Statements" as an overall heading to the main audit report

Emphasis-of-Matter Paragraphs

Matters that are of such importance that they are **fundamental to** the **users' understanding** of the F/S may warrant an additional emphasis-of-matter paragraph in the report. An emphasis-of-matter paragraph is appropriate when the client has **properly accounted for and disclosed** the item, but the auditor is concerned users might miss the information provided by the client. (AU-C 706)

Paragraph Requirements

An emphasis-of-matter paragraph should:

- Include a clear reference to the matter being emphasized and where the matter is addressed in the F/S

- Indicate that the auditor's opinion is not modified with respect to the matter

- Be included in a *separate section* of the report with an *appropriate heading*

  - Heading must include "Emphasis of Matter" if KAMs are also reported.

  - Heading may be tailored to describe the nature of the matter (eg, "Emphasis of Matter—Litigation").

  - Placement of the section depends on the relative importance of the matters emphasized. When a KAM section is also presented, the emphasis of matter section should appear before or after the KAM section, as appropriate.

Examples of Matters that *May Need* Emphasis

Examples of circumstances that may lead to the addition of an **optional** emphasis-of-matter paragraph include:

- Substantial doubt about the entity's ability to continue as a going concern has been alleviated by management's plans

- Significant related-party transactions

- Material uncertainties (eg, an unresolved lawsuit)

- Important subsequent events

- A major catastrophe that had, or continues to have, a significant effect on the entity's F/S

Examples of Matters that *Require* Emphasis

In addition, there are some circumstances in which the inclusion of such a paragraph is **mandatory:**

- A justified change in accounting principles affecting consistency

- F/S prepared in accordance with a special-purpose framework

- The auditor's opinion on revised F/S differs from the opinion previously expressed, although an other-matter paragraph may be used instead

Other-Matter Paragraphs

An other-matter paragraph is used to communicate matters that are not otherwise reported or disclosed in the F/S, but are **relevant to users' understanding** of the audit, the auditor's responsibilities, or the auditor's report. (AU-C 706)

Paragraph Requirements

An other-matter paragraph should:

- Indicate that such matters are not required to be reported or disclosed

- Not include matters reported as KAMs

- Be reported in a separate section of the audit report with an appropriate heading, such as "Other Matter"

  o Heading may be tailored to describe the nature of the matter
  (eg, "Other Matter—Scope of the Audit").

  o Placement of the section depends on the relative importance of the matters presented.

    ▪ If the matter relates to other reporting responsibilities, it may be included in the Report on Other Legal and Regulatory Requirements section.

    ▪ If the matter relates to the entire audit report, it may be included in a separate section following the Report on Other Legal and Regulatory Requirements section.

Examples of Matters that *Require* an Other-Matter Paragraph

Certain circumstances require the auditor to include an other-matter paragraph. Examples include when:

- The auditor's opinion on revised F/S differs from the opinion previously expressed, although an emphasis-of-matter paragraph may be used.

- The report of another auditor who reported on prior period F/S is not presented with comparative F/S.

- Prior periods presented in comparative F/S were reviewed or compiled, or they have not been audited, reviewed, or compiled.

- The F/S are prepared in accordance with a special-purpose framework and are restricted to internal use.

- The auditor is reporting on compliance with contractual agreements or regulatory requirements.

 Standard GAAS Report with Examples of Additional Sections & Paragraphs

INDEPENDENT AUDITOR'S REPORT

To: Addressee

Report on the Audit of the Financial Statements

Opinion

***

Basis for Opinion

***

Substantial Doubt About the Company's Ability to Continue as a Going Concern

The accompanying financial statements have been prepared assuming that the Company will continue as a going concern. As discussed in Note X to the financial statements, the Company has suffered recurring losses from operations, has a net capital deficiency, and has stated that substantial doubt exists about the Company's ability to continue as a going concern. Management's evaluation of the events and conditions and management's plans regarding these matters are also described in Note X. The financial statements do not include any adjustments that might result from the outcome of this uncertainty. Our opinion is not modified with respect to this matter.

Emphasis of Matter — Litigation

As discussed in Note X to the financial statements, the Company is a defendant in a lawsuit [briefly describe the nature of the litigation consistent with the Company's description in the note to the financial statements]. Our opinion is not modified with respect to this matter.

Key Audit Matters

Key audit matters are those matters that were communicated with those charged with governance and, in our professional judgment, were of most significance in our audit of the financial statements of the current period. These matters were addressed in the context of our audit of the financial statements as a whole, and in forming our opinion thereon, and we do not provide a separate opinion on these matters.

[Description of each key audit matter]

Other Matter

The financial statements of the Company for the year ended December 31, 20X0, were audited by another auditor, who expressed an unmodified opinion on those statements on March 31, 20X1.

Responsibilities of Management for the Financial Statements
***

Auditor's Responsibilities for the Audit of the Financial Statements
***

Report on Legal and Regulatory Requirements

[The form and content of this section of the auditor's report would vary depending on the nature of the auditor's other reporting responsibilities.]

[Auditor's signature]
[Auditor's city and state]
[Date of auditor's report]

8.03 Modified Opinions

Overview

As previously mentioned, there are four types of opinions under GAAS (AICPA) for nonissuers: one of them is the standard unmodified opinion and the other three are modified opinions—**qualified, adverse,** and **disclaimer**—which **depend on** the **nature and severity** of the matters encountered during the audit. (AU-C 705)

Modified Opinions	Will be expressed if ...	Key Report Language
Qualified opinion	F/S are fairly presented, except for...	"... except for..., the [F/S] present fairly...."
Adverse opinion	F/S are materially misstated	"... [F/S] do not present fairly..."
Disclaimer of opinion	Sufficient appropriate audit evidence could not obtained to conclude that F/S are fairly presented	"We do not express an opinion..."

Nature of Matters

The nature of matters encountered during the audit fall into **two categories**:

> A **misstatement** is a difference between the *reported* amount, classification, presentation, or disclosure of a F/S item and the amount, classification, presentation, or disclosure that is *required* under the AFRF.

- **Misstatements** – Such misstatements may be a result of one of the following **departures** from the applicable financial reporting framework (AFRF):

  - Inappropriate selection of accounting policies

  - Improper application of accounting policies (eg, consistency, errors)

  - Inappropriate/inadequate F/S presentation or disclosure

- **Possible Misstatements** – The auditor was **unable to obtain sufficient appropriate audit evidence** to determine that misstatements do not exist. Thus, there may be misstatements going undetected because the auditor's scope was limited to some extent, or in the case of uncertainties, the information was just unavailable.

Severity of Matters

The severity of matters hinges on the materiality and pervasiveness of the effects of the matters on the F/S.

- **Materiality**, as previously discussed, is a matter of professional judgment as to whether misstatements and omissions, individually or taken together, are **likely** to **influence** the judgment of a reasonable F/S **user**.

- **Pervasiveness** relates to the **extent of** the **effects** of a matter on the F/S. A matter is pervasive if the effects are:

  o Not confined to a specific element, account, or item of the F/S,

  o Could represent a substantial portion of the F/S, or

  o Relate to disclosures that are fundamental to the users' understanding of the F/S.

Modifying the Report

The following chart shows how the opinion must be modified considering the nature, materiality, and pervasiveness of the matters encountered in the audit.

Nature of Matters	Severity of Effects or Possible Effects on F/S		
	Immaterial	Material but Not Pervasive	Material and Pervasive
Misstated F/S (Not AFRF/GAAP) • Inappropriate accounting policies selected • Improper application of accounting policies (eg, inconsistency, errors), or • Inadequate presentation/ disclosure	Unmodified	Qualified	Adverse
Scope Limitation/Uncertainties (Possible Misstatements) Unable to obtain sufficient appropriate audit evidence		Qualified	Disclaimer*

When a scope limitation is management-imposed, the auditor may decide to withdraw from the audit instead, if allowable by law.

Qualified Opinion

Applicability

The auditor must issue a qualified opinion when either type of matter is considered **material but not pervasive**. That is, a qualified opinion is required when either:

- Known misstatements, individually or in the aggregate, are material but not pervasive; or

- Due to a scope limitation, possible undetected misstatements could be material but not pervasive.

Form and Content of Report

The same basic elements are required in an auditor's report expressing a qualified opinion as in an unmodified report; however, the headings and content of the opinion and basis for opinion sections will be modified as appropriate (see example report that follows).

- The **opinion** must include one of the following phrases depending on the nature of the matters:

  - **Material Misstatements** – "...*except* for the effects of the matter[s] described..." or

  - **Scope Limitation** – "...*except for* the *possible* effects of the matter[s] described..." *

*Notice that this language bases the qualification of the opinion on the possible effects of the scope limitation, rather than on the limitation itself.

- The basis for qualified opinion section should:

  - *Describe* and *quantify* (or state that it is not practicable to quantify) the financial effects of any material misstatements on the F/S

  - Explain how any qualitative disclosures are misstated

  - Describe the nature of any omissions and include the information if it is reasonably obtainable (ie, the auditor should not be preparing the information)

  - Describe the scope limitation if the report is modified due to the inability to obtain sufficient appropriate audit evidence

  - State whether the audit evidence obtained is sufficient and appropriate to provide a basis for their opinion (appropriately modified for the type of opinion)

 Qualified Opinion Due to Material Misstatement—Material but Not Pervasive (GAAS)

INDEPENDENT AUDITOR'S REPORT

To: Addressee

Qualified Opinion

We have audited the financial statements of ABC Company, which comprise the balance sheets as of December 31, 20X1 and 20X0, and the related statements of income, changes in stockholders' equity, and cash flows for the years then ended, and the related notes to the financial statements.

In our opinion, except for the effects of the matter described in the Basis for Qualified Opinion section of our report, the accompanying financial statements present fairly, in all material respects, the financial position of ABC Company as of December 31, 20X1 and 20X0, and the results of its operations and its cash flows for the years then ended in accordance with accounting principles generally accepted in the United States of America.

Basis for Qualified Opinion

ABC Company has stated inventories at cost in the accompanying balance sheets. Accounting principles generally accepted in the United States of America require inventories to be stated at the lower of cost or market. If the Company stated inventories at the lower of cost or market, a write down of $XXX and $XXX would have been required as of December 31, 20X1 and 20X0, respectively. Accordingly, cost of sales would have been increased by $XXX and $XXX, and net income, income taxes, and stockholders' equity would have been reduced by $XXX, $XXX, and $XXX, and $XXX, $XXX, and $XXX, as of and for the years ended December 31, 20X1 and 20X0, respectively.

We conducted our audits in accordance with auditing standards generally accepted in the United States of America (GAAS). Our responsibilities under those standards are further described in the Auditor's Responsibilities for the Audit of the Financial Statements section of our report. We are required to be independent of ABC Company and to meet our other ethical responsibilities, in accordance with the relevant ethical requirements relating to our audits. We believe that the audit evidence we have obtained is sufficient and appropriate to provide a basis for our qualified audit opinion.

Responsibilities of Management for the Financial Statements

[Same language as unmodified report]

Auditor's Responsibilities for the Audit of the Financial Statements

[Same language as unmodified report]

[Auditor's signature]
[Auditor's city and state]
[Date of the auditor's report]

Qualified Opinion Due to Scope Limitation—Material but Not Pervasive (GAAS)

INDEPENDENT AUDITOR'S REPORT

To: Addressee

Qualified Opinion

***

In our opinion, except for the **possible** effects of the matter described in the Basis for Qualified Opinion section of our report....

Basis for Qualified Opinion

ABC Company's investment in XYZ Company, a foreign affiliate acquired during the year and accounted for under the equity method, is carried at $XXX on the balance sheet at December 31, 20X1, and ABC Company's share of XYZ Company's net income of $XXX is included in ABC Company's net income for the year then ended. We were unable to obtain sufficient appropriate audit evidence about the carrying amount of ABC Company's investment in XYZ Company as of December 31, 20X1, and ABC Company's share of XYZ Company's net income for the year then ended because we were denied access to the financial information, management, and the auditors of XYZ Company. Consequently, we were unable to determine whether any adjustments to these amounts were necessary.

***

Responsibilities of Management for the Financial Statements

[Same language as unmodified report]

Auditor's Responsibilities for the Audit of the Financial Statements

[Same language as unmodified report]

[Auditor's signature]
[Auditor's city and state]
[Date of the auditor's report]

Adverse Opinion

Applicability

An adverse opinion is required to be issued when **known misstatements**, individually or in the aggregate, are both **material and pervasive**.

Form and Content of Report

The same basic elements are required in an auditor's report expressing an adverse opinion as in an unmodified report; however, the headings and content of the opinion and basis for opinion sections will be modified as appropriate (see example report that follows).

- The **opinion** must include the following language: "*... because of the significance of the matter[s]* described ... the accompanying financial statements *do not present fairly* ... in accordance with [GAAP]."

- The content requirements for the **basis for adverse opinion** section are the same as for a qualified opinion.

- An audit report with an adverse opinion should not include a KAM section. A KAM section in an adverse report would distract the reader from the fact that the F/S are materially misstated.

 Adverse Opinion Due to Material Misstatement—Material & Pervasive (GAAS)

INDEPENDENT AUDITOR'S REPORT

To: Addressee

Adverse Opinion

We have audited the consolidated financial statements of ABC Company and its subsidiaries, which comprise the consolidated balance sheet as of December 31, 20X1, and the related consolidated statements of income, changes in stockholders' equity, and cash flows for the year then ended, and the related notes to the financial statements.

In our opinion, because of the significance of the matter discussed in the Basis for Adverse Opinion section of our report, the accompanying consolidated financial statements do not present fairly the financial position of ABC Company and its subsidiaries as of December 31, 20X1, or the results of their operations or their cash flows for the year then ended in accordance with accounting principles generally accepted in the United States of America.

Basis for Adverse Opinion

As described in Note X, ABC Company has not consolidated the financial statements of subsidiary XYZ Company that it acquired during 20X1 because it has not yet been able to ascertain the fair values of certain of the subsidiary's material assets and liabilities at the acquisition date. This investment is therefore accounted for on a cost basis by the Company. Under accounting principles generally accepted in the United States of America, the subsidiary should have been consolidated because it is controlled by the Company. Had XYZ Company been consolidated, many elements in the accompanying consolidated financial statements would have been materially affected. The effects on the consolidated financial statements of the failure to consolidate have not been determined.

We conducted our audit in accordance with auditing standards generally accepted in the United States of America (GAAS). Our responsibilities under those standards are further described in the Auditor's Responsibilities for the Audit of the Financial Statements section of our report. We are required to be independent of ABC Company and to meet our other ethical responsibilities, in accordance with the relevant ethical requirements relating to our audit. We believe that the audit evidence we have obtained is sufficient and appropriate to provide a basis for our adverse audit opinion.

Responsibilities of Management for the Financial Statements

[Same language as unmodified report]

Auditor's Responsibilities for the Audit of the Financial Statements
[Same language as unmodified report]

[Auditor's signature]
[Auditor's city and state]
[Date of the auditor's report]

Disclaimer of Opinion

Applicability

A disclaimer of opinion is required to be issued when either:

- There is a **scope limitation*** or **uncertainty** of such magnitude (ie, likely multiple uncertainties) that could result in **undetected misstatements** that are both **material and pervasive**; or

- The auditor is **not independent**, but is required by law/regulation to report on the F/S.

*Note that it would be preferable to withdraw from an engagement when a scope limitation is imposed by management. However, it becomes more impractical to do so as the audit progresses. Thus, if the audit is nearly complete when the limitation is imposed, the auditor is more likely to issue a disclaimer of opinion.

Form and Content of Report

The same basic elements are required in an auditor's report expressing a disclaimer of opinion as in an unmodified report; however, the headings and content of the opinion and basis for sections will be modified as appropriate (see example report that follows).

- The disclaimer of opinion section must say:
  - o "We do not express an opinion...", and
  - o "*Because of the significance of the matter[s]* described ..., we have *not been able to obtain sufficient appropriate audit evidence* to provide a basis for an audit opinion on the [F/S].
  - o "We *were engaged to audit* the [F/S]..." instead of "We *have audited* the [F/S]..."
- The basis for disclaimer of opinion section should:
  - o Not refer to the auditor's responsibilities section of the report (like the other reports do)
  - o Not state that the audit evidence obtained is sufficient and appropriate (because the opposite is true)
  - o Describe any known matters and their effects that would have required modification of the report
- The **auditor's responsibilities** section must be reduced to include only statements regarding:
  - o The auditor's responsibility to conduct an audit in accordance with GAAS and to issue a report
  - o The auditor's inability to obtain sufficient appropriate audit evidence due to the matters described in the Basis for Disclaimer of Opinion section
  - o The auditor's requirement to be independent and to meet other ethical responsibilities
- An audit report with a Disclaimer of Opinion should *not* include:
  - o A KAM section, as it would mislead the reader into thinking the F/S are more credible than they are with respect to KAMs discussed.
  - o An Other Information section (discussed later) regarding information included in an annual report other than the audited F/S and the auditor's report.

Disclaimer of Opinion Due to Auditor's Inability to Obtain Sufficient Appropriate Audit Evidence About a Single Element of the F/S (GAAS)

INDEPENDENT AUDITOR'S REPORT

To: Addressee

Disclaimer of Opinion

We were engaged to audit the financial statements of ABC Company, which comprise the balance sheet as of December 31, 20X1, and the related statements of income, changes in stockholders' equity, and cash flows for the year then ended, and the related notes to the financial statements.

We do not express an opinion on the accompanying financial statements of ABC Company. Because of the significance of the matter described in the Basis for Disclaimer of Opinion section of our report, we have not been able to obtain sufficient appropriate audit evidence to provide a basis for an audit opinion on the financial statements.

Basis for Disclaimer of Opinion

ABC Company's investment in XYZ Company, a joint venture, is carried at $XXX on the Company's balance sheet, which represents over 90 percent of the Company's net assets as of December 31, 20X1. We were not allowed access to the management and the auditors of XYZ Company. As a result, we were unable to determine whether any adjustments were necessary relating to the Company's proportional share of XYZ Company's assets that it controls jointly, its proportional share of XYZ Company's liabilities for which it is jointly responsible, its proportional share of XYZ Company's income and expenses for the year, and the elements making up the statements of changes in stockholders' equity and cash flows.

Responsibilities of Management for the Financial Statements

[Same language as unmodified report]

Auditor's Responsibilities for the Audit of the Financial Statements

Our responsibility is to conduct an audit of ABC Company's financial statements in accordance with auditing standards generally accepted in the United States of America and to issue an auditor's report. However, because of the matter described in the Basis for Disclaimer of Opinion section of our report, we were not able to obtain sufficient appropriate audit evidence to provide a basis for an audit opinion on these financial statements.

We are required to be independent of ABC Company and to meet our other ethical responsibilities, in accordance with the relevant ethical requirements relating to our audit.

[Auditor's signature]
[Auditor's city and state]
[Date of the auditor's report]

Piecemeal Opinions & Other Considerations

A "piecemeal opinion" is the inappropriate expression of an unmodified opinion on a single financial statement or specific parts of a financial statement in the same report as an adverse or disclaimer of opinion on the *F/S as a whole*. Such piecemeal opinions result in a contradictory effect. While this type of combination of opinions is not allowed with respect to the same AFRF, the auditor can:

- In an initial audit, express an unmodified opinion regarding the financial position (B/S) and a disclaimer of opinion regarding the results of operations (I/S) and cash flows (eg, a scope limitation may prevent the auditor from obtaining sufficient appropriate audit evidence regarding an item that affects the I/S and cash flows but does not affect the B/S.) The difference here is that the auditor is not disclaiming an opinion on the *F/S as a whole*.

- Express an unmodified opinion on F/S prepared under one AFRF and express an adverse opinion on the same F/S under a different AFRF within the same report.

Summary—Audit Report Structure

Before considering any additional sections or explanatory language, the audit report structure is very comparable across the different types of opinions. There are, however, some differences in headings and wording, which are indicated in italics below. Unless otherwise indicated, any section with a modified title also has modified wording.

Section Order	Standard Unmodified	Qualified	Adverse	Disclaimer of Opinion
1	Opinion	*Qualified* Opinion	*Adverse* Opinion	*Disclaimer of* Opinion
2	Basis for Opinion	Basis for *Qualified* Opinion	Basis for *Adverse* Opinion	Basis for *Disclaimer of* Opinion
Any	Responsibilities of Management for the Financial Statements	Standard	Standard	Standard
Any	Auditor's Responsibilities for the Audit of the Financial Statements	Standard	Standard	Standard heading, *Modified wording*

8.04 Departures from Reporting Framework

Overview

Now that we've covered four types of opinions and what they entail when drafting the audit report, let's take a deeper dive into the nature of the matters the auditor faces in arriving at such conclusions. Recall that there are two main categories of matters the auditor may encounter in forming their opinion on the F/S:

- **Material misstatements** exist due to a departure from the AFRF (eg, GAAP)

- A **scope limitation** exists that may result in undetected material misstatements (discussed in more depth later)

In this section, we'll focus on the three types of departures from GAAP that may cause material misstatements and how the auditor should address such departures. In doing so, we'll also be reviewing the auditor's **overall reporting responsibilities** and how they overlap here—remember TIPIC**ANOE**?

- **A**ccounting principles in accordance with AFRF

- **N**o new principles – consistency/comparability

- **O**mitted disclosures – none

- **E**xpress an opinion

	Nature of Matters Resulting in Misstatements	Severity of Effects on F/S			
		Immaterial	Material but Not Pervasive	Material and Pervasive	
A	Inappropriate selection of accounting policies				
N	Improper application of accounting policies (eg, inconsistency, errors)	Unmodified	Qualified	Adverse	E
O	Inadequate presentation/disclosure				

Inappropriate Selection of Accounting Policies

In a **standard report**, the opinion paragraph **explicitly states** that the F/S are in **conformity with GAAP**. First and foremost, this means that management must select accounting policies to apply that are consistent with GAAP. For nonissuers, the FASB Accounting Standards Codification (ASC) is the only authoritative source of GAAP. Issuers must also consider requirements imposed by the SEC in addition to the requirements of the FASB.

Justified Departures

In unusual circumstances, a new type of transaction or legislation may arise that causes existing authoritative principles to be inapplicable. In this case, it might be misleading to apply such principles, and GAAP would require the transaction to be presented in a more appropriate, reasonable manner. Justified departures of this nature still warrant an **unmodified opinion**, but an **emphasis-of-matter paragraph** will be included to describe the departure and circumstances.

Inappropriate Departures

When management has not prepared the F/S in conformity with GAAP, the auditor should first suggest that the statements be corrected. If **management refuses to correct** the **departure**, then the auditor will normally issue a **qualified** opinion (ie, the F/S are fairly presented, except for the specific departure from GAAP).

In rare cases, a departure from GAAP will be so extreme that it makes the **F/S as a whole misleading**; in such cases, the auditor will issue an **adverse** opinion, stating the F/S are not fairly presented.

Improper Application of Accounting Policies

Once management has selected the most appropriate accounting policies, the policies must continue to be consistently and properly applied. Material misstatements may result if the selected policies are applied:

- Inconsistently from period to period or to similar types of transactions/events; or

- Incorrectly, whether intentionally (ie, fraud) or unintentionally (ie, error).

Evaluating Consistency

AU-C 708 requires the auditor to evaluate the consistency of the F/S for the periods presented and communicate in the auditor's report when the **comparability** of F/S from one period to the next is **materially affected** by either of the following*:

- A change in accounting principle – Includes a change in:

  o The **method of applying** an accounting principle

  o An accounting **estimate** that is **inseparable** from the effect of a change in accounting principle—eg, a change in the method of depreciation may be inseparable from a change in the estimated remaining useful life of the asset

- An **adjustment to correct a material misstatement** in previously issued F/S – Includes a change from an **unacceptable principle to an acceptable one**, as well as other material corrections.

*Note that a change in classification of an item on the F/S, if material, may represent a change in accounting principle or a correction of an error (eg, reclassifying cash flows from operating activities to investing activities   due to a mistake in previous years' F/S).

The periods that the auditor must evaluate for consistency depend on the periods covered by the auditor's opinion.

- When only the **current period** F/S are covered by the auditor's report, the auditor evaluates whether the current period F/S are consistent with the immediately preceding period. This is true regardless of whether such prior F/S are presented along with the F/S being reported on.

- When **multiple periods** of F/S are covered by the auditor's report, the auditor evaluates consistency between all periods covered. The auditor also should evaluate the consistency between the earliest period presented and the immediately preceding period, but only if such preceding year is presented along with the F/S covered by the auditor's report.

When there is a **change in accounting principle**, the auditor determines whether:

- The new principle is in accordance with the AFRF.

- The accounting for the effect of the change is in accordance with the AFRF.

- Disclosures related to the change are appropriate and adequate.

- There is justification that the change is preferable (eg, an accounting pronouncement requires the change).

If any of the above conditions are not met, the auditor should evaluate whether the change constitutes a **material misstatement**, which would require a **qualified or adverse** opinion.

If all the above conditions are met and the change has a material effect on the comparability of the F/S (but does not result in a material misstatement), the auditor will issue an **unmodified opinion** and add an **emphasis-of-matter** paragraph* that includes:

- A reference to the footnote in which the client discusses the change

- A sentence mentioning that the opinion is not modified

*Paragraph is included in future reports until the new accounting principle has been applied in all periods presented.

Change in Principle – Concur – Unmodified

Emphasis of Matter

As discussed in **Note X** to the consolidated financial statements, in [insert years(s) of F/S representing the change], the company adopted new guidance *[insert description of new accounting guidance]*. **Our opinion is not modified with respect to this matter.**

Other changes that result in an **unmodified opinion** and an **emphasis-of-matter** paragraph include:

- A change in reporting entity that has nothing to do with a change in ownership (eg, switching from reporting on affiliated entities individually to consolidated F/S)

- A significant change in accounting principle by an investee that is accounted for under the equity method of accounting

- An adjustment to correct a material misstatement in previously issued F/S

Notice that **consistency is implied** in the audit report. That is, there is no mention of consistency in the audit report unless there is an inconsistency that has a material effect on the comparability of the F/S.

Inadequate Presentation or Disclosure

The only mention of disclosures in the audit report is in the first paragraph of the opinion section, which indicates that the notes are among the financial information that is being audited. They are not mentioned again unless the disclosures are considered incorrect, incomplete, or otherwise unsatisfactory. In an unmodified report, the auditor **implies** that **disclosures are adequate** by not indicating otherwise in the report.

Material misstatements from inadequate presentation or disclosure may arise, for example, when:

- The F/S do not include all disclosures required by the AFRF.

- The disclosures are not presented in accordance with the AFRF.

- The F/S do not provide sufficient disclosures beyond those required by the AFRF to achieve fair presentation.

- Information required to be presented (eg, a statement of cash flows) has been omitted.

8.05 Scope Limitations & Uncertainties

Overview

Let's continue our deep dive into the nature of the matters the auditor faces in forming an opinion on the F/S. Here, we'll focus on the different types of scope limitations, including uncertainties, that may result in undetected material misstatements in the F/S.

Nature of Matters Resulting in Possible Misstatements	Severity of Possible Effects on F/S		
	Immaterial	Material but Not Pervasive	Material and Pervasive
Scope Limitation/Uncertainties Unable to obtain sufficient appropriate audit evidence	Unmodified	Qualified	Disclaimer*

*When a scope limitation is management-imposed, the auditor may decide to withdraw from the audit instead, if allowable by law.

Scope Limitations

Sometimes the problem isn't GAAP, but GAAS. Instead of the auditor drawing the conclusion that the statements depart from GAAP, the auditor is prevented from performing an audit in accordance with GAAS and is unable to draw any conclusion. When the auditor is **unable to obtain sufficient appropriate audit evidence**, it may not be possible to express an opinion on certain accounts/disclosures or perhaps on the F/S as a whole. (AU-C 705)

When circumstances prevent an auditor from performing a procedure, the auditor's initial response will be to determine if there are **alternative procedures** that can provide **satisfactory** evidence. If so, these alternative procedures will be performed, and there is no injury to the audit. A **standard report** with an unmodified opinion can be issued; there is no need to mention the use of alternative tests from those originally contemplated.

- If the procedures that the auditor was unable to perform are considered *unconditional* requirements (ie, the auditor *must* do something), there are no acceptable alternative procedures.

- If the procedures that the auditor was unable to perform are *presumptively mandatory* requirements (ie, the auditor *should* do something), the auditor must document how alternative procedures were able to accomplish the objectives that the replaced procedures were intended to accomplish.

Thus, when essential procedures or acceptable alternative **procedures cannot be performed**, the auditor faces a **scope limitation**. This may result from:

- Circumstances beyond the control of the auditor and the client
  - For example, accounting records have been seized by a government agency or destroyed in an accident.
- Circumstances related to the nature or timing of the auditor's procedures
  - For example, the auditor missed the physical inventory count and cannot obtain sufficient appropriate evidence through alternative procedures.
- Management-imposed limitations
  - For example, management prevents the auditor from requesting certain external confirmations of account balances.

A scope limitation will result in a **qualified opinion** when the auditor is unable to obtain sufficient appropriate audit evidence, but possible undetected **material** misstatements would **not** be **pervasive**. If, on the other hand, the possible effects of an undetected misstatement could be **material and pervasive**, the auditor will issue a **disclaimer of opinion**.

Uncertainties

Occasionally, an auditor is unable to determine the effects of an item on the F/S because the condition's resolution is uncertain (eg, an unresolved lawsuit). Assuming the auditor has been able to obtain all information that is, or should be, available about the matter (ie, there is **no scope limitation**) and it supports management's assertions, an **unmodified opinion** would normally be issued. (AU-C 705)

If the auditor is concerned a user might not notice certain information provided by the client in the F/S and notes, the auditor has the option of adding an **emphasis-of-matter** paragraph to the audit report. The auditor will normally consider the likelihood of the loss and its materiality, but the decision on whether to add this paragraph is based on the auditor's judgment.

Going Concern Doubt

Events/conditions may indicate that there could be substantial doubt as to whether the entity has the ability to continue as a going concern. In this case, the auditor will make inquiries of management and **gather reliable audit evidence** to determine whether such events/conditions actually indicate a going concern issue. (AU-C 570)

Going concern issues primarily relate to **cash flow**, since a company is most likely to fail if it is unable to pay its debts as they come due. **Risk factors** that may produce substantial doubt as to the going concern status of the client include, for example:

- Several years of operating losses
- Negative working capital
- Defaults or restructuring of debts
- Losses of key customers or suppliers
- Denial or losses of licenses or patents

If a going concern issue is present, the auditor will address whether management's plans to mitigate the adverse effects of the events/conditions are likely to be adequate to alleviate the issue. Such **mitigating factors** may include plans to improve cash flow by:

- Increasing ownership equity through stock issuances for cash

- Borrowing money or restructuring debt

- Disposing of marketable assets that are not needed in the operations of the business

- Delaying or reducing optional expenditures, such as research and development

Plans that **increase** cash **mitigate** going concern doubts

If the auditor concludes that there is substantial doubt as to the ability of the client to continue as a going concern for a reasonable period of time (ie, one year after the balance sheet date), the auditor must determine the adequacy of the client's disclosure of these matters.

- If **disclosure is adequate**, the auditor will issue a report with an **unmodified opinion** and the report will have a **Going Concern section** drawing attention to the matter, as previously discussed.

    o When such doubt has been **alleviated**, the auditor may choose to include an **emphasis-of-matter** paragraph instead.

- If the client has **not properly disclosed** a going concern doubt (or other material uncertainty), it will be considered inadequate disclosure and, thus, require a **qualified opinion**.

- In rare cases, the going concern uncertainty may be considered extreme or there may be multiple uncertainties that make it **impossible to form an opinion** on the statements taken as a whole, requiring a **disclaimer of opinion**.

Summary of Nonstandard GAAS Reports

Situation	Opinion	Section Where Explanation Appears*	Management's Responsibility	Auditor's Responsibility
Material Departure	Qualified or Adverse	Basis for ____ Opinion	Standard	Adequate Basis for Qualified or Adverse
Justified Departure	Unmodified	Emphasis of matter	Standard	Standard
Inconsistent - Properly rep & justifiable (concur)	Unmodified	Emphasis of matter	Standard	Standard
Inconsistent - Not properly rep or not justifiable	Qualified or Adverse	Basis for ____ Opinion	Standard	Adequate Basis for Qualified or Adverse
Inadequate Disclosure (Omitted Disclosure)	Qualified or Adverse	Basis for ____ Opinion	Standard	Adequate Basis for Qualified or Adverse

Situation	Opinion	Section Where Explanation Appears*	Management's Responsibility	Auditor's Responsibility
No statement of cash flows	Qualified	Basis for ____ Opinion	Standard	Adequate Basis for Qualified
Contingent liability	Unmodified	Emphasis of matter	Standard	Standard
Going concern doubts exist	Unmodified	Going concern section	Standard	Standard
Going concern doubts alleviated	Unmodified	Emphasis of matter	Standard	Standard
Scope limit - Mat & Not pervasive	Qualified	Basis for ____ Opinion	Standard	Adequate Basis for Qualified
Scope limit - Mat & pervasive	Disclaimer	Basis for ____ Opinion	Standard	Inability to obtain evidence
Scope limit - imposed by mgmt	Disclaimer	Basis for ____ Opinion	Standard	Inability to obtain evidence
Group Financial Audit (Division of Responsibility)	Unmodified w/ reference to report of other	Not required	Standard	Reference to % or $ audited by other

*Some matters that would ordinarily appear in an Emphasis of Matter section may be included in a Key
  Audit Matters (KAM) section instead, if the auditor is engaged to report KAMs.

8.06 Comparative Financial Statements

Overview

When the F/S of the previous year are shown alongside those of the current year, the auditor will have additional audit procedures to perform. If the auditor of the current year also audited the previous year, then the standard report will simply be updated so that both years are included in the audit report. The report date should be the completion of fieldwork for the most recent audit. (AU-C 700)

The report requirements will vary, however, depending on whether the report:

- Includes a different opinion on prior period F/S than was previously expressed
- Covers prior period F/S audited by a predecessor auditor
- Covers a prior period that was not audited

Required Procedures

When reporting on comparative F/S, the auditor is required to perform procedures in addition to those required when reporting on F/S for a single period. The auditor will determine whether the:

- Comparative F/S are **presented in accordance with AFRF** requirements.
- Comparative **F/S and disclosures agree with** those reported in the **prior period**, or they have been:
  - Restated to correct a departure in the prior period, or
  - Retrospectively adjusted for a change in accounting principle.
- **Accounting principles** and **policies** applied in the comparative F/S and disclosures **are consistent** with those applied in the current period, or that there has been a change in accounting principles that has been properly accounted for and disclosed.

During the current period's engagement, the auditor may become aware of a **material misstatement** in the comparative F/S. Upon performing procedures to determine if, in fact, such a misstatement does exist, and the comparative F/S are restated, the auditor should determine that the comparative F/S agree with the restated F/S.

When reporting on comparative F/S, the auditor will obtain **management representations** for all periods referred to in the report.

Opinion Expressed in Prior Year has Changed

In some cases, the auditor's opinion on the previous year will be different than the opinion expressed on those statements in the earlier report. One example might be if the previous opinion was qualified due to inadequate disclosure of a lawsuit, and the lawsuit was settled during the current year (or the client agrees to disclose the suit in the notes to the current comparative F/S).

When the auditor's opinion has changed, the opinion will reflect the current situation, but an **other-matter paragraph** will **refer to** the **earlier report** indicating:

- o The date of the previous report
- o The type of opinion previously expressed
- o The substantive reasons for the different opinion
- o That the auditor's opinion on the amended F/S differs from the previous opinion

Prior Period Audited by a Predecessor Auditor

When a predecessor auditor examined the F/S of the earlier year, the successor's comparative report of the current year can only express an opinion on the current year since that is the only year the successor audited. There are two ways of handling the earlier year.

1. Reissue the Report

The predecessor's report can be reissued and included along with the successor's report.

- In this case, the predecessor must:
    - o **Read** the current period **F/S**
    - o **Compare the F/S** that they reported on with the current period F/S.
    - o Obtain **representation letters** from **management** and the **successor auditor** stating that there are no events or other information that has come to their attention that would require revisions to the F/S or the reissued audit report.
- When there is no reason to revise the report, the report will be reissued with the **original report date**.
- If the successor is aware of a reason for revision, they should arrange for a three-way meeting (including the client) to discuss the appropriateness of the predecessor applying certain procedures to verify the need for changes. Any **revisions** would result in the predecessor's report being **dual-dated** to refer to any new information obtained.

2. Reference the Report

When the predecessor does not reissue their report, the successor will issue an **unmodified report** and add an **other-matter paragraph** that states the following:

- That the prior period F/S were audited by another auditor
- Date of predecessor's report
- Type of opinion
- Reasons for modification of the opinion, if applicable
- Nature of any explanatory paragraphs

Prior Period Audited by Predecessor Auditor	
Report reissued	**Report not reissued**
<ul><li>Read and compare current F/S with P/Y</li><li>Obtain representation letters from management and successor</li><li>If no adjustment to P/Y F/S, use original report date</li><li>If P/Y F/S are restated, dual-date report</li></ul>	<ul><li>Other-matter paragraph:<ul><li>Prior period was audited by another</li><li>Report date</li><li>Opinion</li><li>Reasons opinion is modified, if applicable</li><li>Nature of explanatory paragraphs, if any</li></ul></li></ul>

Prior Period Was Not Audited

In some cases, an auditor will audit the current period's F/S while the prior period's statements were **reviewed** or **compiled**. When that is the case, if the report on the prior period's F/S is not reissued, the auditor will provide an **other-matter paragraph** in the current period's audit report. It will state the following:

- The **service** performed in the prior period
- The **date** of the report on that service
- A description of any **material modifications** noted in the report
- When the service was a **review**, a statement that the service was substantially less in scope than an audit and does not provide the basis for the expression of an opinion on the F/S as a whole
- When the service was a **compilation**, a statement that no opinion or other form of assurance is expressed on the F/S

If **no audit, review, or compilation** was performed in relation to prior-period F/S that are presented on a comparative basis with the current period's audited F/S, those F/S should clearly indicate their status. The report will include an **other-matter paragraph** that will indicate that the *auditor did not audit, review, or compile those F/S and that the auditor does not assume any responsibility for them.*

8.07 PCAOB Audit Reports

Overview

Audit reports prepared for a company that reports to the SEC (ie, **public companies/issuers**) are subject to the requirements of the Public Company Accounting Oversight Board (PCAOB); thus, such reports must be prepared differently under AS 3101 and 3105.

For example, a "clean," unmodified report under the PCAOB standards is instead called an **"unqualified report,"** and the basis for the opinion must refer to "the standards of the Public Company Accounting Oversight Board (United States)," instead of "generally accepted auditing standards."

> **Unqualified PCAOB Report**
> 1. Opinion
> 2. Basis for Opinion
>   - Critical Audit Matters
>   - Explanatory paragraph(s), if any

To make the audit report easier to read and more helpful to investors, the PCAOB made major changes to the requirements for audit reports of public companies in 2017. Now that the GAAS report has also been revised, we can see that there are many similarities and a few key differences (shown in the following table).

GAAS vs. PCAOB Reports		
Section/Element	**GAAS (Nonissuer)**	**PCAOB (Issuer)**
Opinion	1st section	
Basis for Opinion	2nd section	
Going Concern	3rd section, if applicable	Included in Emphasis of Matter paragraph
Key/Critical Audit Matters (KAMs vs. CAMs)	Required only if engaged to report KAMs	Required
	4th section, if applicable	Order is flexible
Emphasis of Matter	Similar	
Other Matter		
Management Responsibilities	Separate sections; order is flexible	Included in Basis for Opinion section
Auditor's Responsibilities		
Report on Other Legal and Regulatory Requirements	Required, If applicable	N/A

Auditor Tenure	N/A	Required

Basic Elements of a PCAOB Report

- **Title** – "Report of Independent Registered Public Accounting Firm"

- **Addressees** – *Shareholders and the board of directors*, or their equivalents. Additional addressees are permitted.

- **Opinion** – First section is titled *"Opinion on the Financial Statements"* and includes the following:

  - Name of the company whose F/S were audited

  - A statement identifying each F/S and any related schedule(s) audited

  - The date of, or period covered by, each F/S and related schedule identified in the report

  - A statement indicating that the F/S, including the related notes and any related schedule(s), identified and collectively referred to in the report as the F/S, were audited

  - An opinion that the F/S present fairly, in all material respects, the financial position of the company as of the B/S date and the results of its operations and its cash flows for the period then ended in conformity with the AFRF

  - identification of the AFRF

- **Basis for Opinion** – Second section is titled *"Basis for Opinion"* and includes statements that:

  - The F/S are the responsibility of the company's management.

  - The auditor's responsibility is to express an opinion on the F/S based on the audit.

  - The audit was conducted in accordance with the standards of the PCAOB.

  - PCAOB standards require that the auditor plan and perform the audit to obtain reasonable assurance about whether the F/S are free of material misstatement, *whether due to error or fraud.*

  - The audit included:

    - Performing procedures to assess the risks of material misstatement of the F/S, whether due to error or fraud, and performing procedures that respond to those risks

    - Examining, on a test basis, evidence regarding the amounts and disclosures in the F/S

    - Evaluating the accounting principles used and significant estimates made by management

    - Evaluating the overall presentation of the F/S

  - The auditor believes that the audit provides a reasonable basis for the auditor's opinion.

  - The auditor is a public accounting firm registered with the PCAOB (United States) and is required to be independent with respect to the company in accordance with the U.S. federal securities laws and the applicable rules and regulations of the SEC and the PCAOB.

- Signature, Tenure, Location, and Date

- o Signature of auditor's firm
- o The year the auditor began serving consecutively as the entity's auditor (or the earliest year of which the auditor has knowledge)
- o The city and state (or city and country, if non-U.S. auditor)
- o Date of the report

Critical Audit Matters (CAM) Paragraph

CAMs must be communicated or state that no CAMs were present.

- A CAM is a matter that:
  - o Was communicated (or required to be communicated) to the audit committee,
  - o Relates to accounts or disclosures that are *material* to the F/S, and
  - o Involves especially challenging, subjective, or complex auditor judgment.
- When determining whether a matter involves **especially challenging, subjective, or complex auditor judgment,** the auditor considers:
  - o Their assessment of the risk of material misstatement
  - o The degree of auditor judgment related to areas in the F/S that involved the application of significant judgment or estimate by management
  - o The nature and timing of significant unusual transactions and the extent of audit effort and judgment related to these transactions
  - o The degree of auditor subjectivity in applying audit procedures to address a matter or in evaluating the results of those procedures
  - o The nature and extent of audit effort required to address a matter, including specialized skill or knowledge needed to do so
  - o The nature of audit evidence obtained regarding a matter
- In the CAM paragraph, the auditor must:
  - o Identify the CAM
  - o Describe the principal considerations that led to the determination that the matter was a CAM
  - o Describe how the CAM was addressed in the audit
  - o Reference the relevant F/S accounts or disclosures
- Communication of CAMs is **not required for** audits of:
  - o Brokers and dealers
  - o Investment companies other than business development companies
  - o Employee stock purchase, savings, and similar plans

o Emerging growth companies

Critical Audit Matters (CAM) Section Needed?

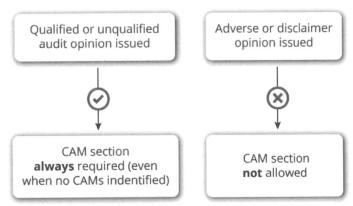

Explanatory Language

In addition to these basic elements and a CAM paragraph, an unqualified report may also **require explanatory language** in certain circumstances, such as:

- There is substantial doubt about the company's ability to continue as a going concern.

- The auditor refers to the report of other auditors as the basis, in part, for their own report.

- There is a change between periods in accounting principles or in the method of application that has a material effect on the F/S.

- There has been a change in a reporting entity.

  o This requirement does not apply when the change results from the creation, cessation, or purchase/disposition of a subsidiary or other business unit.

- A material misstatement in previously issued F/S has been corrected.

- The auditor performs an integrated audit and issues separate reports on the company's F/S and internal control over financial reporting.

- Supplementary information required by the AFRF has been omitted; the presentation of such info departs materially from the AFRF requirements; the auditor is unable to complete prescribed procedures with respect to such info; or the auditor is unable to remove substantial doubts about whether the supplementary information conforms to the requirements of the AFRF.

- Other information in a document containing audited F/S is materially inconsistent with information appearing in the F/S.

The auditor may also decide to **emphasize certain matters** even though they are **not required**, such as:

- Significant transactions (eg, related party transactions)

- Important subsequent events

- Accounting matters, other than changes in accounting principle, affecting the comparability of the F/S with those of the preceding period

- Uncertainties (eg, regarding significant litigation or regulatory actions)
- The entity's status as a component of a larger business enterprise

Standard Unqualified PCAOB Report without Critical Audit Matters

REPORT OF INDEPENDENT REGISTERED PUBLIC ACCOUNTING FIRM

To the shareholders and the board of directors of X Company

Opinion on the Financial Statements

We have audited the accompanying balance sheets of X Company (the "Company") as of December 31, 20X2 and 20X1, the related statements of [*titles of the financial statements, eg, income, comprehensive income, stockholders' equity, and cash flows*], for each of the three years in the period ended December 31, 20X2, and the related notes [*and schedules*] (collectively referred to as the "financial statements"). *In our opinion*, the financial statements *present fairly*, in all material respects, the financial position of the Company as of [at] December 31, 20X2 and 20X1, and the results of its operations and its cash flows for each of the three years in the period ended December 31, 20X2, in conformity with [*the applicable financial reporting framework - AFRF*].

Basis for Opinion

These financial statements are the responsibility of the Company's management. *Our responsibility* is to express an opinion on the Company's financial statements based on our audits. We are a public accounting firm registered with the Public Company Accounting Oversight Board (United States) ("PCAOB") and are required to be independent with respect to the Company in accordance with the U.S. federal securities laws and the applicable rules and regulations of the Securities and Exchange Commission and the PCAOB.

We conducted our audits in *accordance with the standards of the PCAOB*. Those standards require that we plan and perform the audit to obtain *reasonable assurance* about whether the financial statements are free of material misstatement, whether due to error or fraud. Our audits included performing procedures to assess the risks of material misstatement of the financial statements, whether due to error or fraud, and performing procedures that respond to those risks. Such procedures included examining, on a test basis, evidence regarding the amounts and disclosures in the financial statements. Our audits also included evaluating the accounting principles used and significant estimates made by management, as well as evaluating the overall presentation of the financial statements. We believe that our audits provide a *reasonable basis* for our opinion.

Critical Audit Matters

Critical audit matters are matters arising from the current period audit of the financial statements that were communicated or required to be communicated to the audit committee and that: (**1**) relate to accounts or disclosures that are material to the financial statements and (**2**) involved our especially challenging, subjective, or complex judgments. We determined that there are no critical audit matters.

[Signature]
We have served as the Company's auditor since [year].
[City and State or Country]
[Date]

Alternative paragraph for report with Critical Audit Matters

Critical Audit Matters

The critical audit matters communicated below are matters arising from the current period audit of the financial statements that were communicated or required to be communicated to the audit committee and that: (**1**) relate to accounts or disclosures that are material to the financial statements and (**2**) involved our especially challenging, subjective, or complex judgments. The communication of critical audit matters does not alter in any way our opinion on the financial statements, taken as a whole, and we are not, by communicating the critical audit matters below, providing separate opinions on the critical audit matters or on the accounts or disclosures to which they relate.

[Include critical audit matters]

Departures from Unqualified Opinions (AS 3105)

Qualified Opinion

The same basic elements are required in an auditor's report expressing a qualified opinion as in an auditor's report expressing an unqualified opinion, including the communication of critical audit matters (CAM), if applicable. The auditor should consider whether matters for which the auditor qualified the opinion are also CAMs.

- The opinion paragraph must include the words "except" or "exception" in phrases such as "except for" or "with the exception of."

- One or more paragraphs *immediately following* **(After)** the opinion paragraph should disclose all of the substantive reasons for the qualified opinion.

- **Scope Limitation** - Where a qualified opinion results from a scope limitation or an insufficiency of evidence, the auditor's report should describe the basis for departure from an unqualified opinion in a separate paragraph *immediately following* the opinion paragraph and refer to that description in both the Basis for Opinion section and Opinion on the Financial Statements section of the report.

   Qualified PCAOB Report Example

REPORT OF INDEPENDENT REGISTERED PUBLIC ACCOUNTING FIRM

To the shareholders and the board of directors of X Company

Opinion on the Financial Statements

We have audited the accompanying balance sheets of X Company (the "Company") as of December 31, 20X2 and 20X1, the related statements of [titles of the financial statements, eg, income, comprehensive income, stockholders' equity, and cash flows] for each of the years then ended, and the related notes [and schedules] (collectively referred to as the "financial statements"). In our opinion, **except for** the effects of the adjustments, if any, as might have been determined to be necessary had we been able to examine evidence regarding the foreign affiliate investment and earnings, as described below, the financial statements present fairly, in all material respects, the financial position of X the Company as of December 31, 20X2 and 20X1, and the results of its operations and its cash flows for the years then ended in conformity with accounting principles generally accepted in the United States of America.

We were unable to obtain audited financial statements supporting the Company's investment in a foreign affiliate stated at $_____ and $_____ at December 31, 20X2 and 20X1, respectively, or its equity in earnings of that affiliate of $_____ and $_____, which is included in net income for the years then ended as described in Note X to the financial statements; nor were we able to satisfy ourselves as to the carrying value of the investment in the foreign affiliate or the equity in its earnings by other auditing procedures.

Basis for Opinion

These financial statements are the responsibility of the Company's management. Our responsibility is to express an opinion on the Company's financial statements based on our audits. We are a public accounting firm registered with the Public Company Accounting Oversight Board (United States) ("PCAOB") and are required to be independent with respect to the Company in accordance with the U.S. federal securities laws and the applicable rules and regulations of the Securities and Exchange Commission and the PCAOB.

Except as discussed above, we conducted our audits in accordance with the standards of the PCAOB. Those standards require that we plan and perform the audit to obtain reasonable assurance about whether the financial statements are free of material misstatement, whether due to error or fraud. Our audits included performing procedures to assess the risks of material misstatement of the financial statements, whether due to error or fraud, and performing procedures that respond to those risks. Such procedures included examining, on a test basis, evidence regarding the amounts and disclosures in the financial statements. Our audits also included evaluating the accounting principles used and significant estimates made by management, as well as evaluating the overall presentation of the financial statements. We believe that our audits provide a reasonable basis for our opinion.

Critical Audit Matters

[Paragraph explaining CAM, if applicable, and list of critical audit matters or statement that there were no such matters.]

[Signature]
We have served as the Company's auditor since *[year]*.
[City and State or Country]
[Date]

Adverse Opinion

When the auditor expresses an adverse opinion, the report must include the same basic elements as a report for an unqualified opinion, modified appropriately. However, a report containing an adverse opinion **does not include the CAM paragraph** as readers are more interested in knowing why an adverse opinion is expressed.

The auditor's report must describe in a separate paragraph(s) all the substantive reasons for the adverse opinion and the principal effects of the subject matter of the adverse opinion on financial position, results of operations, and cash flows, if practicable.

- If the effects are not reasonably determinable, the report should say so.

- If the effects are disclosed in a note to the F/S, the *explanatory paragraph* (After) should refer to the applicable note.

Adverse PCAOB Report Example

REPORT OF INDEPENDENT REGISTERED PUBLIC ACCOUNTING FIRM

To the shareholders and the board of directors of X Company

Opinion on the Financial Statements

We have audited the accompanying balance sheets of X Company (the "Company") as of December 31, 20X2 and 20X1, the related statements of *[titles of the financial statements, eg, income, comprehensive income, stockholders' equity, and cash flows]* for each of the years then ended, and the related notes [and schedules] (collectively referred to as the "financial statements"). In our opinion, because of the effects of the matters discussed in the following paragraphs, the financial statements do not present fairly, in conformity with accounting principles generally accepted in the United States of America, the financial position of the Company as of December 31, 20X2 and 20X1, or the results of its operations or its cash flows for the years then ended.

As discussed in Note X to the financial statements, the Company carries its property, plant and equipment accounts at appraisal values, and provides depreciation on the basis of such values. Further, the Company does not provide for income taxes with respect to differences between financial income and taxable income arising because of the use, for income tax purposes, of the installment method of reporting gross profit from certain types of sales. Accounting principles generally accepted in the United States of America require that property, plant and equipment be stated at an amount not in excess of cost, reduced by depreciation based on such amount, and that deferred income taxes be provided.

Because of the departures from accounting principles generally accepted in the United States of America identified above, as of December 31, 20X2 and 20X1, inventories have been increased $_____ and $_____ by inclusion in manufacturing overhead of depreciation in excess of that based on cost; property, plant and equipment, less accumulated depreciation, is carried at $_____ and $_____ in excess of an amount based on the cost to the Company; and deferred income taxes of $_____ and $_____ have not been recorded; resulting in an increase of $_____ and $_____ in retained earnings and in appraisal surplus of $_____ and $_____, respectively. For the years ended December 31, 20X2 and 20X1, cost of goods sold has been increased $_____ and $_____, respectively, because of the effects of the depreciation accounting referred to above and deferred income taxes of $_____ and $_____ have not been provided, resulting in an increase in net income of $_____ and $_____, respectively.

Basis for Opinion

[Same basic elements as the Basis for Opinion section of the auditor's unqualified report]

[Signature]
We have served as the Company's auditor since *[year]*.
[City and State or Country]
[Date]

Disclaimer of Opinion

When an auditor has not been able to perform sufficient procedures to form an opinion, the auditor must disclaim an opinion. In this case, the report must include the same basic elements of the unqualified option, modified as follows.

- The first section will be titled, "Disclaimer of Opinion on the Financial Statements" and it will contain:

  o The name of the company whose F/S the auditor was engaged to audit

  o Identification of each financial statement and any related schedules that the auditor was engaged to audit

  o Statements that "we were engaged to audit," rather than "we have audited"

- The second section will be titled "Basis for **Disclaimer** of Opinion."

- The CAM section should be **omitted**. CAM requirements do not apply to disclaimers of opinions.

 Disclaimer of Opinion Example - PCAOB Report

REPORT OF INDEPENDENT REGISTERED PUBLIC ACCOUNTING FIRM

To the shareholders and the board of directors of X Company

Disclaimer of Opinion on the Financial Statements

We were engaged to audit the accompanying balance sheets of X Company (the "Company") as of December 31, 20X2 and 20X1, and the related statements of [titles of the financial statements, eg, income, comprehensive income, stockholders' equity, and cash flows], and the related notes [and schedules] (collectively referred to as the "financial statements"). As described in the following paragraph, because the Company did not take physical inventories and we were not able to apply other auditing procedures to satisfy ourselves as to inventory quantities and the cost of property and equipment, we were not able to obtain sufficient appropriate audit evidence to provide a basis for an audit opinion on the financial statements, and we do not express, an opinion on these financial statements.

The Company did not make a count of its physical inventory in 20X2 or 20X1, stated in the accompanying financial statements at $_____ as of December 31, 20X2, and at $_____ as of December 31, 20X1. Further, evidence supporting the cost of property and equipment acquired prior to December 31, 20X1, is no longer available. The Company's records do not permit the application of other auditing procedures to inventories or property and equipment.

Basis for Disclaimer of Opinion

These financial statements are the responsibility of the Company's management. We are a public accounting firm registered with the Public Company Accounting Oversight Board (United States) ("PCAOB") and are required to be independent with respect to the Company in accordance with the U.S. federal securities laws and the applicable rules and regulations of the Securities and Exchange Commission and the PCAOB.

[Signature]
We have served as the Company's auditor since *[year]*.
[City and State or Country]
[Date]

Departure from a Generally Accepted Accounting Principle

The auditor should express a qualified or adverse opinion. For a qualified opinion, the report should describe the **basis for departure** from an unqualified opinion in a separate paragraph **immediately following the opinion** paragraph and refer to that description in the Basis for Opinion section of the report.

Such paragraph should also disclose the effects of the subject matter of the qualification on financial position, results of operations, and cash flows, if practicable. If not reasonably determinable, the report should say so. If disclosed in a note to the financial statements, the explanatory paragraph should refer to the applicable note.

Reference to the Use of a Specialist

An audit report may refer to the use of a specialist if such a reference will facilitate an understanding of a CAM or the reason for explanatory language or a departure from an unqualified opinion. Otherwise, no reference should be made to the work of a specialist in the auditor's report.

Audits in Accordance with GAAS & Another Set of Standards

An auditor may be engaged to perform an audit in accordance with some set of standards, other than PCAOB standards, but in addition to auditing standards generally accepted in the United States of America (GAAS). The auditor may accept such an engagement but would be required to perform the engagement in accordance with GAAS as well as the other set of standards.

- If the audit was conducted applying both sets of standards in their entirety, the audit report would indicate that the audit was conducted in accordance with GAAS and the other set of standards, naming the source of the standards.

- On the other hand, if the second set of standards was not applied in its entirety, the report will indicate compliance with GAAS, excluding any mention of the other standards.

If the second set of standards is PCAOB standards, the content of the report will depend on whether the audit was within the jurisdiction of the PCAOB.

- If the audit is not within the jurisdiction of the PCAOB, the report will refer to the PCAOB standards in addition to GAAS.

- The report will follow the guidelines of one prepared in accordance with the PCAOB standards and indicate that it was also performed in accordance with GAAS.

Summary of Nonstandard PCAOB Reports

Situation	Opinion	Basis for Opinion	CAM*	Additional Paragraph
Material Departure	Qualified	Adequate basis for qualified opinion	Standard	Immediately after opinion paragraph
	Adverse	Adequate basis for adverse opinion	None	Immediately after opinion paragraph
Justified Departure	Unqualified	Standard	Standard	Emphasis of matter - after CAM
Inconsistent - Properly rep & justifiable (concur)	Unqualified	Standard	Standard	Emphasis of matter - after CAM
Inconsistent - Not properly rep or not justifiable	Qualified	Adequate basis for qualified opinion	Standard	Immediately after opinion paragraph
	Adverse	Adequate basis for adverse opinion	None	Immediately after opinion paragraph
Inadequate Disclosure	Qualified	Adequate basis for qualified opinion	Standard	Immediately after opinion paragraph

Situation	Opinion	Basis for Opinion	CAM*	Additional Paragraph
(Omitted Disclosure)	Adverse	Adequate basis for adverse opinion	None	Immediately after opinion paragraph
No statement of cash flows	Qualified	Adequate basis for qualified opinion	Standard	Immediately after opinion paragraph
	Adverse	Adequate basis for adverse opinion	None	Immediately after opinion paragraph
Other Audit Participants	Unqualified	Standard	Standard	Not required, location unspecified
Contingent liability	Unqualified	Standard	Standard	Emphasis of matter - after CAM Not Required
Going concern doubts	Unqualified	Standard	Standard	Emphasis of matter - after CAM
Scope limit - Mat & Not pervasive	Qualified	Standard	Standard	Immediately after opinion paragraph
Scope limit - Mat & pervasive	Disclaimer	Inability to obtain evidence	None	Immediately after disclaimer paragraph
Scope limit - imposed by mgmt	Disclaimer	Inability to obtain evidence	None	Immediately after disclaimer paragraph
Balance sheet only	Amended	Amended	Standard	Emphasis of matter - after CAM Not Required

*Note, as applied in this chart, "Standard" does not differentiate between a CAM paragraph that states there are no CAMs and a CAM paragraph that lists CAMs; that is, they are both considered "Standard."

AUD 9
Statements on Standards for Accounting & Review Services

9.01 Association with Financial Statements & SSARS Engagement Basics

Overview

When a CPA is associated with a client's financial statements (F/S), there are numerous types of engagements that may be entered into. The nature of the engagement will determine which standards the CPA must follow.

- When associated with the F/S of a **publicly held entity**, the accountant will follow the requirements of the Public Company Accounting Oversight Board (**PCAOB**).

- When the CPA is associated with the F/S of a **nonpublic, nongovernmental entity**:

  - The accountant may be engaged to **audit** F/S, in which case the accountant will follow Generally Accepted Auditing Standards (**GAAS**) in the form of the clarified Statements on Auditing Standards (clarified SAS) issued by the Auditing Standards Board (ASB) of the AICPA.

  - The accountant may be engaged to **review, compile or prepare** the F/S, in which case the accountant will follow Statements on Standards for Accounting and Review Services (**SSARS**) issued by the Accounting and Review Services Committee (ARSC) of the AICPA.

Audits & Reviews

Audits and reviews are considered **assurance** and **attest** engagements.

- In an **assurance engagement**, the accountant evaluates the *accuracy or completeness* of information provided by management or gathers evidence that will serve as a basis for the expression of an opinion or conclusion on the information in a report.

- An **attest engagement** is an engagement that requires independence as defined by the AICPA professional standards.

Compilations

Compilations are **nonassurance** engagements. A report is issued but it does not contain the expression of an opinion or conclusion, nor does it express any assurance.

Compilations are sometimes classified as attest engagements and sometimes not. This is because a CPA is allowed to perform a compilation when not independent. Thus, a compilation may be considered an attest engagement when the accountant is independent, but nonattest when the accountant lacks independence. For simplification purposes, we have labeled compilations as **nonattest** since they technically do not require independence.

Preparation Engagements

Preparation engagements are **nonassurance, nonattest** engagements. The accountant is not required to be independent or verify the accuracy or completeness of the information, nor does the accountant prepare a report.

- The client selects the applicable financial reporting framework (AFRF), but the accountant takes responsibility for the preparation and fair presentation of the F/S.

- The client must specifically request that the accountant prepare the F/S for the engagement to fall under SSARS. For example, the preparation of F/S as part of a bookkeeping engagement is not considered a preparation engagement under SSARS.

Association with F/S Summary				
	Preparation	Compilation	Review	Audit
Applicable standards	SSARS	SSARS	SSARS, GAAS, or PCAOB	GAAS or PCAOB
Attest engagement	No	Depends on independence	Yes	Yes
Level of assurance	None	None	Limited assurance	Reasonable assurance

Downgrading an Engagement

Occasionally, an accountant will be in the midst of an audit of a nonpublic entity, and the client will request that the engagement be downgraded to a review or compilation. Similarly, an accountant performing a review may be asked to downgrade to a compilation. In such circumstances, the accountant should carefully consider:

- The **reasons** offered by the client for the downgraded engagement (Change in circumstances or a misunderstanding of the nature of an audit, review or compilation).

- The **additional effort** and **additional cost** needed to complete the original engagement.

If the request of the client is reasonable, the accountant will switch to the downgraded engagement. It is important that the report resulting from such an engagement make **no reference** to the original engagement or the reasons for the downgrade, as it would only serve to confuse the reader as to the nature of the work performed by the accountant. If the reasons are not justifiable, the accountant should consider withdrawing from the engagement.

If, while auditing an entity's F/S, management refuses to allow the accountant to correspond with the entity's legal counsel, the accountant is generally precluded from changing to a review engagement.

General Principles for SSARS Engagements

All SSARS engagements are required to be performed in accordance with AR-C 60, *General Principles for Engagements Performed in Accordance With Statements on Standards for Accounting and Review Services*. The five general principles are summarized below.

Ethical Requirements

The accountant is required to comply with all relevant ethical requirements, including those imposed by the AICPA Code of Professional Conduct, state boards of accountancy, or other applicable regulatory agencies.

Professional Judgment

Decisions are required to be made throughout a SSARS engagement and an informed decision can be made only by applying the accountant's knowledge and experience to the facts and circumstances. Informed decisions also may require consultation with others and should lead to judgments that reflect applications of SSARS and accounting principles that are both *competent and appropriate*.

Conduct of the Engagement in Accordance with SSARSs

Conducting an engagement in accordance with SSARSs requires the accountant to be familiar with, and apply, all relevant AR-C sections, including information provided in the application and other explanatory material sections.

In some cases, the accountant may be required to comply with requirements in addition to those of SSARS. This would be the case, for example, if laws or regulations imposed other requirements or the accountant is engaged to compile or review F/S in accordance with SSARS and some other set of standards, such as International Standards issued by the International Federation of Accountants.

As is the case in auditing standards, SSARS impose *two types of requirements*.

- An **unconditional requirement** is associated with the word **"must"** or the phrase **"is required to."**

- A **presumptively mandatory requirement**, associated with the word **"should,"** is also required when relevant. In rare circumstances, however, the accountant may need to perform alternative procedures (eg, when a procedure presumptively required would be ineffective). In such cases, the accountant must document the reason for the departure and an indication of how the alternative procedures performed achieved the objectives of the requirement.

In addition to the specific relevant requirements of SSARS, the accountant **should consider** interpretive publications, but is not required to apply the guidance in them.

Engagement Level Quality Control

The engagement partner is responsible for:

- The overall quality of the engagement

- The engagement's direction, planning, supervision, and performance

- The report, if any

- Compliance with the firm's quality control policies and procedures, including those related to client/engagement acceptance or continuance, engagement team qualifications, and engagement documentation

- Identifying and communicating circumstances that may affect the client or engagement acceptance or continuance decision

- Being aware of potential noncompliance with ethical requirements

Acceptance & Continuance of Client Relationships and Engagements

Before accepting or continuing an engagement or a relationship with a client, the accountant should ascertain that:

- All ethical requirements will be satisfied.

- Reliable information needed to complete the engagement will be available.

- There is no reason to doubt the client's integrity.

- The FRF selected by management is acceptable.

- Management has acknowledged responsibility for:

  o Selecting the FRF to be applied

    ▪ Could be a *general purpose framework* (eg, GAAP or IFRS) or a *special purpose framework*, such as the tax basis, cash basis, a contractual or regulatory basis, or some other framework like FRF for SMEs (Financial Reporting Framework for Small to Medium Sized Enterprises).

    ▪ A *fair presentation framework* acknowledges that, in rare circumstances, it may be necessary to provide disclosures beyond those specifically required by the FRF, or that it may be necessary to depart from a requirement of the FRF to achieve fair presentation of the F/S.

  o The design, implementation, and maintenance (DIM) of internal control

    ▪ If the accountant accepts this responsibility, independence would be impaired and no assurance can be provided (ie, a review cannot be performed).

  o Preventing and detecting fraud

  o Compliance with applicable laws and regulations

  o The accuracy and completeness of information provided by management

  o Providing the accountant with access to all relevant information and to persons within the entity, as considered appropriate by the accountant

General Principles for SSARS Engagements
1. Ethical requirements
2. Professional judgment
3. Conduct of engagement in accordance with SSARSs
4. Engagement level quality control
5. Acceptance & continuance

International Reporting Issues

AR-C 100[1] provides guidance on performing **compilations and reviews** under *either* of the following circumstances:

- The F/S have been prepared in accordance with an *FRF generally accepted in another country.*

- The engagement is to be performed in accordance with *both SSARS and another set of standards* (eg, ISRS 4410 or ISRE 2400).

Considerations for Acceptance

In a compilation or review of F/S prepared in accordance with an **FRF generally accepted in another country**, in determining whether the FRF selected by management is acceptable, the accountant should obtain an understanding of:

- The purpose for which the F/S are prepared and whether the FRF applied is a fair presentation framework

- The intended users of the F/S

- The steps taken by management to determine that the AFRF is acceptable

The accountant should obtain an understanding of the *legal responsibilities* involved when the engagement is to be performed in accordance with **both SSARSs and another set of standards** and *both* of the following are true:

- The F/S are intended for use only outside of the U.S.

- The accountant plans to use the report form and content of the other set of standards.

Reporting

- If the F/S will be **used in the U.S.**, the accountant should report in accordance with SSARS.

- If the F/S will be **used only outside the U.S.**, the accountant has a choice of using:

  o A report in accordance with SSARSs that includes:

    ▪ AR-C 80 (Compilations) or AR-C 90 (Reviews) requirements, as applicable

    ▪ A reference to the note, if applicable, that describes the basis of presentation of the F/S, including the country of origin if the FRF is generally accepted in another country

  o The report form and content in accordance with another set of standards, if:

    ▪ The report would be issued in the other country in similar circumstances.

    ▪ The accountant has obtained sufficient appropriate review evidence to support the conclusion expressed in the review report, if applicable.

- The accountant has complied with the reporting standards of the other set of standards and identifies those standards in the report.

- If the F/S will be **used both inside and outside the U.S.**, the accountant *may* issue two reports to comply with both of the above reporting requirements.

9.02 Preparation Engagements

Overview

An engagement to prepare financial statements (F/S) is a **nonassurance, nonattest** engagement. In a preparation engagement, the accountant prepares F/S in accordance with an applicable financial reporting framework (AFRF) based on information provided by management. (AR-C 70[2])

- The accountant is *not required* to verify the accuracy or completeness of the information provided by management.

- Also, as it is a nonattest engagement, the accountant is *not required* to evaluate independence.

Although the accountant may be asked to perform two separate engagements in relation to the same F/S, the accountant would not have two SSARS engagements in relation to a single set of F/S performed simultaneously. For example, if a CPA is engaged to compile or review (or audit) a client's F/S or prospective F/S, but the client has not prepared the F/S and expects the CPA to do so, the CPA is involved in two related engagements. There is:

- An engagement to prepare the F/S, which is a form of **bookkeeping engagement** and is **not subject to SSARS;** and

- A compilation or review engagement, which would be subject to SSARS.

When a CPA is engaged to prepare F/S that will not be compiled, reviewed, or audited by the same CPA, the preparation engagement is a nonattest engagement that is **subject to SSARS**.

Requirements in a Preparation Engagement

As is true of all SSARS engagements, an accountant engaged to prepare F/S for a client is required to adhere to the *General Principles for Engagements Performed in Accordance With SSARS* (AR-C 60). In addition, there are specific requirements that apply to a preparation engagement.

Engagement Letter

The accountant is required to reach an agreement with the client on the terms of the engagement, which should be documented in an engagement letter that is signed by *both* the client and the accountant's firm. The agreement should include:

---

[2] *AR-C 70 also applies when the accountant is engaged to prepare historical financial information other than F/S. In such cases, the requirements are adapted, as appropriate.*

- That the objective of the engagement is for the accountant to prepare the F/S in accordance with the AFRF

- Management's responsibilities

- The accountant's responsibilities to comply with SSARS

- Limitations of an engagement to prepare F/S

- Identification of the AFRF

- Whether certain conditions are expected to exist, such as:

  o A known departure from the AFRF, or

  o The omission of substantially all disclosures required by the AFRF

- An agreement by management that *each page* of the F/S will include a statement indicating that *no assurance is provided*

  o The accountant is not precluded from preparing a client's F/S when the client cannot, or will not, agree to include a statement that *no assurance is provided* on each page of the F/S. As an alternative, the accountant will:

    ▪ Issue a disclaimer, indicating the lack of assurance, that will accompany the F/S; or

    ▪ With the client's permission, compile the F/S and issue a compilation report, or withdraw from the engagement.

Performance Requirements

In a preparation engagement, in addition to requirements under AR-C 60, the accountant is required to:

- Obtain an understanding of the AFRF that will be used in the preparation of the F/S, including an understanding of any of the client's significant accounting policies.

- Prepare the F/S in accordance with the AFRF from the information provided by management.

- Include "no assurance is provided" on *every page* of the F/S; or provide a disclaimer indicating the lack of assurance; or compile the F/S.

- If the F/S are being prepared in accordance with a special purpose framework, include a description of the AFRF, which may simply be a line in the title to the F/S, such as "Statement of Assets and Liabilities – Tax Basis."

- Discuss with management the implications of significant judgments affecting the F/S that the accountant assisted in making so that the client can take responsibility for them.

- Bring to the attention of management any indication that information provided for the preparation of the F/S is incomplete, inaccurate, or otherwise unsatisfactory, requesting additional or corrected information.

- Disclose any known material misstatements.

The accountant **may** prepare F/S that **omit substantially all disclosures** required by the AFRF, provided the omission was **not for** the purpose of **misleading users**. The omission should, however, be disclosed in the F/S.

As an accountant is not required to verify the accuracy or completeness of information underlying the F/S, they are not expected to detect material misstatements. They may not, however, ignore incomplete, inaccurate, or otherwise unsatisfactory information. In this case, the accountant should request additional or corrected information. If management fails to provide such information, the accountant should disclose a material misstatement or withdraw from the engagement.

Documentation

The accountant's documentation for a preparation engagement is required to include:

- The engagement letter
- A copy of the F/S

Preparing Prospective Financial Information

The preparation of prospective financial information requires management to make various significant assumptions about what will occur in the future, including the state of the economy, the industry in which the entity operates, the regulatory environment, and numerous other items. Because an understanding of these assumptions is essential to a user's understanding of the prospective financial information, the accountant should not prepare prospective financial information that does not include a *summary of significant assumptions*.

A financial projection is a unique type of prospective financial information in that it illustrates what management believes will result from the occurrence or nonoccurrence of a future transaction or event. As a result, the accountant should not accept an engagement to prepare a financial *projection* that does not include both:

- Identification of the hypothetical assumptions upon which the projection is based
- A description of the limitations on the usefulness of the presentation

Summary of Preparation Engagement

- **No assurance** – No opinion or conclusion
- **Nonattest** – Not required to evaluate independence
- Engagement letter:
  - Objective is to prepare F/S in accordance w/ AFRF
  - Management's responsibilities
  - Accountant's responsibilities
  - Limitations of engagement
  - Identify AFRF
  - Explain known departures from AFRF
  - Each page of F/S state "no assurance is provided"

- **Understanding** of **AFRF** & significant accounting policies
- May omit substantially all disclosures if not for purpose of misleading users
- No report

9.03 Compilation Engagements

Overview

AR-C 80 indicates that the **objectives** in a compilation engagement are to:

- Apply accounting and financial reporting expertise to assist management in the presentation of financial statements (F/S), and

- Issue a report without providing assurance that there are no material modifications that should be made to the F/S for them to be in accordance with the applicable financial reporting framework (AFRF).

A CPA also may be engaged to compile other historical financial information, pro forma financial information (AR-C 120), or prospective financial information.

- **Pro forma financial information** is historical financial information adjusted to reflect what management believes would have happened in that period if an event or circumstance had or had not occurred. It may, for example, show what management believes its prior period's results would have been if they had purchased a particular machine or if they had not lost a major customer to a competitor.

- **Prospective financial information** is any information about the future, presented as one or more elements, items, or accounts or as complete F/S. Examples include a financial forecast and a financial projection.

  - A **financial forecast** reports what management believes its future results of operations and financial position will be based on their assumptions about conditions in which the entity will be operating. These assumptions may relate to the economy, the industry in which the entity operates, the availability of human and physical resources, and a variety of other factors.

  - A **financial projection** incorporates the same assumptions as applicable to a financial forecast but it also considers a hypothetical assumption related to the occurrence or nonoccurrence of some significant event or transaction.

  - All prospective F/S should include a summary of significant assumptions. In addition, financial projections should include an indication of the *hypothetical assumption* upon which it is based and an indication of the limitations on the usefulness of such a presentation.

Requirements in a Compilation Engagement

As is true of all SSARS engagements, an accountant engaged to compile F/S for a client is required to adhere to the *General Principles for Engagements Performed in Accordance With SSARS* (AR-C 60). In addition, there are specific requirements that apply to a compilation engagement.

Acceptance and Continuance

The accountant must determine whether they are independent in relation to the entity. In addition, prior to accepting the engagement, the accountant should obtain the client's agreement that it understands and accepts its responsibility:

- For the preparation and fair presentation of the F/S
- To include the compilation report in any document containing the compiled F/S

A condition for accepting a compilation engagement is that management must acknowledge and understand their responsibility for the preparation and fair presentation of the F/S, which includes providing:

- All informative disclosures required by the AFRF
- A description of the AFRF if it is a special purpose framework, including significant differences from GAAP
- A description of significant interpretations of the contract that affects the framework if the special purpose framework is a contractual basis of accounting
- Any additional disclosures required to achieve fair presentation under the special purpose framework

Engagement Letter

The accountant is required to reach an agreement with the client on the terms of the engagement, which should be documented in an engagement letter that is signed both by the client and the accountant's firm. The agreement should include:

- The objective of the compilation engagement
- Management's responsibilities
- The accountant's responsibilities
- Limitations of an engagement to compile F/S
- Identification of the AFRF
- The expected form and content of the compilation report

The engagement letter should also indicate circumstances under which the report may differ in form or content from that which is expected. For example, the engagement letter would indicate if the report will disclose a lack of independence.

Performance Requirements

In a compilation engagement, in addition to requirements under AR-C 60, the accountant is required to:

- Obtain an **understanding** of the AFRF that will be used in the preparation of the F/S, including an understanding of any of the client's significant accounting policies
- **Read** the F/S
  - The accountant's knowledge of the client, the AFRF, and management's significant accounting policies is taken into account.

- o The accountant considers if the F/S appear to be free of obvious material misstatements and appropriate in form.

In performing the engagement, the accountant may become aware of actual or suspected deficiencies in the F/S.

- An awareness that information provided by management is *incomplete, inaccurate, or otherwise unsatisfactory* will require the accountant to inform management and request additional or corrected information.

- The accountant should *propose revisions* when the accountant becomes aware that the:

  - o AFRF is not adequately described

  - o F/S require revision to be in accordance with the AFRF

  - o F/S are misleading

Under certain circumstances, the accountant is required to **withdraw** from the engagement, informing management of the reasons. This will be the case if:

- Management is unable or unwilling to *provide information* the accountant considers necessary to satisfactorily complete the engagement; or

- The F/S contain *departures* from the AFRF and management will not make proposed changes or disclose the departures.

  - o The accountant would not be required to withdraw if disclosure of the departures in the compilation report would sufficiently inform users.

Unmodified Compilation Report

Whenever an accountant compiles F/S, those F/S must be accompanied by the accountant's compilation report. When the F/S are prepared in conformity with GAAP and nothing makes it appear that the F/S are not appropriate in form or are inaccurate, incomplete, or otherwise unsatisfactory, the accountant will issue an unmodified compilation report.

The accountant's standard written compilation report will **include certain elements**:

- An indication that management is responsible for the F/S

- Identification of the F/S that were compiled, the entity for which they were compiled, and the date or period covered by the F/S

- An indication that the compilation was performed in accordance with SSARS, promulgated by the ARSC of the AICPA

- An indication that the accountant:

  - o Did not audit or review the F/S

  - o Was not required to perform any procedures to verify the accuracy or completeness of the information provided by management

  - o Does not express an opinion, a conclusion, nor provide any assurance on the F/S

- The accountant's signature or that of the accountant's firm

- An indication of the city and state in which the accountant practices

- Date – The report is dated as of the date on which all requirements under AR-C 80.

Standard Compilation Report

INDEPENDENT* ACCOUNTANT'S COMPILATION REPORT

Board of Directors and Stockholders
X Company

Management is responsible for the accompanying financial statements of X Company, which comprise the balance sheet as of December 31, 20X2, and the related statements of income, changes in stockholders' equity, and cash flows for the year then ended, and the related notes to the financial statements in accordance with accounting principles generally accepted in the United States of America. We have performed a compilation engagement in *accordance with* Statements on Standards for Accounting and Review Services (SSARS) promulgated by the Accounting and Review Services Committee (ARSC) of the AICPA. We did not audit or review the financial statements nor were we required to perform any procedures to verify the accuracy or the completeness of the information provided by management. *We do not express* an opinion, a conclusion, nor provide any form of assurance on these financial statements.

Signature of Accountant or Firm
Accountant's city and state
Date: Completion of the compilation

* The report title should only include the word independent when the accountant is independent.

Notice that there are four elements in the report (**CARD**):

- **Compiled** – The compiled statements are identified.

> The mnemonic **CARD** reminds us that the compilation report is small enough to fit on a small card.

- **AICPA standards** – The reference to SSARS distinguishes the accountant's work from similar work that might be performed by a non-CPA.

- **Responsibility of management** – We emphasize that these are the F/S of management, they are not the accountant's.

- **Don't express an opinion or provide assurance** – We explicitly state that we didn't audit or review and do not express an opinion or provide assurance, so that the user of the statements will not misunderstand our involvement.

The accountant may request that each page of the F/S state *"See Accountant's Compilation Report."* Notice that the CPA is referred to as an accountant and **not** as an auditor, since no audit was performed.

Comparative F/S

A CPA may be engaged to compile comparative F/S. The standard compilation report on comparative F/S is only different from the standard report on a single year's statement in that both dates are indicated and items are referred to in the plural, such as F/S and compilations.

When comparative F/S include statements from one or more prior periods that had been reviewed or audited, the report will include the same language as an unmodified compilation report on comparative F/S. An **explanatory paragraph** will be added, however, indicating:

- The prior F/S had been audited or reviewed.

- The date and type of report originally issued on the prior period F/S, and the reasons for a modification to the prior period report, if applicable.

Prospective Financial Information

When reporting on prospective financial information, in addition to the requirements associated with a compilation report, the report will include a statement that the:

- Forecasted or projected results may not be achieved

- Accountant assumes no responsibility to update the report for events and circumstances occurring after the date of the report

Modified Reports

There are several reasons to issue a modified compilation report. These include:

- A lack of independence

- F/S prepared in accordance with a special purpose framework

- Omission of substantially all disclosures required by the AFRF

- Known departures from the AFRF

- Supplementary information accompanying the F/S

- Required supplementary information

Lack of Independence

When the accountant is not independent of the entity, the report will be modified to indicate the lack of independence.

- The indication will be in a separate final paragraph of the report.

- The accountant may, but is not required to, disclose the reasons for the lack of independence.

  o The description may be as brief or extensive as the accountant feels appropriate under the circumstances.

  o If disclosure is made, all *reasons* impairing independence must be disclosed.

- If the accountant uses a title on the compilation report, it should not include the word independent.

F/S Prepared in Accordance with Special Purpose Framework

The accountant may be engaged to compile F/S that are prepared in accordance with an FRF other than GAAP.

- A *general purpose framework* is one that is widely recognized and about which it is reasonable to expect that users will be knowledgeable (eg, GAAP and IFRS).

- Special purpose frameworks (aka, Other Comprehensive Bases of Accounting, or OCBOAs). include the cash or modified cash basis, tax basis, contractual or regulatory basis, IFRS for SMEs (small to medium sized enterprises), or FRF for SMEs promulgated by the AICPA.

When F/S are prepared in accordance with a special purpose framework, the accountant's compilation report will be modified as follows:

- If the special purpose framework is a result of management's election, the report will refer to management's responsibility for determining that the special purpose framework is appropriate under the circumstances.

- If the special purpose framework is a contractual or regulatory FRF, the report will either describe the purpose for which the F/S are prepared or refer to a note in the F/S that does so. A separate paragraph should be added that states the F/S may not be suitable for another purpose.

Additional modifications to the accountant's compilation report may be necessary when certain circumstances apply:

- Unless disclosures are omitted, the report will be modified if the F/S do not include:

  o A description of the special purpose framework, including the differences between the framework and GAAP

  o A summary of significant accounting policies

  o Informative disclosures comparable to those required by GAAP

- If the F/S are prepared in accordance with a contractual basis, the report will be modified if significant interpretations of the contract affecting the framework are not adequately described.

Omission of Substantially All Required Disclosures

The accountant may compile F/S that omit substantially all disclosures required by the AFRF. The report will be modified by adding a separate paragraph indicating that:

- Management has elected to omit substantially all disclosures required by the AFRF.

- The information, had it not been omitted, may influence conclusions about the entity's performance or financial position.

- The F/S are designed exclusively for those knowledgeable about such matters.

The accountant may not report on statements that omit disclosures if the omissions were intended to mislead the user. This might be the case, for example, if the client is trying to conceal a large potential loss due to a pending lawsuit from a potential lender.

Known Departures

When the accountant is aware of a departure from the AFRF, the report may not be modified to indicate that the F/S are not in conformity with the AFRF.

- If the accountant believes that modifying the report to disclose the departure is adequate, it should be disclosed in a separate paragraph of the report. The effects of the departure on the F/S should be disclosed if such effects are known.

- If the accountant does not believe that disclosure will adequately describe the deficiencies in financial reporting, the accountant should *withdraw* from the engagement and provide no further services in relation to those F/S.

Supplementary Information Accompanies the F/S

When supplementary information accompanies compiled F/S, the accountant will indicate that either the supplementary information was or was not compiled and if the accountant is reporting on the supplementary information.

Required Supplementary Information

When the AFRF under which the F/S were prepared requires supplementary information (RSI), the accountant's report will be modified to indicate:

- Whether the RSI is included, partially included, or omitted

- Whether or not the RSI that is included was compiled by the accountant and is being reported upon.

Documentation

The accountant's documentation for a compilation engagement is required to include:

- The engagement letter

- A copy of the F/S

- A copy of the report

Compilation of Pro Forma Financial Information

Pro forma financial information consists of historical financial information that is derived from historical F/S of an entity, but modified to reflect what management believes the F/S would have looked like if certain decisions had or had not been made, affecting the period being presented. These decisions may relate to a specific transaction or event, such as a business combination, disposal of a business segment, making a significant capital expenditure, or a change in the form of business organization. (AR-C 120)

An accountant may assist a client in presenting pro forma financial information without issuing a compilation report. Such an engagement is a nonattest engagement and the accountant is subject to the applicable sections of the code of professional conduct, but there are currently no professional standards to be followed in its conduct.

When an accountant is engaged to report on pro forma information, the accountant is required to comply with the applicable standards. As a result, when engaged to report on pro forma financial information, the accountant would perform a compilation in accordance with SSARS.

Acceptance and Continuance

As a prerequisite to acceptance, management is required to acknowledge and accept its responsibilities, which include responsibility for the preparation and fair presentation of the pro forma financial information in accordance with the AFRF. Even if the accountant prepares the pro forma financial information, which would be done in a nonattest bookkeeping engagement, the client is required to take responsibility for the preparation and fair presentation of the information.

Due to the unique nature of pro forma financial information, the client is required to agree that, in any document containing the compiled pro forma financial information, the following will be included:

- The complete F/S for the entity for the immediately preceding period

  o In some cases, the F/S for the most recent period may not have yet been prepared. When that is the case, the F/S for the period preceding that are to be included.

- If the pro forma financial information is for an interim period, the historical financial information for that period

  o If the F/S for that interim period are not available, those for the most recent period available should be included.

- If the pro forma financial information is related to a business combination, the financial information for all significant constituent entities

  o The included F/S, either those of the entity or those of all constituent entities in the case of a business combination, are to have been subjected to a compilation, review, or audit.

- The accountant's audit, review, or compilation report on the included F/S

  o Making the report available is sufficient.

Pro forma financial information is to be accompanied by a summary of significant assumptions so that users will understand not only the framework but also management's plans that are being considered or events that are being planned for.

The client is expected to agree to obtain the accountant's permission to include the compilation report in any document containing the pro forma financial information when it indicates that the information has been compiled. The permission should be obtained prior to the inclusion of the information.

Engagement Letter

The terms of the engagement should be agreed upon and documented In an engagement letter. The engagement letter should include:

- The objectives of the engagement
- Management's responsibilities
- The accountant's responsibilities
- The limitations of the compilation engagement
- Identification of the AFRF, according to which the pro forma financial information has been prepared

- The expected form and content of the accountant's compilation report with an indication that circumstances may require a report that may differ in form or content

Compilation Procedures

As is the case in all compilations, the accountant is required to have or obtain an understanding of the FRF in accordance with which the pro forma financial information is being prepared. This will include the client's significant accounting policies and, if a business combination is involved, those of the constituent entities.

The same procedures as those required for any compilation are required, however, they may need some modification to adapt to the fact that the information is pro forma, as opposed to historical, financial information. In addition, the accountant should:

- Obtain an understanding of the event or transaction underlying the pro forma financial information

- Ascertain that management has fulfilled its responsibilities to include the historical financial information indicated above, that the information has been subjected to a compilation, review, or audit, and that the report has been included in the document or made readily available

Compilation Report

The accountant's compilation report is required to be in writing and to comply with all of the requirements delineated in AR-C 80, as discussed above. In addition, the report should include a reference to the historical F/S from which the information was derived, indicating whether the information had been subjected to an audit, a review, or a compilation. Any modifications of the report on the historical information should be referenced and the nature and limitations of pro forma financial information should be described.

Compilation Report – Pro Forma

ACCOUNTANT'S COMPILATION REPORT

Management is responsible for the accompanying *pro forma* condensed balance sheet of X Company as of December 31, 20X1, and the related pro forma condensed statement of income for the year then ended (pro forma financial information), based on the criteria in Note 1. The historical condensed financial statements are derived from the financial statements of X Company, on which we performed a compilation engagement, and of A Company, on which other accountants performed a compilation engagement. The pro forma adjustments are based on management's assumptions described in Note 1. We have performed a compilation engagement in accordance with Statements on Standards for Accounting and Review Services promulgated by the Accounting and Review Services Committee of the AICPA. We did not examine or review the pro forma financial information nor were we required to perform any procedures to verify the accuracy or completeness of the information provided by management. Accordingly, we do not express an opinion, a conclusion, nor provide any form of assurance on the pro forma financial information.

The objective of this pro forma financial information is to show what the significant effects on the historical financial information might have been had the underlying transaction (or event) occurred at an earlier date. However, the pro forma condensed financial statements are not necessarily indicative of the results of operations or related effects on financial position that would have been attained had the above-mentioned transaction (or event) actually occurred at such earlier date.

An additional paragraph may be added to emphasize certain matters relating to the compilation engagement or the subject matter. If it refers to information that is properly accounted for and disclosed, an emphasis-of-matter paragraph will be used. If it is to provide information about the engagement or the subject matter that is not required to be disclosed but, in the accountant's judgment, will be useful to the users of the information, it will be in an other-matter paragraph.
The report will also include the accountant's city and state, the date of the report, and the accountant's signature or that of the firm.

Documentation for Compilation of Pro Forma Financial Information

As is true for all professional engagements, documentation should be sufficient to provide a clear understanding of the work performed. It should include, at a minimum:

- The engagement letter
- The results of procedures performed
- A copy of the pro forma financial information
- A copy of the compilation report

Summary of Compilation Engagement

- Engagement letter:
  - Objective is to assist management in presentation of F/S & report in accordance with SSARS without giving assurance
  - Management's responsibilities
  - Accountant's responsibilities
  - Limitations of engagement
  - Identify AFRF
  - Expected form & content of report
- Understanding of AFRF & significant accounting policies
- Read F/S

- Report Required:
  - Management responsible for F/S
  - Reference SSARS
  - Compiled F/S; did not audit, review or verify accuracy or completeness
  - No opinion, conclusion, or assurance
- Modify report for:
  - Lack of independence (nonattest) – Disclose and do not include "Independent" in title
  - Special purpose framework
  - Omission of substantially all disclosures
  - Known departures from AFRF
  - Supplementary information
  - Required supplementary information

9.04 Review Engagements

Overview

In a review of financial statements (F/S), the accountant expresses a **conclusion** regarding whether the entity's F/S are in accordance with an applicable financial reporting framework (AFRF). The conclusion is based on obtaining **limited assurance,** primarily through the performance of **inquiries and analytical procedures**. (AR-C 90)

Before diving into the details on how a review engagement is performed, let's take a brief look at the different types of conclusions that may be issued.

Inquiries & analytical procedures

Limited assurance

Conclusion on whether F/S are fairly presented

3 Types of Conclusions		Expressed if the accountant …	Key Report Language
Unmodified conclusion	Standard conclusion	Has no reason to believe F/S are not prepared in accordance with [GAAP*].	"…we are not aware of any material modifications that should be made to the … [F/S]…"
Modified conclusions	Qualified conclusion	Has no reason to believe F/S are not prepared in accordance with [GAAP], **except for**...	"… **except for** …, we are not aware of any material modifications that should be made to the …[F/S]…"
	Adverse conclusion	Believes F/S are **not in accordance** with [GAAP]	"…due to the significance of the matter(s) described …, the [F/S] are **not in accordance** with [GAAP].

GAAP is an example of an AFRF.

Applicable Engagements

In addition to *historical F/S*, reviews may be performed in accordance with SSARS in relation to *other historical financial information*, but **not** the following types of engagements:

- **Pro forma financial information** – Historical financial information adjusted to reflect what management believes would have happened if an event or circumstance had or had not occurred. Statements on Standards for Attestation Engagements (SSAEs) apply to reviews of pro forma financial information.

- **Reviews of interim financial information** to which audit standards (ie, AU-C 930 or AS 4105) apply.

General Requirements

In addition to the general principles in AR-C 60 for all SSARS engagements, AR-C 90 provides the following specific requirements that apply to review engagements.

Acceptance and Continuance

An engagement to review F/S should **only** be accepted **if** the accountant:

- Is **independent** of the entity (ie, independence cannot be impaired).

- Has determined that there are **no scope limitations** on the ability to apply adequate review procedures.

- Has obtained an agreement that **management** understands and **accepts** its **responsibilities** to:

  o Prepare and present the F/S fairly in accordance with the AFRF, which includes:

    ▪ Providing all disclosures required by the FRF or as necessary for fair presentation

    ▪ Describing the FRF if it is a special purpose framework, including significant differences from GAAP

    ▪ Describing significant interpretations of the contract when the FRF is a contractual basis of accounting

  o Provide, at the end of the engagement, a letter confirming certain representations made (ie, management representation letter)

  o Include the review report in any document containing the reviewed F/S (unless agreed otherwise)

Engagement Letter

The terms of the engagement should be documented in an engagement letter that is *signed by both the client and the accountant* prior to the engagement. The agreement should include:

- The objectives of the engagement

  o To obtain limited assurance as a basis for reporting whether there are any material modifications that should be made to the F/S to be in accordance with the AFRF

  o To report on the F/S as a whole and communicate as required

- Management's responsibilities

- The accountant's responsibilities

- Limitations of a review engagement, including a statement that a review is substantially less in scope than an audit and does not contain an opinion on the F/S

- Identification of the AFRF

- The expected form and content of the review report and a statement that there may be circumstances in which the form and content may vary from what is expected

Materiality

Materiality for the F/S as a whole should be determined and applied in designing and evaluating review procedures. Materiality should be revised if the accountant becomes aware of information that would have caused the accountant to set a different materiality level initially.

Industry Understanding

The accountant should obtain an understanding of the industry in which the entity operates, including accounting principles and practices generally used, sufficient to enable the accountant to review F/S that are appropriate for an entity operating in that industry.

Client Knowledge

The accountant should obtain an understanding of the client's business and its accounting policies and practices sufficient to enable the accountant to identify:

- Areas in the F/S that may represent a higher risk of material misstatement so that procedures may be designed to address those areas.

- Any policies or practices that may be unusual compared to those generally used in the industry.

Review Procedures

Based on the accountant's understanding of the entity, its industry, and the risk of issuing an inappropriate review report, the accountant should design and perform **analytical procedures**, make **inquiries,** and perform other procedures to obtain **sufficient appropriate review evidence** that the F/S are not in need of **material modification** to be in accordance with the AFRF. Such procedures should be focused on:

- All material items in the F/S, including disclosures

- The areas that represent the greatest risk of material misstatement

Analytical Procedures

Analytical procedures consist of the performance of three essential steps:

- The accountant uses their understanding of the industry, client knowledge, and general knowledge about business, accounting and the economy to **develop expectations**.

- The accountant will **compare** the **client's data to expectations** to determine if variances are within a reasonable range. Note that the accountant's expectations developed for performing analytical procedures in a review of F/S may be less precise than in an audit.

- Any **significant differences** are **investigated** by inquiring of management and performing other review procedures, if necessary. Note that management's responses are not required to be corroborated with other evidence in a review.

Specific analytical procedures that the accountant should perform include:

- Comparing current period data to prior period data
- Considering plausible relationships among financial and nonfinancial data
- Comparing amounts reported in the F/S, or ratios derived from those amounts, to the accountant's expectations
- Comparing disaggregated revenue data (eg, revenue reported by month), when applicable

Inquiries

Making inquiries of management and others with knowledge of, or responsibility for, the F/S or other accounting matters is another significant means by which the accountant obtains review evidence. Inquiries regarding the following matters should be made in every review engagement.

- The preparation and fair presentation of the F/S in accordance with the AFRF, including how management determined reasonable, significant accounting estimates
- Related party relationships and transactions, including the purpose of those transactions
- Whether there are significant, unusual, or complex situations, transactions, or events that may have affected the entity's F/S, including, for example, uncorrected misstatements previously identified and significant journal entries or adjustments.
- Results of analytical procedures requiring further clarification or support
- The existence of any actual, suspected, or alleged fraud or noncompliance with laws and regulations
- Subsequent events
- Going concern issues, including management's assessment of going concern

- Material commitments, contractual obligations, or contingencies, including disclosures
- Material nonmonetary transactions.
- Communications from regulatory agencies, if any
- Litigation, claims, and assessments, if any
- Actions taken at meetings of the board, stockholders, or other relevant groups
- Any other matters considered necessary

Other Procedures

The accountant should also:

- **Read the F/S** to evaluate whether any information has come to their attention that indicates that the F/S are not in conformity with the AFRF.
- **Read any other accountants' reports** on F/S related to significant components (eg, a subsidiary) of the F/S being reviewed, and evaluate the effect, if any, on the reviewed F/S.
- **Reconcile the F/S** to underlying accounting records.
- Remain alert for information that may indicate previously unidentified **related party relationships or transactions.**
  - o Inquire about the nature of any **significant unusual transactions** that are identified and whether related parties were involved.

When there is an indication that **fraud or noncompliance with laws or regulations** has occurred, the accountant should:

- Communicate identified/suspected fraud to senior management or those charged with governance.
- Communicate to management identified/suspected noncompliance with laws and regulations.
- Request management's assessment of the effects on the F/S and consider the effect on the accountant's conclusion.
- Determine whether there is a responsibility to report such occurrences to a party outside the entity.
- Consider obtaining legal advice and withdrawing from the engagement if it cannot be determined that the F/S are not materially misstated due to fraud and the entity is in compliance with laws and regulations.

If the **AFRF requires management to evaluate** the entity's ability to continue as a **going concern** for a *reasonable period of time* (one year, generally) in preparing the F/S, the accountant should perform review procedures (inquiries usually) to ascertain whether:

- The going concern basis of accounting is appropriate
- Management's evaluation identified any conditions/events that raised substantial doubt about the entity's ability to continue as a going concern

- Management has plans to mitigate any matters that raised substantial doubt (eg, management may plan to sell assets, restructure debt, reduce expenses, increase ownership equity, etc.)

- The related disclosures in the F/S are adequate

If conditions/events that raise substantial doubt exist but the **AFRF does not require management to evaluate going concern** matters, then the procedures above should still be performed, except for inquiries regarding management's evaluation, as it wasn't required.

If matters come to the accountant's attention that indicate the **F/S may be materially misstated**, **additional procedures** should be performed to enable the accountant to conclude whether the F/S are, or are not likely to be, materially misstated.

Evaluating Review Evidence

If information provided by the entity is found to be incorrect, incomplete, or otherwise unsatisfactory, the accountant should:

- Request that management consider the implications to the F/S and communicate the results of that consideration to the accountant.

- Consider if management's response indicates that the F/S may be materially misstated.

If sufficient appropriate review evidence has not been obtained from the procedures performed, the accountant should perform other procedures that are necessary to form a conclusion on the F/S. If the accountant is not able to obtain the evidence necessary to form a conclusion, the accountant should withdraw from the engagement.

Written Representations from Management

The accountant is **required to obtain** written representations from management in the form of a representation letter addressed to the accountant (ie, a **Management Representation Letter**).

- Representations are dated as of the date of the review report—that is, the date on which the accountant has determined that sufficient appropriate review evidence has been obtained.

- **Required representations** include that management:

  o Has fulfilled its responsibility to prepare and fairly present the F/S in accordance with the AFRF

  o Is responsible for the design, implementation, and maintenance (DIM) of internal control relevant to reliable financial reporting (including the prevention and detection of fraud)

  o Has given the accountant access to all relevant information, as agreed upon

  o Has been complete and truthful in its responses to inquiries

  o Ensures that all transactions have been recorded and are reflected in the F/S (completeness)

  o Has disclosed any knowledge or suspicions of fraud, including allegations by others

  o Has disclosed known or suspected circumstances involving noncompliance with applicable laws or regulations that may affect the F/S

- Believes that uncorrected misstatements are immaterial to the F/S, individually or in the aggregate (a summary of such items should be attached)

- Has disclosed and appropriately accounted for known or threatened litigation and claims that may affect the F/S

- Believes that significant assumptions used in preparing the F/S are reasonable

- Has disclosed and appropriately accounted for all known related party relationships and transactions

- Has disclosed all information relevant to using the going concern assumption in the F/S

- Has adjusted for or disclosed subsequent events requiring recognition or disclosure

- In addition, the accountant may require management to provide written representations regarding any matters that, in the accountant's professional judgment, are significant and relevant.

- If management does not provide the required representations or there is reason to doubt the integrity of management and the reliability of the written representations, the accountant should withdraw from the engagement.

Unmodified Review Report

When the accountant reviews F/S and nothing comes to the accountant's attention indicating that the F/S are in need of material modification in order to be in conformity with the AFRF, the accountant will issue an *unmodified* review report. The accountant's standard written review report will include certain elements:

- A title with the word *independent*

- An appropriate addressee

- An **Introductory Paragraph** that:

  - Identifies the F/S that were reviewed, the entity for which they were reviewed, and the date or period covered by the F/S

  - States that the F/S were reviewed

  - Indicates that a review consists primarily of applying analytical procedures to information provided by management and making inquiries of management

  - States that a review is substantially less in scope than an audit, which contemplates expressing an opinion on the F/S taken as a whole, and, as a result, no such opinion is expressed

- A section headed **"Management's Responsibilities"** that indicates that management is responsible for the *preparation and fair presentation of the F/S* in accordance with the AFRF, which includes designing, implementing, and maintaining (DIM) internal control over financial reporting (ICFR)

- A section with the heading **"Accountant's Responsibility"** that indicates that the accountant:

  - Is responsible for conducting the engagement in accordance with SSARS, promulgated by the ARSC

- o Is required to obtain limited assurance as a basis for reporting whether the accountant is aware of any material modifications needed for the F/S to be in accordance with the AFRF

- o Believes that evidence obtained is sufficient to support the accountant's conclusion

- o Is required to be **independent** of the entity and to meet the accountant's other ethical responsibilities

- A section with an appropriate heading that contains the **accountant's conclusion** and that identifies the country of origin of the AFRF, if applicable

- The signature of the accountant or their firm

- The city and state in which the accountant practices

- Date – No earlier than the date on which the accountant has obtained sufficient appropriate review evidence as the basis for the accountant's conclusion

There are 8 key elements an accountant must be **FAMILIAR** with in an *unmodified report* review report for nonpublic clients.

Standard Unmodified Review Report (Nonissuers)

INDEPENDENT ACCOUNTANT'S REVIEW REPORT

Board of Directors and Stockholders
X Company

F/S being
reviewed

We have *reviewed* the accompanying financial statements of X Company, which comprise the balance sheet as of December 31, 20X2, and the related statements of income, changes in stockholders' equity, and cash flows for the year then ended, and the related notes to the financial statements. A review includes primarily applying *analytical procedures* to management's financial data and making *inquiries* of company management. A review is substantially *less in scope than an audit,* the objective of which is the expression of an opinion regarding the financial statements as a whole. Accordingly, *we do not express such an opinion.*

AICPA
standards
(SSARS)

Management
Responsibilities

Management's Responsibility for the Financial Statements

Management is responsible for the preparation and fair presentation of these financial statements in accordance with accounting principles generally accepted in the United States of America; this includes the *design, implementation, and maintenance [DIM] of internal control* relevant to the preparation and fair presentation of financial statements that are free from material misstatement, whether due to fraud or error.

Inquiry &
analytical
procedures

Less in
scope
than audit

Accountant's Responsibility

Our responsibility is to conduct the review engagement in accordance with Statements on Standards for Accounting and Review Services (SSARS) promulgated by the Accounting and Review Services Committee (ARSC) of the AICPA. Those standards require us to perform procedures to obtain limited assurance as a basis for reporting whether we are aware of any material modifications that should be made to the financial statements for them to be in accordance with accounting principles generally accepted in the United States of America. We believe that the results of our procedures provide a reasonable basis for our conclusion.

Incapable
of opinion

Assurance
provided
(limited)

We are required to be independent of X Company and to meet our other ethical responsibilities, in accordance with the relevant ethical requirements related to our review.

Accountant's Conclusion (Limited Assurance)

Refer to
AFRF

Based on our review, we are not aware of any material modifications that should be made to the accompanying financial statements in order for them to be in accordance with accounting principles generally accepted in the United States of America.

Joe Schmoe, CPA
Dallas, TX
March 29, 20X3

Modified Review Reports

There are several reasons an accountant may modify a review report. Factors may include:

- A modified conclusion
- Comparative F/S
- Emphasis-of-matter and other-matter paragraphs
- Other reporting responsibilities
- F/S are prepared in accordance with a special purpose framework
- Restrictions on the use of the report
- Going concern considerations

- Subsequent events
- Work of other accountants
- Supplementary information accompanying reviewed F/S
- Required supplementary information

Modified Conclusions

If the accountant determines that the **F/S are materially misstated**, the accountant should express a modified conclusion. When the accountant concludes that the effects of the matter(s) giving rise to the modification are:

- **Material** but **not pervasive** to the F/S, a **qualified** conclusion is expressed.
- **Material and pervasive** to the F/S, an **adverse** conclusion is expressed.

Severity of Effects on F/S	Immaterial	Material but Not Pervasive	Material and Pervasive
Type of Conclusion	Unmodified	Qualified	Adverse

In the **basis for conclusion paragraph**, the accountant should:

- **Describe and quantify** the **financial effects** of the material misstatement, provided the misstatement relates to *specific amounts* in the F/S. If the effects are unknown, the accountant is not required to determine the effects and should state in the report that such determination has not been made by management.
- **Explain how disclosures are misstated**, if applicable.
- **Describe** the nature of any **omitted information** and include the omitted disclosures when feasible.

Example of Review Report with Qualified Conclusion (Nonissuers)

INDEPENDENT ACCOUNTANT'S REVIEW REPORT

Board of Directors and Stockholders
X Company

★★★

Basis for Qualified Conclusion

As disclosed in Note X to these financial statements, accounting principles generally accepted in the United States of America require that inventory cost consist of material, labor, and overhead. Management has informed us that the inventory of finished goods and work in process is stated in the accompanying financial statements at material and labor cost only, and that the effects of this departure from accounting principles generally accepted in the United States of America on financial position, results of operations, and cash flows have not been determined.

Accountant's Conclusion

Based on our review, **except for the effect of the matter described in the Basis for Qualified Conclusion paragraph, we are not aware of any material modifications that should be made to the accompanying financial statements** in order for them to be in accordance with accounting principles generally accepted in the United States of America.

Joe Schmoe, CPA
Dallas, TX
March 29, 20X3

***Paragraphs omitted are the same for modified reports as they are for unmodified reports.

 Example of Review Report with Adverse Conclusion (Nonissuers)

INDEPENDENT ACCOUNTANT'S REVIEW REPORT

Board of Directors and Stockholders
XYZ Company

★★★

Basis for Adverse Conclusion

As disclosed in Note X to these financial statements, the Company has not consolidated the financial statements of subsidiary ABC Company it acquired during 20X1 because it has not yet been able to ascertain the fair values of certain of the subsidiary's material assets and liabilities at the acquisition date. This investment is therefore accounted for on a cost basis by the Company. Under accounting principles generally accepted in the United States of America, the subsidiary should have been consolidated because it is controlled by the Company. Had XYZ Company been consolidated, many elements in the accompanying consolidated financial statements would have been materially affected. The effects on the consolidated financial statements of the failure to consolidate have not been determined.

Accountant's Conclusion

Based on our review, **due to the significance of the matter described in the Basis for Adverse Conclusion paragraph, the financial statements are not in accordance** with accounting principles generally accepted in the United States of America.

Joe Schmoe, CPA
Dallas, TX
March 29, 20X3

***Paragraphs omitted are the same for modified reports as they are for unmodified reports.

Comparative Financial Statements

When reporting on comparative F/S and there are no departures from the AFRF, nor any other circumstances requiring modification of the report, the only change to the report will be reference to all periods included and the use of plurals when referring to the reviews performed and the statements reviewed.

The accountant may be engaged to report on comparative F/S in which the prior year's F/S had been **audited** but the audit report on the prior period's F/S is not being reissued. The accountant's review report will be the same as an unmodified report for comparative F/S with the addition of an **other-matter paragraph** to describe the circumstances.

Emphasis-of-Matter & Other-Matter Paragraphs

An **emphasis-of-matter paragraph** is used whenever an accountant wishes to draw attention to a matter that has been *properly accounted for and disclosed* in the F/S but, in the accountant's judgment, merits special attention in the report. For example, an emphasis-of-matter paragraph is required when a material misstatement is corrected in previously issued F/S.

An emphasis-of-matter paragraph will:

- Have a heading specifying "Emphasis of a Matter" or another suitable heading
- Include a clear reference to where the matter is described in the F/S
- Specify that the accountant's conclusion is not modified with respect to the matter being emphasized

An **other-matter paragraph** is appropriate when it is necessary to communicate a matter that is *not presented or disclosed* in the F/S (nor is it required to be), but which is relevant to enable users to better understand the review, the accountant's responsibilities, or the report.

Other Reporting Responsibilities

An accountant may be requested to address other reporting responsibilities in the review report. Such other reporting responsibilities should be addressed in a separate section in the report under an appropriate heading, such as "Report on Other Legal and Regulatory Requirements." This section should follow the section titled "Report on the Financial Statements."

F/S Prepared in Accordance with Special Purpose Framework

When F/S are prepared in accordance with a special purpose financial reporting framework, the accountant should include an **emphasis-of-matter** paragraph and modify the conclusion if the F/S do not include:

- A description of the special purpose framework, including how it differs from GAAP
- A summary of significant accounting policies
- Disclosures that are comparable to those that would be required under GAAP

If the special purpose framework is a result of management's election, the report will refer to management's responsibility for determining that the special purpose framework is appropriate under the circumstances.

For F/S prepared in accordance with the **provisions of a contract**, the report should be modified if the F/S do not adequately describe any significant interpretations of the contract on which the F/S are based. An emphasis-of-matter paragraph should be added that states the F/S **may not be suitable for another purpose**. The report should also include an other-matter paragraph that **restricts the use** of the report.

Restricting Use of the Report

A review report should include an alert that restricts its use when the report subject matter is based on measurement or disclosure criteria that is available to and suitable for a limited number of users. Thus, the alert should state that the report is intended solely for the information and use of the identified specified parties.

Going Concern Considerations

If substantial doubt about the entity's ability to continue as a going concern exists, the accountant should include an **emphasis-of-matter paragraph** in a separate section in the report with the heading "Substantial Doubt About the Entity's Ability to Continue as a Going Concern."

If adequate disclosure is not made in the F/S, the accountant should also:

- Express a modified conclusion
- State, in the Basis for Conclusion section, that the F/S do not adequately disclose the matter, and whether:
  - Substantial doubt exists about the entity's ability to continue as a going concern, or
  - Substantial doubt about the entity's ability to continue as a going concern has been alleviated by management's plans.

Subsequent Events & Subsequently Discovered Facts

The accountant should request that management consider whether each **subsequent event** requiring adjustment of, or disclosure in, the F/S is appropriately reflected in the F/S. If the subsequent event is **not adequately accounted for or disclosed**, a **modified conclusion** should be expressed.

The accountant is not required to perform any procedures between the date of the report and the date the F/S are released. However, the accountant may become aware of **subsequently discovered facts before the report is released**. When this occurs, the accountant should:

- Discuss the matter with the client
- Determine if the F/S need revision in terms of adjustment or additional disclosure
- Determine how management intends to address the matter in the F/S, if necessary

If management revises the F/S appropriately, the accountant will:

- Apply review procedures to the revision; and
- Either:
  - Date the report as of the later date on which the additional procedures were completed; or

- o Dual date the report with the original date and the later date with respect to the revision, indicating that subsequent review procedures were limited to that matter.

If management does not revise the F/S, the accountant should modify the report or withdraw, as appropriate.

If the accountant becomes aware of such information **after the report has been released**, the accountant will follow the same procedures by discussing it with the client and evaluating the client's intended means of addressing the matter. If management's response is to appropriately revise the F/S, the accountant will:

- Either apply the later date to the report or dual date it

- Determine if management is taking the appropriate steps to make certain that those who received the previously issued F/S are appropriately informed about the matter and instructed not to use the reviewed F/S

If the F/S are revised due to subsequently discovered facts, the accountant's conclusion may differ from that in the original report. When that is the case, the revised report will include an emphasis-of-matter paragraph to disclose the matter.

If the client does not make appropriate revisions to the F/S, which have not yet been issued to third parties, the accountant should notify the client that the reviewed F/S should not be made available to third parties. If management persists in not taking appropriate action, the accountant may be required to take additional action to prevent the use of the report (eg, seek legal advice and/or inform known users).

Work of Other Accountants

The accountant may rely upon the work of other accountants who may have performed reviews or audits on significant components of the reviewed F/S, such as consolidated subsidiaries. If the accountant decides not to take responsibility for that work, the report should reference the audit or review of the other accountant and indicate:

- That the accountant used the work of other accountants

- The magnitude of the portion of the F/S attested to by the other accountants

Note, however, that another accountant's report **cannot be referenced** if:

- It is restricted for limited use.

- The F/S are prepared based on a different FRF. Exceptions apply when:

  - o The measurement, recognition, presentation, and disclosure criteria applicable to all material items in the component's F/S are similar to the criteria applicable to all material items in the reporting entity's F/S (eg, GAAP and IFRS would be considered similar); and

  - o Sufficient appropriate review evidence has been obtained for purposes of evaluating the appropriateness of adjustments needed to convert the component's F/S to the FRF used by the reporting entity without assuming responsibility for, or being involved in, the work of the other accountants.

Supplementary Information

When **supplementary information (SI) accompanies reviewed F/S**, the accountant will indicate the degree of responsibility the accountant is taking in relation to the SI. This may be done in either an other-matter paragraph in the review report or a separate report on the SI.

When the AFRF **requires supplementary information (RSI)**, the accountant's report will be modified to include an emphasis of matter paragraph that will indicate whichever of the following are applicable:

- The RSI is included and:
  - The accountant performed a compilation engagement upon it;
  - The accountant reviewed it; or
  - The accountant did not compile, review, or audit it.
- The RSI is omitted.
- Some RSI is presented in accordance with prescribed guidelines and some is missing.
- There are departures from the prescribed guidelines.
- There are unresolved doubts as to whether the RSI is presented in accordance with the prescribed guidelines.

When some or all RSI presented was not compiled or reviewed by the accountant, an other-matter paragraph will be included to describe the circumstances.

Documentation

The accountant's documentation for a review engagement should include:

- The engagement letter
- Communication with management regarding fraud or noncompliance with applicable laws and regulations
- Communication with management if the accountant expects the report to include an emphasis-of-matter or other-matter paragraph
- Communication with other accountants that have audited or reviewed significant components of the F/S
- Representation letter
- Reviewed F/S
- Review report

Summary of Review Engagement

- **Engagement letter:**
  - o Objectives: report whether F/S need material modifications & communicate as required
  - o Management's responsibilities
  - o Accountant's responsibilities
  - o Limitations of engagement
  - o Identify AFRF
  - o Expected form & content of report
- Set **materiality** for F/S as a whole
- **Understanding** of:
  - o AFRF & significant accounting policies
  - o Client's business & industry
- Perform **inquiries & analytical procedures**
- **Read** F/S
- **Reconcile** F/S to underlying records
- Obtain **management representation letter**

- **Report required**:
  - o 1st paragraph
    - Identify F/S, entity, & period covered
    - Primarily analytical procedures & inquiries
    - Less in scope than audit & no opinion expressed
  - o Management responsibilities for F/S & ICFR
  - o Accountant's responsibilities
    - Reference SSARS
    - **Independence** required (attest)
  - o **Conclusion** – Limited assurance
- **Modify report** for:
  - o Qualified or adverse conclusion
  - o Comparative F/S – prior year audited
  - o Special purpose framework
  - o Report restriction
  - o Going concern considerations
  - o Subsequent events
  - o Work of other accountants
  - o Supplementary information
  - o Other explanatory paragraphs
  - o Other reporting responsibilities

9.05 Comparison of Engagement Types

GAAS & SSARS Engagements

Let's recap the differences between the **four types of engagements** available for nonpublic entities as a hierarchy. Although the following summary is not exhaustive, it covers nearly all the differences addressed on previous CPA exams.

Summary of SSARS & GAAS Engagement Requirements				
Task	Audit	Review	Compilation	Preparation
Obtain signed **engagement letter**	✓	✓	✓	✓
Obtain **understanding** of AFRF & significant accounting policies	✓	✓	✓	✓
Read F/S & notes to ensure free of material error and in appropriate form	✓	✓	✓	✗
Issue a **report**	✓	✓	✓	✗
Reference **subsequent events** with a material effect on the F/S in the report	✓	✓	✗	✗
Evaluate client's assessment of entity's ability to continue as a **going concern** (if required by AFRF)	✓	✓	✗	✗
Obtain **knowledge** of the accounting principles & practices of the entity's industry	✓	✓	✗	✗
Have a general **understanding** of client's business transactions & accounting records	✓	✓	✗	✗
Set **materiality** for F/S as a whole	✓	✓	✗	✗
Make **inquiries** of company personnel	✓	✓	✗	✗
Perform **analytical procedures**	✓	✓	✗	✗
Obtain a **management representation letter**	✓	✓	✗	✗
Maintain **independence**	✓	✓	✗	✗

Summary of SSARS & GAAS Engagement Requirements				
Task	Audit	Review	Compilation	Preparation
Communicate with predecessor accountant to obtain access to their audit documentation	✓	✗	✗	✗
Obtain **understanding** of **internal controls**	✓	✗	✗	✗
Assess RMM (risk of material misstatement)	✓	✗	✗	✗
Perform inquiries of client's attorney to address **litigation, claims, & assessments**	✓	✗	✗	✗
Perform **substantive procedures** involving inspection, observation, and confirmation	✓	✗	✗	✗

9.06 Review of Interim Financial Statements

Overview

While the annual financial statements (F/S) of a **public** client (issuer) may be audited, the quarterly (interim) information typically is not. Instead, the auditor of the annual F/S will normally perform a **review of interim financial information** under **PCAOB** standards (AS 4105).

Like all reviews, this engagement consists principally of **inquiries** of company personnel and **analytical procedures** applied to financial data. It also results in the expression of **limited assurance** (negative assurance) by the accountant. The report will indicate that the accountant is unaware of any material modifications that should be made to the interim information for it to conform to GAAP.

For **nonpublic** entities, these interim reviews are performed under **GAAS** (AU-C 930) when:

- The entity's latest annual F/S have been audited;
- The auditor either:
  - Has been engaged to audit the entity's current year F/S, or
  - Audited the entity's latest annual F/S and expects to be engaged to audit the current year F/S; and
- The same FRF used to prepare the annual F/S is used for the interim financial information.

If all these **conditions** are **not met**, a review of interim financial information is required to be performed in accordance with **SSARS** (AR-C 90).

Required Procedures

Many of the procedures required for an interim review are similar to that of a review under SSARS. Some of the procedures that are more specific to interim reviews under GAAS and PCAOB standards include:

- Performing procedures to obtain or **update** their **understanding of the entity and its environment**, including **internal control**, such as:
  - Reading prior year audit documentation or previous review documentation
  - Reading the most recent financial information (annual or interim period)
  - Reviewing the results of audit procedures performed with respect to the current year's F/S
  - Inquire of management about:
    - Changes in business activities
    - The identity of related parties and the nature of related party transactions
    - Any significant changes in internal control, such as changes in policies, procedures, and personnel, as well as the nature and extent of such changes

- **Comparing quarterly interim financial information** with comparable information for the immediately preceding interim period
- **Reading the minutes** of meetings of stockholders and board of directors
- Obtaining **reports from component auditors**, who have reviewed the interim financial information of significant components of the reporting entity, its subsidiaries, or its other investees
- Inquiring of management about:
    o Whether the interim financial information has been prepared in conformity with GAAP consistently
    o Unusual or complex situations that may affect the interim financial information
    o Significant transactions recorded near the end of the interim period
    o Events occurring after the date of the interim financial information that could have a material effect
    o Significant deficiencies in internal control
- **Reading other information (OI)** that accompanies the interim financial information for material inconsistencies
- Evaluating management's quarterly certifications about ICFR

Report Requirements

The reports under SSARS, GAAS, and PCAOB standards are all a little different (see table below).

- The primary differences between the SSARS and GAAS reports is the **order** of the report and the **GAAS** report has **no Accountant's Responsibility** section.
- **SSARS** presents the **conclusion** in the **last section** while both **GAAS** and **PCAOB** standards put the conclusion in the **first** section of the report.
- Furthermore, the **PCAOB** report:
    o Is generally the shortest as it has **no management or accountant responsibilities sections** (see example report below).
    o Must be titled "Report of Independent Registered Public Accounting Firm."
    o Must refer to "the standards of the Public Company Accounting Oversight Board (United States)," not SSARS or GAAS.

Differences Between Unmodified Interim Review Reports			
Section	SSARS	GAAS	PCAOB
1	Introduction	Results of Review of Interim Financial Information (Includes introduction & accountant's conclusion)	
2	Management Responsibilities*	Basis for Review Results	
3	Accountant's Responsibility	Management Responsibilities*	N/A
4	Accountant's Conclusion	N/A	

*Shortened heading

 Review of Interim Financial Information or F/S (Issuers)

REPORT OF INDEPENDENT REGISTERED PUBLIC ACCOUNTING FIRM

To the shareholders and the board of directors of ABC Company

Results of Review of Interim Financial Information

We have reviewed the accompanying [describe the interim financial information reviewed] of ABC Company (the "Company") and consolidated subsidiaries as of September 30, 20X1, and for the three-month and nine-month periods then ended, and the related notes [and schedules] (collectively referred to as the "interim financial information"). Based on our review, **we are not aware of any material modifications that should be made** to the accompanying interim financial information for it to be in conformity with accounting principles generally accepted in the United States of America.

Basis for Review Results

This interim financial information is the responsibility of the Company's management. We conducted our review in accordance with the standards of the **Public Company Accounting Oversight Board (United States)** ("PCAOB"). A review of interim financial information consists principally of applying **analytical procedures and making inquiries** of persons responsible for financial and accounting matters. It is **substantially less in scope** than an audit conducted in accordance with the standards of the PCAOB, the objective of which is the expression of an opinion regarding the financial statements taken as a whole. Accordingly, we **do not express such an opinion**.

Signature
City and State or Country
Date (completion of the review procedures)

Note that each page of the interim financial information should be marked as unaudited.

AUD 10
Other Services
& Reports

AUD 10: Other Services & Reports

10.01 Supplemental Information

Overview

There are six different standards that apply to **supplemental information** (ie, information that is not part of the basic F/S): three of them apply to audits of nonpublic entities issued by the ASB and the other three apply to publicly traded entities under the PCAOB auditing standards. While there are slight differences in how the standard-setters define the three categories of supplemental information, they basically can be reduced to the following:

- **Other Information (OI)** – unaudited supplemental information voluntarily provided in the annual report (eg, financial summaries or highlights)

- **Supplemental Information (SI)** – audited supplemental information, voluntarily or required to be provided (eg, additional details on items in or related to F/S, consolidating information, historical summaries, statistical data)

- **Required Supplemental Information (RSI)** – unaudited supplemental information that is required to be provided (eg, certain disclosures required by FASB, GASB, or FASAB outside the basic F/S)

We will focus our discussion on the three standards issued by the ASB and highlight the differences found in the PCAOB's parallel standards. The following diagram has been provided to show how all this information is related and can overlap.

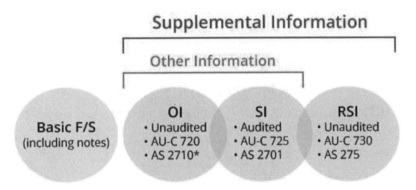

An auditor of a public entity is technically required to follow AS 2710 rather than AU-C 720; however, there are no fundamental differences to note between the two.

Other Information (OI) Included in Annual Reports

In addition to the audited financial statements (F/S) and the auditor's report, an annual report may contain other financial and nonfinancial information (ie, OI). Examples of OI include financial summaries or highlights, financial ratios, and names of officers and directors. (AU-C 7201)

Unless the auditor is engaged to perform procedures in relation to other information (OI), the auditor's **opinion does not cover** it. A discrepancy between the OI and the information in the audited F/S, however, could undermine the credibility of the F/S; therefore, the auditor should:

- Obtain a written acknowledgement regarding which documents will make up the annual report and the manner and timing of release of such documents

- Obtain the final version of such documents, preferably prior to the date of the auditor's report

  o If the auditor will receive the documents after the date of the report, the auditor should obtain a written representation from management that such documents will be provided to the auditor prior to being released to third parties

- **Read** the **OI** and compare certain information in the OI to the F/S to determine if there are any **material inconsistencies** between the OI and the F/S. While reading the OI, the auditor should remain alert to any:

  o Material inconsistencies between the OI and the auditor's knowledge obtained in the audit, or

  o Material misstatements of fact or other misleading information in the OI.

  Note that the auditor is not required to check the OI for completeness.

If material inconsistencies exist, the auditor should determine whether the:

- F/S or OI is materially misstated

- Auditor needs to update their understanding of the entity and its environment

If it is determined that the **OI needs correction**, and the **client refuses** to do so, the auditor's actions will depend on when the OI was obtained.

- Prior to the report date – The auditor should:

  o **Describe it in the report**, or disclaim an opinion if the refusal casts doubt on the client's integrity and the overall reliability of audit evidence;

  o **Withhold** the report; or

  o **Withdraw** from the engagement, if possible.

- **After the report date** – The auditor should take appropriate action, which may include seeking legal advice and exercising professional judgment about how to inform those who have received the F/S.

If it is determined that the **F/S need correction** or the **auditor's understanding** of the entity and its environment **needs to be updated**, the auditor should respond in accordance with relevant auditing standards, such as:

---

[1] *AU-C 720 does not apply to audited SI under AU-C 725 or RSI under AU-C 730.*

- AU-C 560, Subsequent Events and Subsequently Discovered Facts
- AU-C 450, Evaluation of Misstatements Identified During the Audit
- AU-C 315, *Understanding the Entity and Its Environment and Assessing the Risks of Material Misstatement*

The auditor should include a **separate section** in the auditor's report with an appropriate heading, such as "Other Information" and state that:

- Management is responsible for the OI.
- The OI does not include the F/S and the auditor's report.
  - The auditor should also identify the OI in the report.
- The auditor's opinion on the F/S does not cover the OI and the auditor does not express an opinion or any assurance on it.
  - The auditor is responsible to read the OI and consider whether a material inconsistency exists between the OI and the F/S or the OI otherwise appears to be materially misstated.
- If, based on the work performed, the auditor concludes that an uncorrected material misstatement of the OI exists, the auditor is required to describe it in the auditor's report.

If an uncorrected material misstatement of the OI exists, the section will also state that the auditor has concluded that an uncorrected material misstatement of the OI exists and provide a description of it in the auditor's report.

Supplementary Information (SI) in Relation to F/S as a Whole

The auditor may be engaged to report on whether supplementary information (SI) is fairly stated, in all material respects, in relation to the F/S as a whole. (AU-C 725) The auditor may only accept such an engagement if the following **conditions** are met:

- The SI and the F/S were derived from the same records.
- They relate to the same period.
- The F/S were audited and a report was issued that was neither adverse nor contained a disclaimer of opinion.
- Either the SI will accompany the F/S or the F/S will be readily available.

In addition to the procedures performed during the audit, to express an opinion regarding the SI, the auditor should perform **additional procedures** that include:

- Making inquiries of management regarding the purpose of the SI, how it was prepared, and significant assumptions.
- Evaluating whether form and content comply with applicable criteria, whether the criteria have been consistently applied, and whether the SI is appropriate and complete.
- Comparing and reconciling the SI to the underlying accounting records.
- Obtaining written representations from management regarding:
  - Its responsibility for the SI
  - Its belief that it is fairly presented in accordance with applicable criteria

- o Its consistency
- o Its significant assumptions
- o The availability of the audited F/S if they do not accompany the SI

If the **SI is presented with the F/S**, the auditor should report on the SI in either:

- a **separate section** of the audit report, with an appropriate title (eg, "Supplemental Information"), or
- a **separate** report.

If the **F/S are not presented with the SI**, the auditor should report on the SI in a **separate report**, which should include a reference to the report on the F/S, the date of that report, the nature of the opinion, and any report modifications.

Remember that the accuracy or inaccuracy of SI does **not** affect the auditor's opinion on the basic F/S, since such information is outside those statements. However, if the auditor expresses an adverse or disclaimer of opinion on the basic F/S, the auditors are precluded from expressing an opinion on the SI.

If the SI is determined to be materially misstated, the auditor should discuss the matter with management and propose a revision. If management refuses to revise the SI, the auditor should modify the opinion on the SI and describe the misstatement in the report, or withhold the report on the SI if a separate report is to be issued.

PCAOB Requirements for SI under AS 2701

An auditor of a public entity is required to follow PCAOB AS 2701, which is very similar to AU-C 725, but there are some additional requirements.

- The required procedures set forth for SI are basically the same as under AU-C 725; however, the PCAOB requires the auditor to perform "audit procedures necessary to obtain sufficient appropriate audit evidence" to support the auditor's opinion on the SI. The nature, timing, and extent of these procedures are dependent upon the risk of material misstatement of the SI, materiality considerations, audit evidence supporting the F/S, and the type of opinion expressed on the F/S.

- In addition to the written representations required from management under AU-C 725, AS 2701 specifically requires the auditor to obtain a statement from management that:
  - o Identifies any applicable regulatory requirements for the form and content of the SI
  - o Provides that the SI complies, in all material respects, with such requirements

- With regard to the evaluation of audit results on SI, AS 2701 provides that the auditor should:
  - o Evaluate whether the SI, including its form and content, is fairly stated in relation to the F/S as a whole, and is presented in conformity with relevant regulatory requirements or other applicable criteria.
  - o Accumulate misstatements identified regarding the SI and communicate them to management to give them an opportunity to make corrections.
  - o Evaluate whether uncorrected misstatements are material, taking into account relevant quantitative and qualitative factors.
  - o Evaluate the effect of uncorrected misstatements related to the SI in evaluating the results of the financial statement audit.

- ○ Evaluate the effect of any modifications to the audit report on the F/S when forming an opinion on the SI.
  - ▪ If a qualified opinion is expressed on the F/S and the basis for the qualification also applies to the SI, the auditor should describe the effects of the qualification on the SI and express a qualified opinion on the SI as well.
  - ▪ If an adverse opinion is expressed on the F/S or an opinion is disclaimed, the auditor should also express an adverse opinion, or disclaim an opinion, on the SI, as appropriate.
- If it is determined that the SI is materially misstated in relation to the F/S as a whole, the auditor should describe the material misstatement in the auditor's report on the SI and express a qualified or adverse opinion on the SI.
- If the auditor is unable to obtain sufficient appropriate audit evidence to support an opinion on the SI, the auditor should disclaim an opinion on the SI. In those situations, the auditor's report on the SI should describe the reason for the disclaimer and state that the auditor is unable to and does not express an opinion on the SI.
- The auditor may express an opinion on some SI but disclaim an opinion on other SI. For example, if the SI consists of more than one schedule, and the auditor is able to support an opinion on one schedule but not the other, the auditor may express an opinion on the schedule for which sufficient appropriate evidence was obtained and disclaim an opinion on the other schedule.

Required Supplementary Information (RSI)

In some cases, supplementary information is required by the applicable financial reporting framework (AFRF). This is, for example, often the case when the framework is established by a regulatory agency, such as FASB, GASB, or FASAB.

With regard to **Required Supplementary Information (RSI)**, the auditor must apply **limited procedures** to see if the required info has been provided and whether or not it appears to be correct. Examples of this information as it relates to GASB include management's discussion and analysis, budgetary comparison schedules, and schedules of funding progress and employer contributions for other post-employment benefits and pensions.

The **required procedures** include:

- Inquiring of management about its methods of preparing the information:
  - ○ Are the methods of measurement or presentation in accordance with prescribed guidelines?
  - ○ Are such methods consistent with prior periods and, if not, why?
  - ○ Were there any significant assumptions or interpretations?
- Comparing information for consistency
- Obtaining written representations from management regarding their responsibility for the RSI and the methods of preparation

The procedures do not constitute an audit of the RSI; thus, no opinion on the RSI is required and the opinion on the F/S will not be affected. However, the auditor should include a **separate section** in the audit report with an appropriate title (eg, "Required Supplemental Information"), that explains the following circumstances, as applicable:

- The RSI is included and the auditor applied the appropriate procedures.
- The RSI is omitted.
- Some RSI is missing.
- The information is not in compliance with applicable requirements.
- The auditor is not able to complete required procedures.
- There is substantial doubt about the conformity of the RSI.

PCAOB Requirements for RSI under AS 2705

With respect to supplemental information required by FASB, GASB, and FASAB, an auditor of a public entity is required to follow PCAOB AS 2705, which is very similar to AU-C 730, but there are some differences.

- If an entity voluntarily provides SI that is RSI to other entities, the auditor is required to either apply the procedures under AS 2705 or provide a disclaimer on the information in an explanatory paragraph, unless the entity itself specifies that the information was not subjected to such procedures.
- In addition to the limited procedures required by AU-C 730, PCAOB AS 2705 requires the auditor to:
  - Consider whether representations on RSI should be included in specific written representations obtained from management under AS 2805, Management Representations;
  - Apply additional procedures, if any, that other statements or interpretations prescribe for specific types of RSI; and
  - Make additional inquiries if the auditor believes that the information may not be measured or presented within applicable guidelines.
- Though under AU-C 730 the auditor is required to include a separate RSI section in the audit report even if no issues are found, AS 2705 requires an explanatory paragraph only in the following circumstances:
  - The RSI is omitted.
  - There is a material departure from prescribed guidelines.
  - The auditor is not able to complete required procedures.
  - There is substantial doubt about the conformity of the RSI.

Note: AS 2701 (Auditing SI Accompanying Audited F/S) applies instead of AS 2705 if the auditor is engaged to audit the RSI.

Summary – OI, SI, and RSI		
Situation	**Effect on Fieldwork**	**Effect on Report**
Voluntary by client (**OI**)	Read for inconsistencies	• Separate OI section – report inconsistencies • Withhold report, or • Withdraw
Engaged to Audit (**SI**)	Audit Procedures	• Separate SI section, or • Separate report
Required by FASB/GASB (**RSI**)	Limited Procedures	• GAAS – Separate RSI section • PCAOB – Explanatory paragraph only for exceptions

Segment Information (>10%)—Notes to the F/S

Annual financial statements of public entities are required to contain segment information (FASB ASC 280) about a company's operations in different industries, foreign operations and export sales and major customers. This is part of the basic F/S. If it is omitted or contains a material misstatement (disagreement), the auditor will either qualify or give an adverse opinion on the financial statements taken as a whole.

10.02 Special Reports

Overview

An accountant may be asked to prepare a **special report** in certain engagements, including:

- Reporting on F/S that are prepared in conformity with some special purpose framework, often referred to as an other comprehensive basis of accounting (**OCBOA**) other than GAAP.

- Completing **prescribed report forms** of a government agency on behalf of the client.

- Reporting on the client's **compliance** with aspects of **contracts or regulatory requirements** in connection with an **audit.**

Audits of F/S Prepared in Accordance with Special Purpose Frameworks

A special purpose framework is a financial reporting framework (FRF) other than GAAP, often referred to as an OCBOA. Examples are the income tax basis, the cash basis, a contractual basis, a basis used by a regulatory agency (restricted use), or an "other basis of accounting." To be considered a special purpose framework, there must be a definite set of criteria that would enable the auditor to determine conformity with the approach. (AU-C 800)

- An entity may prepare its F/S using a framework based on GAAP with certain differences.

    - This is **not** considered a special report.

    - The auditor will consider differences to be departures from GAAP and would issue a qualified or adverse opinion, as appropriate.

Prescribed forms of government agencies often require special handling because they may include specific representations that the accountant is expected to make.

Third parties dealing with the client may request reports on compliance with agreements related to the F/S. For example, a creditor may wish the auditor to provide a report on whether the client's working capital ratio has been maintained through the year at the level required by a loan agreement.

Forming an Opinion & Reporting

When an auditor accepts an engagement to examine F/S that are intended to conform to a comprehensive basis of accounting other than GAAP, the audit will still conform to generally accepted auditing standards (GAAS), and the opinion may still be unmodified, qualified, or adverse, depending on whether the statements conform to the OCBOA.

When forming an opinion and reporting on F/S prepared in accordance with a special purpose framework, the auditor should address the following considerations.

- Regardless of whether the going concern basis of accounting is relevant to the special purpose F/S, the auditor should still:

    - Determine whether there are conditions or events that raise substantial doubt about the entity's ability to continue as a going concern

    - Assess whether financial statement disclosures are adequate if such doubt exists

- Whether the F/S adequately refer to or describe the AFRF, including:
  - Whether the F/S are *suitably titled* (eg, "Statement of Income—Regulatory Basis" instead of "Statement of Income").
  - Whether the F/S include a summary of *significant accounting policies*.
  - Whether the F/S adequately describe the *material differences* in how the special purpose framework differs from GAAP.
  - If the F/S are prepared in accordance with a contractual basis of accounting, whether the F/S adequately describe any *significant interpretations of the contract* on which the F/S are based.
- Whether the F/S are fairly presented:
  - When the special purpose F/S contain items that are similar to those in F/S prepared in accordance with GAAP, whether the F/S include informative disclosures similar to those required by GAAP.
  - Whether additional disclosures are necessary to achieve fair presentation (eg, disclosures regarding related-party transactions, restrictions on assets/owners' equity, subsequent events, and significant uncertainties).
- Whether the auditor's report requires:
  - A description of the purpose for which the F/S were prepared or a reference to a note in the F/S with this information (generally for *regulatory or contractual basis* of accounting)
  - An explanation of management's responsibility for the F/S that references its responsibility for determining that the AFRF is acceptable in the circumstances (necessary when management has a choice of FRFs)
  - An emphasis-of-matter paragraph that:
    - Alerts users with respect to the special purpose framework and that it is a basis of accounting other than GAAP used to prepare the F/S
    - Refers to the notes in the F/S that describes the framework
    - Indicates the F/S may not be suitable for another purpose (when a description of the purpose of the F/S is included)
  - An other-matter paragraph that restricts the use of the report to certain parties to avoid misunderstandings (generally when the F/S are prepared under a *regulatory or contractual basis* of accounting)
  - An opinion as to whether the F/S are presented fairly in accordance with GAAP in addition to the opinion regarding the special purpose framework, instead of the other-matter and emphasis-of-matter paragraphs described above (only applicable for *Regulatory Basis F/S for General Use*)

Special Purpose Framework Report (OCBOA) Example

INDEPENDENT AUDITOR'S REPORT

To: The Board of Directors of X Company

Report on the Audit of Financial Statements

Opinion

We have audited the financial statements of ABC Partnership, which comprise the **statement of assets and liabilities arising from cash transactions** as of December 31, 20X1, and the related statement of revenue collected and expenses paid for the year then ended, and the related notes to the financial statements.

In our opinion, the accompanying financial statements present fairly, in all material respects, the assets and liabilities arising from cash transactions of ABC Partnership as of December 31, 20X1, and its revenue collected and expenses paid during the year then ended **in accordance with the cash basis of accounting** described in Note X.

Basis for Opinion

We conducted our audit in accordance with auditing standards generally accepted in the United States of America (GAAS). Our responsibilities under those standards are further described in the Auditor's Responsibilities for the Audit of the Financial Statements section of our report. We are **required to be independent** of ABC Partnership, and to meet our other ethical responsibilities, in accordance with the relevant ethical requirements relating to our audit. We believe that the audit evidence we have obtained is sufficient and appropriate to provide a basis for our audit opinion.

Emphasis of Matter — Basis of Accounting

We draw attention to Note X of the financial statements, which describes the basis of accounting. The financial statements are prepared on the cash basis of accounting, which is a basis of accounting other than accounting principles generally accepted in the United States of America. Our opinion is not modified with respect to this matter.

Responsibilities of Management for the Financial Statements

Management is responsible for the preparation and fair presentation of the financial statements in accordance with the cash basis of accounting described in Note X, and for determining that the cash basis of accounting is an acceptable basis for the preparation of the financial statements in the circumstances. Management is also responsible for the design, implementation, and maintenance of internal control relevant to the preparation and fair presentation of financial statements that are free from material misstatement, whether due to fraud or error.

Auditor's Responsibilities for the Audit of the Financial Statements

Our objectives are to obtain reasonable assurance about whether the financial statements as a whole are free from material misstatement, whether due to fraud or error, and to issue an auditor's report that includes our opinion. Reasonable assurance is a high level of assurance but is not absolute assurance and therefore is not a guarantee that an audit conducted in accordance with GAAS will always detect a material misstatement when it exists. The risk of not detecting a material misstatement resulting from fraud is higher than for one resulting from error, as fraud may involve collusion, forgery, intentional omissions, misrepresentations, or the override of internal control. Misstatements are considered material if there is a substantial likelihood that, individually or in the aggregate, they would influence the judgment made by a reasonable user based on the financial statements.

In performing an audit in accordance with GAAS, we:

- Exercise professional judgment and maintain professional skepticism throughout the audit.

- Identify and assess the risks of material misstatement of the financial statements, whether due to fraud or error, and design and perform audit procedures responsive to those risks. Such procedures include examining, on a test basis, evidence regarding the amounts and disclosures in the financial statements.

- Obtain an understanding of internal control relevant to the audit in order to design audit procedures that are appropriate in the circumstances, but not for the purpose of expressing an opinion on the effectiveness of ABC Partnership's internal control. Accordingly, no such opinion is expressed.

- Evaluate the appropriateness of accounting policies used and the reasonableness of significant accounting estimates made by management, as well as evaluate the overall presentation of the financial statements.

- Conclude whether, in our judgment, there are conditions or events, considered in the aggregate, that raise substantial doubt about ABC Partnership's ability to continue as a going concern for a reasonable period of time.

We are required to communicate with those charged with governance regarding, among other matters, the planned scope and timing of the audit, significant audit findings, and certain internal control-related matters that we identified during the audit.

Report on Other Legal and Regulatory Requirements

[Form and content of this section of the auditor's report will vary depending on the nature of the auditor's other reporting responsibilities.]

L.F. Rosenthal, CPA
Auditor's city and state
March 1, 20X2

Note: An accountant may be asked to compile or review OCBOA statements of a nonpublic entity. In that case, the accountant will apply SSARS to such an engagement, as discussed earlier.

Completing a Prescribed Audit Report Form of a Government Agency on Behalf of the Client

When an accountant is asked to follow an audit report form, layout or wording prescribed by law or a regulatory agency (AU-C 800), the report should only refer to GAAS if the report includes all the following:

- Title
- Addressee
- Introductory paragraph identifying the special purpose financial statements audited
- Description of management's responsibility
  - For the preparation and fair presentation of the special purpose statements
  - For determining that the applicable financial reporting framework is acceptable under the circumstances
- When prepared in accordance with a regulatory or contractual basis, a description of the purpose for which the financial statements are prepared
- Description of the auditor's responsibility to express an opinion, including:
  - Reference to GAAS and, if appropriate, the law or regulation
  - Description of an audit in accordance with the standards
- Opinion paragraph
- Emphasis-of-matter paragraph
- Other-matter paragraph restricting the use of the report
- Auditor's signature and city and state
- Date of report

If the report is intended for general distribution, the auditor will not include the emphasis-of-matter or other-matter paragraph and will, instead, express an opinion as to whether or not the financial statements are in conformity with GAAP.

If the prescribed form of the report differs significantly from GAAS, and the auditor is worried that users might misunderstand the audit report, the auditor may:

- Reword the prescribed form and sign it, or

- Attach a separate audit report to the form, or

- The auditor should NOT accept the audit engagement (unless required by law or regulation).

Reporting on Compliance with Contracts or Regulatory Requirements in Connection with Audited F/S

When the auditor is asked to verify compliance with contractual agreements (such as a loan agreement) or regulatory requirements related to the F/S, the resulting report is generally referred to as a "by-product report." (AU-C 806) Such report should include:

- The accountant's findings in an other-matter paragraph or a separate report.
    - The auditor should state that nothing came to the auditor's attention to suggest the client had not complied with all requirements if:
        - The auditor found no instances of noncompliance,
        - An unmodified or qualified opinion has been expressed on the related F/S, and
        - The applicable requirements relate to accounting matters subjected to audit procedures during the audit of the F/S.
    - Otherwise, each instance of noncompliance should be described.
    - If an **adverse opinion or disclaimer of opinion** has been expressed on the F/S, a compliance report should *not* be issued unless there are instances of noncompliance.

- A statement indicating that the audit was not directed primarily toward obtaining knowledge regarding compliance, and thus, had additional procedures been performed, other matters may have come to the auditor's attention regarding noncompliance.

- A description and the source of *significant interpretations* made by management relating to the provisions of the contractual or regulatory requirement.

- An alert that restricts the use of the report.

Note: AU-C 935, Compliance Audits, applies if the auditor is engaged, or required by law, to perform a compliance audit in accordance with GAAS, GAGAS, or some other governmental audit requirement that requires the expression of an opinion on compliance. AT-C 315, Compliance Attestation, applies if the auditor is engaged to perform a separate attestation engagement on an entity's compliance with certain requirements or the effectiveness of the entity's internal control over compliance with certain requirements. These engagements are discussed later in this section.

Overview

Ever since the first accounting firm was asked to count the ballots at the Academy Awards, CPA firms have been expanding into areas beyond historical F/S. These now include engagements to verify the accuracy and security of websites, the truth of advertising claims, the completeness of personal disclosures by political candidates, internal control opinions, prospective information and compliance with contracts or laws and regulations.

The AICPA uses the term **attestation engagement** to refer to three types of engagements performed under the attestation standards (SSAEs[2]) related to **subject matter or an assertion** that is the responsibility of another party.[3] (AT-C 105)

In this section, we'll focus our attention on:

- The concepts that are common to all attestation engagements, and

- The three levels of attestation engagements (**ERA**):

  - **Examination –** An engagement in which the accountant (practitioner) expresses an **opinion** (*reasonable assurance*) about the subject matter or assertion of another party. The work performed will involve a level of service comparable to audits of historical F/S.

  - **Review –** An engagement in which the accountant expresses a **conclusion** with **limited assurance** (ie, *negative assurance*) on the subject matter or assertion. Procedures such as inquiry of the other party as to the methods used and analytical procedures applied to numerical information related to the assertion will be performed.

  - **Agreed-upon procedures –** An engagement in which the accountant issues a report on their **findings** (*no opinion or conclusion*) regarding **specific procedures** applied to subject matter. The procedures will depend on the agreement made among the parties to the engagement.

> The mnemonic **ERA** reminds us that attestation standards are part of a new era in which accountants are performing engagements that go beyond reports on historical F/S.

The different types of subject matters will be covered in the next section.

---

[2] *Statements on Standards for Attestation Engagements*

[3] *SSAEs do not apply to other professional services for which other standards are established, such as audits under the SASs, compilations and reviews of F/S under the SSARSs, (3) tax services under the SSTSs, or litigation services under the SSCSs.*

Common Concepts

The following requirements are applicable to all attestation engagements. (AT-C 105)

Preconditions for Acceptance

- All attestation engagements require that the accountant be **independent** of the party whose assertion is being evaluated, unless the accountant is required by law or regulation to accept the engagement.

- The **responsible party** (eg, senior management), not the accountant, assumes responsibility for the subject matter.

- The **subject matter is appropriate**. That is, can it be identified and measured or evaluated against specific criteria?

- The **criteria** to be applied is **appropriate** and will be available to the users.

- The accountant expects to be able to obtain sufficient evidence to provide an opinion, conclusion, or findings. This means the accountant will have **access to all relevant information** as well as individuals who may provide such evidence.

- The accountant's opinion, conclusion, or findings will be contained in a **written report**, as appropriate.

Prescribed Forms

When an accountant is required to use a specified report form, layout, or wording prescribed by law or a regulatory agency, and the *prescribed form is unacceptable*, the auditor should:

- Reword the prescribed form, or

- Attach a separate, appropriately worded report.

Change of Engagement

If the client decides to *change the terms of the engagement* after acceptance, the accountant should only agree to such a change when there is *reasonable justification* for doing so. If the change is made during the engagement, evidence obtained prior to the change cannot be disregarded. As long as the accountant complies with the standards for the new level of service, the accountant should issue the appropriate report and should *not* make reference to:

- The original engagement,

- Any procedures performed, or

- Any scope limitations that resulted in the changed engagement.

Using the Work of Another

When the accountant uses the *work of another accountant*, the accountant should:

- Determine whether the other accountant is independent and understands the applicable ethical requirements.

- Determine whether the other accountant is professionally competent.

- Communicate the scope and timing of the other accountant's work.
- Evaluate whether the other accountant's work is adequate.
- Determine whether the report should reference the work of the other practitioner.

Engagement Documentation Requirements

With regard to engagement documentation, the accountant should:

- Prepare it on a timely basis (ie, as the work is performed or shortly after).
- Assemble the final engagement file within 60 days of the accountant's report release date.
- Retain all documentation after the documentation completion date for the appropriate retention period. If it is necessary to add or discard any documentation after such time, the specific reasons for the changes, who made the changes, and the date of such changes should be documented.
- Adopt reasonable procedures to keep the documentation confidential and prevent unauthorized access.
- Include written justification for departing from any presumptively mandatory requirements (ie, requirements specified with "should" rather than "must") and how alternative procedures achieved the intent of the requirement.

Examination Engagements

In addition to the concepts applicable to *all attestation engagements*, all *examination engagements* (eg, the examination of prospective financial information) are subject to another set of requirements specific to examinations under AT-C 205.

An examination, you might remember, is a level of service comparable to audits of historical F/S, involving the expression of an **opinion** (*reasonable assurance*) about the subject matter or written assertion of another party. With this type of engagement, the accountant should:

- Specify the terms of the engagement in an **engagement letter** or other written agreement, including:
  - o The objective and scope of the engagement
  - o Responsibilities of the practitioner
  - o A statement that the engagement will be conducted in accordance with SSAEs
  - o Responsibilities of the responsible/engaging party
  - o Inherent limitations of the engagement
  - o The criteria for measuring, evaluating, or disclosing the subject matter
  - o An agreement by the engaging party (eg, those charged with governance) to provide a representation letter at the conclusion of the engagement
- Request a **written assertion** from the responsible party regarding measurement/evaluation of the subject matter.
  - o If the responsible party is *not* the engaging party and refuses to comply, the accountant must disclose the refusal in the report and restrict the report to the engaging party.

- o If the responsible party *is* also the engaging party and they refuse to comply, the accountant must withdraw from the engagement, or disclaim an opinion if law/regulation prevents withdrawal.

- Establish an **overall engagement strategy**, which sets the scope, timing and direction of the engagement and assists in the development of the engagement plan.

- Develop an **engagement plan** that includes the nature, timing, and extent of procedures to be performed, including risk assessment procedures.

- Obtain an **understanding** of the subject matter and relevant circumstances (including internal controls over the preparation of the subject matter) to be able to:

  - o Identify and assess the risks of material misstatement, and

  - o Design procedures to respond to such risks and obtain reasonable assurance to support the opinion.

- Consider **materiality** for the subject matter when establishing the overall engagement strategy, and reconsider materiality if new information brings it into question.

- Obtain **sufficient appropriate evidence** to reduce attestation risk to an acceptably low level.

- Design and perform **tests of controls** if:

  - o The accountant intends to rely on the operating effectiveness of controls in determining the nature, timing, and extent of other procedures;

  - o If other procedures will not provide sufficient appropriate evidence alone; or

  - o If the subject matter itself is internal control.

- Design and perform **tests of details** or **analytical procedures** (unless the subject matter is internal control).

- Consider and inquire as to whether there are any indications of **fraud or noncompliance** with laws/regulations.

- Consider and inquire about **subsequent events** (ie, events occurring after the period covered by the engagement up to the report date) and **subsequently discovered facts** (ie, facts discovered after the report date).

- Request **written representations** (in the form of a letter to the accountant as of the date of the report) from:

  - o The responsible party regarding the assertion, relevant matters, their responsibilities, subsequent events, immaterial uncorrected misstatements, etc.; and

  - o The engaging party (if a separate party) regarding the responsible party's responsibilities, their lack of knowledge of any material misstatements, subsequent events, etc.

- **Read other information** in the document that will contain the accountant's report to identify any material inconsistencies.

- **Evaluate the results** of the procedures, **form an opinion,** and **prepare a written report** on a written assertion or on the subject matter directly.

  - o If the accountant was *unable to obtain sufficient appropriate evidence or the subject matter is not in accordance with the specified criteria*, in all material respects, and the effect of any such insufficiencies are *material*, the opinion should be modified and a separate paragraph describing such matters should be included in the report.

    - ▪ **Qualified opinion** – Effects are *material, but not pervasive*

- **Adverse opinion** – Misstatements are *material and pervasive*

- **Disclaimer of opinion** – Unable to obtain sufficient appropriate evidence (ie, scope limitation) and effects *could be material and pervasive*

o When the opinion is modified, external specialists can be referenced in the report if it is relevant to the opinion; however, they should not be referenced when the opinion is unmodified.

o The report should include a separate paragraph that restricts the use of the report when:

- The criteria used are appropriate for, or available to, only specified parties, or

- The responsible party is *not* the engaging party and refuses to comply with the request for written representations, but does provide oral responses, the report should be restricted to the engaging party.

 CPA candidates could be asked to prepare an examination report on the exam starting with a report example, such as one of those that follow. This does not mean that you need to memorize each report; just be familiar with their differences.

 Examination Report on Subject Matter – Unmodified Opinion

INDEPENDENT ACCOUNTANT'S REPORT

To: Appropriate addressee

We have **examined** [identify the subject matter, for example, the accompanying schedule of investment returns of XYZ Company for the year ended December 31, 20XX]. XYZ Company's management is responsible for [identify the subject matter, for example, presenting the schedule of investment returns] in accordance with (or based on) [identify the criteria, for example, the ABC criteria set forth in Note 1]. Our responsibility is to express an **opinion** on [identify the subject matter, for example, the schedule of investment returns] based on our examination.

Our examination was conducted in accordance with **attestation standards** established by the American Institute of Certified Public Accountants. Those standards require that we plan and perform the examination to obtain reasonable assurance about whether [*identify the subject matter, for example, the schedule of investment returns*] is in accordance with (or based on) the **criteria**, in all material respects. An examination involves performing procedures to obtain evidence about [*identify the subject matter, for example, the schedule of investment returns*]. The nature, timing, and extent of the procedures selected depend on our judgment, including an assessment of the risks of material misstatement of [*identify the subject matter, for example, the schedule of investment returns*], whether due to fraud or error. We believe that the evidence we obtained is sufficient and appropriate to provide a reasonable basis for our opinion.

[Include a description of significant **inherent limitations**, if any, associated with the measurement or evaluation of the subject matter against the criteria.]

[*Additional paragraph(s) may be added to **emphasize certain matters** relating to the attestation engagement or the subject matter.*]

In our opinion, [identify the subject matter, for example, the schedule of investment returns of XYZ Company for the year ended December 31, 20XX or the schedule of investment returns referred to above], is presented **in accordance with** (or based on) [identify **the criteria**, for example, the ABC criteria set forth in Note 1], in all material respects.

Asher P. Levy, CPA
Santa Ana, CA
March 1, 20XX

Examination Report on Subject Matter – Qualified Opinion

INDEPENDENT ACCOUNTANT'S REPORT

To: Appropriate addressee

***

Our examination disclosed [describe condition(s) that, individually or in the aggregate, resulted in a material misstatement or deviation from the criteria].

In our opinion, **except for** the material misstatement [or deviation from the criteria] described in the preceding paragraph, [identify the subject matter, for example, the accompanying schedule of investment returns of XYZ Company for the year ended December 31, 20XX, or the schedule of investment returns referred to above], is **presented in accordance** with (or based on) [identify **the criteria**, for example, the ABC criteria set forth in Note 1], in all material respects.

Alexes B. Ruiz, CPA
Santa Ana, CA
March 1, 20XX

Examination – Disclaimer of Opinion

INDEPENDENT ACCOUNTANT'S REPORT

To: Appropriate addressee

We were engaged to examine [identify the subject matter, for example, the accompanying schedule of investment returns of XYZ Company for the year ended December 31, 20XX], in accordance with (or based on) [identify the criteria, for example, the ABC criteria set forth in Note 1]. XYZ Company's **management is responsible** for [identify the subject matter, for example, presenting the schedule of investment returns]. **Our responsibility** is to express an opinion on [identify the subject matter, for example, the schedule of investment returns] based on conducting the examination in accordance with attestation standards established by the American Institute of Certified Public Accountants.

[Include a paragraph to describe scope limitations.]

Because of the limitation on the scope of our examination discussed in the preceding paragraph, the scope of our work was not sufficient to enable us to express, and **we do not express**, an opinion on whether [*identify the subject matter, for example, the accompanying schedule of investment returns of XYZ Company for the year ended December 31, 20XX, or the schedule of investment returns referred to above*] is in accordance with (or based on) [*identify the criteria, for example, the ABC criteria set forth in Note 1*], in all material respects.

Darren Chris, CPA
Santa Ana, CA
March 1, 20XX

Review Engagements

As previously discussed, a review engagement under the attestation standards is one in which the accountant expresses a **conclusion** with **limited assurance** (ie, negative assurance) about whether the *subject matter or assertion* of another party is fairly stated. Procedures for such engagements are generally limited to **inquiries** and **analytical procedures**.

As we have already covered reviews of F/S under SSARSs (in another section), the concepts common to all attestation engagements, as well as examination engagements under the attestation standards (ie, SSAEs) in great detail, we will only discuss the differences in the reporting requirements under AT-C 210 here.

In a review engagement, the accountant will evaluate the results of the procedures and **form a conclusion** as to whether there are any material modifications that need to be made to:

- The subject matter in order for it to be in accordance with the criteria, or
- The responsible party's assertion in order for it to be fairly stated.

In forming this conclusion, the accountant should evaluate whether sufficient appropriate evidence was obtained and whether any uncorrected misstatements are material, individually or collectively.

- If the accountant is aware of an uncorrected misstatement in the subject matter, the accountant should consider whether **qualification of the conclusion** is sufficient to disclose the matter (if not, withdraw).

  o **Qualified conclusion** – Effects are *material, but not pervasive*

    ▪ Include a separate paragraph in the report providing a description of the misstatement.

    ▪ Report directly on the subject matter rather than the assertion (even if it acknowledges the misstatement).

  o **Withdraw, if possible** – Unable to obtain sufficient appropriate evidence (ie, scope limitation) or misstatements are *material and pervasive*

    ▪ This generally includes being unable to obtain written representations. In some cases, oral representations may be accepted.

Please note that reviews are generally *prohibited* for the following:

- Prospective financial information
- Internal control
- Compliance with laws, rules, regulations, contracts, and grants

 CPA candidates could be asked to prepare a review report on the exam starting with a report example, such as one of those that follow. This does not mean that you need to memorize each report; just be familiar with their differences.

Review Report on Subject Matter – Unmodified Conclusion

INDEPENDENT ACCOUNTANT'S REVIEW REPORT

To: Appropriate addressee

We have **reviewed** [identify the subject matter, for example, the accompanying schedule of investment returns of XYZ Company for the year ended December 31, 20XX]. XYZ Company's management is responsible for [identify the subject matter, for example, presenting the schedule of investment returns] in accordance with (or based on) [identify the **criteria**, for example, the ABC criteria set forth in Note 1]. Our responsibility is to express a **conclusion** on [identify the subject matter, for example, the schedule of investment returns] based on our **review**.

Our **review** was conducted in accordance with attestation standards established by the American Institute of Certified Public Accountants. Those standards require that we plan and perform the **review** to obtain **limited assurance** about whether any material modifications should be made to [identify the subject matter, for example, the schedule of investment returns] in order for it to be **in accordance with** (or based on) the **criteria.** A review is substantially **less in scope than an examination,** the objective of which is to obtain reasonable assurance about whether [identify the subject matter, for example, the schedule of investment returns] is in accordance with (or based on) the criteria, in all material respects, in order to express an opinion. Accordingly, we **do not express such an opinion.** We believe that our review provides a **reasonable basis for our conclusion.**

[Include a description of significant inherent limitations, if any, associated with the measurement or evaluation of the subject matter against the criteria.]

[Additional paragraph(s) may be added to emphasize certain matters relating to the attestation engagement or the subject matter.]

Based on our review, we are **not aware of any material modifications that should be made** to [identify the subject matter, for example, the accompanying schedule of investment returns of XYZ Company for the year ended December 31, 20XX], in order for it be **in accordance with** (or based on) [identify the criteria, for example, the ABC criteria set forth in Note 1].

Kristin Charberts, CPA
Santa Ana, CA
March 1, 20XX

Review Report on Subject Matter – Qualified Conclusion

INDEPENDENT ACCOUNTANT'S REVIEW REPORT

To: Appropriate addressee
***

Our review disclosed [describe condition(s) that, individually or in the aggregate, resulted in a **material misstatement or deviation** from the criteria].

Based on our review, **except for the matter(s) described** in the preceding paragraph, we are **not aware of any material modifications** that should be made to [*identify the subject matter, for example, the accompanying schedule of investment returns of XYZ Company for the year ended December 31, 20XX*], in order for it to be in accordance with (or based on) [*identify the criteria, for example, the ABC criteria set forth in Note 1*].

Wendy Robson, CPA
Santa Ana, CA
March 1, 20XX

Agreed-Upon Procedures Engagements

AT-C 215 provides requirements applicable to agreed-upon procedures engagements in addition to the requirements applicable to all attestation engagements under AT-C 105.

As previously discussed, an agreed-upon procedures engagement is one in which the practitioner issues a report on their **findings** (*no opinion or conclusion*) with regard to **specific procedures** applied to subject matter. The procedures:

- Will depend on the agreement made among the parties to the engagement.
- May be developed over the course of the engagement with the assistance of the practitioner.
- Must be agreed to and acknowledged as appropriate by the engaging party prior to the issuance of the report.
  - If necessary, other parties may also need to agree to the appropriateness of the procedures to be performed.
  - The engaging parties and intended users assess for themselves the engagement findings and draw their own conclusions from the work performed.

With regard to this type of engagement, the practitioner should:

- *Not* accept the engagement if the practitioner believes the intended purpose of the engagement is not clear or the engaging party will not have a basis for agreeing and acknowledging that the procedures are appropriate.
- *Not* agree to perform procedures that are described by terms that are too generic or open to interpretation (eg, general review, limited review, check, or test). Also, merely reading certain information about the subject matter does not constitute a procedure that is worthy of being reported upon.
- **Obtain evidence** from applying only the agreed-upon procedures; the practitioner does not need to perform additional procedures beyond the scope of the engagement.
- **Request a written representation letter** from the engaging party that states that:
  - The responsible party is responsible for the subject matter.
  - It has obtained agreement and acknowledgment as to the appropriateness of the procedures from all necessary parties (if applicable).
  - All relevant information and access as agreed upon has been provided.
  - All known matters contradicting the subject matter and any communication from regulatory agencies or others affecting the subject matter have been disclosed to the practitioner.
  - It is not aware of any material misstatements in the subject matter.
- **Include in the report**, among other things:
  - Identification of the engaging party, subject matter, responsible party, and intended purpose of the engagement
  - A description of:
    - The **procedures performed**, including their nature, extent, and timing (if applicable)
    - The **findings** (avoiding any vague or ambiguous language)
    - Any **exceptions** found and the agreed-upon **thresholds** (ie, materiality limits) for reporting such exceptions

- Reservations or restrictions concerning procedures/findings, if applicable
- Any matters brought to the practitioner's attention outside of the agreed-upon procedures if they significantly contradict the subject matter or assertion (eg, a material weakness in internal control)
- The nature of the assistance provided by a practitioner's external specialist, If applicable

o Statements that indicate:

- The engaging party acknowledged that the procedures performed are appropriate to meet the intended purpose of the engagement.
- The report may not be suitable for any other purpose.
- Procedures performed may not address all the items of interest to a report user and may not meet the needs of all users and, as such, users are responsible for determining whether the procedures performed are appropriate for their purposes.
- An agreed-upon procedures engagement involves the practitioner performing specific procedures that the engaging party has agreed to and acknowledged to be appropriate for the intended purpose of the engagement and reporting on findings based on the procedures performed.
- The engagement was conducted in accordance with attestation standards established by the AICPA.
- The practitioner was not engaged to and did not conduct an examination or review, the objective of which would be the expression of an opinion or conclusion, respectively. Thus, no opinion or conclusion is expressed.
- Had additional procedures been performed, other matters might have come to the practitioner's attention that would have been reported.
- The practitioner is required to be independent of the responsible party and to meet other ethical responsibilities, in accordance with the relevant ethical requirements relating to the agreed-upon procedures engagement.

o An **alert that restricts the use** of the report, if appropriate

CPA candidates could be asked to prepare a review report on the exam starting with a report example, like the one that follows. This does not mean that you need to memorize each report; just be familiar with it.

Agreed-Upon Procedures Report Example (with optional restriction alert)

INDEPENDENT PRACTITIONER'S REPORT

To: Appropriate addressee

We have performed the procedures enumerated below on [identify the subject matter, for example, the financial accounts of the engaging party during the year ended December 31, 20XX]. [The responsible party] is responsible for [the subject matter].

[The engaging party] has agreed to and acknowledged that the procedures performed are appropriate to meet the intended purpose of [identify the intended purpose of the engagement, for example, assisting users in understanding the financial accounts of the engaging party during the year ended December 31, 20XX]. **This report may not be suitable for any other purpose.** The procedures performed may not address all the items of interest to a user of this report and may not meet the needs of all users of this report and, as such, users are responsible for determining whether the procedures performed are appropriate for their purposes.

The procedures and the associated findings are as follows:

*[Include paragraphs to describe the **procedures performed** detailing the nature and extent, and if applicable, the timing, of each procedure and to describe the **findings** from each procedure performed, including sufficient details on **exceptions found**.]*

We were engaged by *[the engaging party]* to perform this agreed-upon procedures engagement and conducted our engagement in accordance with **attestation standards** established by the AICPA. We were not engaged to and did not conduct an examination or review engagement, the objective of which would be the expression of an opinion or conclusion, respectively, on *[identify the subject matter]*. Accordingly, **we do not express such an opinion or conclusion**. Had we performed additional procedures, other matters might have come to our attention that would have been reported to you.

We are required to be **independent** of *[the responsible party]* and to meet our other ethical responsibilities, in accordance with the relevant ethical requirements related to our agreed-upon procedures engagement.

This report is intended solely for the information and use of *[identify the specified parties, for example, the engaging party and the State of XXX]*, and is not intended to be, and should not be, used by anyone other than these specified parties.

[Additional paragraphs may be added to describe other matters.]

Jae Evers, CPA
Santa Ana, CA
March 1, 20XX*

* The report should be dated no earlier than the date on which the practitioner completed the procedures and determined the findings.

Summary of Differences Between Services

SSAE Comparison Chart (ERA)			
Requirements	**Examination**	**Review**	**Agreed-Upon Procedures**
Maintain independence	Yes	Yes	Yes
Obtain signed engagement letter	Yes	Yes	Yes
Request written assertion regarding measurement/evaluation of subject matter	Yes	Yes	No
Obtain understanding of subject matter and relevant circumstances	Sufficient to assess RMM	Sufficient to achieve objectives of engagement	No
Consider materiality	Yes	Yes	No, unless thresholds are agreed-upon

SSAE Comparison Chart (ERA)			
Requirements	**Examination**	**Review**	**Agreed-Upon Procedures**
Obtain sufficient appropriate evidence	Yes	Yes	No
Design/perform tests of controls	If relying on controls	No	No
Testing of subject matter	Tests of details / analytical procedures	Generally only inquiries / analytical procedures	Agreed-upon procedures
Inquire about fraud or noncompliance	Yes	Yes	No
Inquire about subsequent events	Yes	Yes	No

Request written representations from responsible/engaging parties	Yes	Yes	Yes
Read other information for material inconsistencies	Yes	Yes	No
Written report	Opinion	Conclusion	Findings
Level of assurance	Reasonable	Limited	None
Restriction on use	If necessary	If necessary	If necessary

Prospective Financial Statements

Prospective financial statements (AT-C 305) present expected or hypothetical future results of an entity. There are two different types of prospective statements:

- **Forecast** – This presents what management **expects to occur** in the future based on expected conditions and expected courses of action.

- **Projection** – This presents what management believes will occur given certain **hypothetical assumptions** based on a "what if" scenario.

For example, a drug manufacturer might be expecting to receive government approval for a new drug and will prepare a financial forecast based on expected results over the next few years given approval of the drug. The manufacturer may also prepare a financial projection on expected results over the next few years in the event the new drug does not receive approval.

Although a financial **forecast** is based on certain *significant assumptions* made by management about the future, the assumptions are general in nature, regarding factors that will affect the entity's performance. These may include the economy; competition; the availability of resources, capital, and employees; demand; and comparable factors. As a result, a forecast is appropriate for either **general or limited use.**

A financial **projection** is based on *hypothetical propositions*, which are assumptions about events or transactions that may not actually be expected to occur. As a result, a projection is only appropriate for **limited use** by parties with whom the entity is negotiating directly and who are aware of the use of the assumptions.

When third-party users seek some level of assurance regarding prospective F/S, a practitioner may perform an attestation engagement to provide that assurance. There are two different types of engagements that a practitioner may undertake in connection with prospective F/S:

- **Examination** – The practitioner expresses an opinion on the prospective statements.

- **Agreed-Upon Procedures** – The practitioner applies tests that are the result of an agreement between the CPA, the client, and a third party with whom the client is negotiating.

  Note: As previously mentioned, a review of prospective F/S is not allowed. Also, while compilations of prospective F/S are allowed, they are not attestation engagements and are thus covered under SSARS.

As is true for all attestation engagements, the practitioner is required to comply with the requirements of the section of the attestation standards that is applicable to the specific engagement, as well as with AT-C 105, *Concepts Common to All Attestation Engagements*, discussed above.

Examinations of Prospective Financial Statements

The objective of an examination of prospective financial is for the practitioner to obtain, and to convey in a written report, reasonable assurance that the presentation of prospective information conforms, in all material respects, to the guidelines established by the AICPA for the presentation of prospective information and that the assumptions underlying the forecast, or the assumptions underlying the projection, are suitably supported and provide a reasonable basis for the responsible party's forecast, or the responsible party's projection given the hypothetical assumptions.

Before a practitioner agrees to be associated with a projection, the practitioner should determine that the projection will only be distributed to parties that are negotiating directly with the responsible party since a projection is not appropriate for general use.

A practitioner should *not* agree to:

- Examine a forecast if the responsible party does not agree to disclose significant assumptions.

- Examine a projection if the responsible party either does not agree to disclose significant assumptions or does not identify the hypothetical assumptions or describe the limitations of the presentation.

- Examine a partial presentation that does not describe the limitations on the usefulness of the presentation.

As preconditions for an examination engagement, the practitioner should understand the guidelines for preparation and presentation in the AICPA guide and have or obtain knowledge of the industry in which the entity operates and the accounting principles and practices appropriate for it.

The practitioner should obtain a written assertion from the client and develop an overall strategy for the engagement that sets the scope, timing, and direction of the engagement. The procedures applied in the examination engagement should take into account the nature and materiality of the information; knowledge obtained in the current and previous engagements; the competence of the responsible party; the extent to which the prospective financial information is affected by the responsible party's judgment; and the available support for the responsible party's assumptions.

The practitioner will perform those procedures the practitioner considers necessary to report on whether the assumptions are suitably supported and provide a reasonable basis for the forecast or provide a reasonable basis for the projection taking into account the hypothetical assumption. The practitioner will evaluate the preparation and presentation of the prospective financial information to obtain reasonable assurance as to whether the presentation reflects the identified assumptions; computations are mathematically accurate; assumptions are internally consistent; accounting principles applied are appropriate; the prospective financial information is presented in accordance with AICPA guidelines; and that the assumptions are adequately disclosed.

The report following an **examination** must include the following:

- A title that includes the word independent.

- An appropriate addressee.

- Identification of the prospective financial information being reported on and the time period it relates to.

- An indication that the prospective financial information was evaluated against guidelines established by the AICPA.

- A statement identifying the responsible party, indicating their responsibility for the preparation and presentation of the prospective financial information in accordance with the AICPA guidelines.

- The practitioner's responsibility for expressing an opinion on the prospective financial information.

- A statement that the examination was performed in accordance with the AICPA attestation standards, which require the practitioner to plan and perform the engagement to obtain reasonable assurance that the AICPA guidelines were followed and that the practitioner believes that the examination provided a reasonable basis for the opinion.

- A description of the nature of an examination.

- An **opinion** as to whether the statements conform to AICPA presentation guidelines and the underlying assumptions provide a reasonable basis for the presentation.

- A warning (Caveat) that the prospective **results may not be achieved.**

- A statement that the practitioner has **no responsibility to update** the report for events occurring after the report date.

- The manual or printed signature of the practitioner or the practitioner's firm.

- The practitioner's city and state.

- The date of the report.

- For **projections**, a separate paragraph with an indication of the **limitations on the usefulness** of the presentation.

  o "The accompanying projection and this report are intended solely for the information and use of [*identify specified parties, for example, XYZ Company and DEF National Bank*], and are not intended to be and should not be used by anyone other than these specified parties."

 Examination Report of a Financial Forecast

INDEPENDENT PRACTITIONER'S REPORT

To: Appropriate addressee

We have **examined** the accompanying forecast of XYZ Company, which comprises the forecasted balance sheet as of December 31, 20XX, and the related forecasted statements of income, retained earnings, and cash flows for the year then ended, based on the guidelines for the presentation of a forecast established by the American Institute of Certified Public Accountants. XYZ Company's management is responsible for preparing and presenting the forecast in accordance with the guidelines for the presentation of a forecast established by the American Institute of Certified Public Accountants. Our responsibility is to express an opinion on the forecast based on our examination.

Our examination was conducted in accordance with **attestation standards established by the American Institute of Certified Public Accountants**. Those standards require that we plan and perform the examination to obtain reasonable assurance about whether the forecast is presented in accordance with the guidelines for the presentation of a forecast established by the American Institute of Certified Public Accountants, in all material respects. An examination involves performing procedures to obtain evidence about the forecast. The nature, timing, and extent of the procedures selected depend on our judgment, including an assessment of the risks of material misstatement of the forecast, whether due to fraud or error. We believe that the evidence we obtained is sufficient and appropriate to provide a reasonable basis for our opinion.

In our opinion, the accompanying forecast is presented, in all material respects, in accordance with the guidelines for presentation of a forecast established by the American Institute of Certified Public Accountants, and the underlying assumptions are reasonably supported and provide a reasonable basis for management's forecast.

There will usually be **differences** between the forecasted and actual results, because events and circumstances frequently do not occur as expected, and those differences may be material. We have **no responsibility to update** this report for events and circumstances occurring after the date of this report.

Jessica Daubson, CPA
Santa Ana, CA
March 1, 20XX

For **agreed-upon procedures**, the report must include the following:

- The **findings** of the practitioner resulting from the procedures.

- A statement that the procedures applied **may not be sufficient**, and that the specified users accept responsibility for this fact.

- A warning (Caveat) that the prospective **results may not be achieved.**

- A statement that the practitioner has **no responsibility to update** the report for events occurring after the report date.

- A separate paragraph with an indication of the **limitations on the usefulness** of the presentation.

- A summary of **significant assumptions** is also required.

Summary – Prospective Financial Statements
- **Forecast** (General Use) → Expects to occur
- **Projection** (Limited Use ⇒ Add a Middle ¶) → "Hypothetical" – May or may not occur; Can only give it to people directly negotiating with you
1. **Examination → Giving an Opinion**
a. Met AICPA minimum presentation guidelines
b. F/S reasonable given assumptions
o If not, called partial presentation (limited use)   } Opinion
2. **Agreed-Upon Procedures**
a. Only going to do procedures you told us to do
b. Distribution & Use is Limited   ▼   Independent Findings
- Included in both reports   Disclaimer
1. Results may *not* be achieved
2. *No* responsibility to update

Compliance Attestation

AT-C 315 provides the aspects a practitioner should consider with respect to attestation engagements related to an entity's compliance with specified laws, regulations, rules, contracts or grants, including reports on the effectiveness of internal controls over compliance with those requirements. There are two different types of engagements that are covered under AT-C 315:

- **Examination –** The practitioner obtains reasonable assurance and expresses an opinion on:

- o The entity's compliance with specified requirements of laws, regulations, rules, contracts, or grants; or

- o An assertion about compliance with such requirements.

Note that AT-C 315 does NOT apply to examination engagements with respect to internal control over compliance with specified requirements; such engagements are covered only under AT-C 105 and 205. AU-C 940, An Audit of an Entity's Internal Control Over Financial Reporting That Is Integrated With an Audit of Its Financial Statements, can also be used for guidance.

- **Agreed-Upon Procedures –** The practitioner applies tests that are the result of an agreement between the CPA, the client, and a third party with whom the client is negotiating. The agreed-upon procedures may relate to:

  - o Compliance with specified requirements as described above or

  - o Internal control over compliance with such requirements.

As previously mentioned, a review is not allowed for testing compliance with laws, rules, regulations, contracts, or grants. AT-C 315 also does not apply to situations covered under AU-C 806, *Reporting on Compliance With Aspects of Contractual Agreements or Regulatory Requirements in Connection With Audited Financial Statements*, as previously discussed; and AU-C 935, *Compliance Audits,* discussed later.

Among the **requirements specific to an examination** of compliance with specified requirements, the practitioner should:

- Determine that management:

  - o Accepts responsibility for such compliance with specified requirements, including its internal control over compliance; and

  - o Evaluates the entity's compliance, which may include documentation, written policies, accounting manuals, etc.

- Request a **written assertion** from management. If management refuses, the practitioner should withdraw from the engagement, if possible.

- Design the engagement to detect **material noncompliance**, whether intentional or not.

- Consider **materiality** with establishing the overall engagement strategy.

- *Obtain an understanding of specified requirements*. This should include obtaining an understanding of the applicable laws, rules, regulations, etc. as well as relevant knowledge obtained in previous engagements, and discussing such matters with appropriate personnel (eg, internal auditors).

- Evaluate the following factors when the client has **multiple components** (eg, locations, branches, etc.):

  - o How the compliance requirements apply at each level of the organization

  - o Materiality

  - o Centralization of records

  - o The control environment, including management's direct control over delegation of authority and its ability to supervise the various components

  - o Nature and extent of operations at the various components

  - o The similarities of operations over compliance for the various components

- *Obtain an understanding of relevant I/C over compliance* sufficient to plan the engagement and *assess control risk* for compliance with specified requirements.

- *Review any relevant reports and communications with regulatory agencies* and inquire of the regulatory agencies as to any current or ongoing examinations.
- Obtain **written representations** that:
  - Acknowledge management's responsibility for establishing and maintaining effective I/C over compliance,
  - Provide that management has evaluated the entity's compliance with specified requirements, and
  - Provide management's understanding of any compliance requirements subject to interpretation.

Note that these are in addition to the representations required for examination engagements in general under AT-C 205, as previously discussed, and refusal to provide any written representation constitutes a scope limitation sufficient to preclude an unmodified opinion or cause the practitioner to withdraw, if possible.

- Form an **opinion** based on the practitioner's evaluation of (1) the nature and frequency of any noncompliance instances found and (2) whether such noncompliance is material in relation to the nature of the compliance requirements.
  - If there is material noncompliance, it should be described and the opinion should be modified.

With respect to an **agreed-upon procedures engagement** related to compliance with specified requirements or I/C over compliance, the practitioner should:

- Determine that management:
  - Accepts responsibility for such compliance with specified requirements, including its internal control over compliance; and
  - Evaluates the entity's compliance with specified requirements or I/C over compliance.
- *Obtain an understanding of specified requirements.* Same considerations as for an examination (see above).
- Obtain written representations that:
  - Acknowledge management's responsibility for establishing and maintaining effective I/C over compliance,
  - Provide that management has evaluated the entity's compliance with specified requirements or I/C over compliance, as appropriate,
  - Provide management's understanding of any compliance requirements subject to interpretation, and
  - Provide that management has disclosed any known noncompliance occurring after the period covered by the practitioner's report.

Note that these are in addition to the representations required for agreed-upon procedures engagements in general under AT-C 215, as previously discussed.

Management's Discussion & Analysis (MD&A)

Publicly held entities are required to provide a set of disclosures referred to as Management Discussion and Analysis (MD&A) in accordance with certain rules prescribed by the SEC. In addition, some nonpublic entities prepare MD&A and management asserts that it is presented in accordance with SEC requirements. A CPA may be engaged to perform either an examination or a review of MD&A for either type of entity. (AT-C 395)

- An *examination* would ordinarily be performed in conjunction with an audit of the F/S.

- A *review* may be performed for an annual period, an interim period, or a combination of an annual and an interim period.

Such an engagement may only be accepted if the most recent period covered by the MD&A was audited by the CPA and all other periods covered by the MD&A were audited by either the CPA or a predecessor.

As a result of the engagement, the CPA will issue either an examination report or a review report, as appropriate. Both reports address the same issues:

- Does the MD&A include all of the required elements?

  o An examination report will indicate that the presentation *includes all required elements*.

  o A review report will indicate that *nothing came to the practitioner's attention* to indicate that all required elements were not included.

- Was the historical financial information included in MD&A accurately derived from the F/S?

  o An examination report will indicate that the historical financial information *was accurately derived* from the F/S.

  o A review report will indicate that *nothing came to the practitioner's attention* to indicate that the historical financial information was not derived from the F/S.

- Do the underlying information, determinations, estimates, and assumptions provide a reasonable basis for the disclosures included in MD&A?

  o An examination report will indicate that the information, determinations, estimates, and assumptions *provide a reasonable basis for the disclosures*.

  o A review report will indicate that *nothing came to the practitioner's attention* that the information, determinations, estimates, and assumptions did not provide a reasonable basis for the disclosures.

Various Engagements

There are various other types of engagements that a practitioner may perform that are each lightly tested on the exam.

Condensed Financial Statements or Selected Data

A client may wish to present condensed F/S or selected data in an advertisement, brochure, or other presentation which doesn't include the basic F/S and notes. The practitioner may issue a report on such information as long as they audited the basic F/S from which the condensed data is derived. The report on the condensed F/S must:

- Refer to the audit, providing the report date and type of opinion expressed.

- State whether the condensed data is fairly stated in all material respects in relation to the complete F/S.

Pro Forma Financial Statements

A practitioner may be asked to report on pro forma F/S (AT-C 310) that are derived from historical F/S. This refers to a presentation in which information is restated for an event that actually hadn't occurred. For example, a client that is considering a change in accounting principle might want to see how the F/S of the preceding year would have appeared had the change been made earlier. As long as the F/S from which the pro forma statements were derived were audited an examination engagement of this type is permitted. Similarly, as long as the F/S from which the pro forma statements were derived were *audited or reviewed,* a review engagement of this type may be performed.

Note: AT-C 310 covers examination and reviews of the information. Note: Agreed-upon procedures engagements are also allowed, but they are subject only to the applicable rules for agreed-upon procedures engagements under AT-C 215 as well as the common concepts under AT-C 105, not AT-C 310. Compilations of pro forma financial information are covered by SSARS, not SSAE; specifically, AR-C 120.

The examination (or review) report must:

- Refer to the audit (or review), providing the report date and type of opinion (or conclusion) expressed.

- Provide **reasonable assurance** (or limited if a review) as to the assumptions and presentation of the pro forma data being reasonable. Should also obtain a management representation letter.

SSARS 22 expands the applicability of the SSARS to apply when the CPA is engaged to compile or issue a **compilation report** on *pro forma* financial information. The CPA's compilation or review report, or the auditor's report on the historical F/S, should be included (or incorporated by reference) in the document containing the *pro forma* financial information. No management representation letter is required.

 Examination Report on Pro Forma Financial Information – Unmodified Opinion

INDEPENDENT PRACTITIONER'S REPORT

We have **examined** the pro forma adjustments giving effect to the underlying transaction (or event) described in Note 1 and the application of those adjustments to the historical amounts in the accompanying pro forma condensed balance sheet of X Company as of December 31, 20X1, and the related pro forma condensed statement of income for the year then ended (pro forma financial information), based on the criteria in Note 1. The historical condensed financial statements are derived from the historical financial statements of X Company, which were **audited by us**, and of Y Company, which were audited by other accountants, appearing elsewhere herein [or "and are readily available"]. The pro forma adjustments are based on **management's assumptions** described in Note 1. X Company's management is responsible for the pro forma financial information. Our responsibility is to express an opinion on the pro forma financial information based on our examination.

Our examination was conducted in accordance with attestation standards established by the American Institute of Certified Public Accountants. Those standards require that we plan and perform the examination to obtain reasonable assurance about whether, based on the criteria in Note 1, management's assumptions provide a reasonable basis for presenting the significant effects directly attributable to the underlying transaction (or event), and, in all material respects, the related pro forma adjustments give appropriate effect to those assumptions, and the pro forma amounts reflect the proper application of those adjustments to the historical financial statement amounts. An examination involves performing procedures to obtain evidence about management's assumptions, the related pro forma adjustments, and the pro forma amounts in the pro forma condensed balance sheet of X Company as of December 31, 20X1, and the related pro forma condensed statement of income for the year then ended. The nature, timing, and extent of the procedures selected depend on our judgment, including an assessment of the risks of material misstatement of the pro forma financial information, whether due to fraud or error. We believe that the evidence we obtained is sufficient and appropriate to provide a reasonable basis for our opinion.

The objective of this pro forma financial information is to show what the significant effects on the historical financial information might have been had the underlying transaction (or event) occurred at an earlier date. However, the pro forma condensed financial statements are not necessarily indicative of the results of operations or related effects on financial position that would have been attained had the above-mentioned transaction (or event) actually occurred at such earlier date.

In our opinion, based on the criteria in Note 1, management's assumptions provide a **reasonable basis** for presenting the significant effects directly attributable to the above-mentioned transaction (or event) described in Note 1, and, in all material respects, the related pro forma adjustments give appropriate effect to those assumptions, and the pro forma amounts reflect the proper application of those adjustments to the historical financial statement amounts in the pro forma condensed balance sheet of X Company as of December 31, 20X1, and the related pro forma condensed statement of income for the year then ended.

***

F/S in Conformity with Accounting Principles of Another Country

An accountant may be auditing a U.S. entity which requires F/S that are in conformity with the accounting principles of **another country** and are intended for use **outside the U.S.** This might be as part of an attempt to raise capital in the other country or because the U.S. entity is a subsidiary to be consolidated with a parent of the other country. SAS 124 (AU-C 910) requires the auditor to obtain an understanding of the purpose of the F/S, whether the reporting framework applied provides fair presentation of the F/S, the intended users of the F/S, and the steps taken by management to determine whether the reporting framework is acceptable. The audit will still conform to GAAS, but the report must indicate conformity with the principles of the other country and be presented in either of the following ways.

- A U.S.-style report modified to express an opinion on conformity with the principles of the other country (essentially comparable to a special report on OCBOA statements) with an explanatory paragraph "emphasizing a matter."

- A report in which the form and content is consistent with that of the other country if such a report would be issued by auditors in the other country in similar circumstances; the auditor understands and has obtained sufficient appropriate audit evidence to support the report; and the auditor has complied with the other country's reporting standards and identifies the other country in the report. Issuing such a report may require the auditor to:

  o Report on statutory compliance or otherwise understand the local laws and regulations.

  o Obtain an understanding of applicable legal responsibilities, in addition to the auditing standards and the financial reporting framework generally accepted in the other country.

In instances where a report that is to be *used in the United States* was prepared in accordance with a financial reporting framework generally accepted in another country, the auditor is **required** to include an **emphasis-of-matter paragraph** to highlight the foreign financial reporting framework, but permits the auditor to express an unqualified opinion. This paragraph would follow the basis for opinion paragraph.

Trust Services—System and Organization Controls (SOC) Reports

Trust Services are governed by SSAE (Statements on Standards for Attestation engagements) and represent attest engagements in which a CPA assesses a client's commercial internet site and reports on whether the system meets one or more of the following **principles:**

- Security

- Availability for operation

- Processing integrity

- Online privacy

- Confidentiality

For each principle reported, the auditor considers each of the following **four criteria:**

- Policies

- Communications

- Procedures

- Monitoring

Service organizations are entities that provide services—such as payroll or web-hosting—to other entities. SOC for Service Organizations reports are issued by an independent CPA to assist service organizations in building trust and confidence in the service provided and controls related to those services. There are three types of such services.

SOC 1® – SOC for Service Organization: ICFR

Report on Controls at a Service Organization Relevant to User Entities' Internal Control over Financial Reporting

Reports prepared in accordance with AT-C 320, Reporting on an Examination of Controls at a Service Organization Relevant to User Entities' Internal Control Over Financial Reporting, are intended to meet the needs of user entities and user auditors in considering the controls at the service organization and their impact on the user entities' F/S. User entities are entities that use the service organizations' services. User auditors are the auditors of user entities. Use of these reports is **restricted** to the management of the service organization, user entities, and user auditors. There are two types of reports for ICFR engagements:

- Type 1 – Report on the fairness of the presentation of management's **description** of the service organization's system and the **suitability of the design of the controls** to achieve the related control objectives included in the description as of a specified date.

- Type 2 - Report on the fairness of the presentation of management's **description** of the service organization's system and the **suitability of the design and operating effectiveness of the controls** to achieve the related control objectives included in the description throughout a specified period.

SOC 2® – SOC for Service Organizations: Trust Services Criteria

Report on Controls at a Service Organization Relevant to Security, Availability, Processing Integrity, Confidentiality or Privacy

These reports are designed to meet the needs of users that seek **detailed** information and assurance about the controls at a service organization relevant to security, availability, and processing integrity of the systems the service organization uses to process users' data and the confidentiality and privacy of the information processed by these systems. The emphasis within SOC 2 reports is not on ICRF, but the operational fitness of the system. These reports can play an important role in:

- Oversight of the organization

- Vendor management programs

- Internal corporate governance and risk management processes

- Regulatory oversight

Similar to a SOC 1 report, there are two types of reports, with similar differences: A type 1 report is on management's **description** of a service organization's system and **the suitability of the design of controls**. A type 2 report is on management's description of a service organization's system and **the**

suitability of the design and operating effectiveness of controls. Use of these reports are **restricted**.

SOC 3® – SOC for Service Organizations: Trust Services Criteria for General Use Report

These reports are intended to meet the needs of users who seek assurance about the controls at a service organization relevant to security, availability, processing integrity confidentiality, or privacy, but do not seek or have the knowledge required to make effective use of the detail in a SOC 2 Report. Since SOC 3 reports are **general-use reports**, they can be freely distributed.

10.05 Government Reporting

Overview of Compliance Audits

Compliance audits can be program-specific or organization wide and are generally performed along with financial statement (F/S) audits to determine if an entity is complying with applicable laws, regulations, or other contractual requirements. They are required for entities (ie, nonprofits and governmental organizations, and sometimes businesses) receiving some sort of financial assistance, such as cash, a loan, or interest-rate subsidy, from federal, state, or local governmental entities.

Generally Accepted Government Auditing Standards (GAGAS) (oftentimes interchangeably referred to as simply **Government Auditing Standards (GAS)** or the **"Yellow Book"**) and other specific governmental audit requirements (eg, the **Single Audit Act**, as amended) add layers of audit requirements for certain entities in addition to GAAS. That is, if GAGAS applies, so does GAAS; and if the Single Audit Act applies, then GAGAS and GAAS also apply.

The following chart breaks down these layers of audit requirements by who they are generally applicable to, the authoritative guidance supporting them, and the organizations they're issued by.

Audit Type	Applicable to	Authoritative Guidance	Issued by
GAAS F/S Audits	All entities requiring a F/S audit	All AU-C sections apply, except AU-C 935, *Compliance Audits** which only applies if a government compliance audit is also required.	AICPA
GAGAS Financial Audits	Certain governmental entities and nongovernmental entities (eg, contractors, nonprofits) receiving / administering governmental assistance, depending on program requirements	Government Auditing Standards for financial audits**	U.S. Government Accountability Office (GAO)
Single audits	Nonfederal entities (eg, cities, universities, and nonprofits) receiving *major* federal financial assistance (ie, ≥ $750,000 within a fiscal year)	Single Audit Act, as amended OMB Audit Requirements for Federal Awards (2 CFR 200)	Office of Management and Budget (OMB)

PCAOB AS 6110 (and other relevant PCAOB standards) may apply instead. Also note that AU-C 935 is not applicable when an examination in accordance with attestation standards (AT-C 315) is required.

**GAGAS also covers performance audits (discussed later) and attestation engagements.*

GAAS Financial Statement Audits

Required Procedures

In an audit in accordance with GAAS ("GAAS F/S audit"), tests of compliance will be focused on **violations of laws and regulations** that have a *direct and material effect* on the amounts in the organization's F/S. (AU-C 250)

Reporting Requirements

A **standard audit report** is normally issued; however, if material noncompliance is detected, it is disclosed and treated as a departure from the applicable financial reporting framework (eg, GAAP), resulting in a qualified or adverse opinion (disagreement).

Note that the following types of reports are NOT required:

- *Report on compliance with laws and regulations*
- *Report on internal control (I/C)*

- *Report on noteworthy accomplishments of the program or recommendations for actions to improve operations*

GAGAS Financial Audits

All of the above GAAS requirements apply to compliance audits in accordance with GAGAS ("GAGAS financial audit"), plus more.

Additional Required Procedures

The auditor must design the audit to provide reasonable assurance of detecting material misstatements resulting from **noncompliance with contract provisions or grant agreements** that have a *direct and material effect* on the F/S.

If relevant and necessary to achieve audit objectives, auditors should perform procedures to determine the following for each *finding* (ie, any matter that is required to be reported):

- *Criteria* – What are the laws, regulations, etc. that apply?
- *Condition* – What is the situation that exists?
- *Cause* – For example, is there an I/C deficiency?
- *Effect* – What are the actual or potential consequences?

Note that the consideration of I/C deficiencies may include deficiencies that result in waste or abuse.

- *Waste* is defined as "the act of using or expending resources carelessly, extravagantly, or to no purpose." It primarily relates to "mismanagement, inappropriate actions, and inadequate oversight." It can include activities that do not include abuse or a violation of law.
- *Abuse* is defined as "behavior that is deficient or improper when compared with behavior that a prudent person would consider reasonable and necessary business practice given the facts and circumstances, but excludes fraud and noncompliance with provisions of laws, regulations, contracts, and grant agreements." Abuse may also include misuse of authority or position for personal financial benefit or for the benefit of a close family member or business associate.

Additional Reporting Requirements

In addition to an audit report on the F/S required by GAAS, GAGAS requires the auditor to report on:

- Internal control
  - Describe the **scope of the auditors' testing of I/C** over financial reporting and compliance with laws, regulations, and provisions of contracts or grant agreements.
  - State whether the tests performed provided sufficient, appropriate evidence to support opinions on the effectiveness of I/C and on compliance. Note, however, that an **opinion on I/C is not required**.
  - Report **significant deficiencies and material weaknesses** in I/C over financial reporting as findings.
- **Compliance** with laws and regulations
  - Report identified or suspected **material noncompliance or fraud**.

The auditor should also provide written communication to the audited entity officials regarding identified or suspected noncompliance or fraud that are *less than material but warrant attention* from those charged with governance.

Material noncompliance with laws and regulations and instances of fraud should be communicated directly to parties outside the audited entity (eg, a federal inspector general) under two circumstances:

- If the **auditee fails to communicate** the issues to **parties specified by law or regulation** even after being notified by the auditor of the failure to do so

- If the **auditee fails to respond** to such issues when it involves funding received directly or indirectly from a government agency, even after being notified of management's failure to respond, the auditor should report the failure directly to the **funding agency**.

The three reports required under GAAS and GAGAS can be provided separately, or they can be combined into one or two reports (ie, one on the F/S and one combined on compliance and I/C). The following is an example from AU-C 935.

 Combined Report on Compliance with Applicable Requirements & I/C Over Compliance

INDEPENDENT AUDITOR'S REPORT

[Addressee]

Report on Compliance

Opinion on [indicate the reporting level pursuant to governmental audit requirement]

We have audited Example Entity's compliance with the [identify the applicable compliance requirements or refer to the document that describes the applicable compliance requirements] applicable to Example Entity's [identify the government program(s) audited or refer to a separate schedule that identifies the program(s)] for the year ended June 30, 20X1.

We have audited Example Entity's compliance with the [identify the applicable compliance requirements or refer to the document that describes the applicable compliance requirements] applicable to Example Entity's [identify the government program(s) audited or refer to a separate schedule that identifies the program(s)] for the year ended June 30, 20X1.

In our opinion, Example Entity complied, in all material respects, with the compliance requirements referred to above that are applicable to [indicate the reporting level pursuant to governmental audit requirement] for the year ended June 30, 20X1.

Basis for Opinion

We conducted our audit of compliance in accordance with auditing standards generally accepted in the United States of America (GAAS); the standards applicable to financial audits contained in Government Auditing Standards (*Government Auditing Standards*) issued by the Comptroller General of the United States; and [*insert the name of the governmental audit requirement or program-specific audit guide*]. Our responsibilities under those standards and [insert the name of the governmental audit requirement or program-specific audit guide] are further described in the Auditor's Responsibilities for the Audit of Compliance section of our report.

We are required to be independent of Example Entity and to meet our other ethical responsibilities, in accordance with relevant ethical requirements relating to our audit. We believe the audit evidence we have obtained is sufficient and appropriate to provide a basis for our opinion. Our audit does not provide a legal determination of Example Entity's compliance with the compliance requirements referred to above.

Responsibilities of Management for Compliance

Management is responsible for compliance with the requirements referred to above and for the design, implementation, and maintenance of effective internal control over compliance with the requirements of laws, statutes, regulations, rules, and provisions of contracts or grant agreements applicable to the Example Entity's government programs.

Auditor's Responsibilities for the Audit of Compliance

Our objectives are to obtain reasonable assurance about whether material noncompliance with the compliance requirements referred to above occurred, whether due to fraud or error, and express an opinion on Example Entity's compliance based on our audit. Reasonable assurance is a high level of assurance but is not absolute assurance and therefore is not a guarantee that an audit conducted in accordance with GAAS, *Government Auditing Standards*, and [*insert the name of the governmental audit requirement or program-specific audit guide*] will always detect material noncompliance when it exists. The risk of not detecting material noncompliance resulting from fraud is higher than for that resulting from error, as fraud may involve collusion, forgery, intentional omissions, misrepresentations, or the override of internal control. Noncompliance with the compliance requirements referred to above is considered material if there is a substantial likelihood that, individually or in the aggregate, it would influence the judgment made by a reasonable user of the report on compliance about Example Entity's compliance with the requirements of the government program as a whole.

In performing an audit in accordance with GAAS, Government Auditing Standards, and [insert the name of the governmental audit requirement or program-specific audit guide], we:

- Exercise professional judgment and maintain professional skepticism throughout the audit.

- Identify and assess the risks of material noncompliance, whether due to fraud or error, and design and perform audit procedures responsive to those risks. Such procedures include examining, on a test basis, evidence regarding Example Entity's compliance with the compliance requirements referred to above and performing such other procedures as we considered necessary in the circumstances.

- Obtain an understanding of Example Entity's internal control over compliance relevant to the audit in order to design audit procedures that are appropriate in the circumstances and to test and report on internal control over compliance in accordance with [*insert the name of the governmental audit requirement or program-specific audit guide*], but not for the purpose of expressing an opinion on the effectiveness of Example Entity's internal control over compliance. Accordingly, no such opinion is expressed.

We are required to communicate with those charged with governance regarding, among other matters, the planned scope and timing of the audit and any significant deficiencies and material weaknesses in internal control over compliance that we identified during the audit.

Report on Internal Control Over Compliance

A *deficiency* in internal control over compliance exists when the design or operation of a control over compliance does not allow management or employees, in the normal course of performing their assigned functions, to prevent, or detect and correct, noncompliance on a timely basis. A *material weakness* in internal control over compliance is a deficiency, or combination of deficiencies in internal control over compliance, such that there is a reasonable possibility that material noncompliance with a compliance requirement will not be prevented, or detected and corrected, on a timely basis. A *significant deficiency in internal control over compliance* is a deficiency, or a combination of deficiencies, in internal control over compliance that is less severe than a material weakness in internal control over compliance, yet important enough to merit attention by those charged with governance.

Our consideration of internal control over compliance was for the limited purpose described in the first paragraph of this section and was not designed to identify all deficiencies in internal control over compliance that might be material weaknesses or significant deficiencies in internal control over compliance. Given these limitations, during our audit we did not identify any deficiencies in internal control over compliance that we consider to be material weaknesses, as defined above. However, material weaknesses or significant deficiencies in internal control over compliance may exist that have not been identified.

Our audit was not designed for the purpose of expressing an opinion on the effectiveness of internal control over compliance. Accordingly, no such opinion is expressed.

The purpose of this report on internal control over compliance is solely to describe the scope of our testing of internal control over compliance and the results of that testing based on the [*insert the name of the governmental audit requirement or program-specific audit guide*]. Accordingly, this report is not suitable for any other purpose.

[Auditor's signature]
[Auditor's city and state]
[Date of the auditor's report]

Single Audits

All of the above GAAS and GAGAS requirements apply to compliance audits in accordance with the Single Audit Act ("single audits"), plus even more.

- As mentioned above, a **single audit**, which generally *covers all operations of an auditee*, is required for nonfederal entities (eg, cities, universities, and nonprofits) receiving more than $750,000 in federal financial assistance within a fiscal year.

- There is, however, an election to have a **program-specific audit** instead of a single audit for entities that exceed the $750,000 limit but only spend awards under one federal program. This election is not allowed if the program requires a financial statement audit though. While you should know about the election, the requirements of a program-specific audit are likely beyond the scope of the exam; thus, we will only be discussing single audit requirements below.

Additional Required Procedures

In addition to GAAS and GAGAS procedures, the auditor must test both:

- Compliance with requirements of major federal financial assistance programs*.

- Internal control over compliance with the requirements of such programs.

Note that the auditor uses a risk analysis to determine which programs are considered major. Also, materiality is set at the level of each major program rather than the overall F/S of the entity, so this will involve greater audit fieldwork effort than a GAAS audit.

Additional Reporting Requirements

In addition to the first three reports required by GAAS and GAGAS, single audits also require the auditor's reports to include the following:

- Schedule of federal award expenditures, which requires an opinion.

- Schedule of findings and questioned costs, which includes:

  - A **summary of audit results** for financial statements, internal control, and compliance

  - Findings related to the F/S (also required under GAGAS)

  - Findings and questioned cost for federal awards

Single audits require audit **opinions** (or disclaimers of opinion) on all of the following items. When there are material weaknesses, noncompliance, or misstatements in the schedule, respectively, these opinions may be *qualified or adverse*.

- The financial statements

- Compliance with laws and regulations applicable to each major program

- Whether the schedule of federal awards expenditures is fairly stated

All reports issued in connection with audits under GAGAS and the Single Audit Act are directed to specific agencies, but are available for public inspection.

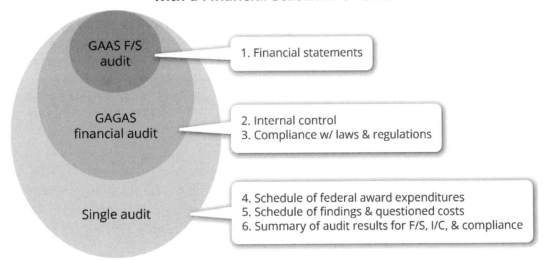

Report Requirements for Compliance Audits Performed in Conjunction with a Financial Statement Audit

- GAAS F/S audit → 1. Financial statements
- GAGAS financial audit → 2. Internal control / 3. Compliance w/ laws & regulations
- Single audit → 4. Schedule of federal award expenditures / 5. Schedule of findings & questioned costs / 6. Summary of audit results for F/S, I/C, & compliance

GAGAS Performance Audits

Required Procedures

Performance audits are primarily designed to determine the **economy, efficiency, and effectiveness** of a program in achieving its goals. Such audits also include consideration of fraud, compliance with laws and regulations, and I/C related to achieving program goals if they are significant to audit objectives. If I/C is significant to audit objectives, the auditor should:

- Obtain an understanding of I/C

- Assess I/C to the extent necessary to address audit objectives

- Evaluate I/C deficiencies and determine if such deficiencies were the cause of other audit findings (ie, any noncompliance, fraud, waste or abuse found)

Reporting Requirements

The auditor's report will include:

- Objectives and scope (including any limitations) of the audit

- Methodology of the audit (including any significant assumptions made, techniques used, and criteria applied)

- The auditor's findings, conclusions, and recommendations for corrective action of significant findings, if any

- A summary of responsible official's views on the auditor's findings

- The nature of any confidential information omitted from the report

When I/C is significant to audit objectives, the report will also include:

- The scope of work on I/C
- Significant I/C deficiencies

AUD 11
Research
Appendix

11.01 Research Task Format – Audit

Overview

Research is tested in its own independent task-based simulation (TBS) problem. Each Audit exam will include at least 1 research type TBS. The Candidates will be asked to search through the database to find an appropriate reference that addresses the issue presented in the research problem. The candidate will choose the code title for the appropriate body of authoritative literature from the drop-down list and then enter a specific reference number applicable to their given scenario.

Using the Authoritative Literature, the candidate will search for keywords associated with the question using the search box, which will pull up all references within the literature to those keywords. From there, the candidate should use the "search within" function to find specific instances of keywords within each subsection. Keywords will be highlighted in the text and the candidate can go through them to find the relevant text that answers the research problem.

Research questions will also alert the candidate if they have correctly formatted their answer by displaying "Your response is correctly formatted" in a box below the candidate response if the candidate has entered reference numbers correctly. For example, single-digit reference numbers (such as "paragraph 3") may be formatted as a two-digit response (such as "paragraph "03"). A good tool is to also use the Authoritative Literature to look up answers to other TBS in the exam, for example, if they ask you about an audit report, use the Authoritative Literature to assist you in solving this type of TBS.

Professional Authoritative Literature for Audit Research Questions

The first step in performing a research question for the AUD exam is to determine what set of standards the question relates to. Standards tested on the AUD exam include Statements on Auditing Standards (SAS) for nonpublic U.S. entities, **AU-C**; auditing standards for public U.S. entities, **PCAOB-AS**; Statements on Standards for Attestation Engagements (SSAE), **AT-C**; Statements on Standards for Accounting and Review Services (SSARS) standards for reviews, compilations, or preparation engagements of nonpublic entities, **AR-C**; the AICPA Code of Professional Conduct, **ET**; the bylaws applicable to members of the AICPA, **BL**; standards for valuation services, **VS**; standards for consulting services, **CS**; standards for personal financial planning services, **PFP**; requirements for continuing professional education, **CPE**; tax services, **TS**, peer review standards, **PR**, and quality control standards, **QC**.

The primary source of authoritative literature for the performance of an audit of a nonpublic entity in the U.S. consists of **Statements on Auditing Standards (SAS)** issued by the Auditing Standards Board (ASB), the senior technical body of the AICPA designated to issue pronouncements on auditing matters applicable to the preparation and issuance of audit reports for nonissuers.

In performing a research question related to auditing standards for nonpublic entities, after determining that the appropriate source will be SASs, the **AU-C literature**, the next step would be to determine which section of the standards the information is likely to be included in.

AU-C – Statements on Auditing Standards (SASs)

The sections of the auditing standards for **nonpublic entities** are:

- AU-C 200 – Overall objectives of the independent auditor and the conduct of an audit in accordance with GAAS

- AU-C 210 – Terms of engagement

- AU-C 220 – Quality control for an engagement conducted in accordance with GAAS

- AU-C 230 – Audit documentation

  o AU-C 9230 – Audit documentation – auditing interpretation of section 230

- AU-C 240 – Consideration of fraud in a financial statement audit

- AU-C 250 – Consideration of laws and regulations in an audit of financial statements

- AU-C 260 – The auditor's communication with those charged with governance

- AU-C 265 – Communicating internal control related matters identified in an audit

  o AU-C 9265 – Communicating internal control related matters identified in an audit – auditing interpretation of section 265

- AU-C 300 – Planning an audit

- AU-C 315 – Understanding the entity and its environment and assessing the risks of material misstatement

- AU-C 320 – Materiality in planning and performing an audit

- AU-C 330 – Performing audit procedures in response to assessed risks and evaluating the audit evidence obtained

- AU-C 402 – Audit considerations relating to an entity using a service organization

- AU-C 450 – Evaluation of misstatements identified during the audit

- AU-C 500 – Audit evidence

  o AU-C 9500 – Audit evidence – auditing interpretation of section 500

- AU-C 501 – Audit evidence – Specific consideration for selected items

- AU-C 505 – External confirmations

- AU-C 510 – Opening balances – Initial audit engagements, including reaudit engagements

- AU-C 520 – Analytical procedures

- AU-C 530 – Audit sampling

- AU-C 540 – Auditing accounting estimates, including fair value accounting estimated, and related disclosures

- AU-C 550 – Related parties

- AU-C 560 – Subsequent events and subsequently discovered facts

- AU-C 570 – The auditor's consideration of an entity's ability to continue as a going concern

- o AU-C 9570 – The auditor's consideration of an entity's ability to continue as a going concern – auditing interpretation of section 570
- AU-C 580 – Written representations
- AU-C 585 – Consideration of omitted procedures after the report release date
- AU-C 600 – Special considerations – Audits of group financial statements (including the work of component auditors)
  - o AU-C 9600 – Special considerations – Audits of group financial statements (including the work of component auditors): auditing interpretation of section 600
- AU-C 610 – Using the work of internal auditors
- AU-C 620 – Using the work of an auditor's specialist
  - o AU-C 9620 – Using the work of an auditor's specialist: auditing interpretations of section 620
- AU-C 700 – Forming an opinion and reporting on financial statements
  - o AU-C 9700 – Forming an opinion and reporting on financial statements – auditing interpretation of section 700
- AU-C 701 – Communicating key audit matters in the independent auditor's report
- AU-C 703 – Forming an opinion and reporting on financial statements of employee benefit plans subject to ERISA
- AU-C 705 – Modifications to the opinion in the independent auditor's report
- AU-C 706 – Emphasis-of-matter paragraphs and other-matter paragraphs in the independent auditor's report
- AU-C 708 – Consistency of financial statements
- AU-C 720 – The auditor's responsibilities relating to other information included in annual reports
- AU-C 725 – Supplementary information in relation to the financial statements as a whole
- AU-C 9725 – Supplementary information in relation to the financial statements as a whole: auditing interpretation of section 725
- AU-C 730 – Required supplementary information
- AU-C 800 – Special considerations – Audits of financial statements prepared in accordance with special purpose frameworks
- AU-C 805 – Special considerations – Audits of single financial statements and specified elements, accounts, or items of a financial statement
  - o AU-C 9805 – Special considerations – Audits of single financial statements and specified elements, accounts, or items of a financial statement: auditing interpretation of section 805
- AU-C 806 – Reporting on compliance with aspects of contractual agreements or regulatory requirements in connection with audited financial statements
- AU-C 810 – Engagements to report on summary financial statements

- AU-C 905 – Alert that restricts the use of the auditor's written communication
- AU-C 910 – Financial statements prepared in accordance with a financial reporting framework generally accepted in another country
- AU-C 915 – Reports on application of requirements of an applicable financial reporting framework
- AU-C 920 – Letters for underwriters and certain other requesting parties
- AU-C 925 – Filings with the U.S. Securities and Exchange Commission under the Securities Act of 1933
- AU-C 930 – Interim financial information
- AU-C 935 – Compliance audits
- AU-C 940 – An audit of internal control over financial reporting that is integrated with an audit of financial statements
- AU-C 945 – Auditor involvement with exempt offering documents

Once the appropriate section has been identified, scanning the section, if relatively short, or using a word search, if the section is longer, will generally be sufficient to quickly identify the specific paragraph being sought.

Sample research question

Identify the section of professional standards that describes from whom written representation should be obtained.

Answer: Written representations are considered a form of audit evidence. Written representations is the title of AU-C 580, which is where the answer is most certainly to be found. Scrolling in that section, under requirements, the first caption is "Management From Whom Written Representations Are Requested" and paragraph AU-C 580.09 indicates "The auditor should request written representations from management with appropriate responsibilities for the financial statements and knowledge of the matters concerned."

Solution: AU-C 580.09

PCAOB-AS – PCAOB Auditing Standards

The PCAOB standards applicable to public companies (ie, issuers) are:

General Auditing Standards

- 1000 – General Principles and Responsibilities
  - **AS 1001: Responsibilities and Functions of the Independent Auditor** – Requires the auditor to comply with PCAOB standards and distinguishes between the auditor's responsibilities and those of management.
  - **AS 1005: Independence** – Requires the auditor to be independent in mental attitude in all matters relating to the engagement.

- o **AS 1010: Training and Proficiency of the Independent Auditor** – Requires the auditor to have adequate technical training and proficiency as an auditor.

- o **AS 1015: Due Professional Care in the Performance of Work** – Requires the auditor to apply due professional care in the planning and performance of the engagement and in the preparation of the report.

- 1100 – General Concepts

  - o **AS 1101: Audit Risk** – Requires the auditor to consider risk in both an integrated audit and in an audit of financial statements, consisting of audit risk, which is made up of the risk of material misstatement and detection risk (RMM & DR).

  - o **AS 1105: Audit Evidence** – Describes what constitutes and requires the auditor to perform procedures to obtain sufficient appropriate audit evidence.

  - o **AS 1110: Relationship of Auditing Standards to Quality Control Standards** – Requires the auditor's firm to establish quality control policies and procedures to provide reasonable assurance that the firm will comply with applicable PCAOB standards in the performance of its audit engagements.

- 1200 – General Activities

  - o **AS 1201: Supervision of the Audit Engagement** – Requires the auditor to supervise the engagement team to assure that work is performed as directed and that conclusions reached are supported.

  - o **AS 1205: Part of the Audit Performed by Other Independent Auditors** – Indicates when an auditor may serve as a principal auditor and the effect on the auditor's procedures and the report in circumstances when the auditor does and does not make reference to the other auditor in the report.

  - o **AS 1210: Using the Work of an Auditor-Engaged Specialist** – Provides guidance to auditors using a specialist when performing an audit under PCAOB standards.

  - o **AS 1215: Audit Documentation** – Requires the auditor to establish a written record to support conclusions reached and all representations made by the auditor, including those in the audit report.

  - o **AS 1220: Engagement Quality Review** – Requires that audit engagements, reviews of interim financial, and attestation engagements be subjected to an engagement quality review and concurring approval of issuance.

- 1300 – Auditor Communications

  - o **AS 1301: Communications with Audit Committees** – Requires the auditor to communicate to the audit committee relevant information regarding the audit, including the overall strategy and timing, and obtain any information relevant to the audit from the audit committee.

  - o **AS 1305: Communications About Control Deficiencies in an Audit of Financial Statements** – Requires the auditor to communicate all significant deficiencies and material weaknesses detected during the audit, in writing, to management and the audit committee prior to the issuance of the auditor's report on the financial statements.

Audit Procedures

- 2100 – Audit Planning and Risk Assessment

  - **AS 2101: Audit Planning** – Requires the auditor to plan the audit so that it can be conducted effectively, including the establishment of an overall audit strategy and an audit plan that incorporates planned risk assessment procedures and planned responses to identified risks of material misstatement.

  - **AS 2105: Consideration of Materiality in Planning and Performing an Audit** – Requires the auditor to consider quantitative and qualitative factors in determining what constitutes a potential material misstatement to the financial statements and to plan and design audit procedures that are expected to be effective in detecting them.

  - **AS 2110: Identifying and Assessing Risks of Material Misstatement** – Establishes guidelines for the performance of risk assessment procedures, enabling the auditor to obtain an understanding of the entity and its environment, including its internal control, as a basis for designing and applying responses to identified risks of material misstatement.

- 2200 – Auditing Internal Control Over Financial Reporting

  - **AS 2201: An Audit of Internal Control Over Financial Reporting That Is Integrated with An Audit of Financial Statements** – Establishes requirements for engagements in which the auditor is engaged to examine management's assessment of internal control that is relevant to financial reporting.

- 2300 – Audit Procedures in Response to Risks – Nature, Timing, and Extent

  - **AS 2301: The Auditor's Responses to the Risks of Material Misstatement** – Requires the auditor to design and implement appropriate responses to identified risks of material misstatement including responses that have an overall effect on how the audit is conducted and the effects on the nature, timing, and extent of audit procedures to be performed.

  - **AS 2305: Substantive Analytical Procedures** – Establishes guidelines for circumstances in which the auditor is using analytical procedures as substantive tests based on the nature of the assertion begin tested, the existence of predictable relationships among data, the availability of reliable information upon which to base expectations, and the precision of expectations developed by the auditor.

  - **AS 2310: The Confirmation Process** – Defines the confirmation process; discusses the relationship of confirmations to the assessment of audit risk; identifies factors affecting the reliability of confirmations; indicates alternative procedures to be applied when responses to confirmations are not received; addresses the evaluation of the results of confirmation procedures; and specifically addresses the confirmation of accounts receivable.

  - **AS 2315: Audit Sampling** – Provides guidance for the planning, performing, and evaluating of audit samples.

- 2400 – Audit Procedures for Specific Aspects of the Audit

  - **AS 2401: Consideration of Fraud in a Financial Statement Audit** – Establishes requirements and provides direction to address the auditor's responsibility to obtain reasonable assurance that the financial statements are not materially misstated as it relates to fraud.

- o **AS 2405: Illegal Acts by Clients** – Establishes the auditor's responsibility for considering the possibility of illegal acts by a client and guidance on the auditor's responsibility when a possible illegal act is detected.

- o **AS 2410: Related Parties** – Establishes requirements for the auditor's consideration of the client's identification of related parties and related party transactions, as well as how they are accounted for and disclosed.

- o **AS 2415: Consideration of an Entity's Ability to Continue as a Going Concern** – Establishes the auditor's responsibility to evaluate whether there is substantial doubt as to an entity's ability to continue as a going concern for a reasonable period of time, including auditing procedures to be performed and any reporting responsibilities.

- 2500 – Audit Procedures for Certain Accounts or Disclosures

- o **AS 2501: Auditing Accounting Estimates, Including Fair Value Measurements** – Establishes guidance regarding obtaining sufficient appropriate audit evidence to support significant estimates in the financial statements.

- o **AS 2505: Inquiry of a Client's Lawyer Concerning Litigation, Claims, and Assessments** – Requires the auditor to perform certain procedures to obtain evidence about litigation, claims, and assessments, including inquiries of client management; obtaining a description and evaluation of litigation, claims, and assessments from management; examining relevant documents; obtaining written assurance from management regarding disclosure of unasserted claims; and requesting that management send an inquiry letter to lawyers consulted or retained in relation to those matters.

- o **AS 2510: Auditing Inventories** – Indicates that the observation of inventories is a generally accepted audit procedure and places a burden on the auditor to justify the opinion expressed on the financial statements when inventory has not been observed.

- 2600 – Special Topics

- o **AS 2601: Consideration of an Entity's Use of a Service Organization** – Provides guidance to auditors of entities that use service organizations that become part of its information system and for auditors that issue reports related to the processing of transactions by a service organization for use by the auditors of the entity using it.

- o **AS 2605: Consideration of the Internal Audit Function** – Provides guidance to the auditor on the consideration of the work of internal auditors in forming an opinion on the financial statements and for obtaining direct assistance from internal auditors in performing the audit in accordance with PCAOB standards.

- o **AS 2610: Initial Audits—Communications Between Predecessor and Successor Auditors** – Requires an auditor in an initial engagement to communicate with the predecessor auditor as a prerequisite for accepting the engagement and establishes guidance for communication with the predecessor when the auditor discovers misstatements in financial statements reported on by the predecessor.

- 2700 – Auditor's Responsibilities Regarding Supplemental and Other Information

  o **AS 2701: Auditing Supplemental Information Accompanying Audited Financial Statements** – Requires the auditor to perform audit procedures in relation to supplemental information to support an opinion as to whether or not the supplemental information is fairly stated.

  o **AS 2705: Required Supplementary Information** – Provides guidance to auditors as to the nature of procedures to apply to supplemental information required by the FASB, GASB, or FASAB and indicates when the auditor is required to report on required supplemental information.

  o **AS 2710: Other Information in Documents Containing Audited Financial Statements** – Establishes requirement for auditor to read other information included in documents that include the financial statements, excluding registrations statements filed with the SEC, to make certain that there are no inconsistencies with information included in the audited financial statements.

- 2800 – Concluding Audit Procedures

  o **AS 2801: Subsequent Events** – Requires the consideration of subsequent events by management and evaluation by the auditor, including those representing conditions existing at the balance sheet date and requiring adjustment to the financial statements, and those representing conditions that came into existence after the balance sheet date and requiring disclosure.

  o **AS 2805: Management Representations** – Requires the auditor to obtain written representations from management as a component of an audit performed in accordance with PCAOB standards, including guidance as to specific representations to be obtained.

  o **AS 2810: Evaluating Audit Results** – Provides guidance to the auditor in determining the appropriateness and sufficiency of audit evidence.

  o **AS 2815: The Meaning of "Present Fairly in Conformity with Generally Accepted Accounting Principles"** - Requires the auditor to determine, based on the requirements of the SEC, the accounting principles applicable to the company under audit and requires the auditor to determine if the principles applied by the entity are generally accepted, are appropriate under the circumstances, and if the financial statements are informative in relation to matters that will affect the use of the financial statements.

  o **AS 2820: Evaluating Consistency of Financial Statements** – Requires the auditor to evaluate the consistency of the financial statements, provides guidance for the evaluation, and describes the effects of the evaluation on the auditor's report.

- 2900 – Post-Audit Matters

  o **AS 2901: Consideration of Omitted Procedures After the Report Date** – Requires the auditor to evaluate whether the opinion expressed can be supported despite the omitted procedure and, if not, requires the auditor to perform the procedure or a satisfactory alternative. If unable to do so, the auditor should consult with legal counsel as to responsibilities and the best course of action. If performance indicates that facts existing at the financial statement date would have affected the report, the auditor should follow the guidance in AS 2905.

- ○ **AS 2905: Subsequent Discovery of Facts Existing at the Date of the Auditor's Report** – Upon discovery of facts not known to the auditor at the date of the report that would have been investigated if known at the time, requires the auditor to determine if the information is reliable and if it existed as of the date of the report. If so, the auditor is further required to determine if the information would have affected the auditor's report and if there are parties likely to be relying on the financial statements that would attach importance to the information. Requires the auditor, upon making such a determination, to work with the client and perform procedures to make certain that the report is not inappropriately relied upon.

Auditor Reporting

- 3100 - Reporting on Audits of Financial Statements

  - ○ **AS 3101: The Auditor's Report on an Audit of Financial Statements When the Auditor Expresses an Unqualified Opinion** – Provides guidelines for the preparation of a standard audit report.

  - ○ **AS 3105: Departures from Unqualified Opinions and Other Reporting Circumstances** – Provides guidelines for the preparation of reports containing a qualified opinion, adverse opinion, or disclaimer of opinion, as well as other reporting circumstances, such as comparative financial statements.

  - ○ **AS 3110: Dating of the Independent Auditor's Report** – Requires the auditor to date the report no earlier than the date on which sufficient appropriate audit evidence is obtained and provides guidance for reporting events occurring after the date of the report but before its issuance and the reissuance of a report.

- 3300 – Other Reporting Topics

  - ○ **AS 3305: Special Reports** – Provides guidance for preparing reports related to financial statements prepared in accordance with a comprehensive basis of accounting other than GAAP; related to specified elements, accounts, or items of a financial statement; to compliance with aspects of contractual agreements or regulatory requirements; to presentations designed to comply with contractual agreements or regulatory provisions; and related to financial information presented in prescribed forms or requiring a prescribed form or report.

  - ○ **AS 3310: Special Reports on Regulated Companies** – Requires reports on regulated companies to address whether the financial statements present fairly, in all material respects, the financial position of the entity as of the balance sheet date and the results of its operations and cash flows for the period then ended in conformity with accounting principles generally accepted in the United States of America unless statements are for filing with its supervisory agency.

  - ○ **AS 3315: Reporting on Condensed Financial Statements and Selected Financial Data** – Provides guidance for reporting on condensed information presented by a public entity that I required to provide complete audited financial statements to a regulatory agency at least annually and for reporting on selected financial data derived from audit financial statements presented in a document containing audited financial statements.

  - ○ **AS 3320: Association with Financial Statements** – Specifies that an accountant is associated with financial statements upon consenting to the inclusion of the auditor's name in a report, document, or written communication containing the statements, whether audited or unaudited.

Matters Relating to Filings Under Federal Securities Laws

- o **AS 4101: Responsibilities Regarding Filings Under Federal Securities Statutes** – Establishes the auditor's responsibility for financial representations in documents filed under federal securities statutes.

- o **AS 4105: Reviews of Interim Financial Information** – Establishes standards and provides guidance related to the nature timing, and extent of procedures that should be performed in a review of interim financial information.

Other Matters Associated with Audits

- o **AS 6101: Letters for Underwriters and Certain Other Requesting Parties** – Provides guidance for performing engagements to provide comfort letters to underwriters and others in relation to financial statements and financial information included in registration statements filed with the SEC.

- o **AS 6105: Reports on the Application of Accounting Principles** – Provides guidance to an accountant preparing a written report on the application of accounting principles to specified transactions, or the type of opinion that may be rendered on a particular entity's financial statements or providing oral advice to be used by a principal to a transaction in determining how accounting principles apply to a specific transaction or the type of opinion that may be rendered on a particular entity's financial statements.

- o **AS 6110: Compliance Auditing Considerations in Audits of Recipients of Governmental Financial Assistance** – Provides guidance to an auditor engaged to audit a governmental entity under PCAOB standards and to report on compliance with laws and regulations under Government Auditing Standards.

- o **AS 6115: Reporting on Whether a Previously Reported Material Weakness Continues to Exist** – Allows an auditor to report on whether a previously reported material weakness continues to exist if the auditor has audited the entity's financial statements and internal control or has been engaged to do so.

Sample research question

Assume that you are assigned to the audit of Roger Corporation, an issuer company. Your firm is performing its first integrated audit for the company, and the partner on the engagement has asked you to research professional standards to identify the factors that should be considered in planning the audit and may affect the firm's audit procedures. Identify and insert the reference in the following box.

Answer: An audit of internal control over financial reporting that is integrated with an audit of financial statements is the topic of AS 2201. Scrolling quickly down that section, there is a heading "Planning the Audit," under which paragraph 2201.09 indicates "The auditor should properly plan the audit of internal control over financial reporting and properly supervise the engagement team members. When planning an integrated audit, the auditor should evaluate whether the following matters are important to the company's financial statements and internal control over financial reporting and, if so, how they will affect the auditor's procedures."

Solution: PCAOB AS 2201 Par. 09

AT-C – Statements on Standards for Attestation Engagements (SSAEs)

When a CPA performs an **attestation engagement**, the authoritative literature is the **Statements on Standards for Attestation Engagements (SSAEs),** which are issued by senior technical bodies of the AICPA designated to issue pronouncements on attestation matters. The primary objective of attestation standards (**AT-C**) is to provide guidance for performing and reporting on attestation engagements.

Although attestation engagements are not audits of financial statements, to which SASs apply, or reviews of financial statements, to which SSARS apply, they are similar in many respects. Attestation engagements consist of *examinations*, in which the accountant expresses an opinion; *reviews*, in which the accountant expresses a conclusion; and *agreed-upon procedures* engagements, in which the accountant expresses findings. They are distinct from audits and reviews of financial statements in that, instead of comparing financial information to an applicable financial reporting framework, attestation engagements involve reporting on the reliability of subject matter or an assertion about the subject matter, as measured against suitable and available criteria.

The **Attestation Standards** (**AT-C**) are organized as follows:

AT-C 100 – Common Concepts

- AT-C 105 – Concepts common to All Attestation Engagements

AT-C 200 – Level of Service (ERA)

- AT-C 205 – Examination Engagements
- AT-C 210 – Review Engagements
- AT-C 215 – Agreed-Upon Procedures Engagements

AT-C 300 – Subject Matter

- AT-C 305 – Prospective Financial Statements
- AT-C 310 – Reporting on Pro Forma Financial Information
- AT-C 315 – Compliance Attestation
- AT-C 320 – Reporting on an Examination of Controls at a Service Organization Relevant to User Entities' Internal Control Over Financial Reporting
- AT-C 395 – Management's Discussion and Analysis

Sample research question

In anticipation of a merger, the president of Welcore Inc., a nonpublic audit client of your firm, would like to present a projection to shareholders that is intended to present what the president believes to be the likely impact of the transaction. The president has asked you to perform an examination of the projection so that you can express an opinion as to whether the prospective financial information is presented in accordance with the guidelines for the presentation of prospective financial information, as established by the AICPA, and whether the assumptions underlying the projection are suitably supported and provide a reasonable basis for the president's projection, given the hypothetical assumptions regarding the business combination. Which section of the Professional Standards addresses this issue?

Answer: Prospective financial statements are addressed in AT-C 305, Prospective Financial Information. Scrolling down that section, there is a heading entitled "Objectives of an Examination Engagement." Paragraph .07 under that heading begins with "In conducting an examination of prospective financial information, the objectives are…"

Solution: AT-C 305.07

AR-C – Statements on Standards for Accounting & Review Services (SSARS)

SSARS apply to *preparation engagements, compilations and reviews* of *nonpublic* company financial statements. They do not cover preparing a trial balance, assisting in adjustments, consulting on accounting or tax matters, preparing tax returns, preparing manuals, and processing financial data, which are considered bookkeeping services. They apply exclusively to nonpublic entities, also referred to as nonissuers.

SSARS concern the preparation of financial statements for a client, which does not involve the issuance of a report, or the compilation or review of financial statements, both of which do require the accountant to issue a report. The principals and requirements related to preparation, compilation, and review engagements are not limited to financial statements. They may also be applied to engagements for the preparation, compilation, or review of financial information.

The sections of the standards related to preparation engagements, compilations, and reviews are (**AR-C**):

- AR-C 60 – General Principles for Engagements Performed in Accordance With Statements on Standards for Accounting and Review Services
- AR-C 70 – Preparation of Financial Statements
- AR-C 80 – Compilation Engagements
- AR-C 90 – Review of Financial Statements
- AR-C 100 – Special Considerations – International Reporting Issues
- AR-C 120 – Compilation of Pro Forma Financial Information

Sample research question

The president of Enright Corporation, a client, asked you to perform a review of the financial statements for the current year only. You have completed your fieldwork and find you can issue an unmodified review report. Which section of the Professional Standards indicates what, is required to be included in an unmodified review report for the financial statements of a single year?

Answer: Reviews of financial statements are the subject matter of AR-C 90. Scrolling in AR-C 90, there is a heading entitled "Reporting on the Financial Statements" followed by a sub-heading entitled "Accountant's Review Report." Paragraph .76 under that sub-heading begins with "The written review report should include..."

Solution: AR-C 90.76

ET – Code of Professional Conduct

The AICPA Code of Professional Conduct **(ET)** was created to provide guidance and rules to all members of the AICPA—those in public practice, in industry, in government, and in education—in the performance of their professional responsibilities. It includes principles and rules as well as interpretations and guidance. The principles provide a framework upon which the rules are based, which in turn govern the performance of professional responsibilities.

The Code is divided into 4 chapters consisting of a preface that applies to all members, part 1 for members in public practice, part 2 for members in business, and part 3 for other members. A rule is specific in a numbered paragraph, followed by interpretations and guidance. As an example, the Independence rule is in part 1 and is paragraph 1.200.001. The rule is followed by "Interpretations under the Independence Rule" in paragraphs 1.200.005 through 1.297.030.03.

Preface – All Members

- ET 0.100 – Overview of the Code of Professional Conduct
- ET 0.200 – Structure and Application of the AICPA Code
- ET 0.300 – Principles of Professional Conduct
- ET 0.400 – Definitions
- ET 0.500 – Nonauthoritative Guidance
- ET 0.600 – New, Revised, and Pending Interpretations and Other Guidance
- ET 0.700 – Deleted Interpretations and Other Guidance

Part 1 – Members in Public Practice

- ET 1.000 – Introduction
- ET 1.100 – Integrity and Objectivity
- ET 1.200 – Independence
- ET 1.300 – General Standards
- ET 1.310 – Compliance With Standards

- ET 1.320 – Accounting Principles
- ET 1.400 – Acts Discreditable
- ET 1.500 – Fees and Other Types of Remuneration
- ET 1.600 – Advertising and Other Forms of Solicitation
- ET 1.700 – Confidential Information
- ET 1.800 – Form of Organization and Name

Part 2 – Members in Industry

- ET 2.000 – Introduction
- ET 2.100 – Integrity and Objectivity
- ET 2.300 – General Standards
- ET 2.310 – Compliance With Standards
- ET 2.320 – Accounting Principles
- ET 2.400 – Acts Discreditable

Part 3 – Other Members

- ET 3.000 – Introduction
- ET 3.400 – Acts Discreditable

Sample research question

You work with a CPA firm as an assistant. The senior on the XYZ audit has asked you to determine whether you are eligible to work on the XYZ audit since he knows that you own 100 shares of XYZ worth $700 in total. He has asked you to research the following: He thinks that he recalls the issue relates to whether you are or are not a "covered member." He would like you to find the definition of a covered member in the professional standards. What section and paragraph addresses the definition of a covered member.

Answer: Definitions are provided in the preface to the Code of Professional Conduct in section ET 0.400. The definitions are listed in alphabetical order and "Covered member" is defined in paragraph .12.

Solution: ET 0.400.12

BL – Bylaws of the AICPA

Bylaws of the American Institute of Certified Public Accountants **(BL)** govern matters of membership and governance of the Institute. These are contained in the same publication as the Code of Professional Conduct.

The sections of the Bylaws are as follows:

- BL 100 – Name and Purpose

- BL 200 – Admission to, and Retention of, Membership and Association
- BL 300 – Organization and Procedure
- BL 400 – Financial Management and Controls
- BL 500 – Meetings of the Institute and the Council
- BL 600 – Election of Council, Board of Directors, and Officers of the Institute
- BL 700 – Termination of Membership and Disciplinary Sanctions
- BL 800 – Amendments
- BL 900 - General

VS – Statements on Standards for Valuation Services

The AICPA Statement on Standards for Valuation Services **(SSVS)** establishes standards for AICPA members who are engaged to, or, as part of another engagement, estimate the value of a business (including not-for-profit entities or activities), business ownership interest, security, or intangible asset. Although the SSVS have been codified, there is only one section, VS 100, Valuation of a Business, Business Ownership Interest, Security, or Intangible Asset.

CS – Statement on Standards for Consulting Services

The AICPA Statement on Standards for Consulting Services **(SSCS)** provides behavioral standards for the conduct of consulting services. The SSCS includes the General Standards found in Rule 201 of the AICPA Professional Code of Conduct plus three additional standards found in Rule 203, including Client Interest, Understanding with the Client and Communication with the Client.

Consulting services differ fundamentally from the CPA's function of attesting to the assertions of other parties. In an attest service, the practitioner expresses a conclusion about the reliability of a written assertion that is the responsibility of another party, the asserter. In a consulting service, the practitioner develops the findings, conclusions, and recommendations presented. The nature and scope of work is determined solely by the agreement between the practitioner and the client. Generally, the work is performed only for the use and benefit of the client.

The only section of SSCS is CS 100, Statements on Standards for Consulting Services.

PFP – Personal Financial Planning

The AICPA Statement on Standards in Personal Financial Planning Services **(PFP)** establishes responsibilities in providing personal financial planning services. The only section of PFP is PFP 100, Statement on Responsibilities in Personal Financial Planning Practice.

CPE – Continuing Professional Education

The AICPA Statement on Standards for Continuing Professional Education Programs **(CPE)** establishes a framework for the development, presentation, measurement, and reporting of CPE programs and thereby help to ensure that accounting professionals receive the quality continuing professional education necessary to satisfy their obligations to serve the public interest.

TS – Statements on Standards for Tax Services

The AICPA's Statements on Standards for Tax Services (SSTSs) are enforceable tax practice standards for members of the AICPA. The SSTSs apply to all members regardless of the jurisdictions in which they practice and the types of taxes with respect to which they are providing services. The SSTSs are organized into the following sections from which to choose:

- TS 100 – Tax Return Positions
- TS 200 – Answers to Questions on Returns
- TS 300 – Certain Procedural Aspects of Preparing Returns
- TS 400 – Use of Estimates
- TS 500 – Departure From a Position Previously Concluded in an Administrative Proceeding or Court Decision
- TS 600 – Knowledge of Error – Return Preparation and Administrative Procedures
- TS 700 – Form and Content of Advice to Taxpayers

PR – Peer Review Standards

The Standards for Performing & Reporting on Peer Reviews and Interpretations provide information on administering, planning, performing, reporting on and the acceptance of peer reviews of CPA firms (and individuals) enrolled in the AICPA Peer Review Program.

QC – Quality Control Standards

The AICPA Statements on Quality Control Standards **(SQCSs)** govern quality control standards established by the AICPA. The AICPA's Quality Control Standards do not address the quality-control ramifications of the Sarbanes-Oxley Act nor do they address the quality control ramifications of the PCAOB standards that must be followed by auditors of issuers. NOTE: the CPA exam will cover only those standards currently in force.

There is only one section of the SQCS, QC 10, A Firm's System of Quality Control.

Sample research question

Assume that you are employed by Wilson & Wilson CPAs. One of the partners has asked you to research the professional standards for the section that identifies the elements of a firm's quality control standards. Identify the section and place the reference in the box below.

Answer: QC 10.17

Professional Standards Selections	
AU-C	U.S. Auditing Standards
PCAOB-AS	PCAOB Auditing Standards
AT-C	Attestation Services
AR-C	Statements on Standards for Accounting & Review Services
ET	Code of Professional Conduct
BL	Bylaws
VS	Statements on Standards for Valuation Services
CS	Statement on Standards for Consulting Services
PFP	Personal Financial Planning
CPE	Continuing Professional education
TS	Statements on Standards for Tax Services
PR	Peer Review Standards
QC	Quality Control Standards

AUD 12
Final
Review

12.01 AUD Final Review

You finished your AUD Course...now what?
A quick guide to the final days leading up to, and following, the CPA exam

FINAL REVIEW

Now is the time to make connections and solidify your understanding of the topics you found most challenging, and to review the most heavily tested topics on the exam.

- ❑ Review your SmartPath data to ensure you have hit all targets. Revisit any areas marked "Needs Improvement."

- ❑ Reread your course notes and review your digital flash cards.

- ❑ If it is included in your program package, use the Cram Course to do a final review of the most heavily tested topics.

- ❑ Take at least one Full CPA Practice Exam in your QBank to hone your test-taking skills in an environment that follows the same 5-testlet, 4-hour structure of the exam.

- ❑ Checkout an AICPA Sample Test at www.cpa-exam.org to familiarize yourself with the exam format and welcome (instruction) screens.

12.02 AUD Exam Overview

DAY OF THE EXAM

- ❑ Get a good night's rest before heading into your exam.

- ❑ Arrive to the Prometric testing center at least 60 minutes before your appointment so you have time to park, check-in, and use the restroom before your exam begins.

- ❑ Bring your Notice to Schedule (NTS) and two forms of acceptable identification (see Intro for more details).

- ❑ Proceed through check-in: store belongings, get fingerprinted, have photo taken, sign log book, get seated, write your Launch Code (from your NTS) on your noteboard.

- ❑ Don't stress. You've prepared for this; now, just breathe and power through!

DURING THE EXAM

- ❑ Remember your AUD Exam time strategy, and jot down the times at which you want to be at your benchmarks:
  - o Use 75 seconds per multiple choice question as a benchmark
  - o Allocate 15-25 minutes per task-based simulation, depending on complexity

- Plan to use no more than 10 minutes per research question
- Take the standard 15-minute break after the 3rd testlet – it does not count against your time
- (Remember that any other break will count against your time)

AUD: 4 Hour Exam			Break		
Testlet 1	Testlet 2	Testlet 3		Testlet 4	Testlet 5
36 MCQs	36 MCQs	2 TBSs		3 TBSs	3 TBSs
45 min	45 min	30 min		60 min	60 min

- You will be given 10 minutes to review the welcome screens and exam instructions. You should already be familiar with these screens after taking the AICPA Sample Test and can bypass them during your exam.

- Once you begin testing, make sure to read each question carefully, paying close attention to the keywords that dictate the question's intention (eg, *except, is greater than, always, never*).

- Take note if your questions are getting more difficult. That's a good sign! A progressively harder exam indicates that you are performing well.

AFTER THE EXAM

- Remember, it is normal to not feel great afterwards. It's a tough exam and designed to challenge your confidence and competencies.

- Relax and celebrate! You've earned it.

- Your scores will be released within a couple of weeks.

- GOOD LUCK!!!